DATE DUE

International
Environmental
Negotiation

International Environmental Negotiation

edited by
Gunnar Sjöstedt

A Publication of the
Processes of International Negotiation (PIN) Project.
International Institute for Applied Systems Analysis, Laxenburg, Austria

Editorial Committee:
Gunnar Sjöstedt
Guy-Olivier Faure
Victor A. Kremenyuk
Winfried Lang
Jeffrey Z. Rubin
Bertram I. Spector
I. William Zartman

SAGE Publications
International Educational and Professional Publisher
Newbury Park   London   New Delhi

For information address:

SAGE Publications, Inc.
2455 Teller Road
Newbury Park, California 91320

SAGE Publications Ltd.
6 Bonhill Street
London EC2A 4PU
United Kingdom

SAGE Publications India Pvt. Ltd.
M-32 Market
Greater Kailash I
New Delhi 110 048 India

Printed in the United States of America

Library of Congress Cataloging-in-Publication Data

Main entry under title:

International environmental negotiation / edited by Gunnar Sjöstedt.
    p.   cm.
Includes bibliographical references and index.
ISBN 0-8039-4760-7
    1. Environmental policy—International cooperation. I. Sjöstedt, Gunnar.
HC79.E51536   1993
363.7'0526—dc20   92-26749

93 94 95 96 97 10 9 8 7 6 5 4 3 2 1

Sage Production Editor: Astrid Virding

Contents

Foreword

The rapid, worldwide economic development of the past 100 years has been based on the classic economic concept that air and water are free resources and that land and minerals are inexhaustible. The consequences of this development seem inevitable: a world-threatening increase in environmental pollution and a scarcity of natural resources. Fortunately, this threat has not gone unheeded. During the past 50 years, as pollution and resource scarcity have grown from local and regional problems to international and global problems, they have become issues for negotiation, high on the agendas of all developed and developing nations.

In 1992, the United Nations held the World Conference on Environment and Development to underscore the importance of environmental issues and to emphasize the strong relationship among them. How well these issues are managed will determine the course of human and world events in the centuries to come.

The most fundamental need for achieving successful solutions to the many international environmental and developmental issues is a new approach to the process of international negotiation. This approach should start with a logical and open analysis of the situation, and then provide options for managing the issues. The approach must also provide a negotiation process based on the premise that a negotiated solution makes winners, or at least survivors, of all parties.

Many of the environmental problems that we face today are unlike problems the world faced less than a century ago. Today, the increasing toxicity of the air we breathe, the water we drink, and the earth we walk on is so critical to the lives and well-being of all of us, that environmental negotiation is nothing less than an exercise in negotiating the survival of society.

Thus this book on international negotiations concerning environmental issues should be viewed from two perspectives. First, it should be regarded as an exposition of the development of such negotiations and of some of the issues that need to be addressed. Second, this book should be viewed as an experiment in developing a new approach to international negotiations—an approach that takes into account the complex interrelationships of modern society: an approach that recognizes that individual negative effects, which may emerge from the negotiation process, will most likely negatively affect both participants and nonparticipants.

International negotiation is an ancient art, older than any nation, probably as old as organized tribes themselves. Even so, throughout early history, the degree of commercial, social, and political intercourse between nations was relatively limited. Most nations were agrarian-based and generally self-sufficient. What trade and commerce existed among them dealt largely with luxuries, not commodities that were essential to meet the basic needs of people. Consequently, international negotiation was mostly bilateral and directed at resolving disputes over territorial ownership or rights, such as rights of navigation and safe passage.

Generally, international negotiation was employed to resolve a conflict or dispute at one specific time, after which the matter was considered closed. The matter stayed closed until the nations' leaders or their interests changed. Then, when a new conflict arose, another negotiated settlement was required.

Breakdowns in negotiations occurred regularly because the issues usually involved the rights, powers, and egos of rulers. Once a deadlock was reached and negotiations broke down, war broke out, almost as a natural extension of the negotiation process. The purpose of the war was to break the deadlock by force of arms and to create a new relationship for negotiations. The negotiations would then continue under the pressure of the victor, and the dispute would be successfully settled, at least for a while. Force, or the potential of force, was a major variable in the negotiation process.

During the past century, however, the nature of interrelationships among nations has changed. The change has increased the complexity of the approach to the negotiation process and the complexity of achieving a successful outcome. A major element at the root of the change was the emergence of science and, in turn, its influences on technology. The result has been a major transformation in the whole fabric of international social and economic intercourse. The evolution of first energy-related and mechanical technologies, then transportation and logistics technologies, and finally information and communications technologies has given rise to two major trends affecting the behavioral framework of nations.

The first trend is the rapid and broad-based economic growth of about one third of the world's population. The wealth created has allowed for, and has been enhanced by, an unprecedented rise in mass education, which has led to a rise in representative government and individual freedoms, both social and economic. The second trend is the worldwide integration of manufacturing and commerce and their service "handmaidens," international banking and finance. This trend was aided by the development of communication and information technologies and the parallel development of technologies for transportation and distribution systems. The resulting economic and social interdependence of nations has brought about fundamental changes in the way nations must deal with each other.

At the start of the Industrial Revolution, international trade and commerce were sufficiently limited; a nation could remain independent and develop economically at its own pace. No nation was threatened economically by another nation that was developing more rapidly. For example, if one nation developed superior products, its neighbors were not threatened by any resulting domination of international markets, domestic economic imbalances, foreign debt, or foreign ownership of domestic assets.

Today, the opposite situation prevails. No nation, however large or wealthy, can remain isolated for long and continue to maintain parity in economic and social progress with other nations. Every nation is now forced to compete against every other nation and against complex, interlocking, interdependent world networks of nations acting as one.

The trend toward commercial integration is, in my view, largely responsible for the emergence of the European Community, first as an economic and then as a political unit. The trend has also been a major force in the opening up of Asia, including the People's Republic of China. And it is largely responsible for the recent dramatic changes in the Soviet Union and Eastern Europe. There is no doubt that the seriously flawed political structures in many countries were the primary cause of their economic and social decline. But without the increased internationalization of economic development, the changes that occurred in these countries would have been delayed.

In addition to the possible benefits of technology, several disadvantages are also important to consider in discussing the theory and practice of international negotiation. The first disadvantage is the rise in the potential for mass destruction—overtly, through military means and, subtly, through the effect that economic development can have on the environment.

A second drawback now, and one that is likely to be the most important in years to come, is the growing disparity in social, political, economic, and technological development between North and South nations. This threat to humankind is real, and no solution is in sight. If current trends continue, within 50 years, 80% of the world's population will live in grossly underdeveloped areas, while the remaining 20%, although economically rich, will be morally choking on human poverty and physically choking on a degraded environment.

Such a threat adds an important dimension to the challenge of international negotiations on every issue. Not only are economic, environmental, social, and political risks interdependent, but the reduction of these risks will increasingly depend on the actions of the 80% of the population that does not have the social and political structures or the economic ability to take any action.

As developed nations have painfully learned—through wars in Vietnam and Afghanistan and through dozens of equally unsuccessful and devastating regional conflicts—war can no longer be viewed as a natural extension of the negotiation process. On an international scale, the ability of powerful nations to deliver total, bilateral destruction within hours or days has made an all-out war impractical as a means of breaking a negotiation deadlock. Likewise, the economic equivalent of war—excessive tariffs and duties, sanctions, and blockades—has also been shown, so far, to be ineffective. In most cases, these economic measures are too slow and too difficult to enforce to be effective. Developed nations, therefore, have no alternative but to negotiate.

What directions must international negotiation take in the future? To help answer this question, it might be beneficial to examine the nature of some new issues and conflicts that are likely to arise.

International issues of health and safety, education, human rights, product standards, treatment and disposal of industrial waste, and various assaults on the environment call for new approaches in negotiation practice. On each issue a process leading to a fair outcome has to be implemented. Thus, both multilateral, multinational, and multiparty negotiation and the development of international institutions, which openly and systematically analyze the issues and provide a range of options for negotiating solutions, will become increasingly important.

The issues that the world now faces inherently transcend national boundaries, international groupings, and continents. Foremost among them is the accelerating degradation of the environment. An example can demonstrate its importance. If the population of the world had remained what it was about 200 years ago, with all inhabitants living at today's per capita income of the United States, the rate of destruction and exhaustion of the so-called free economic resources (air, water, and land) could continue at its current level almost indefinitely, assuming that some technology would evolve to adjust for the eventual exhaustion of some mineral resources. The world environment is robust enough to recover sufficiently from that degree of destruction.

However, the world population is now 5 billion people, approximately five times the number it was less than 200 years ago. In another half century or so, it will be 10 billion. And most current estimates indicate that the population at the end of the next century will be about 15 billion, well above any imagined population that can sustain itself even at the current U.S. living standard.

Let us look at the issue of climate change and the greenhouse effect. In the United States, the amount of gases emitted that contribute to the greenhouse effect is on average more than four times the world per capita level. If the entire world were to rise to the U.S. level of emissions and, at the same time, increase in population two to three times, as is projected, the total emission of greenhouse gases would increase 8 to 12 times.

Since there are clear indications of climate change at current levels of emissions, a 10-fold increase would be intolerable and lead to tragic, irreversible consequences. Unfortunately, the changes required in world economics, social habits, and the energy infrastructure would take decades, half-centuries, or even centuries to achieve. Thus we are faced with negotiating solutions over long periods with little certainty of their effects or outcomes.

Meanwhile, our streams, rivers, lakes, and coastal waters are becoming dangerously polluted. Land erosion, soil degradation, and water pollution caused by energy-intensive farming are endangering agriculture itself and the health of humans and animals. Regionally, deforestation—in the Southern Hemisphere through physical destruction and in the Northern Hemisphere through acid rain—is threatening the diversity of the world's plants and animals. Globally, the greenhouse effect and the depletion of ozone through chemical emissions are rising threats to the ability of the world to sustain itself. Thus locally, regionally, internationally, and globally, the environmental issue is not one of merely maintaining a serene and enjoyable landscape. It is an issue of critical importance at many levels: human rights, health, social, economic, intellectual, philosophical, and political.

Examination of the process of environmental negotiation, therefore, takes on a special timeliness and importance, not only in its own right, but also because this type of negotiation is inevitably tied to critical economic, political, social, and technological issues. By nature, environmental issues require negotiated solutions, not solutions brought about by force or the threat of force. Solutions must be recognized as mutually beneficial and equitable, and they must provide instruments for monitoring and managing the results of negotiated decisions over a long period. Monitoring and managing results are increasingly important factors in many other areas of negotiation.

A careful, systematic analysis is required at the beginning of the negotiation process. This analysis should consider the situation, its origins and interrelationships to other issues, and the likely social, economic, and environmental results of the negotiation outcome. Such an analysis can also assist in developing the follow-up monitoring and managing of results to ensure that the desired results are achieved. In many cases results might take years or decades to achieve, making continued management of the process a necessity.

For these reasons, the need continually to improve the framework and process of international negotiation is a central concern of the International Institute for Applied Systems Analysis (IIASA). The constructive policy alternatives that systems analysis provides may be extremely important in resolving a wide variety of international issues. However, any attempt at a systematic approach is worthless if it is not combined, from the outset, with a policy management.

The increasingly important field of environmental negotiation presents a great opportunity to examine recent approaches to the solutions that have been negotiated for several complex international issues. It is hoped that the examination of the theories and the case studies in the following chapters, along with the suggestions for future investigations, will contribute significantly to the understanding of international and multilateral negotiation.

—Robert H. Pry
Director of IIASA
1986-1990

Preface

This book is the second in a series conceived and coordinated by the steering committee of the Processes of International Negotiation (PIN) Project at the International Institute for Applied Systems Analysis (IIASA) in Laxenburg, Austria. The steering committee is an international group of researchers representing different approaches to the study of negotiation. Several of the members also have a considerable amount of experience in training diplomats or practicing negotiation at an international or regional level. Except for the leader of the PIN Project, Bertram I. Spector, the steering committee members are not resident at IIASA. They include: Guy-Olivier Faure of Sorbonne University (Paris), Victor Kremenyuk of the Academy of Sciences of Russia, Winfried Lang of the Austrian Ministry of Foreign Affairs, Jeffrey Z. Rubin of Tufts University, I. William Zartman of Johns Hopkins University, and myself from the Swedish Institute of International Affairs.

The book series, as well as other numerous research activities conducted by the project, is in response to a growing concern among the public and government officials interested in the state of affairs of international negotiation. The first book in the series, *International Negotiation: Analysis, Approaches, Issues,* edited by Victor Kremenyuk, was published by Jossey-Bass Publishers in 1991. Its purpose was to take stock of the state of the art in research approaches and perspectives, discuss what is known about the principal properties of international negotiation, and review developments in significant issue areas, as well as in the education and training of diplomats. That work serves as the general theoretical frame of reference for the subsequent studies conducted by the PIN Project Steering Committee.

It is quite natural that this second book should deal with international environmental negotiations. There were at least three important reasons for this selection. First, environmental problems have required more and more attention in recent years. The strongest manifestation is the international process culminating in the 1992 UN Conference on Environment and Development (UNCED) in Brazil. We have all become strongly aware of the rapidly growing damage to the ecosystem caused by pollution. Likewise, the transboundary, and ultimately global, character of environmental problems is becoming increasingly clear. There is an urgent need to accelerate international negotiations on environmental issues and to find internationally accepted and viable solutions to them.

Second, international environmental negotiations appear to have several qualities that make them particularly difficult to deal with at the negotiating table. For example, issues are highly complex and characterized by insufficient knowledge and background information when negotiations commence. As well, the outcomes of environmental negotiations often are represented by formulas that distribute painful short-term economic costs to attain comparatively uncertain long-term gains accrued by future generations. These special difficulties make it urgent to increase understanding of international environmental negotiations through concentrated research.

Third, environmental issues represent a high-priority research area at IIASA, where scientific research on global and regional policy problems predominates. We believe that our focus on the behavioral process of how nations cooperate to resolve their common environmental problems will serve as a meaningful complement to the technical assessments of other IIASA projects.

The ambitious goal of this book is to support the many ongoing regional and global processes of international negotiations concerning environmental problems. An important purpose is to draw lessons from earlier processes of negotiations on the environment that may be useful and instructive for practitioners engaged in present or future bargaining on these issues. This objective is partially realized in Chapter 12 on one practitioner's perspectives. However, it is our conviction that the current foundation of cumulated knowledge about international environmental negotiations, on which policy recommendations ultimately rest, is not fully satisfactory. We believe that future effective policy advice must rely on an improved understanding of these negotiations that can only be attained by means of continued systematic research. This assessment explains the thrust of the present project: to draw useful lessons for practitioners and for researchers.

The book is organized in three sections. Part I summarizes the history of international environmental negotiations. It also lays out the theoretical premises for the empirical case studies in Part II. This framework offers a theoretical outlook on negotiation as a mechanism of conflict resolution. It also postulates a list of attributes that identifies what is unique or common about the process of international environmental negotiations. Particularly, environmental negotiations are characterized by multiple parties playing multiple roles, the existence of multiple conflicting issues, meaningless national boundaries, high scientific and technical uncertainty, issue-specific power asymmetry among negotiating parties, shared or joint interests, negative perceptions of immediate outcomes, long time frames to resolution, changing diplomatic personalities and experts, an active audience represented by public opinion and interest groups, institutionalized solutions, and the necessary establishment of new rules and regimes.

Part II of the book contains a set of carefully selected historical cases of global, regional, and bilateral environmental negotiations. These negotiations have been conducted in the past two decades. Some of them are still taking place at the time of writing. These case studies cover important topics like ozone depletion, acid rain in Europe and North America, water pollution in rivers (the Rhine) and in the sea (the Mediterranean), nuclear pollution, the transport of hazardous waste, land destruction, and biological diversity. Most of the case studies have been written by practitioners who participated in the negotiations they describe.

The last case study of Part II (Chapter 11) represents a creative bridge from the empirical investigations of the case studies to the more theoretical analyses of Part III. This chapter is a systematic attempt to draw useful lessons for the current negotiations on climate change from the earlier Law of the Sea negotiations. But Chapter 11 not only formulates concrete advice pertaining to climate change. It also evaluates the theoretical question of how lessons learned from the experience of one round of negotiations can be applied to understanding another round of negotiations concerned with a different issue.

Part III contains analytical observations and conclusions drawn from the case studies. Chapter 12 treats the analytical and prescriptive observations of an experienced practitioner. Chapter 14 contains the comments of an experienced scholar who assesses the lessons learned from research. Two other authors address the crucial question of how conflict resolution can be facilitated by external intervention; one of these concerns the role of international organizations (Chapter 13), whereas the other deals with the role of third-party mediators (Chapter 15). Finally, the concluding chapter offers policy recommendations for practitioners and identifies further topics for research that seek to support greater effectiveness in future environmental negotiations.

This book is the result of a stimulating team effort. Its main engine has been the PIN Project's Editorial Committee. The design of this book project and the selection of authors is the result of the collective work of this committee.

In July 1990, a two-day conference was held at IIASA to discuss the first drafts of the introductory, analytical, and case study chapters. We are grateful that the authors were able to attend this useful meeting. We are also greatly indebted to the discussants at this meeting—Gerhard Hafner, Alexandre Kiss, Martine Remond-Gouilloud, and Rüdiger Wagner. As discussants, they helped the editorial committee in a very constructive way and provided advice to the case study authors on how to finalize their chapters.

We are also grateful to the former Director of IIASA, Robert H. Pry, who inspired and encouraged the editorial committee to undertake this book project on international negotiations on the environment. We are equally grateful for the support we have received from the present Director of IIASA, Peter de Jánosi.

We owe many thanks to Fred Syzdlik, Sharyn Cooper, and Wendy Caron who have worked diligently to polish the prose and to give a coherent style to the language.

Finally, very special thanks go to Ulrike Neudeck, who is the assistant to the PIN Project. Ms. Neudeck not only typed the manuscript and inserted the editor's corrections, she also organized the meetings of the editorial committee as well as the July 1990 conference. Until the appointment of a PIN Project leader in August 1990, she, in fact, took care of all of the executive functions of this project.

—Gunnar Sjöstedt
Swedish Institute of International Affairs
Stockholm

Part I

BACKGROUND AND
CONCEPTUAL FRAMEWORK

In the Foreword, Robert H. Pry points out that international negotiations on environmental issues is a relatively recent phenomenon. The 1972 UN conference on the environment held in Stockholm is a landmark. The Stockholm Conference set the agenda for the negotiations and cooperation concerning environmental problems over the following decades. The 1992 UN Conference on the Environment and Development (UNCED) in Rio de Janeiro was intended to produce a new agenda and a new plan of international action on the environment for the 1990s and beyond.

The environmental agenda may be of recent origin, but it establishes an immense enterprise for continued work. It includes many very broad issues. Here belong, notably, issues like climate change, the ozone layer, other types of air pollution problems, forestry, ocean use and management, management of freshwater resources, desertification and land use, human settlements, hazardous waste, biodiversity, and biotechnology.

The breadth of this agenda is one typical feature of the international negotiations on the environment. Another equally typical characteristic of environmental negotiations is complexity. Take, for instance, the case of climate change, which is one of the key issues in the UNCED process. The interplay between human activities and nature that produces climate change is not yet completely understood; this, in itself, represents one kind of issue complexity. Another kind of complexity is due to the fact that the issue of climate change is physically linked with other problem areas defined as separate issues in the UNCED process, notably the depletion of the earth's ozone layer and air pollution in general, as well as the problems of deforestation and biodiversity.

A third and related type of complexity concerns the forums in which environmental negotiations take place. Negotiations on the environment are often conducted at two levels simultaneously: regionally and globally. At the regional and global levels environmental problems are addressed in a multitude of negotiation processes, in various ways engaging numerous international agencies. The relatively new negotiations on the sustainable management of forest ecosystems represent a good illustration. The forest issue appeared in earnest during the preparatory process for the UNCED. The consultations on forests involved many international institutions and organized activities, such as the Food and Agriculture Organization; the World Meteorological Organization; the United Nations Environment Program; the International Tropical Timber Organization; the United Nations Education, Scientific, and Cultural Organization; the Tropical Forestry Action Plan; and World Wildlife Fund.

Their multidimensional complexity indicates that environmental negotiations may have a special character differentiating them from other negotiations. This suspicion is further substantiated when a closer look is taken at environmental issues and at the demands they put on negotiators. It seems that, in a general sense, environmental negotiations have characteristics of their own that in significant ways distinguish them from other kinds of negotiations. It is the purpose of this volume to assess these typical and special features of environmental negotiations. The ultimate aim of the study is not only scientific elucidation. It is the belief of the editors that a better understanding of these processes will facilitate future environmental negotiations. Special features may represent obstacles and pitfalls whose negative effects can be downgraded or neutralized if negotiators are aware of them.

The section that follows offers a general introduction to international environmental negotiation and a conceptual structure that provides a concrete framework for the remainder of the volume. First, Victor Kremenyuk and Winfried Lang reflect on the history of environmental negotiations and present the personal perspectives of a senior diplomat in this area.

Chapter 2, by Guy-Olivier Faure and Jeffrey Z. Rubin, introduces a large set of propositions that identifies what is typical or very special about environmental negotiations. These propositions are evaluated in the case studies analyzed in Part II. Faure and Rubin also offer a theoretical framework that deals with the essence of environmental negotiations by laying bare their basic elements: actors, strategies, structure, process, and outcome.

1

The Political, Diplomatic, and Legal Background

VICTOR A. KREMENYUK

WINFRIED LANG

Negotiations on environmental issues have become a highly visible part of diplomacy. It would be incorrect, however, to regard such negotiations as purely diplomatic activities, because they draw a significant number of people from the sciences, politics, pressure groups, and various mass movements. At the same time, environmental negotiations parallel other activities in international politics: They change public opinion, inspire advances in technology, and affect the way nations conduct their foreign policies.

Negotiations on the environment constitute an important part of domestic and world politics and involve people who demand profound, effective, and timely solutions. This political attention complicates the decision-making process, sometimes slowing it down and making it vulnerable to various factors. It also heightens the sense of urgency surrounding the issues under discussion, adding to the importance of the negotiations, and placing constraints on how the negotiations are conducted as well as their eventual outcome.

Therefore, in studying environmental negotiations, it is useful to regard them not only as a specialized type of international negotiations, but also within a broader diplomatic and political context. Of course, they also have an inherent legal and scientific context, which will be discussed later.

Negotiation as Part of the Process

Environmental negotiations can be regarded as part of the larger process of international relations, capable of changing relationships among nations through cooperation and joint problem solving. In fact, the entire international atmosphere has changed and now provides a much sounder basis for relationships among former antagonists. Nations realize that a reliance on coercion to impose one's own solution, even when there is a striking asymmetry of power, is futile and counterproductive. The result is a growing awareness of the importance of negotiation. Most governments consider negotiation the only reasonable way of handling their differences with other nations. The public, too, is inclined to regard negotiation as the only way of making life secure.

The trend today is to use negotiation to identify common interests, bring parties closer together, and work out acceptable solutions to a variety of issues. This increased interest requires more research, new tools and methods of training, and a constructive approach to negotiation on the part of negotiators and decision makers (Kokoshin, Kremenyuk, & Sergeev, 1989).

The increasing number of negotiations in most fields is due to the crucial changes along the East-West axis that have swept through international relations in the past decade. The existing structures and alignments underwent even more change when the Cold War was declared over. This change inspired new negotiations on different issues and took different forms: summit conferences, meetings of ministers, and gatherings of technical experts. The end of the Cold War precipitated a host of talks on arms control and disarmament, regional conflicts, trade and development, human rights, and the environment. To a lesser degree, international relations have also experienced changes along the North-South cross section. And here, too, the number of negotiations is growing.

One result of the changes in international relations was the emergence of a largely reformed system of international negotiations that incorporated talks on such topics as arms control and disarmament, trade and development, environment, and regional conflicts. The priorities assigned to these talks varied in importance; for many years, arms control and disarmament were ranked as the primary concern of governments, while trade and development issues were given secondary importance.

During the long Cold War years, environmental issues, to the extent that their international dimension had been recognized, received relatively little attention. Although they were sometimes discussed and even resolved, in the general context of East-West relations environmental issues largely were disregarded. The 1972 United Nations Conference on Human Environment (UNCHE), held in Stockholm, represented the first serious attempt to deal with these issues. But it proved only that, because there was little awareness of the urgency of these issues, the international community was not able to concentrate fully on the environment. The former Soviet Union was not a participant in this landmark conference.

Environmental negotiations inevitably touch upon important issues such as national sovereignty, and paradoxically they sometimes develop out of conflicting interests. So it is then clear that in times of sharp, ideological discord and military rivalry, governments will not be inclined to focus much attention on environmental issues.

In response, grass roots movements sprang up around the world. Organizations such as Greenpeace formed and gained political clout. Under the growing pressure of the problems, which in addition to their technical makeup were acquiring important political elements, environmental issues began to appear on the agendas of national governments as well as bilateral and multilateral talks at the international level. Concern for the environment and discontent over how world leaders were handling the situation also became an important force behind the antinuclear proliferation and testing movement.

Finally, there was an appropriate response to the environmental problem from the highest level of government. At their annual meeting in July 1989 the leaders of the seven major industrial powers—Great Britain, the Federal Republic of Germany, France, Italy, Japan, Canada, and the United States—agreed that environmental issues should be given utmost attention. It was recommended that a series of negotiations be carried out in this area. In his address to the superpower summit, Soviet President Mikhail Gorbachev strongly supported this recommendation (Kremenyuk, 1989). The change in attitude of the developed nations helped to pave the way toward the 1992 United Nations Conference on Environment and Development (UNCED) in Brazil.

Regardless of recent developments, negotiations on the environment continue to be secondary to some other negotiations. Security and economic issues are still the primary concerns of governments. There are signs, however, that priorities are shifting as nations begin to understand that environmental issues can threaten national and international security just as much as military issues. Environmental negotiations are likely to play a much more important role in the future. Environmental issues require a high degree of problem solving and international cooperation. Thus they contribute to the overall efficiency of international negotiations, regarded as a holistic system.

In summary, two overlapping developments directly contributed to the state of environmental negotiations. The first was the easing of tensions between the East and West that forged a new relationship between former antagonists. The second was the growing concern over the harmful effects on the environment from industrial and social development. At the same time, scientific research supported the seriousness of the concern over the environment and emphasized the necessity for immediate international cooperation.

This chapter examines international environmental negotiations from several viewpoints, including its inherent characteristics, political dimensions, actors, obstacles, and constraints. The chapter discusses treaty-making as the most advanced type of negotiation, and the roles played by the lawyer-diplomat and the scientist in the course of negotiation and in treaty-making.

Characteristics of Negotiations

Every negotiation has its own characteristics, depending on the area in which it takes place. The characteristics relate to the issues being discussed, the participants or actors, and the solution or outcome of a negotiation. Environmental negotiations have special characteristics, but they also share common features with other types of negotiation (Lang, 1991b).

An *environmental issue* can be defined, generically, as a natural phenomenon that needs protection from the detrimental effects of human activity. For example, an issue might involve a geographic area within a nation's borders that has been damaged by the emission of hazardous substances from another nation; or, it might concern a region that includes the territories of several nations, all of them emitting hazardous substances and all suffering from those emissions; or, it could be a vast area of the earth, the so-called common heritage or global commons, that is being endangered by major polluters. What is common to these descriptions is the basic issue of how to reduce or modify a certain human activity that threatens nature and people (see Chapter 2).

In this respect, the conflict that usually develops around environmental issues is double structured. On one hand, there is a conflict between nature and humanity in which human activity threatens not only the most vulnerable elements of nature but also the health and well-being of humanity. This conflict typically emerges following the announcement of new scientific evidence defining humanity's latest devastating effect on the environment. Often such an announcement generates media attention and promotes public campaigns to examine not only the evidence but also the proposed solutions to environmental problems.

On the other hand, problem solving generates conflict, pitting one against another, polluters against those victimized by pollution. This conflict can be evident directly as an immediate health threat or indirectly as feelings of outrage when parts of the wildlife are affected by the deterioration of the environment. At the international level, conflict is generated between nations because of the transboundary flows of pollutants. This brings governments into conflict with one another.

International environmental negotiations seem to group nations into two camps: polluters and victims. Initially, the developed nations produced the bulk of pollutants and hazardous materials, and the developing nations were victims of this industrial growth. But, in time, the developed nations have become concerned about the quality of the environment, while some of the developing nations, especially those with rapid population growth, have become polluters themselves. This role reversal explains some of the complexity of negotiations on environmental issues and illustrates that different aspects of the social and political lives of nations—sovereignty, borders, the decision-making process, and the level of economic development—can also become a matter for discussion.

Political Dimensions of Negotiation

Negotiations are further complicated when environmental issues acquire, almost automatically it seems, a political dimension, which carries with it technological, economic, and scientific dimensions. The political repercussions have both domestic and international dimensions. Domestically, environmental issues inevitably involve the interests of industry and labor. Internationally, they affect a nation as a whole—the polluter or the victim of pollution or both. A nation's ability to deal with environmental issues is influenced by its existing internal and external situation; the more this situation is beset by tension and confrontation, the less the prospects of a solution, and vice versa. So, environmental issues may generate either confrontation or cooperation in international relations, depending upon political circumstances.

Environmental negotiations may be classified by the level of political activity—neighborhood, regional, global—that takes place around them. Neighborhood negotiations are concerned with environmental problems in the immediate vicinity. Potential threats to the environment, real or imagined, may include a nuclear power plant in a neighboring state, a polluted river or lake that straddles a border, or toxic fumes being emitted from a factory in a neighboring state. Regional negotiations deal with problems that reach beyond the vicinity of contiguous states, such as long-range, transboundary air pollution and the pollution of international rivers that flow through several countries. Environmental problems in partially enclosed areas like the Baltic Sea or the Mediterranean Sea are treated as regional issues. Global negotiations relate to problems concerning the globe as a whole, such as the depletion of the ozone layer, global warming, dangers to the marine environment, and the transport of hazardous waste.

As a part of the diplomatic process, environmental negotiations to some extent depend on the other issues that nations bring to the discussions. Issues are constantly being jockeyed for a higher position on the agenda. As an environmental issue becomes more threatening and takes on global dimensions, it gains importance in the eyes of the public and of governments. The need to solve the environmental problem demands more cooperation and dominates all other issues. The perception of what constitutes a major threat to national and international security also changes (Zhurkin, Karagnov, & Kortunov, 1987).

Governments as Actors

Because the conduct of international negotiations is still mainly the prerogative of national governments, the main actors are governments and their agents, and primarily foreign ministries. Almost all developed and developing nations have created special agencies responsible for pollution control and for formulating their governments' policies in this area. These agencies participate in the negotiation process to provide their own view of the desirable solution. The participation of functional agencies, while it adds to bureaucratic meddling, brings to the process an expertise and a vested interest that participants must contemplate along with other political considerations.

Many factors determine a government's action in environmental negotiations. Among them are the nation's environmental policy, the feasibility of the solutions, the nation's location, its dependence on energy sources, the nature and size of perceived threats, and its international status.

National environmental policy. This is the dominant factor in determining a nation's behavior. Environmental policy is usually the result of balancing economic and ecological considerations, and is influenced by foreign policy and political expediency.

Economic feasibility. This is the major reason governments do not enter into formal agreements or they extricate themselves from existing ones. Economic feasibility depends on the level of socioeconomic development in a nation and the level of environmental awareness in its society, an alertness that is promoted mostly by nongovernmental organizations and interests (Sands, 1989).

Geography. A downstream nation is more likely to ask for strict controls of water pollution than an upstream nation. Likewise, so-called transit countries may be concerned with hazardous waste transports through their own territory by nations that import or export hazardous waste.

Dependence on energy resources. Nations that rely heavily on brown coal, such as those in Central and Eastern Europe, are reluctant to agree to restrictions on sulfur emissions. For a nation to reduce its dependence on brown coal, it may have to switch to nuclear energy, which, in turn, might be opposed by its neighbors.

Nature and size of perceived threats. A country that has renounced all uses of nuclear energy will regard a nuclear power plant in a neighboring country as a threat, and will try to cease its operation. A less ambitious strategy would aim at supervising the safety requirements of the plant, but this also could be regarded as infringing on the neighboring country's national sovereignty.

International status. A nation that is a member of an economic union like the European Community (EC), which has its own stance on environmental matters, has much less leeway in its actions than a nonmember nation. A member nation has to follow the policies approved by its fellow members in that supranational organization.

Other Actors

Governments predominate in environmental negotiations, but other important actors are also interested in the way the negotiations are handled. Such important actors as the EC or the United Nations Environment Program (UNEP) have acquired a growing role in managing the issues of the environment. The whole body of actors in this area also includes international agencies and committees following the situation in specific areas (for example, Antarctica) or the state of affairs with specific wildlife species (fish, birds, mammals, and so on).

In addition to the growing number of international legal actors, who are able to make legally binding commitments, there are other concerned parties whose roles also should be assessed. One such interested party is the industrialist, whose activity produces the pollution. Major corporations are interested in the outcome of negotiations because the negotiated agreements may require them to spend more money to reduce pollution. Other interested parties include scientists, public movements and organizations, and the mass media, all of whom, by their participation, contribute to the delicate and complicated process of negotiation and make it a highly politicized domestic matter.

An interesting and unusual relationship develops among the parties involved in environmental negotiations. Seemingly, they all have a common interest: to ensure a healthier environment. However, the costs of achieving a healthier environment usually puts them at odds with each other.

It would be naive and simplistic to assume that industry is interested only in making as much profit as possible and ignores the public good on environmental issues. Usually, environmental problems have a direct relevance to the interests of all: business, labor, local communities, scientists, and the public. Likewise, the decisions negotiated on environmental issues can have major economic consequences for many, such as cuts in industrial production, reduction in employment, or the introduction of quotas. The interests of all parties usually can be aligned in negotiation. But often the responsibility falls on those who play the major roles, governments, to find a solution.

Agreements on environmental issues such as pollution control are often fragile and subject to criticism from all sides. Negotiators are aware of this danger and, therefore, try to avoid politicizing issues. Instead, they negotiate on a kind of objective basis, such as scientific evidence and legal constraints, to protect themselves and the purpose of their negotiations.

Treaty-Making

Treaty-making has three optional outcomes. First, it may codify measures to control the environment. Second, it may set a precedent that can be used in similar cases elsewhere. Third, it may turn the outcome of negotiations into a symbiosis of legal and scientific data, in which law provides the binding power.

Treaty-making is one of three types of negotiation discussed in this chapter. The other two are soft-law making and consultation. Treaty-making is the most common type of negotiation, because it provides the only means of arriving at legally binding rules. Witness the number of bilateral and multilateral conventions on environmental issues recently (Kiss, 1989; Lang, 1989; UNEP, 1989a). However, treaty-making will always be avoided by participants who do not wish to enter into commitments that they cannot control or comply with.

Soft-law making refers to the process that originally developed economic codes of conduct in North-South relations. Soft law, in the form of guidelines, declarations, conclusions, and principles, does not carry the force of law, but reflects a high degree of political commitment on the part of governments. Soft-law making may serve as a stepping stone toward more binding agreements. Negotiators sometimes choose this approach to overcome the initial resistance of some participants and to get them used to the control measures.

Consultation, the third type of negotiation, takes place on an ad hoc basis or periodically, bilaterally or multilaterally, and mostly on regional issues. Consultation permits nations to talk below the level of legal or quasi-legal commitments, so that parties can elaborate on or implement technical measures that have been decided unilaterally or in conjunction with similar measures in neighboring states.

Role of the Lawyer-Diplomat

A key representative of the participants in a negotiation is the lawyer-diplomat. These specialists apply treaty-drafting skills to construct obligations as well as ambiguities. Ambiguities in treaties are mostly intentional; they avoid the destructive effects that some treaty obligations may have on national sovereignty. Lawyer-diplomats draft vague compromises in a form that is firm and solemn (Birnie, 1988). This activity, traditionally called *treaty-making,* is part of a broader "process of commitment." The process begins with a nation formulating its national policies, which then are communicated to other states and may become a commitment. The commitment then ultimately comes into effect as part of a treaty (Chen, 1989).

Treaty-making, however, is more than the legal reflection or confirmation of a political compromise. It has to strike a balance between the stability of expectations and the necessity of change, a delicate yet vital task for negotiators (Chen, 1989). In the field of environmental protection it is a major challenge for the lawyer-diplomat to embody change and flexibility within the terms of a treaty. A treaty is the legal expression of a political understanding, based on scientific and technological evidence and the balance of economic interests. It reflects the legal status quo between nations. However, new scientific evidence or the development of alternative technologies may require a modification of the terms of the treaty.

If this need for modification is not perceived the same way by different nations, and one nation prefers, for reasons of its economic interests, to maintain the legal status quo, serious problems may arise. Or, perhaps a small group of nations that are parties to a treaty may agree on a subsequent treaty that replaces the original one. The new agreement affects the rights and obligations of all the nations that belong to the original agreement. Thus treaty-making and treaty-amending do not take place in a legal vacuum.

Environmental negotiations usually encounter numerous obstacles before an issue is successfully resolved (Fouéré, 1988). One obstacle is that the scientific community, made up of representatives from different national backgrounds, does not always agree on data and long-term trends. Such a consensus is, however, the basis on which negotiators try to build an agreement. Also, differences may arise over the cost-benefit analysis of proposed measures, and whether short-term costs outweigh long-term benefits. Furthermore, nations that have yet to establish an infrastructure for environmental protection as part of their national policy encounter major difficulties when they try to meet their obligations under an international agreement. One should not lose sight of the fact that the political will to abide by rules does not always coincide with the ability to do so.

Treaty-making is subject to political and legal constraints that lawyer-diplomats, as members of a national delegation, have to accept as the framework that both enables and restricts their actions. Among the political constraints are the instructions that lawyer-diplomats receive from their government or the chief negotiator. The terms of a political compromise already arrived at by the chief negotiator may also be perceived as a constraint. For example, during the actual drafting session, the lawyer-diplomats have to translate the terms of the compromise into treaty language. They may realize, in creating the final draft, that the ambiguities purposely left in the original political understanding (because full agreement could not be achieved) cannot appropriately be reflected in treaty language. In such instances, the lawyer-diplomats must ask the political negotiators to clarify the agreement or renegotiate it. In multilateral negotiations, this "shuttling" of treaty text between a drafting committee dominated by lawyer-diplomats and the political bodies of the conference is quite common.

Among the legal constraints that figure foremost in treaty-making are each nation's constitutions and laws, into which the rules laid down in a treaty must fit. In most instances national legislation has to be changed as a consequence of treaty-making. Lawyer-diplomats must be aware not only of the constitutional rules determining their actions, but also of all the laws, decrees, and rules at lower levels of government that reflect environmental policy. In federal states, it might only be possible to comply with treaty commitments if the provincial governments or local authorities are willing to comply. In most cases of this kind, the lawyer-diplomats will seek the consent, or at least the advice, of local bodies before formally concluding the draft for a treaty.

No less of a legal constraint on negotiators are existing obligations to other nations, through previous treaties or customary international law. In translating a political compromise into legal terms, lawyer-diplomats need to have a comprehensive knowledge of their country's existing obligations toward other countries or to the international community as a whole. They must draw the attention of the chief negotiator to any discrepancies or conflicting situations early in the negotiations, even though such advice, usually referred to as "legal niceties," is not always appreciated.

The most important guideline for treaty-making is *The Vienna Convention on the Law of Treaties* (Sinclair, 1984). It is a legal instrument that serves to guide the actions of the lawyer-diplomat. It contains most of the rules required for the creation, interpretation, application, and termination of a treaty. Many clauses in this convention can be borrowed directly for the treaty under negotiation, because treaty writers find little in these clauses that is contentious. Yet they are important because they contain rules on how to amend the existing text of a treaty and how to adapt it to changing circumstances.

Considering all the facets and consequences of treaty-making, such as the interpretation of ambiguous terms, the adoption of amendments, and other procedures, one should not lose sight of the fact that these issues are part of the negotiation itself, although they may come to the surface only at a very late stage. The success of lawyer-diplomats depends on their ability to tackle these comparatively minor problems, to ensure that in the future, after the treaty has come into operation, problems do not arise that may jeopardize the interests of their government.

Role of the Scientist

Whereas the basic elements of treaty-making and the role of the lawyer-diplomat are similar in most negotiations, those covering environmental issues also are strongly influenced by scientific evidence. Viewing environmental negotiations from the broadest possible angle, several points should be identified at which scientists may get involved. They are likely to intervene during the prenegotiation phase as well as during the implementation phase. It is often scientists who ring the alarm when new instances of environmental damage or at least new threats of such damage are discovered. In many cases scientists are called upon to participate in the implementation of a treaty or in the monitoring of its strict application.

The impact of scientists in the negotiation process depends mainly on their specific function. Scientists may advise the delegation before it departs for the negotiation or they may accompany the delegation formally as advisers. To be fully incorporated in such delegation implies, however, a more or less complete alignment with the respective political positions and given instructions. Sometimes scientists from various national delegations who are attending a conference meet separately as a scientific committee or as a scientific working group. Agreements achieved in this context, as for example the consensus on the ozone-depletion capacity of certain substances, serve as the basis upon which the treaty itself will be built. Other scientists are invited to attend a negotiation on behalf of green or industrialist lobbies (nongovernmental organizations). In some cases the leeway of these experts, especially in respect to statements to the press, is greater than when they are included in official delegations acting on behalf of governments.

The challenges to scientists and to lawyer-diplomats are quite similar. Scientists are also subject to certain objective constraints; these especially include the state of the art in the respective field, the relative certainty or uncertainty of the evidence available, and the evaluation of this evidence by applying more or less strict standards. Furthermore, scientists may be confronted with more subjective constraints, such as the instructions of the chief delegate, by which they are supposed to abide. Thus a conflict between the positions to be defended and the personal convictions of the scientists, regardless of the strength of the respective arguments, can never be fully eliminated. Such tensions, however, are not limited to the area of negotiations; they are part and parcel of the overall relationship between science and politics, between science and society.

Elements of a Treaty

Before examining specific negotiations, one should be aware of the distinction between the primary and secondary elements of a treaty. Primary elements are those linked directly to the object and purpose of a treaty. If one negotiates a treaty aimed at protecting the ozone layer, the primary elements are those that contain strict rules for reducing emissions of ozone-depleting substances. In a treaty on air pollution, primary elements would contain exact figures related to the reduction or elimination of specific toxic emissions. In a treaty devoted to the transport of hazardous waste, primary elements would refer to the conditions that have to be satisfied before the export or transit of hazardous substances would be approved by authorities.

Secondary elements contribute to the realization and application of the primary elements. Secondary elements include rules on compliance control (verification), state responsibility, and trade restrictions. Secondary elements also refer to all the institutional arrangements that make the primary rules operational, as well as to the amendment procedures that allow the treaty to be modified when circumstances change.

Conclusion

Most of the negotiations examined in the following chapters are multilateral negotiations. The selection of these cases does not imply that bilateral negotiations or bilateral treaties are less important than multilateral ones. However, most international environmental problems concern more than two nations. In addition, multilateral negotiations have more public visibility, even though bilateral negotiations may be more common.

Furthermore, research on multilateral negotiations has the additional advantage that negotiation material, such as records and provisional drafts, is more accessible than that from bilateral negotiations, in which confidentiality is observed to a much higher degree. Also, the actions of lawyer-diplomats can be more easily observed in multilateral negotiations than in bilateral ones, as they shuttle treaty text between the drafting committee and the political bodies of the conference. In bilateral negotiations, the movement between these political and legal levels can rarely be observed.

Multilateral treaty-making is somewhat similar to lawmaking in democratic societies. Interest groups are comparable to political parties; deals leading to the final compromise are struck in a smoky back room; the level of rhetoric of a party does not always match the party's level of real influence. There are also major differences. The most important difference is that parliamentary proceedings results in texts which have the force of law and have to be followed by all government officials, the courts, corporations, and individuals. On the other hand, an international treaty is part of international law. Whether or not it is complied with depends on the political will of the parties, since no international central authority exercises jurisdiction over these matters. Thus, from the outset, environmental treaties have to meet the concerns of all parties involved, to assure their full compliance.

In some instances, treaty-making for environmental issues has developed a specific step-by-step approach (Chossudovsky, 1989). The following chapters will demonstrate this. The first step is often the creation of a framework convention or umbrella treaty that broadly describes duties and areas of cooperation. For example, a first step could involve procedures to observe the condition of the ozone layer or to monitor pollution. It could also include the obligation to agree at a later stage on substantive rules for reducing noxious emissions and limiting environmentally dangerous activities. The second step could be the drafting of additional or supplementary protocols or treaties that contain exact requirements to reduce emissions by a specific amount by a certain date.

Sometimes negotiators also follow a step-by-step approach in drafting restrictions and obligations in the context of such protocols. For example, a protocol might require some sort of reduction by 20% in 3 years, and a further reduction by 50% in 10 years. The constraints that a treaty imposes are frequently incremental so that the parties affected by the constraints can become accustomed to the sacrifice they have to make. Such an incremental approach can also encourage them to switch to alternative technologies and products. Moving from less-restrictive to more-restrictive obligations, in some areas, has helped to overcome the resistance of parties entrenched in environmentally dangerous activities.

Environmental negotiations are similar to other types of negotiations in attributes, but they are also quite different. The dual nature of environmental negotiations poses a challenge to practitioners and researchers. For researchers, the task is to discern what makes a negotiation distinctive and how that distinction affects the negotiation process.

The outcome of any negotiation depends on many factors. But when the outcomes are examined by analysts, experts, and the public, negotiators are certain to encounter critical scrutiny of the results of their endeavors. Negotiators in the area of environmental protection feel special pressure to negotiate a desirable outcome because of this scrutiny. This is another reason for negotiators to base their negotiations on scientific evidence, even though they will be pressured to consider the wide spectrum of opposing opinions and conclusions about that evidence. That pressure is public opinion, which might include harsh attacks on them.

The framework that Guy-Olivier Faure and Jeffrey Z. Rubin describe in Chapter 2 approaches the task of analysis in a way that suggests an interdisciplinary and cross-sectional study of the process and outcome of negotiation. This approach can help researchers find the appropriate tools for further study of negotiation.

The problem still remains, however, of how to apply the theoretical findings of research to the practice of negotiation. Research findings always will be challenged by skeptical practitioners and the public. Therefore, it is useful to keep in mind that with the growing importance of the political aspects of environmental negotiations and with the need to turn negotiated outcomes into law, the negotiation always will be acquiring new dimensions and qualities and will evolve into an open-ended process.

2

Organizing Concepts and Questions

GUY-OLIVIER FAURE
JEFFREY Z. RUBIN

Negotiations—*all* negotiations—are fundamentally alike. Whether the exchange or division of resources through negotiation takes place between husband and wife, labor and management, one business and another, conflicting members of a community or organization, official political representatives of nation states, or parties to an environmental dispute—regardless, all negotiations share several attributes and adhere to a common underlying rationale.

These attributes are as follows: At least two or more parties have divergent interests that they have chosen to reconcile not through the traditional methods of coercion, capitulation, or inaction, but through the process of negotiation. The divergence of interest that forms the raison d'être for negotiation, in turn, has several characteristics: scope and basis among them. Regarding scope, differences that are relatively small in scale (generating relatively little personal involvement and anger) will generally be easier to settle than those that are more intense. Basis, in turn, refers to the apparent reason for the difference in question: typically the division or exchange of either a tangible or an intangible resource.

General Framework

All negotiations can be described and analyzed in terms of several key elements: *actors, structure, strategies, process,* and *outcome(s).* If one conceives of a negotiation as analogous to a theatrical production, then the negotiators themselves are the actors. The various constraints on the negotiators lead them to behave in particular ways that form the structure within which negotiation occurs. These constraints may consist of the audience, the lines that the actors/negotiators have been scripted to say, and so on. Negotiation strategy is a bit like the motivated and end-oriented behavior that guides the players who strut and fret upon the stage. Outcome denotes the result of the negotiation, like the denouement of the dramatic production. Process describes (at a meta-level of analysis) the theme and underlying texture of the exchange.

Actors. The actors may be individuals, groups, organizations, or nations. Usually they are represented at the negotiation table, but occasionally they may exist away from the table. Most often, in the complex circumstances that typically characterize international environmental negotiations, actors include the negotiators and the constituents to whom they are accountable.

Actors differ in the power and authority that have been delegated to them: Some may be relatively free to make binding decisions on behalf of their client(s); others may be required or expected to consult before making even the smallest concession. They differ in personality, and this in turn affects negotiating style. They may differ in status. They may belong to different cultures, which may affect their particular understanding of the situation. They may have personal goals that do not necessarily overlap with those of their constituents.

One thing is certain: Before any adequate analysis of a negotiation can take place, one must know who the actors are. *Who* are the parties to the dispute, both those sitting around the table, as well as those who, while not present at the negotiations, nevertheless have an interest in, and an opportunity to influence, the exchange?

Structure. The second key element of a negotiation is its structure: the set of constraints within which the exchange takes place. Among the components that pertain to any negotiation are such things as the number of parties; power (including the amount of power and its distribution, either symmetrical or asymmetrical); time limits; location of the negotiating site; openness of this site to various observing audiences; opportunities for communication through written, oral, and other means; number of issues; differences among these issues in terms of difficulty; the order in which they must be addressed; and requirements for developing an agenda. In short, structural elements provide the framework for analysis of every aspect of the context in which negotiation occurs.

Although there is no necessary causal link between these structural components and the logic of the negotiation process that ensues, we believe that in order to understand fully any negotiation it is necessary to answer the *what* question: *What* are the physical, social, and issue constraints of the negotiation?

Strategies. The third key element, strategy, refers to the general orientation of the actions that negotiators take to achieve their objectives. Strategic considerations concern decisions to cooperate or compete; decisions to match or exploit the strategy of the other party; decisions to deceive or be forthright; decisions to be flexible or rigid; a plan to start with reward and to turn to punishment only if necessary or to start tough and then relent only if the other side indicates a willingness to move toward agreement. One may play the negotia*tor* as well as the negotia*tion.*

A strategy is an intellectual construct, enacted by means of tactics that can be defined as elementary moves. Among the many tactics that can be utilized by negotiators are benevolent moves (such as compliments or concessions) and coercive ones (such as verbal aggression, threats, or fait accompli actions).

Each consideration, and many others, bears on the general matter of strategic analysis in negotiation. This is the *how* question: *How* do the negotiators move toward their negotiation goals? How do they organize the various tactics that they employ toward this end?

Process. As a key element in negotiation, process can be thought of as the meta-level set of concepts that are used to explain how the interaction takes place. Process focuses on the very dynamics of the negotiation; it focuses neither on the negotiator nor the other party, but on their ongoing interaction.

Negotiation process can be characterized as a succession of stages, including prenegotiation. Or it can be understood as distinct but interconnected subsets of activity, each having its own logic. For example, *demands* (what a negotiator says he or she must have) may be contrasted with *interests* (the needs or concerns that motivate statements of demand); *formula* (the overall or overarching framework within which negotiation transpires) can be distinguished from *detail* (the set of moves, agreements, and so on, that translate a formula into the nuts and bolts of an agreement); *aspiration* (the agreement a negotiator hopes to achieve under the best possible circumstances) contrasts with *expectation* (the agreement one

believes is most likely to result) and with *bottom line* (the point below
which one would rather not negotiate rather than accept the current offer).

These, then, are but a few of the considerations that can be generally
subsumed under the heading of process. This is the *why* question: *Why* do
things proceed as they do in negotiation? What are the meta-level variables
that help to explain what is really going on in the exchange? What is the
rationale for the interaction? What concepts can be used to describe and
understand how things progress?

Outcome. The final key element to examine in any negotiation is its
outcome—the end results to which the parties aspire. Such outcomes, the
results of negotiation, can be understood in many ways. Does the reaching
of an agreement necessarily correspond to a success? How does each party
perceive this result? How does the content of an agreement compare with
the expectations of each negotiator, as well as each side's opening position? What is the quality of the outcome (on the assumption that some
agreements may be objectively better than others)? What is the *joint*
outcome obtained by the parties—including, if necessary, any side payments (in general, the higher the joint outcome, the closer the negotiators
are said to be to the Pareto frontier)? How creative is the agreement? How
satisfied are the negotiators with the results? Has each side obtained what
it deserves (that is, is the agreement fair)? Are there any process-generated
stakes? How stable is the agreement? How implementable is it?

In general, then, outcome questions concern the matter of *what for*:
What are the negotiations *for*? What are the end results that the negotiators
will use to evaluate the success of the proceedings?

Distinctive Attributes of Environmental Negotiations

So far, this chapter has summarized some of the major ways in which
negotiation can be understood in any setting. This book, however, is not
on negotiation in general or, for that matter, on international negotiation per
se (for a comprehensive discussion of the latter subject, see Kremenyuk,
1991). Rather, we are concerned with international environmental negotiation. How are negotiations in the international environmental arena
different than other kinds of negotiation? Are such negotiations qualita-
tively different, or are the differences a matter of degree? Do the negotiations
require the implementation of specific processes to reach agreement?

The remainder of this chapter, therefore, advances the view that international environmental negotiations *do* have a set of distinguishing attributes. These same attributes can be found elsewhere as well, but are

probably present to a greater extent in environmental disputes, and may lead to the implementation of a distinct negotiation rationale.

Multiple parties and multiple roles. International environmental negotiations, almost by definition, involve more than two parties. Even in the instance of bilateral discussions there are likely to be various onlookers (other states, regional or international organizations, the media) with an interest in the outcome, and who function, in effect, as additional negotiating parties. Moreover, even in the simplest international dispute over the environment, issues are likely to be sufficiently complex that a variety of negotiating, decision-making, and advisory roles are necessary. Thus the conclusion of a successful agreement requires input from policymakers, scientists, and engineers, as well as the host of government officials who will be charged with implementing any agreement reached.

Multiple issues. If environmental disputes typically require the participation of many parties, then less obvious, perhaps, may be the fact that multiple issues are often involved as well. What appears to be a relatively straightforward environmental issue soon turns out to have important economic, social, and political implications. And when these negotiations take place in the international arena, the various implications multiply in importance and assume the form of additional issues on the table; moreover, the nature of the agreement reached for one country may have implications, indeed may help create additional issues, for the other nations that are affected by this decision. In short, the parties to environmental negotiations too often assume that they are dealing with a single issue, when in fact the story may be far more complex.

For example, consider the upcoming European Community negotiations over the installation of catalytic exhaust systems in cars as a way of reducing toxic emissions. More is at play than the preservation of forests in some European countries; car manufacturers are faced with significant problems of economics and marketing. Since the installation of catalytic exhaust systems is a relatively expensive and relatively fixed cost (regardless of the vehicle's size), the price of small cars will be increased by a larger proportional amount than the price of large vehicles. As a result, producers of large vehicles will be less disadvantaged than those manufacturing small cars. Negotiations of environmental issues are thus often negotiations about marketing strategies.[1]

Meaningless boundaries. As the soldiers in World War I discovered, poison gas does not respect national borders. Nor does pollution or acid rain. Under these circumstances, the meaninglessness of national boundaries has the effect of reinforcing the importance of interdependence of neighboring countries (while "inviting" interference in the internal affairs of others). These problems are transboundary in nature, even though the solutions are to be enforced on a territorial or national basis. Whereas the presenting problem in most negotiations is relatively straightforward (for example, the renewal of military base rights), it is less self-evident in the instance of environmental disputes.

The transboundary quality of many environmental conflicts can be a two-edged sword in negotiations. On the one hand, it may be more difficult than in other negotiations to evaluate who bears responsibility for the particular problem; on the other hand, provided that every country concerned bears some responsibility, this very ambiguity may also make it more likely that the parties to the dispute will come to understand that they *all* stand to benefit from whatever agreement is reached. If *all* sides stand to lose unless a solution is found to the problem of a decreasing ozone layer and global warming, then all sides stand to benefit from any global agreement on the problem. In environmental matters, zero-sum games (in which one side wins and the other loses) do not exist, since it is always possible for *all sides to lose.*

Scientific and technical uncertainty. It is possible to know the exact dimensions of a piece of land, just as it is possible to calculate precisely a company's industrial output. Environmental disputes, however, do not lend themselves to such precision. In particular, the measures that are continually being invented to resolve the growing number of environmental problems that plague our planet are solutions that are fraught with scientific and technical uncertainty. We are not sure about the reasons underlying the thinning of the global ozone layer, let alone the wisest solution to the problem. Indeed, some scientists even argue that there really is *no* problem with the ozone layer at all. The implication of such uncertainty is that one side's suggested solutions may often be deemed just as feasible (or otherwise) as suggestions advanced by the other. And this situation becomes even more complex when the parties cannot even agree as to whether a problem exists in the first place. Judgments about an environmental problem's existence are often subjective and notoriously unreliable.[2] Small wonder, then, that a nation suspected of polluting the waters may find itself far less convinced that a problem exists than its counterparts.

Power asymmetry. Most environmental problems—whether domestic or international in scope—are initiated by a human hand. Someone *does* something to the environment that has negative consequences for someone else. To be sure, there are many situations where one side's actions hurt itself as readily as they hurt others; however, of particular interest here are the situations where one side initiates a course of action that has negative consequences for the other. The result is typically that the latter cries out for help, or demands that the problem be redressed, or both. Consider a problem of river pollution. The state sitting upstream may think nothing of polluting the river, until the state downstream begins to demand a change. In this instance, since the costs incurred by the upstream and downstream interests are not equivalent, power in the upcoming negotiations is often asymmetrical. The upstream interest (more generally, the side that initiates a course of action that damages the environment in some way) may be far less inclined to take the problem seriously, let alone to bear responsibility for devising an appropriate solution, than the downstream interest (the side that is affected adversely by the former's actions).

Most negotiation analysis has focused on the strategies and tactics that are appropriate for use when parties are roughly equal in power; far less is known about the nature of negotiation under circumstances where parties differ in their dependence on agreement, as well as their motivation to negotiate at all. And as we have suggested here, many if not most environmental negotiations are of the latter sort; hence, understanding of these issues stands not only to increase opportunities for the policymaker and practitioner, but also to increase our theoretical understanding of negotiation processes.

Joint interest. As observed earlier, if poison gas or toxic waste is as likely to harm the offender as the offended, then in principle it should be possible to persuade negotiators that it is in their shared interest to reach agreement. Even the upstream interest in a river dispute may have someone else who is upstream; it therefore makes good sense for the downstream victim to point out to the upstream counterpart that no one really ever gets a free ride in an environmental problem.

In one way or another, because the world is united by so many environmental problems, we are all affected by the behavior of other people. As the English poet John Donne expressed it, "No man is an island unto himself . . . each is part of the main." In the short term, the changes that result from negotiations on the environment may be hard to observe, may seem to have little impact, and may carry nonobvious benefits for the parties involved. But in the long run, the potential for joint gain is truly enormous.

Negative perceptions of immediate outcomes. Environmental negotiations proceed rather differently than those involved, for example, in the acquisition of goods or the termination of war. Whereas a negotiated purchase provides immediate return (in the form of the goods obtained), and the end of a war brings an immediate conclusion to casualties, reaching an agreement on an environmental problem is likely instead to increase the constraints imposed on all concerned.

History has been defined as the science of men's misfortune. Borrowing from the same logic, one could define *environmental negotiation* as a process aimed at distributing misfortune among people. Perceptions of outcomes in environmental negotiations will tend to be only negative in the short term, generating costs, inconvenience, and loss of various advantages. In such cases, negotiation is like a problem of inconvenience distribution, paying now in order to avoid problems in the future.

As long as the painfulness of the situation does not justify immediate action, environmental disputes are evaluated prospectively—which is not the most powerful leverage to get negotiation started or progressing efficiently. Moreover, such negative perceptions influence the attitudes of the negotiators, the process itself, and subsequently the duration and outcome of the negotiation.

Long time frame. Just as it can often take quite a long time for the human abuse of nature's resources to manifest itself as an environmental problem, so too is it the case that the solutions to environmental problems may take a long time to take effect. This creates an important consequence: In environmental negotiations, the people who reach agreement may not be the ones to benefit from the agreement reached. For example, the implementation today of a radical regime to reduce the problem of pollution in the Mediterranean Sea would likely show beneficial results that are realized only by our children, or perhaps our grandchildren. Moreover, unless public opinion applies unusual pressure, the parties may not experience a current crisis as an emergency; rather, they may operate as if there is no need to reach agreement quickly.

International environmental negotiations, then, are unusual in their juxtaposition of short-term and long-range goals and concerns. The participants are constantly challenged to look beyond solutions that promise immediate results (if this is possible), and to consider solutions that are likely to be beneficial in the long term.

Changing actors. In international environmental negotiations, different negotiators may be called on to assist in the exchange before a final agreement is concluded. This is especially likely to be the case in negotiations that are highly technical, and in which the ordinary complexities of international negotiation are compounded by the presence of many experts.

Since environmental negotiations require considerable specialization of expertise, the individuals who help create the general framework of an agreement may not be the best people to work out the scientific or technical details. The experts participating in such negotiations are skilled in their own special domains, of course, but are often quite incompetent in dealing with negotiation processes and techniques. Moreover, such experts are rarely aware of the overall picture. Because of the close relationship required among policymakers and the scientific community, as well as among the sciences themselves (zoology, sociology, chemistry, anthropology), expertise in international environmental negotiations has become increasingly the result of genuinely interdisciplinary analysis.

Public opinion. Many negotiations are played out before an audience of onlookers, and many a skilled negotiator has attempted to master the art of playing to public opinion. It is a risky gambit, but one that negotiators are inclined to resort to nevertheless. Environmental negotiations—especially those that occur in the international arena—are almost certain to be followed with great interest by the news media, and they are likely both to influence and to be influenced by public opinion. This should not be surprising since environmental issues are likely to have an effect on the lives of many citizens; indeed, the negotiations themselves may be a direct result of the trauma expressed in public opinion. The disposal of hazardous waste is an issue that results in newspaper headlines, even as it grabs the attention of citizens; the events at Chernobyl had reverberations that were felt throughout the world, and indeed are still felt today.

The fact that public opinion is so readily engaged in the form of onlookers and influence agents in environmental negotiations makes these negotiations much more difficult to conclude successfully. The presence of onlookers, research indicates, increases the tendency of negotiators to take extreme positions from which they are subsequently unwilling to budge (lest they look soft or weak in the eyes of public opinion); this, in turn, may further complicate the negotiators' task.

Institutionalization of solutions. It is precisely because so many people are affected by international environmental issues that their resolution through negotiation may require some form of institutionalization; regional and international organizations (such as the United Nations Environmental Program) have proven extremely important in this regard. Thus a negotiated agreement on the environment will probably require the support of various government officials who, in turn, may find it necessary to formalize a negotiated understanding with new legislation. Often financial support is required as well. Or perhaps some new organization may be required to ensure that a negotiated agreement meets with compliance. This is likely to be of particular importance in the international arena, where some sort of regional or international organization may be expected or required to monitor the extent of compliance with the terms of a negotiated agreement.

New regimes and rules. A related consideration has to do with the importance in international environmental negotiation of finding some way of replacing old arrangements and rules with new ones. For example, to reduce the amount of freon gas entering the atmosphere, considerably more than a negotiated settlement is called for; even legislation, both domestic and international, will not suffice. Individuals living in countries that have been habitual producers of freon (through aerosol cans, among other things) must learn new rules of behavior. They must change their attitudes to such an extent that, even when not compelled by law, they will work to protect the environment.

This, then, is what we mean by new regimes. In international environmental negotiation, as in other forms of negotiation, new patterns of behavior are often necessary to supplant traditional approaches. Reaching an agreement is only one milestone in a much broader process.

Conclusion

The attributes described in this chapter are especially important in international environmental negotiations. Each attribute may be found in other types of negotiation, although we have argued that they are particularly relevant to environmental issues. Indeed, the case analyses discussed in Part 2 of this volume have, in one way or another, used this list of attributes to offer insights into international environmental negotiation.

Notes

1. To provide another example, it is clear that discussion of the maximum authorized weight per truck axle on European roads involves more than the simple matter of road protection. Technical design and economic problems result, with consequences for manufacturers' ability to make the heavy investment required to produce vehicles conforming to a new standard.

2. We note that in some countries discussions are currently under way concerning the possible harmful effects of laundry detergents. Several research laboratories have stated that the phosphates contained in detergents are destroying river fauna. Other laboratories have argued precisely the opposite, asserting that the products that are used as substitutes for phosphates are even more dangerous for fish than the phosphates themselves.

Part II

CASE STUDIES

The theoretical analysis in Chapter 2 indicates a number of common properties of international negotiations on environmental problems. Guy-Olivier Faure and Jeffrey Z. Rubin convincingly argue that, taking all these special—or typical—characteristics into consideration, there are good reasons to believe that environmental negotiations to some extent fit into a category of their own. The logical conclusion from the assertions made by Faure and Rubin is that in international negotiations on the environment, issues and problems should be approached and dealt with somewhat differently than in the bargaining over other issues such as, say, cultural cooperation, trade, or military disarmament. These propositions are, however, basically hypothetical and remain to be tested empirically.

It is by no means unreasonable to look upon the environment in a holistic perspective. In the final analysis this is indeed the only reasonable perspective. Many discernible ecosystems manifest strong linkage between the air, the sea, and the soil. One illustration is sufficient to color this proposition: If large portions of existing rain forests are cut down, the concentration of carbon dioxide in the atmosphere will, ceteris paribus, increase. Such a development will, in all likelihood, contribute to the greenhouse effect. As a result, the probability of climate change will increase significantly. Such climate change will probably have an effect on the water level in the oceans. Global warming may melt polar ice caps. The melting of ice caps will elevate the sea level in the interconnected oceans of the globe. An elevated sea level will destroy cultivated land near the sea in many countries around the world.

Given this holistic perspective on international environmental issues, however, it is also quite clear that in some respects these problems look quite different to negotiators. Notably, we may take stock of the fact that environmental problems may have a local, regional, or global reach. For instance, the problem of acid rain in industrialized countries has an important transboundary element, but it is still considered to be a regional phenomenon essentially located in Europe and North America. In contrast, climate change is a global problem that will affect countries in all parts of the world, although in quite different ways. For this reason we can expect significant differences in the negotiations on acid rain and climate change, respectively. At least we can safely predict that the circle of participants will be dissimilar in the two cases.

Presumably, the substance of an environmental issue helps to identify the negotiation problem. The nature of the negotiation problem affects how the issue is to be negotiated and what kind of outcome is feasible or probable. For instance, in the search for a solution it is necessary to consider how the problem was produced.

All environmental problems share a common source; deposition of pollutants resulting from human activity. But there are differences with respect to how environmental problems occur. For instance, soil deterioration may also be the result of destruction caused by, for instance, inefficient machinery or overgrazing of cattle or sheep. Deforestation is also an extremely important cause of soil deterioration.

It is noteworthy that the processes producing water and air pollution, respectively, are perceived differently due to the skewedness of human knowledge concerning the environment. The advanced state of the science and practice of meteorology, with its special skill in making predictions, have had great impacts on the way air-pollution problems have been handled in international negotiations. Meteorological tools make it possible to measure and predict transboundary flows of different sorts of pollutants. The knowledge of how pollutants are transported in the seas is much more restricted and diffuse. Currently, it is technically easy to identify which countries are likely to import carbon dioxide depositions from, say, Polish factories. It is much more difficult to clarify how pollutants deposited in the seas are spread. These circumstances are clearly important determinants of the way in which environmental problems are approached in negotiations.

In a comparative case study of environmental negotiations it is vital to capture as many different, significant aspects as possible of this subclass of diplomatic intercourse. This is the ultimate rationale for the selection of cases presented in this section. The cases of environmental negotiations pertain to the following regions or issues:

- Depletion of the ozone layer in the atmosphere (Chapter 3 by Patrick Széll).
- The transport of hazardous waste (Chapter 4 by Willy Kempel).
- Atomic security and the risk of the spread of radioactive pollutants (Chapter 5 by Gunnar Sjöstedt).

- Acid rain in Europe and North America (Chapter 6 by Roderick W. Shaw).
- Environmental problems in the Mediterranean (Chapter 7 by Peter Thacher).
- Environmental problems on the Rhine (Chapter 8 by Christophe Dupont).
- The Sahel problem (Chapter 9 by Michael Mortimore).
- Biological diversity (Chapter 10 by John Temple Lang).

A general criterion for the cases selected is that they are ongoing processes of negotiation and cooperation, although in different stages of maturity. To mention but two extreme cases: The negotiations on the Mediterranean were initiated in the early 1970s and the negotiations on the Sahel were launched in the summer of 1991. All cases are still on the international political agenda.

The issues for negotiation incorporated in this analysis pertain to the three basic layers of the environment: the soil (the Sahel case); accumulation of water (the Rhine and the Mediterranean); and the atmosphere (acid rain and the ozone layer). To this should be added three more environmental problems, more of which can easily be linked exclusively to a particular layer of the environment. Two cases relate to distinct industrial activities that are particularly risky as seen from an environmental point of view. The first of these two cases concerns the treatment of hazardous waste. This is notably the problem of the generation of garbage that cannot satisfactorily be treated in the country of origin. Therefore, a sort of international market has been created for hazardous waste. Relatively poor countries accept hazardous waste from companies in wealthier nations for a fee. The problem is that the authorities of the importing country do not always realize the consequences. Or else the responsible civil servant may have been bought for a fee. Therefore, several countries have accumulated hazardous waste and do not have the capability to cope with it. The possible detrimental effects relate to all environmental layers: air, water, and soil.

Another special case of generation of hazardous waste is the nuclear energy industry. A particular character of this industry is the terrifying magnitude of the consequences should pollution occur. Like hazardous waste in general, emissions of radioactive pollutants are likely to have a destructive effect on all layers of the environment: in the soil, in accumulations of water, as well as in the atmosphere.

The third environmental issue discussed in the book is that of biological diversity. This environmental problem cannot be related to any particular type of source of emission of pollutants. The extermination of species may be the result of pollution in the air, in the water, in the soil, or of a combination of such environmental deterioration. Human activities like hunting and fishing have also led to the virtual disappearance of entire species.

A second criterion for the selection of cases is that international negotiations on all significant geographic levels should be considered. The Rhine case represents a narrow region of few countries immediately involved in the negotiations: the Netherlands, France, the Federal Republic of Germany, and Switzerland. The case of acid-rain negotiations between the United States and Canada belongs to the same category.

Several of the cases investigated in the book belong to a category of larger, somewhat more diffuse but still regionally limited regions. Cases in this category include the Sahel problem, acid-rain negotiations in Europe, and the Mediterranean case.

Negotiations on the depletion of the ozone layer clearly pertain to the global level. The cases of hazardous waste and atomic security may be included in this category. In principle, they refer to problems that may occur anywhere.

A third criterion for the selection of cases is to present useful lessons for the future. Cases in this category highlight successful environmental negotiations: we want to find the conditions necessary for constructive and effective agreements. Therefore, most of the cases are success stories. However, to gain some perspective on these success stories a couple of failures have also been included. The first failure is the case of acid-rain negotiations between the United States and Canada. The second, and still more pronounced, failure concerns the so far abortive negotiations on the Sahel problems, which have not yet been officially launched.

The last chapter in this section is "The Law of the Sea Conference: Lessons for Negotiations to Control Global Warming" by James K. Sebenius. Here an environmental problem of great magnitude is introduced that has not been discussed in any other chapter: the prospect of climate change due to global warming. The chapter contains a study that differs from the other cases of environmental negotiations. This chapter is a transition from the case studies to the analytical chapters in Part 3. Sebenius has not undertaken a case study of a particular process of negotiation. He has, rather, identified lessons from the process of negotiation.

3

Negotiations on the Ozone Layer

PATRICK SZÉLL

This chapter deals with one of the major environmental issues, the depletion of the ozone layer. The main negotiation milestones referred to are the Convention for the Protection of the Ozone Layer (Vienna Convention), 1985; the Protocol on Substances That Deplete the Ozone Layer (Montreal Protocol), 1987; the first Meeting of the Parties (Helsinki), May 1989; and the second Meeting of the Parties (London), June 1990.

Chronology

Twenty years ago, the world was ignorant of the harm that humanity was causing to the ozone layer. Only when two scientists at the University of California, Sherwood Rowland and his postdoctoral student, Mario Molina, advanced the theory that chlorofluorocarbons (CFCs) might be damaging the ozone layer, did the problem receive attention. Initially, scientists, industrialists, and politicians were skeptical. By the late 1970s, however, scientists realized that if use of CFCs was left unchecked it would soon substantially deplete the ozone present in the upper atmosphere. The

31

depletion would allow more of the sun's harmful ultraviolet radiation to reach the earth's surface, causing an increase in certain types of skin cancer and in mutagenic effects, and inhibiting plant growth.

Concern grew to such an extent that, in 1978, the United States banned the main CFCs, numbers 11 and 12, in aerosols for all but essential purposes. In 1980, the members of the European Community (EC) imposed, on a precautionary basis, a limit on production of CFCs and a 30% reduction of the use of CFCs in aerosols. Sweden, Norway, and Canada also moved to reduce the use of the substances relatively early.

At the international level, the governing council of the United Nations Environment Program (UNEP) decided at its fifth session, in May 1977, to promote a "world plan of action on the ozone layer." The council established the Coordinating Committee on the Ozone Layer (CCOL), composed of representatives of government and industry.

The scientific community remained uncertain about the effects of CFCs, however. Scientific advice ranged from warnings that the problem was potentially extremely serious to cautions against overreacting to the situation. Nevertheless, the governing council of UNEP decided, at its ninth session, in May 1981, to start work on a global convention for the protection of the ozone layer. Six months later, this decision was endorsed by the UNEP ad hoc meeting of Senior Government Officials Expert in Environmental Law, held in Montevideo, Uruguay.

Negotiations on the framework convention began in January 1982. Disparate views on the need for action were apparent from the outset. Some nations wanted to accept a general framework convention. They said that their real objectives were a global ban of CFCs 11 and 12 in aerosols (except for essential purposes) and a limit on CFC emissions in nonaerosol uses. Other nations were wary of condemning too hastily chemicals that were nonflammable and relatively nontoxic, and that had proved themselves to be among the most useful, inexpensive, and convenient refrigerants, foam-blowing agents, and solvents available. For these nations, a framework convention would suffice until scientific evidence against CFCs became compelling.

Eight negotiating sessions in three years failed to draw these extreme viewpoints together. By the time the diplomatic conference was held in Vienna in 1985 to adopt the Convention for the Protection of the Ozone Layer (Lang, 1986; Rummel-Bulska, 1986; Sand, 1988; Széll, 1985), it was apparent that nothing more could be achieved than a framework that contained nonspecific obligations for protecting the ozone layer and general requirements for more research and the exchange of information. This limited outcome may be viewed as a victory for the more reluctant nations. However, associated with it was a resolution of the plenipotentiaries that set up workshops on scenarios, costs, and effects. The workshops would be followed, if possible, by a diplomatic conference in 1987.

Immediately after the workshops were held, nations pushed to develop an addendum to the Vienna Convention that would contain specific measures for controlling CFCs. Negotiations of a protocol with teeth started in December 1986. In contrast to the 38 months that it took to negotiate the Vienna Convention, it took only nine months to complete the Montreal Protocol on Substances That Deplete the Ozone Layer (Bunge, 1989; Buxton, 1988; Lang, 1988; Széll, 1988). The speed was remarkable considering that the positions of the protagonists remained, until almost the end, as deeply divided as they had been during negotiation of the Vienna Convention.

Meanwhile, scientific evidence confirming ozone depletion was becoming clearer and more compelling. In particular, in May 1985, scientists with the British Antarctic Survey published data that sent shock waves through scientific and political communities. Their observations at Halley Bay, in Antarctica, pointed to a 40% decrease in total ozone over Antarctica during each austral spring since the 1960s. By 1987, most nations realized that the time had come to adopt specific controls. The only disagreement that remained was how extensive those controls should be in terms of the range of substances and of the degree and timing of the controls.

In Montreal, in September 1987, the nations agreed to control eight substances: five CFCs (numbers 11, 12, 113, 114, and 115) and three bromine compounds (halons 1211, 1301, and 2402). Within 10 years, production and consumption of the CFCs was to be cut back, in three stages, to 50% of their 1986 levels. Production and consumption of the halons would be frozen within three years, except for essential uses such as fire retardants, because no satisfactory substitute was yet available. The halons had a much higher ozone-depleting potential than the CFCs, but were produced in smaller quantities.

Qualifications to this basic agreement were built into the protocol to meet the special circumstances of several nations. Additional controls limiting trade with nonparties were adopted to give these nations an incentive to become parties to the protocol.

Lastly, negotiators agreed to a derogation for the developing nations. The reasons for these exceptions were that developing countries had not caused the damage to the ozone layer, were soon to receive the industrial and social benefits of CFCs and halons, and were justified in wanting those benefits. It was also agreed that developing nations would have 10 years' grace before they had to comply with the control measures, provided that their annual consumption of the eight substances during the period did not exceed 0.3 kilograms per capita. Developing nations were also entitled to receive technical assistance. Many participants from developed countries thought the derogation went too far.

The agreement was remarkable; it was the first environmental treaty to take precise steps to avert a problem before it had begun to take its toll. The recognized need for quick action was symbolized by the provision that the protocol should come into force on January 1, 1989, just 15 months after the Montreal diplomatic conference, provided that:

- By that date, a minimum of 11 instruments of ratification, representing at least two thirds of the estimated 1986 global consumption of the controlled substances, had been deposited.
- The parent Vienna Convention was in force. The Vienna Convention required 20 ratifications and had not yet come into force by the start of the Montreal conference in September 1987.

The Montreal Protocol came into force on schedule. However, as scientific evidence became more conclusive, and concern for the deteriorating condition of the ozone layer grew, it became apparent that the protocol would not be the end of measures to control CFCs, but merely the beginning (Benedick, 1990a). The protocol required that the parties meet not later than one year after it came into force, and at regular intervals thereafter. Within that year (1988) a major working group met in the Hague, in October, and started the process of strengthening the protocol's control measures. Also, a ministerial conference held in London on March 1989 on saving the ozone layer focused on the involvement of developing nations in the protocol.

When the first Meeting of the Parties took place in Helsinki in May 1989 the representatives realized they would have to act quickly to reduce production and consumption of all CFCs and halons. This attitude prevailed even among nations that had felt the Montreal Protocol had gone as far as could be expected to control the substances.

Time did not permit the delegates in Helsinki to amend the protocol formally. Instead, they adopted a declaration that called for phasing out the production and consumption of the five CFCs listed in the Montreal Protocol not later than the year 2000. They also agreed to phase out the use of halons and to reduce dependence on other ozone-depleting substances as soon as was feasible. In addition, in what was to be a significant move with wide-ranging implications, the meeting decided to help developing countries get access to information, research, and training, and to try to set up ways to finance technology transfer and retooling in those countries.

This nonbinding statement of political intent provided the impetus for action at the second Meeting of the Parties, held in London in June 1990. The meeting had before it an even more extensive package of legally binding adjustments and amendments to the protocol than had been envisaged by the Helsinki declaration. In addition to the complete phaseout of the five CFCs and the three halons by 2000, the meeting agreed to phase out 10 other fully halogenated CFCs and carbon tetrachloride by 2000, and to phase out methyl chloroform by 2005. The schedule to reduce the original five CFCs and methyl chloroform would be reviewed in 1992 to determine if it should be accelerated.

In an associated resolution, the ministers resolved to phase out 33 partially halogenated CFCs (HCFCs) no later than 2040, possibly even by 2020. They also resolved to refrain from authorizing, or to prohibit the production or consumption of, 46 other halons.

Thus, after nearly a decade of reluctance and caution, control of CFCs is now almost total. At the same time, it has become more important than ever to ensure that all significant producers and consumers of ozone-depleting substances become parties to the protocol and abide by its terms. The participating nations realized that the environmental good that was achieved by the measures applied by the developed countries would be undone if developing countries—especially those like Brazil, China, and India, with sizable populations and rapid industrial growth—were to stay outside the protocol and continue their uncontrolled use of CFCs. Therefore, the amendment agreed to in London provided developing countries with financial incentives—including technical cooperation and environmentally safe, alternative technologies—so that they could become parties to the protocol. This amendment is likely be an increasingly important part of the protocol in the future.

The developing countries insisted that the financial incentives be in addition to any other contributions they received from developed countries. Bilateral cooperation may be considered part of a nation's contribution, according to criteria yet to be specified, provided it does not exceed 20% of the total. Contributions are to be levied only on developed countries. (The amendment avoids the word *compulsory* in this context.) Funds are to be paid in convertible currency according to the UN's scale of assessment. Payments by developing countries, international organizations, and nongovernmental organizations are also encouraged.

Developed nations will put the money into a new multilateral fund, out of which grants and concessional disbursements will be made to developing countries for expenditures that the parties agree to. The annual Meeting of the Parties is responsible for the policies of the fund, and an executive committee, working with agencies such as the World Bank, is in charge of its operation and administration.

Actors

The main actors involved in the negotiations on the depletion of the
ozone layer were the Toronto Group and the European Community, the
developing nations, the UNEP Secretariat, and other interest groups.

The Toronto Group and the European Community. Two blocs of nations
were the main actors throughout most of the negotiations of the Vienna
Convention and Montreal Protocol. These groups cut across the traditional
alignment of nations (Western countries, Eastern Bloc, and developing
nations) that has characterized so many global negotiations over the years.
The alignment reflected the fact that until 1987 the ozone-layer problem
aroused little interest among developing nations. Instead, it was solely the
concern of countries that produced and used CFCs and halons: the Western
industrialized nations. The former Soviet Union was the only Eastern
European nation to participate regularly in the negotiations.

The protagonists were the Toronto Group (so called because of a meeting
held in Toronto at a critical stage in the Vienna Convention negotiations)
and the EC. The Toronto Group was composed of the United States, Canada,
Sweden, Norway, and Finland, and, later, New Zealand, Australia, and
Switzerland. The EC included its member nations and loosely allied, at
various stages, with Chile, Japan, and the former Soviet Union.

The two opposing groups had fundamentally different objectives. The
Toronto Group wanted to go faster and further than the EC in controlling
CFCs and halons. It wanted to control the consumption of those substances
rather than their production. The EC preferred to control their production.

As with many other environmental initiatives, the Scandinavian countries were the prime movers. In 1981, they urged UNEP to launch its first
binding legal instrument of global scope. The Scandinavians were also the
architects of the aborted scheme for a protocol controlling CFCs in parallel
with the Vienna Convention. During the later stages of the Montreal
Protocol negotiations, New Zealand played a forceful role.

However, the real driving force behind the later stages of the Vienna
Convention negotiations and the entire Montreal Protocol negotiations
was the United States. It was decidedly hostile toward the entire exercise
at the second negotiating session—a point that is often forgotten. But in
1983 the United States changed its national policy, which it proceeded to
advance with the zeal of a convert during the next five years.

Unlike the Toronto Group, the member nations of the EC were not, at
least until 1989, united by a common belief in the scope of the ozone
problem or the best way to tackle it. They marched in step for a reason that
owed little to their individual views on the ecological consequences of

CFCs: their mutual obligations under the Treaty of Rome. In reality, the attitudes of the individual member nations varied greatly. On one extreme were nations that wanted the EC to align itself fully with the Toronto Group; on the other, were nations that wanted no more than limited, precautionary measures until scientific evidence was considerably clearer.

The Toronto Group was well aware of the internal strains within the EC group and tried to exploit them in its negotiating tactics (Benedick, 1989). Even before facing the other participants in plenary sessions, the EC nations and the Commission of the European Communities (CEC) had to expend considerable energy on forging common negotiating positions that the member nations would accept. The process was time-consuming and on more than one occasion it taxed the patience of the other participants.

Under EC law, member nations are required to negotiate as a single unit on any matter that is within exclusive EC competence. Competence is established whenever common rules that bind all members are adopted. This means that member nations are not allowed to act unilaterally on matters covered, or even affected, by common rules. As mentioned earlier, in 1980 the EC had adopted binding measures on CFCs; these were common rules. They were, however, very limited in scope and, therefore, did not confer much exclusive competence on the EC. On the other hand, EC members did not accept, during the London meeting, that the EC possessed any exclusive competence on environmental aid questions.

This said, the EC countries were obliged, under Article 5 of the Treaty of Rome, to seek (though not necessarily to find) a common position on matters outside exclusive EC competence. This rule held the EC member nations together throughout three meetings: the Vienna Convention, the Montreal Protocol, and the negotiations that amended the protocol (Lang, 1986).

The Toronto Group's ability to stick together did not survive the coming into force of the Montreal Protocol. When some members realized they needed more stringent measures than those in the Montreal Protocol, the negotiating positions of Canada, the Scandinavian nations, and, most significantly, the United States started to diverge from the earlier common position. By contrast, the EC members continued to speak with one voice.

The previously unbridgeable gap in attitude between the Toronto Group and the EC narrowed significantly by the time the London meeting convened. The principal difference that remained among Western countries was the rate of progress toward the total phaseout of the ozone-depleting substances. What drew those nations together even further was the developing countries' requests for financial assistance.

Developing countries. When attention switched from control measures to financial mechanisms, the major actors were realigned. The involvement of developing nations in the Vienna Convention was slight; of the first 23 nations to sign, only 5 were from the Group of 77, the group of developing nations. However, developing nations became more involved in negotiating the Montreal Protocol, as evidenced by the 10-year derogation they achieved and the expressed recognition of their need for technical assistance. Nevertheless, only 7 of the first 24 signatories in Montreal were developing nations.

Latterly, however, the developed nations have recognized that the developing nations are critical to the long-term success of the Montreal Protocol. As a result, the developing nations have been able to drive a hard financial bargain in return for their subscribing to the amendments or becoming party to the protocol. The announcement by the Indian and Chinese delegations, at the end of the second Meeting of the Parties, that they would recommend that their governments ratify the Montreal Protocol was a significant moment in the history of the negotiations. A possible new factor is that certain East European countries, seeing themselves in the same economic condition as developing nations, may seek to be classified with them, so they can obtain the same financial advantages under the protocol. Should they succeed, the negotiating leverage of the developing countries will be further enhanced.

In contrast to its forceful, pacesetting role in earlier years, the United States became defensive, even isolated, about several key aspects of the proposed financial package. The U.S. inflexibility was not caused by the annual contribution that it and the other developed nations had to pay into the fund. In economic terms, the substances controlled under the Montreal Protocol were comparatively insignificant. Instead, what concerned the United States, and what all nations realized from early on, was that the financial incentives agreed on for the Montreal Protocol would set the tone for subsequent global environmental treaties. In particular, the United States was worried about the forthcoming Climate Change Convention, during which the sums involved would be vastly greater. Arrangements devised in one multilateral environmental treaty have a tendency to become precedents for others.

The UNEP Secretariat. An increasingly important actor in treaty negotiations held under the auspices of UNEP has been its secretariat, specifically its executive director, M. K. Tolba. The profile of secretariats during negotiations varies considerably from one international organization to another. Some are highly interventionist, such as the CEC, for constitutional reasons, and the secretariat of the Organization for Economic Cooperation and Development, for traditional reasons. Other secretariats, including some within the UN system, are decidedly passive.

In the early years of its involvement in treaty-making, the UNEP Secretariat fell within the passive category. During the Montreal Protocol negotiations, however, the executive director had to take over as mediator when, coincidentally, a deadlock emerged between the protagonists, and the chairman was forced to return home in the middle of the meeting. This experience proved successful and led to further initiatives by Tolba in the form of written communications incorporating proposed compromise texts and informal consultations to narrow the gap on central issues. The secretariat's involvement has become a regular feature of global negotiations within UNEP. However, such involvement is not commonplace in treaty negotiations. It has become acceptable because of the care, skill, objectivity, and restraint with which Tolba performed his catalytic role.

Interest groups. Finally, mention should be made of the role of interest groups in the negotiating process. The presence of these groups in plenary sessions, and sometimes even in working group sessions, has increased over the years. The rules of procedure, adapted from those of the UNEP Governing Council, permitted nongovernmental organizations qualified in fields relating to the protection of the upper atmosphere to participate as observers.

Interest groups have not been allowed to table proposals, and the chair asked for their views only after the participating nations had given theirs. Whether representing the environmentalist cause or the industrialist cause, interest groups remained largely silent during formal negotiating sessions, making no more than occasional, short statements. They sat and listened carefully to the proceedings and used what they learned to brief the press and to lobby legislators and ministers back home before the next round of sessions.

In the ozone negotiations, the tactic of the North American and West European environmental lobbies was to hold press briefings. On the other hand, the tactic of the industrialist lobbies was to send representations to ministers of industry. The purpose was to keep the resolve of the negotiators of certain nations unyielding. The result was that, except on technical questions, the case of the environmental interest groups received most of the headlines in the Western media. Media attention undoubtedly shapes public opinion.

The number of observers from interest groups at negotiations is increasing with the growing concern of citizens for the damage to the atmosphere. The presence of interest groups in the negotiation chamber puts pressure on negotiators, particularly those from countries with vociferous environmental lobbies that know how to manipulate the press and those with powerful industrial lobbies whose leaders can demand the attention of government officials.

Structure

This section examines the structure of the negotiations on ozone-layer depletion and global warming, and notably the following factors: UNEP, meeting locations, format, duration, conduct, and delegations.

UNEP. Negotiations on the Vienna Convention and the Montreal Protocol were conducted entirely within the framework of UNEP. This UN body provides a natural forum for environmental discussions, especially technical discussions.

More than any other organization, UNEP has provided an established framework for supervising and running environmental treaty negotiations. The governing body of UNEP has stimulated the progress that has been made. Moreover, UNEP has been able to offer negotiating nations a secretariat that is technically experienced in atmospheric science and treaty-making. While individual nations could undoubtedly host single meetings, global treaty negotiations, such as those on ozone depletion and global warming, are time-consuming and could not reasonably be left to a single country or a group of countries to host.

Meeting locations. UNEP's headquarters are in Nairobi, but the negotiations on ozone depletion have taken place in other cities, mainly Geneva, where the UN has extensive facilities. Locations other than Geneva have been used for diplomatic conferences and the Meetings of the Parties. Even then, on at least three occasions (Vienna, Montreal, and London), the meetings, though financed by the host country, have been held on UN premises.

In all these locations an important factor has been the ease with which delegations could communicate with their government at home, either from UN premises or their own local missions or embassies. In modern environmental treaty negotiations, particularly during the stage immediately before a legally binding instrument is adopted or amended, delegations have to be able to communicate quickly, easily, and often with their governments to obtain instructions and approval of texts. The practical advantages of meeting in Geneva were so many that countries that might otherwise have offered to host a session, opted instead to make a financial contribution to UNEP for running the session.

Format. The format of the ozone-depletion negotiations followed the pattern used by UNEP in all its treaty negotiations. A legal and technical working group was established to identify the issues; to translate the scientific, economic, and environmental considerations into international policy; and to present that policy to a diplomatic conference in the form of a legally binding instrument.

The process started with a session in which ideas and suggested content were debated in general terms. On the basis of this discussion, a draft text was prepared by, or under the authority of, the secretariat. The draft was discussed paragraph by paragraph with the aim of reaching consensus on as many items as possible. The process culminated with a diplomatic conference (or, in the case of a treaty amendment, a Meeting of the Parties), at which ministers or senior officials negotiated the final, intractable issues before the text was adopted. In practice, because of the short time available for such high-level gatherings (typically, they last two or three days), it is important for negotiators to make sure that few issues are left for ministers to negotiate, and that those that are left are near resolution.

Duration. Since the ozone negotiations began in 1982, the meetings have become increasingly short but more frequent. Pressure from environmentally minded countries has significantly shortened the time for negotiation. In the early 1980s, negotiating sessions of 10 to 14 days were normal. Now, it is unusual for a session to last more than a week. Also, in recent years, negotiating sessions have been held two or three months apart, in contrast to the six-month intervals that were common years earlier.

As the issue of the world's atmosphere has become more politically important, meetings between sessions and informal gatherings of nations have increased substantially. At critical stages of the negotiating process, officials from certain nations may have felt they were permanently in session. If one reason for the increased tempo of negotiations had to be given, it would be the modern practice of setting the date, and even location, of the diplomatic conference for adopting the treaty well before it is clear what the scope and content of that treaty will be. Working toward such an artificially generated deadline undoubtedly produces quick results, but at the price of unrefined notions and rough drafting.

Conduct. Control of the formal proceedings was predominantly in the hands of a chair, who, once elected, kept the role right up to the diplomatic conference or Meeting of the Parties. At the diplomatic conference itself, by tradition, the chair for the proceedings was at the disposal of the host country. Continuity of the chair was critical for the cohesion of the meetings and their smooth progress. The chair's power to propose compromise text to bridge the gap between divergent views can be critical to achieving a successful outcome to negotiations. The key in such circumstances is not to offer the compromise text too early in the debate, however obvious the compromise may be. Patience of this sort was demonstrated in both Vienna and Montreal.

The chair has always been supported by a bureau (usually made up of two vice-chairs and a rapporteur), elected on a basis that ensures equitable geographical distribution of the major posts. The role of the bureau has varied according to the instincts and styles of the chair. Generally, in the more recent ozone negotiations, the bureau was used considerably less than it was in the Meetings of the Parties to the Vienna Convention and Montreal Protocol. Between these meetings, the bureau maintained continuity by supervising the execution of the meeting decisions and by preparing for the next session.

In the Vienna and Montreal negotiations, the chair sometimes relied on groups other than the bureau to move the meetings along. These groups varied from informal consultations on particular issues to small drafting groups composed of three or four individuals selected by the chair. Their task was to produce a compromise formula on a given point. The chair's reason for organizing these smaller meetings was that if the countries involved could agree, then the meeting overall was unlikely to disagree.

Toward the end of each set of negotiations a small legal drafting group was set up, made up of representatives of the languages in which the treaty or amendment was to be adopted. Its job was to analyze the text objectively and to ensure that it was legally accurate and that it would work. This group worked smoothly and comprehensively for the Vienna Convention. However, because of the political tensions that surrounded the closing stages of the Montreal Protocol negotiations, the group was firmly instructed not to modify anything, "not even a comma," in the critical control measures, lest the delicate compromise that the provisions represented would disintegrate.

During the preparations for the London amendments to the Montreal Protocol, another use of the legal drafting group was demonstrated. In those negotiations, the chair set up the group early in the proceedings and made its membership open-ended so that as many as 30 countries participated. The chair told the group to work on problems that were stalled in plenary sessions. This was less a legal drafting group than an extended version of the small drafting group described above. These groups had the advantage of working away from the pressures of plenary sessions. In such an atmosphere, with little formality and no written records, seemingly insurmountable problems were often solved.

Delegations. The size of national delegations to global atmosphere meetings varied greatly. So, too, did the rank of the delegation leader. Some nations consistently appeared with one representative, often from the local mission or embassy. Not surprisingly, these participants were not, for the most part, experts in the matter of the negotiations and tended, therefore, to keep little more than a watchful eye on the proceedings.

At the other extreme, some nations attended with large delegations of 15 or more members. These were usually countries with a strong economic interest in the negotiations. Such large delegations presented no difficulty, except, perhaps, in terms of seating arrangements; they always used a single spokesperson except on scientific or technical matters, when the appropriate delegation expert spoke.

Between these two extremes came the majority of delegations, composed, on average, of two to four members, representing not so much the interests of the different government agencies in their countries, but rather the breadth of disciplines required to be effective participants in the proceedings: scientific, industrial, economic, legal, and political disciplines.

While a number of delegations, particularly from developing nations, were content for their positions to be represented by generalist diplomats from the local mission or embassy, most countries, even if located far from the meeting, were represented by delegations composed of experts from home. Unlike locally based diplomats, experts from home often had the advantage of having worked on ozone questions.

An inevitable hazard of international environmental negotiations is the inefficiency caused by changes of personnel from one meeting to the next. The momentum of the negotiations is inevitably lost while new delegates, especially in delegations that are at the center of the debate, become acclimatized. Personnel changes are inevitable with diplomats and civil servants being moved to new posts. The ozone-layer negotiations had their share of transient participants too. However, one bonus to the Vienna Convention and Montreal Protocol negotiations was the extent to which the meetings took place at a single location, thereby increasing significantly the amount of continuity of representation.

Strategies

This section describes the strategies used by participants outside and inside the negotiation chamber.

Outside the negotiations. The principal tactic used outside the negotiation chamber by some nations and all the pressure groups was to vie for media attention. Press coverage of the negotiations increased greatly with the increased public interest in protecting the world's atmosphere. The Vienna Convention negotiations did not receive much coverage, but media attention grew by the time the Montreal Protocol negotiations began.

Several nations tried to put pressure on other nations, which they thought were dragging their feet, by holding carefully controlled press briefings before, during, and after the meetings. This strategy was only partially successful. It would have been totally successful had the public concern about ozone depletion been as high in the nations that were being accused as it was in the accusing nations.

Environmental pressure groups are constantly increasing their skills in handling the media, and make it a top priority to keep the press informed about what they perceive are unacceptable positions adopted by negotiators in the meeting room. The media relied heavily on leaked information to present up-to-date and critical analysis of national positions.

A second tactic used by participants outside the meeting room was to coax industries in their countries to act in environmentally sound ways. They tried to do this by impressing on the industries the attractive business opportunities that could result from taking a lead in research and technological innovation.

Nations that believed they had strong environmental credentials used international meetings of ministers, and the resulting declarations, to press for more environmental action. One example of this tactic is the resolution adopted at a diplomatic conference, such as the one in Vienna that envisaged a second ozone treaty or the Saving the Ozone Layer Conference held in London that highlighted the role of developing countries. Another example is the declaration of the ministers at the first Meeting of the Parties in Helsinki, which committed nations to phase out the controlled CFCs and halons by the year 2000.

Adoption of such instruments along with or prior to environmental treaties is a comparatively recent phenomenon. Perhaps the first time such a tactic was tried was with the protocols adopted under the Geneva Convention on Long-Range Transboundary Air Pollution. This instrument provided nations that were disappointed with the modest obligations in the protocol with a means of recording their views of what the obligations should have been. Subsequently, the instrument was adapted as a means of achieving high-level political commitment on key issues, such as targets for reducing greenhouse gases.

Inside the negotiations. Inside the negotiation chamber, some nations were reluctant to commit themselves to strong measures to tackle ozone depletion. Even so, they could not oppose the negotiations outright for political reasons. Instead, they resorted to slowing down the process, hoping that, during the delay, science, technology, or politics would vindicate their hesitancy or, at least, the industries in their countries would develop substitute substances or processes. Such tactics have been viewed with distrust by the more environmentally oriented countries.

In practice, however, it has always been possible for a strong actor, like the Toronto Group, to control the timing of events. For example, a delay sought by the EC in 1987 to allow its ministers to agree on a changed position before the next full negotiating session was swept aside as unnecessary, uncooperative, and inimical to the environment. However, countries calling for fast action have to accept that measures that are adopted quickly are weaker than they would be if more time were allowed for negotiation.

In addition, aggressive nations have had to face the dangers of insisting on adoption of measures that are too stringent. For example, toward the end of negotiations on the Vienna Convention, nations wishing to adopt a parallel protocol that contained specific controls on CFCs backed off and consoled themselves with the resolution calling for a second diplomatic conference. They did not want to risk having a convention and protocol to which merely the Toronto Group and its supporters were party.

Critical to the success for those seeking a particular objective was the ability to seize the high ground and defend it staunchly. Such a strategy meant that nations had to advocate the strongest possible case, short of alienating less progressive nations. Less progressive nations were disadvantaged by the fact that they could not exaggerate their resistance for tactical reasons in a negotiation, because of the adverse publicity it would have received. Meanwhile, the more environmentally minded nations overstated their case, knowing that they would be reined in during the compromise process.

The benefits of operating through a group rather than individually have been considered above. In general, countries that operated independently did not make a significant impact on the texts of the ozone agreements. In multilateral negotiations, time constraints and pressure to achieve an outcome place independent voices at a disadvantage. Likewise, those who remained silent added weight to whatever argument eventually prevailed. These harsh facts, among other things, encouraged member states of the EC to negotiate as a unit, despite the absence of exclusive Community competence over ozone-depleting substances. An exception has been, perhaps, the former Soviet Union, which plowed its own furrow from the outset, with much success. In Montreal, for example, the former Soviet Union won a special concession only for itself concerning production facilities that were authorized but not yet in operation by the date that the protocol was adopted.

Outcome and Conclusions

Participants in the Vienna Convention negotiations agreed on a legislative approach that was used for the first time in the environmental field in the Barcelona Framework Convention for the Protection of the Mediterranean Sea Against Pollution, held in 1975 (see Chapter 7). It was UNEP's first Regional Seas Convention. The participants recognized the political impossibility of agreeing on detailed control measures and specific norms for matters covered by the convention. So they agreed to adopt a "gradualistic" approach and create a general framework text that established little more than the institutional organization for continuing talks about Mediterranean pollution. The agreement could be augmented, either immediately (as happened in the case of Barcelona) or subsequently by specific protocols.

One advantage of such a process is that it provides parties with a breathing space, either if they are not yet ready to subscribe to all the specific obligations or if scientific, technical, and economic analysis of pollution problems are not sufficiently advanced to justify specific controls. Another advantage is that the process makes the nations which ratify the agreement members of a permanent forum for discussing problems and launching initiatives. The third advantage is that, when the time is right to consider further legislation, negotiators can concentrate on the substantive details, because the procedures of the parent convention automatically apply.

This approach, which has proved itself over the years, is likely to be adopted for the 1992 global-warming convention. With a deadline of 1992 for finalizing a legal text, and a growing number of countries opposing early action to cut back on greenhouse gases, a repetition of the Vienna Convention experience seems likely. Nations might again adopt a framework convention accompanied by a resolution or declaration outlining further steps and a timetable.

Part of the price that was paid for the speed with which the Montreal Protocol was adopted and amended has been an imprecision in its drafting that had to be fixed later. Key expressions in the protocol—such as "basic domestic needs," "industrial rationalization," and "developing countries"—were deliberately left undefined by the negotiators because of a lack of time. For the protocol to operate effectively, however, ambiguous terms had to be clarified by decisions, binding in nature but not formally part of the protocol, of the first Meeting of the Parties. At the second meeting, participants extensively amended the protocol, which completely altered its principal articles and made several important adjustments. Already, after only three years, the text looks so different from the one adopted in Montreal that it is difficult for anyone but a specialist, who works closely with it, to describe precisely what the protocol requires and where a requirement can be found. To solve this problem, which seems certain to grow, the parties decided at the second meeting to invite the executive director of UNEP to consolidate all the relevant material (which may include items from the *travaux preparatoires*) in a *Montreal Protocol Handbook,* which can be updated regularly.

Paradoxically, successful negotiations on the ozone-layer problem have often involved avoiding, or only lightly touching upon, key issues. But such evasiveness has been only temporary. Either circumstances have demanded that discussions on the issues were soon reopened or the nations committed themselves, by resolution or declaration, to address them again by a specified date.

The Vienna Convention and the Montreal Protocol undoubtedly disappointed the Toronto Group and its supporters (Benedick, 1990b). In their view, both instruments offered too little over too long a period. Scientific findings have, perhaps, vindicated the Toronto Group's opinion, but those who supported the cautious approach would no doubt say that the delay of three or four years before taking strong measures was necessary to enable scientific findings to prove that such action was really required. Those countries would also point out that they had more to lose economically than the advocates of rapid action, if the pressure for action had proved to be misplaced.

Because the Vienna Convention established a dynamic regime, parties have been able to react much more quickly to advances in scientific knowledge. It is safe to say that no nation, not even the Scandinavian ones, expected in 1981, when they decided to prepare a convention, that within a decade measures would be in place that would either phase out or severely cut back almost all ozone-depleting substances by the end of the century.

Resolution of the global ozone-layer problem is now seen as a short-term technical and economic matter, well within the abilities of nations. The controlled substances are, for the most part, not essential and they are being replaced. Global warming, on the other hand, is going to be a larger, harder, and more complex task to tackle effectively. Nations will be faced with new technical and economic problems and with awkward political questions on such fundamental matters as energy patterns and population policies. More interests will be affected than were affected by the ozone negotiations. The argument that protection of the global environment is paramount will not necessarily be easy to mount or win.

In embarking on this daunting and uncertain task, all nations should be reassured that a well-established legal model to use as the basis for negotiation already exists—a model with which the UNEP Secretariat has acquired considerable experience.

4

Transboundary Movements of Hazardous Wastes

WILLY KEMPEL

Waste is generated as a major consequence of almost any human and economic endeavor. Low-toxicity waste can be collected, transported, and disposed of using low-sophistication technologies such as incineration or disposal in landfills. In the case of high-toxic wastes, however, specific methods of handling, transport, and disposal are applied as stipulated by national environmental and health regulations. Space in disposal sites is becoming increasingly scarce in countries generating such wastes, either because national legislation does not permit the disposal of high-toxic wastes or because the economics of existing disposal sites are unacceptably high. The question of exporting such wastes is therefore raised. As these wastes are highly toxic, it is crucial to consider questions of packaging, transportation, and disposal together with the responsibilities and liabilities at each stage of these operations.

As a result of the growing export activity, legal regulations as well as administrative control regimes became more stringent in the early 1980s, primarily at a national level. The first initiatives were taken at the regional level by the European Community (EC) and later by the Organization for Economic Cooperation and Development (OECD). The principal reasons for this interest appear to be twofold: on the one hand, risks had to be minimized on account of potential political problems as a consequence of such hazardous waste exports, therefore stringent rules of conduct had to be applied; on the other hand, exports of hazardous wastes from the waste-generating region had to ensure equal treatment of the receiving states to avoid problems with them or with other states.

The EC adopted Directive 84/631, the Supervision and Control Within the European Community of the Transfrontier Shipment of Hazardous Waste, to control transboundary movements of hazardous wastes within its domain. The OECD initiated similar efforts in 1984, based upon the EC Directive, and attempted to extend its scope by drafting a convention. A further effort focused on reaching an acceptable definition of *hazardous wastes* within the so-called cross-reference system. This meant that waste regarded as hazardous in one EC country is defined as hazardous in all other EC member countries. Furthermore, the means of transportation were defined and standardized to ensure environmentally sound waste management throughout the EC by creating the necessary transparency. Provisions were also made to encourage recycling activities within OECD member states. However, due to varying national practices and standards, progress was slow.

Following numerous reports of illegal hazardous waste shipments, especially from developed to developing countries, the United Nations Environment Program (UNEP) decided to take action. The issue was taken up by the UNEP Governing Council, which initiated regulations at the global level. The basic idea was to establish minimum standards based on prior information about any shipments; general obligations upholding regulations for the safe transport and environmentally sound disposal of such wastes; and regulations concerning responsibility and liability in case of accidents, illegal shipments, or other circumstances obstructing the planned operation. In instances where such minimum standards could not be implemented, transboundary movement could not take place legally, thereby restricting international trade to protect the environment.

With an increasing number of illegal shipments of hazardous wastes from industrialized to developing countries, the issue of such transactions came to the forefront of international politics in the mid-1980s. This situation shaped the framework of the negotiations and would have a major impact on their outcome. Therefore, from the very beginning, the matter was viewed mainly as a North-South issue, although in reality approximately 95% of all transboundary movements take place in a North-North context. Illegal transports of hazardous wastes from developed to developing countries accounted for less than 1% of all transports, but gained somewhat in symbolic and political significance.

The principal problem of transboundary movements of hazardous wastes concerned the toxic nature of the substances and materials, thereby giving the impression that the problem was being exported. As long as such transports were taking place under the single-transport stipulations, not much attention was paid to the risks involved. Once problems gave rise to questions of both private and state responsibility and attendant liability, public opinion came increasingly into play. Further public involvement was generated by documents such as the Cairo Guidelines, which outlined the obligation to reimport hazardous waste shipments in case of illegal activities or the inability to complete the planned transport.

As states by then had become increasingly involved in the issues of transboundary movements of hazardous wastes and their disposal, the time seemed ripe to follow initiatives taken at the regional level and to apply them at the global level. Therefore, at the initiative of Switzerland, negotiations on a global convention started in 1987 in Caracas, Venezuela. The main reason for Switzerland's initiative was that Swiss companies were involved in illegal transports of hazardous wastes to Third-World countries. The second meeting took place in Budapest, Hungary, followed by a series of meetings leading to a plenipotentiary conference in March 1989 that adopted the Basel Convention on the Control of Transboundary Movements of Hazardous Wastes and Their Disposal.

The General Framework of the Negotiations

Actors. International activities regulating transboundary movements of hazardous wastes had been fairly limited until the start of the negotiations on the international convention. Until then, governments and industries were eager to conduct business as usual to avoid both major cost increases and alarming local populations (people living in the vicinity of the collection, storage, or disposal of hazardous wastes). In the global framework, the Cairo Guidelines represented the first attempt to deal with the problem, but only constituted international soft law (declarations that do not carry the force of law). Under the auspices of the EC and the OECD, attempts were made to elaborate on rules and regulations; when negotiations started, a definitive outcome had not yet been achieved.

In view of the issue's political importance, as well as the established international principles that necessitated state interference in case of a threat of major damage, states were becoming the main actors in the negotiations. However, in order to leave as much responsibility as possible in the hands of private citizens, state representatives of industrialized countries were eager to impose direct responsibilities and liabilities on private law entities. Thus national and international decision makers—in the political, economic, and social spheres—were drawn into the process to a greater extent. Representatives of major enterprises that were responsible for the international movement of hazardous wastes or were actual waste generators were allowed to participate at negotiating sessions as nongovernmental organizations (NGOs). During the sessions they lobbied against the imposition of very stringent control regulations to curtail the additional costs that were anticipated. As public law regulations were at stake, NGOs also became increasingly interested and played a key role in the negotiations. In comparing the successes of these different lobbying groups, it should be pointed out that environmental NGOs, such as Greenpeace, were much more effective than industry representatives.

In the course of the negotiations, country representatives became major actors. They represented two categories of states: involved states (large waste exporters, or producers, or major transit countries) and politically interested states (key players in the North-South context or those with a history of problems, especially with illegal transports of hazardous wastes). The first category included countries such as the United States, the member states of the EC (especially the United Kingdom, France, the Netherlands, Belgium, and the Federal Republic of Germany), Canada, Mexico, Switzerland, the former German Democratic Republic, and Romania, as well as the former Soviet Union. The second category included countries such as Brazil, India, Nigeria, Ghana, Senegal, and China, as well as the Organization of African Unity (OAU).

In addition, because of the personalities involved and the flexible nature of the instructions issued to them, several countries with no stated positions on negotiating issues were among the chief members of the negotiating group. Members of the delegations of Lebanon, Egypt, Finland, Sweden, Norway, and Austria serve as examples. These countries played an essential role in the negotiations since their respective capitals had not issued detailed instructions at all or were becoming aware only too late of the political significance of the negotiations. Given the high political sensitivity of the subject, the North-South component gained such prominence that representatives of Third-World countries gained leverage at the negotiating table. This was due particularly to their negotiating position that no transboundary movements of hazardous wastes were to be allowed, except when this was done simultaneously with the transfer of adequate and environmentally sound technology. Although the overwhelming majority of such transports occurs among industrialized countries, mostly for recycling purposes, such a position was unacceptable to the industrialized countries. Similarly, developing countries would not accept the position of developed countries on enlarging the scope of the convention to control *all* wastes in order to ensure their environmentally sound disposal.

Prominent NGOs, such as Greenpeace, were making a direct impact on the negotiations by setting high goals and pursuing a strong course of action. This was communicated through public relations campaigns and other activities at the meetings, through press and television coverage of their positions, and by successfully lobbying developing-country representatives to endorse their postulates and interventions in the capitals of the chief negotiating delegations (mainly Western countries such as the United States, the United Kingdom, the Federal Republic of Germany, and Austria). Thus, developing countries, especially the members of the OAU, took positions that were not in line with their initial negotiating goal (control of transboundary movements of hazardous wastes), but went much further to encompass questions such as the minimization of waste generation and disposal standards.

As regulations directly affected enterprise behavior, several industry representatives, as mentioned earlier, participated in talks and actively lobbied for their particular interests during negotiations. They had full access to formal plenary meetings and were in constant and intensive contact with the delegations of developed countries. Their interests, however, were really not considered, as the crux of negotiations continued to shift from the substantial consideration of technical and administrative details to a highly sensitive political North-South confrontation.

The secretariat also played a distinct role in the negotiations. This role was assumed by UNEP, largely in the person of its politically acute and ambitious executive director, Mostafa Tolba, a powerful player, whose importance evolved during the course of the negotiations. The executive director prepared proposals for each negotiating session (justified by accompanying explanatory "cover" notes); intervened orally at any given time in the ongoing negotiations; approached members of the bureau and active negotiators in an attempt to influence their positions; provided statements to the media before, during, and after negotiating sessions; and successfully pushed for slight changes in rules of procedure, thereby influencing the course of action. When seeking the adoption of compromise solutions, which in principle favored developing-country interests, and to meet the final deadline, the secretariat, as well as the chair of the negotiations, assumed the role of mediator on many occasions.

Structure. Considering the history of the negotiations, it is interesting to note that at the outset of the negotiating process in 1987 in Caracas, Venezuela, there was prevailing consensus for the need to find adequate, simple, and commonly acceptable solutions to the problem. However, during the course of the negotiations, the pattern of behavior changed dramatically. The initial consensus approach was abandoned at a later stage when various delegations and the secretariat started to push to include specific interests not directly related to the core substances of the negotiations. These interests comprised, among other things, obligations relating to the minimization of waste generation, the financing of the buildup of a disposal infrastructure in developing countries, and the adoption—at the national level—by all member states of criminal law provisions in cases of illegal traffic.

As the structure of the negotiations changed in both form and substance, there emerged a growing sensitivity and aggressive pattern of behavior among negotiators. Time constraints played a crucial role. From the outset, a limited number of negotiating sessions was agreed upon and a final deadline was established. The time-sensitive structure and the complexity of the issue left negotiators with no other choice than to extend sessions or add informal meetings to the already overbooked calendar.

The complexity and interdisciplinary nature of the issue produced a great deal of stress that consequently led to the establishment of rigid negotiating fronts. Moreover, only a limited number of countries, partially due to the personalities of their key representatives, negotiated most parts of the final outcome and therefore assumed responsibility in a new area of international diplomacy.

Strategy. As late as 1984, the issue of hazardous wastes had been considered limited in scope and politically easy to handle. In retrospect, however, it is rather surprising that negotiators were not forewarned by the failure of the OECD to produce an agreement in the same problem area.

During the first two negotiating sessions most state representatives, as well as the NGOs, used a deliberate strategy, as a commonly acceptable approach to the issue seemed feasible and apt to serve best the interests of all the parties involved. In early 1988, however, the issues at stake became increasingly politicized, leading negotiators to form coalitions. Although no group behavior was apparent in the beginning, the developing countries increasingly began to align themselves according to their special interests. Industrialized countries reacted quite late to this new development; even at a later stage they were not able to agree on formal strategic alliances but rather coordinated their strategies on an ad hoc basis. The coalition of socialist countries hardly played a real role, partly because only a few were present at the negotiating table; those present finally joined forces with the industrialized countries.

Strategic negotiating techniques included using the rules of procedure as well as press leaks to influence the negotiations. The rules of procedure became increasingly important because several meetings were organized on an ad hoc basis. This meant that in the meetings decisions had to be made on which rules of procedure were to be followed. It was the chair of the negotiations, as well as the members of the secretariat, who tried to influence which rules would be adopted to accelerate progress. The rules of procedure therefore changed from meeting to meeting. At the beginning, it incorporated rules that led to the adoption of any proposal as long as five country delegations were not against it. At a later stage, the procedure changed to accommodate the adoption of any proposal supported by five country delegations. Such interference by the secretariat was accepted because of the charismatic leadership of the UNEP Executive Director, as well as the ready support of the majority of developing countries.

These different rules of procedure led to intensive informal consultations, regular group meetings (i.e., of the coalition of developing countries and of the coalition of industrialized countries), and regular bureau meetings with the participation of the secretariat. The five-member bureau was made up of one country representative from all five UN regional groups and met constantly to evaluate ongoing negotiations, elaborate on the general guidance for the negotiations, and exchange views among the five regions. On some occasions the bureau also elaborated on draft proposals of the text.

In the spring of 1988 several new questions were raised and advanced for inclusion in the convention. These were issues not contained in the initial negotiating mandate of the technical and legal expert group and therefore widened the scope of the undertaking. They related to the following principles: minimization of waste generation at the source (such as production sites and packaging); disposal of wastes on the territory of the waste-generating country, allowing exports only for environmental or substantive economic reasons; exports of hazardous wastes only to countries with at least the same disposal standards as the country of export; and inclusion of disposal standards. These new questions were raised initially by developing countries although proposals of the text were drafted by NGO representatives, mainly Greenpeace. Similarly, these efforts were also the outcome of intensified consultations and consequent dynamic group processes among delegates. Finally, this negotiating phase during the course of 1988 produced specific North-South issues that remained with negotiators until the end of the negotiations in the spring of 1989.

Process. Apart from the group-dynamic processes, the negotiations were greatly influenced by nongovernmental groupings and by individual personalities within the negotiating groups. Dynamic individuals within the delegations frequently presided over small formal and informal working groups during and between negotiating sessions. These individuals were mainly representatives of the European countries, the United States,

Canada, and Lebanon. NGO representatives, mainly from organizations such as Greenpeace or Friends of the Earth, also demonstrated specific drafting capabilities.

From the very beginning, NGO representation was greatly welcomed at the negotiations to show the world community the delegates' sincere willingness to deal with the actual issue. At a later stage, however, NGO participation became somewhat problematic as confidential papers and proposals were leaked from the conference room, putting pressure on those who had agreed on compromises. It was decided, therefore, to split up the meetings into closed sessions excluding NGOs and open ones that permitted NGO representation. However, as some developing countries regularly briefed NGO representatives on the outcome of the closed negotiations, the procedure adopted did not prove effective.

The personalities involved in the negotiations also influenced their outcome. In most cases, political representatives from environmental, economic, and foreign ministries were heads of country delegations. Thus several technical questions became politicized, and indirectly related questions were introduced into the negotiating process. These questions not only related to the disposal of hazardous waste in the country of origin and technical standards for disposal operations, but also dealt with legal issues such as notification obligations when passing seawaters within the 200-nautical-mile Exclusive Economic Zone as defined by Latin American countries, Portugal, and Spain. Other legal issues included the question of liability and responsibility under the convention in a broad sense, which meant that, at one stage of the negotiations, export countries would even be held responsible for accidents during disposal operations in the import country. Time-consuming efforts were required to settle side issues and only a little time remained to deal with the core issues—the control of transboundary movements of hazardous wastes and their disposal. At the same time, delegation heads of several developing countries formed their own specific spheres of interest. As they concentrated largely on detailed questions, they lost sight of the overall context of the negotiations.

Therefore, because an increasing number of technical and detailed questions were raised, governments were left with no opportunity to issue timely instructions. The global context further produced a "no limits" feeling; either more and more questions were left pending or ad hoc compromise solutions were found, since no instructions were issued from the capitals. Regulations on criminal law and on Law of the Sea questions are examples. In the final analysis, however, most negotiators were not empowered to compromise on the whole range of questions concerned and therefore had to withdraw their support of agreements made earlier in the negotiations. At the final meeting of experts, which was followed by a meeting of plenipotentiaries in Basel in the spring of 1989, negotiators therefore had to deal with several unresolved issues.

Outcomes. When negotiations started in 1987, negotiators believed that they could agree upon a substantial international legal instrument to control transboundary movements of hazardous wastes and that they could achieve this goal within the two-year deadline. As the range of questions raised under the new convention was extended and more and more compromise solutions were needed to settle all the issues, the possibility of arriving at a solution within the given time frame was slipping away. Newly introduced issues, as mentioned earlier, were being brought up so late in the course of the negotiations that their inclusion in the text of the convention would have endangered compromises that had already been reached. Therefore, subjects such as disposal standards, the Exclusive Economic Zone, and liability were dealt with in the form of resolutions, and decisions were adopted only at the final ministerial conference.

Perceptions of what the new agreement should contain changed radically during the course of the negotiations. Although at the beginning a control regime for transboundary movements of hazardous wastes had been envisioned, it later included provisions dealing with technology transfer, criminal law, the establishment of a fund and clearinghouse, and a variety of other questions. As different and sometimes contradictory interests prevailed until the end of the negotiations and were then incorporated either in the agreement or in resolutions or decisions adopted at the final meeting, no side really was satisfied with the outcome of the negotiations.

In the final stage of the negotiations, almost every compromise reached up to that point had to be reconsidered and led to compromise solutions that made everyone involved in the negotiations feel they had lost out. Intensive press coverage and NGO activity in the final stage of the negotiations created an atmosphere in which high-ranking government representatives felt obliged to question compromises reached earlier. This holds true especially for ministers and senior officials who were asked by numerous journalists and permanent NGO representatives to participate in media interviews. In examining the final result of these late compromises, however, their often contradictory content in relation to other provisions of the convention puts their usefulness in doubt.

Specific Topics of the Negotiations

Several controversial topics were covered during the negotiations. The main topics of interest included:

- The minimization of waste generation
- Avoidance of waste export
- Responsibility and liability
- Law of the Sea regulations
- Illegal traffic provisions
- Recycling
- Formalities
- Financial aspects
- Standards for disposal

Negotiators from industrialized countries, in particular, viewed the basic approach to the subject as one that controlled private as well as state activities in the field of transboundary movements of hazardous wastes. As the scope of the negotiations enlarged, as a result of lobbying by nongovernmental groups and developing-country delegations, industrialized countries were reluctant to incorporate regulations dealing with the principles of minimizing the generation of wastes, as well as of limiting exports to cases of absolute necessity while ensuring environmentally sound disposal. Only at a later stage, when public opinion pushed for the same direction and industry representatives showed some acceptance of these principles, were industrialized countries ready to accept such provisions.

The concept of state responsibility touched upon basic political principles. Several countries were not ready to assume responsibility for taking action against the illegal activities of private enterprises operating in their territory, or in case of a force majeure, hindering the completion of a transboundary shipment. Despite rigid positions, especially on the part of developing countries who interpreted "state responsibility" to be the "responsibility of the exporting developed country," such regulations were finally adopted.

As transboundary movements of hazardous wastes related directly to national sovereignty, questions about national control over coastal sea areas played an important role. Latin American nations and other states tried to use the negotiations to achieve acceptance of their concept of a 200-nautical-mile Exclusive Economic Zone adjacent to coastal state territories. The nations vying for coastal control proposed that they, as the transit country, be notified of any maritime transports of hazardous wastes within this area. As a compromise could not be arrived at, a complicated solution had to be found that would include the adoption of a resolution, the establishment of a working group, and interagency consultations.

The criteria for and consequences of illegal traffic were among the most disputed items of the negotiations. Apart from the questions of state responsibility in cases of illegal traffic, the obligation to adopt criminal law regulations at the national level was highly disputed but finally was agreed upon. Similarly, the definition of *illegal traffic* produced conflict, especially regarding the notion of "dumping." Industrial interests were advancing counterarguments for comprehensive regulations of hazardous waste exports when such transboundary shipments for recycling purposes were to be excluded from the stringent regulations of the convention. In this case as well, industrialized countries had to yield and accept a comprehensive approach with some less formalized procedures.

Among the most disputed issues in the negotiations were the notification requirements for both the transit and the import states in cases of transboundary movements of hazardous wastes. While developed countries argued in favor of as little formality as possible to guarantee expeditious waste transports (envisioning even simplified procedures such as tacit consent), developing countries argued for stringent provisions to enable transit and import countries—in their view always developing countries— duly to consider every single export application. The final result of the negotiations followed the debate for stringent procedures and therefore favored the arguments of developing countries.

In summing up the outcome of the negotiations on the main issues, there is no doubt that the interests of developing countries prevailed over those of industrialized countries throughout the negotiations as well as in the final stage. The main reason for this prevalence was the basic conceptual difference in viewing the need for a global convention. Developing countries were not convinced of the necessity for such a convention at all and rigidly viewed it as another North-South issue, whereas developed countries attached high political importance to a such a convention and therefore were much more flexible and ready to compromise. This flexibility, however, resulted in minimal coordination efforts among developed countries and moreover created conflicts, especially concerning the questions of "innocent passage" through the Exclusive Economic Zone of maritime countries.

Hazardous Waste Negotiations as Specific Environmental Negotiations

The negotiations on a convention on the control of transboundary movements of hazardous wastes and their disposal are a good case study for examining the distinct and rather specific features of environmental negotiations. In general, their cross-sectoral nature and their international character are of significance.

Multiple parties and multiple roles. While negotiations on the Basel Convention took place, more and more segments of society became involved in the issue. Several national parliaments of Western countries adopted legislation or resolutions blocking all exports of hazardous wastes to developing countries. At the same time, private initiatives were launched in certain regions of Europe supporting the minimization of waste generation and prohibiting the construction of new disposal sites. In the international setting, states, as well as enterprises, showed their concern in quite different ways, depending on the circumstances. Hence, states assumed different roles depending on their position as an export, transit, or import country. Meanwhile, private and state-owned enterprises were faced with the task of finding disposal sites for hazardous wastes, recycling wastes as raw material, and financing more costly waste management programs by passing on the costs to other sectors. This was especially true of large chemical, pharmaceutical, and packaging industries.

Consequently, negotiators as well as lobbying groups were forced to argue in different ways depending on how they saw themselves affected by specific issues. An obvious case in this regard involved the questions of illegal traffic and state responsibility, which developing countries always took to be industrialized countries only. At a very late stage in the negotiations, however, Third-World negotiators realized that the behavior of their own countries and citizens might very likely also fall under these provisions. As a result, developing countries attempted to avoid their responsibilities for environmentally sound waste management by proposing language that would have restricted some obligations to developed countries only. This was, however, not included in the final text of the convention.

Multiple issues. When identifying and analyzing problems related to transboundary movements of hazardous wastes and their disposal, scientific, economic, and political considerations have to be taken into account. This was apparent when the definition of hazardous wastes, one of the key issues under negotiation, was discussed. A strictly scientific definition was deemed insufficient as it would have excluded political considerations as well as economic viability arguments. Therefore, the convention finally dealt only with hazardous wastes and not, as proposed at one stage of the negotiations, with transboundary movement of all categories of wastes.

Meaningless boundaries. In the case of transboundary waterways or shared freshwater basins the meaningless boundaries may be obvious. However, this feature is not as easily identifiable in the context of transboundary movements of hazardous wastes, as permission for entry into a given territory could be denied. Nevertheless, environmentally unsound practices and standards of handling and disposal of hazardous wastes concern neighboring countries as well, which may be affected by the pollution of groundwater, surface water, or the air. The elimination of internationally binding regulations of disposal standards thus came to the forefront of the negotiations.

The question of prohibiting all transboundary movements of hazardous wastes under all circumstance was never really considered. In some cases it proved to be more efficient to allow rather than deny imports to, or transports through, a state's territory, since the transit or receiving country could ensure environmentally sound final disposal of the wastes.

Scientific and technical uncertainty. Most of the case studies in this book confirm the hypothesis of scientific uncertainty in environmental negotiations. With regard to the transboundary movements of hazardous wastes, however, such uncertainties generally do not exist, because toxicity parameters clearly indicate the range of the problems. A degree of uncertainty still relates to the question of identifying standards for environmentally sound disposal or for defining hazardous wastes.

Power asymmetry. As already mentioned, power asymmetry played a role in the negotiations of the Basel Convention. Although a major part of all transboundary movements of hazardous wastes take place among industrialized countries, developing countries acquired a dominant role throughout the negotiations by playing to the media and employing aggressive negotiating tactics. Political success meant putting developed countries on the defensive by overstating the case of (illegal) transports of hazardous wastes from developed to developing countries. This was facilitated by excessive television coverage of the North-South dimensions of the problem, creating false public awareness and concern.

Furthermore, aggressive negotiating tactics by developing-country representatives underscored the postulate for maximum protection of their interests. As developing countries held an overall majority at all stages of the negotiations, their compromise proposals were widely adopted, thereby weighting the regime of the convention (for example, notification requirements and illegal traffic provisions) heavily in their favor. Industrialized countries were mainly concerned about regulations relating to transboundary movements among themselves and thereby left large tracts of the negotiating ground to developing countries. At one stage of the negotiations, however, both sides realized that they would be affected by the whole range of provisions: Intensive rethinking resulted, and all the questions were reconsidered.

Joint interests. At the start of the negotiating process, as was pointed out earlier, the markedly identical interest of most parties (states, NGOs, and media representatives) was apparent. During the course of the negotiations, however, this basic consensus eroded and gave way instead to the pursuance of specific interests. In this situation, an increasing number of parties felt that they might be better off without the envisaged agreement. It was only at the end of the negotiations that the parties realized that implementing international regulations on transboundary movements of hazardous wastes and their disposal would benefit all sides; they therefore adopted the draft convention. However, as rigid positions had prevailed, last-minute compromises were not able to accommodate all interests and some countries were reluctant to sign the agreement.

Negative perceptions of immediate outcomes. During the final days and hours of the negotiations in March 1989 in Basel, the parties present perceived the results primarily as being negative. This frustration was understandable, as no one party achieved its main goals. Developed countries were looking for an agreement to control transboundary movements of hazardous wastes and to rule out possible negative consequences through strict controls. Developing countries viewed the negotiations as a way of receiving a transfer of technology and additional funding for their related activities. At the same time, developing countries overburdened the convention with specific regulations in order to stipulate and guarantee the overall responsibility of exporting countries (that is, developed countries in their understanding). As the negotiating environment was emotionally charged, the compromises achieved often did not represent the best or most rational solutions for either side. The final act was signed by 116 countries, but only about 20 countries signed the convention itself in Basel. As of June 1, 1990, 53 states and the EC have signed the convention, but so far only 7 countries, not regarded as key contracting parties, have ratified it. Twenty ratifications are needed for its entry into force.

Long time frame. The stipulations of the Basel Convention on the Control of Transboundary Movements of Hazardous Wastes and Their Disposal will change patterns of behavior to a considerable extent, to the benefit of all sides, only in the long run; governments will, however, have to deal with the political dimensions of this time lag.

In the short run, however, problems are likely to occur at the national level because of new regulations on exports of hazardous wastes or obligations to comply with disposal standards, thereby creating considerable unproductive investments. Such factors can be expected to play a role as long as costs of inaction do not affect gross national product (GNP) accounting negatively. In the context of hazardous wastes, such real costs would include expenditure on cleaning up polluted disposal sites and long-term consequences of inland water and high-sea pollution.

Changing actors. As environmental issues are of an interdisciplinary nature, different actors are required to deal with different aspects of the same main problem. The alignment of these different approaches at a national as well as international level will prove crucial to the achievement of an effective outcome.

In the case of the Basel Convention, experts highlighted technical aspects that contradicted economic and political concepts. It therefore proved important to ensure continuity in the composition of delegations, especially at the expert level, in order to guarantee a comprehensive overview in the course of the process. However, in the final analysis, some form of bargaining had to take place to accommodate different spheres of interest, while still achieving an acceptable outcome.

Public opinion. The perceptions of the public played a key role in these negotiations. Developing countries, allied with environmental NGOs, had been successful in presenting to the public the problem of preventing hazardous waste shipments, especially illegal ones, from developed to developing countries. While this was, without any doubt, one of the main concerns during the negotiations, public opinion did not allow any strong positions by industrialized countries on substantial technical or administrative issues such as notification procedures, recycling modalities, or disposal standards. Any attempts by industrialized countries to take strong positions were presented to the public as a violation of the justified interests of developing countries or as a cover-up for continuing illegal activities. Since developed countries, throughout the negotiating process, were not able to change this public perception of the problem, they finally had to compromise on their interests and accept highly political language in the framework of a rather technical legal instrument.

Concluding Remarks

Environmental negotiations in today's mostly economically oriented societies present negotiating parties with a variety of challenges. In most negotiations one is confronted by a range of sometimes contradictory aspects of the same problem. Negotiators must wear a number of hats to accommodate national and international interests. As far as the Basel Convention negotiations were concerned, one is tempted to say that unrealistic goals, as well as the pursuit of isolated interests, impeded the realization of the best solution. It was perceived and acknowledged too late that, in the environmental domain, winners and losers can hardly be differentiated.

5

Negotiations on Nuclear Pollution: The Vienna Conventions on Notification and Assistance in Case of a Nuclear Accident

GUNNAR SJÖSTEDT

In January 1988, the former Soviet Union and Sweden concluded an agreement on two conventions. One dealt with early notification; the other, with mutual assistance in case of a nuclear accident (Avtal, 1988). The agreement is notable because the conventions paved the way for an extended period of cooperation between the two countries on the politically sensitive issue of nuclear security.

The Soviet-Swedish bilateral agreement was but a small part of the outcome of the multilateral negotiations on nuclear security that had been held in 1986 under the auspices of the International Atomic Energy Agency (IAEA). This chapter analyzes these talks, hereafter referred to as the Vienna Negotiations. They concerned one of the most serious environmental issues we know today; the spread of radioactive pollutants. This problem was intensified by the Chernobyl catastrophe in April 1986.

In keeping with the general theoretical framework of this book, this chapter examines the *process, actors, strategies, outcome,* and *structure* of the negotiations.

Process

In Chapter 2, Guy-Olivier Faure and Jeffrey Z. Rubin defined *process* as a meta-level concept used to systematize what negotiators do, regardless of the substance and events of a particular negotiation. For analytical purposes, the assessment of the process of the Vienna Negotiations examines the following topics: the initiation of the negotiations, setting the agenda, the bargaining methods, and the termination of the negotiations.

The initiation of the negotiations. People often argue about exactly when a particular round of negotiations started. Usually there is a formal beginning, such as a government conference. The ceremony is, however, often preceded by informal but important prenegotiation meetings. In analyzing a process, the crucial question is: What actions indicate when two or more nations, which are in constant contact with one another, seriously begin a process of negotiation?

In the case of the Vienna Negotiations, the formal start is easy to identify: the speech made by Soviet President Mikhail Gorbachev on May 14, 1986, in which he proposed the creation of a multilateral regime for nuclear security (IAEA: GOV/INF, 1986). The idea of such a regime was not new. Since at least the early 1980s, nuclear security had been a key concern of the IAEA Secretariat. However, the secretariat's initiatives to create a nuclear-security regime had met with limited support from IAEA members. For this reason, the speech by Gorbachev represented a departure from this area. The Federal Republic of Germany recognized it as such and swiftly responded by asking for an immediate meeting with the IAEA Board of Governors to consider the Soviet proposal (Adede, 1987).

On May 21 the board decided to form a group of government experts whose task was to produce two texts on nuclear safety. One text concerned early notification; the other, assistance in case of a nuclear accident or radiological emergency (IAEA: GOV/OR, 1986). The IAEA Secretariat was commissioned to draft proposals that the group of experts would use as the foundation for treaties. The draft proposals were presented to the heads of the permanent delegations to the IAEA on June 30 (Adede, 1987). Only three weeks later, the experts began planning the negotiations on these drafts, and the initiation stage was hence over (IAEA, 1987).

Setting the agenda. Although some of the agenda for the Vienna Negotiations had been predetermined by activities during the initiation stage, much of it remained to be set. For analytical purposes, the process of setting an agenda may in this case be broken into three subprocesses: the first gave general direction to the negotiations; the second decided what matters negotiators should deal with; the third gave political sanction to the agenda.

The general direction for the Vienna Negotiations agenda was determined early, at the meeting of the IAEA Board of Directors in late May. Before this, nuclear security was interpreted in many ways. But the IAEA Board of Directors determined that the Vienna Negotiations should deal with only two specific issues: notification and assistance in case of a nuclear accident (IAEA: GOV/OR, 1986).

Various political statements also shaped and sanctioned the agenda of the negotiations. Particularly significant were declarations of the Occidental Summit in Tokyo in 1986 (the Group of Seven), the European Parliament (International Environmental Reports, 1986), and the United States Congress (U.S. Congressional Records, 1986). The message of these statements, made in reaction to the Chernobyl nuclear accident, was that the IAEA should work faster toward achieving agreement on nuclear security. These political utterances, however, did not dictate the contents of the agenda for the Vienna Negotiations; detailed political direction came from the IAEA Secretariat.

For several years, the IAEA had been working on two conventions concerning notification and assistance respectively (IAEA: INFIRC, 1984, 1985). So when, suddenly, there was an urgent call after the Chernobyl accident to "do something" about nuclear security, the two IAEA draft conventions were available for immediate use. This was the main reason why setting the agenda for the Vienna Negotiations required only a few weeks to conclude. There was no need for complex prenegotiations to make issues negotiable.

Furthermore, the IAEA Secretariat was eager to have the draft agenda informally politically sanctioned before the group of government experts began their meeting on June 30, 1986. Only a few days before, the director general of the IAEA, together with several senior officials of the same organization, met with the heads of the delegations that were going to participate in the negotiations to help them identify and explain the political implications of the two draft texts (Adede, 1987). The IAEA leaders wanted to have the drafts accepted as the substance of the agenda. The government experts would then not have to concern themselves with principles, and could concentrate on details. This strategy of the IAEA leadership was successful, thus contributing specific process characteristics to the Vienna Negotiations.

Bargaining methods. Normally, after an agenda is set, the nations involved in a complex multilateral negotiation begin debating the principles underlying the solutions that are feasible. The purpose is to channel the negotiation in certain directions. During the following stage, the participants make concrete proposals. Then the real exchange of concessions begins. At the end, there is likely to be a period of hard bargaining over unresolved questions. This part of the bargaining process concludes the long march from formula to detail.

The Vienna Negotiations on nuclear security did not fit this model of complex multilateral negotiation. The reason was that setting the agenda went much further than simply identifying the issues to be negotiated. The agenda included proposals for final solutions to problems. These were incorporated into the draft texts on notification and assistance. Setting the agenda even concluded with a detailed organizational plan for the rest of the negotiations, including a tight schedule for only three weeks of talks (Adede, 1987).

The organizational structure put in place for the Vienna Negotiations appears to have significantly influenced the negotiations. Negotiating institutions often represent a trade-off between two requirements: the effective distribution of work and the smooth coordination between the various negotiating bodies. The negotiation work, in this case, was distributed among three working parties. The first working party, chaired by Brazilian Ambassador Poenca Rosa, dealt with the draft text on early notification. The second working party, chaired by East German Deputy Head of Delegation Maser, dealt with the issue of assistance. The third working party, chaired by Egyptian Ambassador Shash, deliberated on the issues that were common to the other two working parties or that overlapped the agendas. This third group also took over some issues from the second group that were politically sensitive, notably the issues of liability, reimbursements for assistance, and immunity of personnel operating in a foreign country (Adede, 1987; IAEA, 1987).

The negotiations were coordinated in at least three different ways. First, the process in Shash's work group was the least obvious, but it assured the political consistency of the two drafts on nuclear security. The second, and most visible coordination of negotiations, was the steering performed by the so-called bureau. Along with the chair for the negotiations, Dutch Ambassador van Gorkom, the bureau consisted of the chairs of the three working parties and four of their secretaries, who were also high officials of the IAEA Secretariat. One secretary, the legal adviser of the IAEA, appears to have played a particularly important role (Adede, 1987).

The third means of coordinating the negotiations was somewhat more diffuse; the functioning of what may be called a hegemonic, consensual knowledge among the negotiators. *Consensual knowledge* is generally understood to mean a common understanding among actors in a certain context, like a negotiation, about the "facts" of an issue and the "objective relationships" between the facts (Haas, 1989). Consensual knowledge refers to cognition rather than attitude. In general terms, consensual knowledge may affect a negotiation in different ways. It provides an elaborate vocabulary that is common to most negotiating teams. More importantly, it indicates how a problem should be approached and what criteria should be used to evaluate the solutions proposed.

Cloaked in international law as it was, hegemonic consensual knowledge was an important factor in the Vienna Negotiations. It meant that the bargaining between nations could be streamlined so that negotiators could concentrate on a few problematic issues. Consensual knowledge did not function without some help. It was guided by the IAEA, notably by the legal adviser in coordinating diplomacy. The legal background of the IAEA Director General also can be noted in this context.

In summary, the organization and functioning of the Vienna Negotiations significantly influenced their outcome. From the beginning agenda-setting dealt with one single text, the one provided by the IAEA Secretariat. The exchange of concessions between nations was essentially a process of editing the draft text. Some bargaining did take place between nations, usually when smaller nations tried to promote their interests. But this bargaining involved exceptions rather than the text itself (see list of reservations in IAEA, 1987).

The termination of the negotiations. The bargaining approach to edit the draft text was manifestly successful. On August 15, 1986, the plenary meeting of the government experts adopted one text on early notification and another on assistance in case of a nuclear accident. Seven days later, the draft texts were sent to the IAEA Board of Governors, along with the summary records of the plenary meeting and a few oral comments by the meeting's chair. These records are significant because they contain a list of formal reservations on particular provisions in the texts.

This list of exceptions paved the way for an agreed termination of the negotiations on nuclear security as delegations could thus eliminate sensitive demands from the text. On September 24 a special session of the IAEA General Conference opened in Vienna, at which the two texts were adopted by consensus. The texts were open for signature on September 26. Thus the Vienna Negotiations on nuclear security were formally and successfully concluded in less than four months (Adede, 1987; IAEA, 1987).

Actors and Strategies

It is sometimes difficult to distinguish between a plurilateral and a multilateral negotiation. Some basic distinctions can be made, however. In a plurilateral negotiation, individual nations can usually pursue their own strategies, whereas in a multilateral negotiation, smaller nations sooner or later have to join larger ones in coalitions. When the number of participants rises above 20, negotiations are likely to take on a multilateral character.

Sixty-two nations, 10 organizations, and the IAEA participated in the Vienna Negotiations (see list of international organizations in IAEA, 1987). The number of participating organizations may seem high, but, except for the IAEA, they were observers that did not take part in the negotiations. The 62 nations were all members of the IAEA and represented about 50% of its membership.

It is difficult to assess the pattern of diplomatic activity in committees like the working parties of the Vienna Negotiations. Records on the participants' performance and effectiveness are simply not available. Therefore, indirect indicators have to be used. One such indicator is the number of formal proposals made by a nation; this indicator has been used in this study (Adede, 1987).

The indicator of formal proposals shows that, to some extent, real bargaining in the Vienna Negotiations contains characteristics of a plurilateral rather than a multilateral process. The majority of participants did not table proposals. For example, on the issue of early notification, only about 40% of the participants took such action. The rate of participation was virtually the same on the issue of assistance. The only difference was that the European Community tabled two proposals on the issue of assistance. Therefore, if we only consider the tabling of significant diplomatic proposals, the Vienna Negotiations resemble plurilateral rather than multilateral negotiations.

Understandably, the passive participants were largely the developing countries. The resources required to make a significant contribution to a complex negotiation cannot be underestimated. It often takes considerable analytical capability to work out and communicate a technically feasible and politically relevant proposal so as to affect the bargaining. Generally, developing countries simply do not have the informational and analytical capabilities to do this.

On any issue, the participation of an individual nation will vary with its interests and technical competence. Interests motivate nations to become active and to table proposals. Technical competence, in turn, allows a nation to make a significant contribution.

TABLE 5.1 The Participation of Nations in the Vienna Negotiations Measured by the Number of Proposals They Tabled in the Working Party on Early Notification

Country	Significant Proposals
USSR	13
France	11
Australia	10
India	10
Spain	10
Finland	9
Switzerland	5
The GDR	5
Others[1]	1-4

NOTE: "Others" includes Algeria, Austria, Canada, Cuba, Czechoslovakia, the EC, Hungary, Iran, Ireland, Italy, Japan, the Netherlands, Nigeria, Turkey, and the United States.

Accordingly, one would expect that the Vienna Negotiations would be dominated by nations that were leaders on specific issues, the nations with the largest civilian and military nuclear capabilities: the United States, the former Sovier Union, France, the United Kingdom, the People's Republic of China, and 5 to 10 so-called nuclear-threshold nations. However, according to the number-of-significant-proposals indicator, a different pattern emerged with respect to both early notification and assistance in case of a nuclear accident (see Tables 5.1 and 5.2).

In the working party on early notification (Table 5.1), only two nuclear powers, the former Soviet Union and France, were exceptionally active. Notice that India, a nation with a highly likely nuclear military capability, also had a high rate of activity.

TABLE 5.2 The Participation of Nations in the Vienna Negotiations Measured by the Number of Proposals They Tabled in the Working Party on Assistance in the Event of a Nuclear Accident

Country	Significant Proposals
Argentina, Canada, the UK	6
Japan	5
Australia, Egypt, Luxembourg	4
Italy, Spain, the FRG	3
Cuba, the EC, France, Mexico, the Netherlands, the People's Republic of China	2
Brazil, Indonesia, Ireland, Iran	1

Table 5.2 shows that in the working party on assistance, the relative passivity of the nuclear powers was still more striking. The former Soviet Union and the United States are conspicuously absent in the circle of active states. France is near the bottom of the table. Of the acknowledged nuclear powers, only the United Kingdom is at the top of the ranking order. Of the other nations near the top, only Argentina qualifies as a nuclear-threshold nation. Thus nations with strong issue-specific capabilities tended to have a low profile in the negotiations.

The performance of each nation in the Vienna Negotiations, to some extent, may be explained by a particular circumstance. For instance, the Netherlands may have played a special role because the chair of the plenary session was from the Netherlands. Finland was probably relatively active in the group on early notification because it represented all the Nordic nations. Egypt and Indonesia aspired to represent other developing countries.

There are other explanations for the way nations participated. There is a correlation between the performance of a nation and its alignment in primary interstate conflicts. Conflicts developed along three axes: North versus South, polluter versus victim, and nuclear versus nonnuclear. As in most international bargaining sessions, the North-South conflict manifested itself in the Vienna Negotiations (Adede, 1987). However, unlike many international economic negotiations, no great Southern alliance of nations developed. One explanation was that the usual Southern alliance strategy of seeking exceptions to the commitments required by the industrialized nations did not work because this strategy was not exclusive to developing countries. In the Vienna Negotiations, nations from all camps requested exceptions to the stipulations of the draft conventions proposed by the IAEA Secretariat. In fact, seeking an exception was a standard negotiating posture. The North-South contention was present, but it did not give the negotiations their main character as had been the case in many other multilateral negotiations.

A more tangible conflict existed between the nations that polluted the environment with radioactive substances and the nations that were the victims of the pollution. This main conflict was, however, not addressed directly. It manifested itself in discussions on details. One issue that did generate conflict between the polluters and the victims was the reimbursement of nations that came to the aid of another nation during a nuclear accident.

Another significant conflict pertained to the possession of nuclear weapons. This conflict affected the text on early notification and developed into an issue over the scope of the convention. A large group of nonnuclear nations wanted the convention to cover notification of accidents at military as well as civilian installations. The nuclear powers, particularly the United States, insisted that military operations should remain outside the scope of the convention. A lengthy deadlock occurred over this issue.

A last-minute compromise was found, designed to satisfy the nuclear powers' demands for independence. Under the compromise, the governments of the nuclear powers declared that they would voluntarily notify other countries about incidents on military installations that might lead to transboundary pollution. The text of Article 3 of the convention on early notification states: "With a view to minimizing the radiological consequences, State Parties may notify in the event of nuclear accidents other than those specified in Article 1." The key word in the article is *may* instead of *should.*

The pattern of conflict indicates a noteworthy characteristic of the Vienna Negotiations that seems to distinguish them from other multilateral negotiations. There was no grouping of rival or cooperating nations that functioned as a driving force in the negotiations. Instead, the IAEA Secretariat played this role. It provided the draft texts, which were generally accepted as a basis for the negotiations. Together with the bureau, the secretariat also played a key role in smoothing out differences between nations and coming up with constructive compromises.

Except for Luxembourg, no country preferred nonagreement to agreement. During the entire process, there was general agreement that the negotiations should produce two conventions. Therefore, most nations that were active in bargaining employed a modifying strategy. The nations concerned did not openly object to the framework of the convention but concentrated their activities on the elements of special significance to them.

The former Soviet Union and the United States, as well as other nations with nuclear weapons, applied a braking strategy. They did not want to block the negotiations and prevent an agreement, which they easily could have done, but neither did they want the conventions to limit their autonomy. The convention texts were extremely sensitive issues because, potentially, they infringed on national security. This was apparent in the discussion on whether the notification agreement should cover military installations. For this reason, the nuclear-weapons powers, the United States especially, used an obvious nonproposal tactic. They let the IAEA, and sometimes other participants, move the negotiations forward while they used their influence to prevent the proposals from putting too many demands on them. Thus the United States succeeded in keeping military installations outside the formal scope of the notification agreement. Nevertheless, the voluntary commitment agreed to in Article 3 should be regarded as a real concession on the part of the nuclear-weapons powers.

Outcome

The outcome of the Vienna Negotiations was concrete in form and substance.

The Convention on Early Notification of a Nuclear Accident stipulates how the authorities of a nation should notify other nations about a nuclear accident that may have cross-border consequences. The convention describes the kind of accidents that require notification and what kind of information nations should provide. The convention also includes procedures for settling disputes about the interpretation of the convention.

The Convention on Assistance in Case of a Nuclear Accident or Radiological Emergency describes when and how nations should provide assistance in the case of a nuclear accident. Article 2 describes the circumstances for providing assistance; Article 3 concerns "the direction and control of assistance." Other parts of the convention refer to competent authorities and points of contact (Article 4); the functions of the IAEA (Article 5); confidentiality and public statements about an accident (Article 6); and other practical matters like reimbursements, privileges, and facilities and conditions for transit. The convention also contains procedures for settling disputes (Article 13).

At first glance, both conventions appear to be noncontroversial. The obligations that the signatories agreed to is behavior that one would normally expect among friendly nations. Also, one may assume that the short negotiation process points to the noncontroversial nature of the conventions. However, such an interpretation of the negotiations would not be entirely correct.

One reason for the short negotiation process is that speed was an objective in its own right. The aim was to conclude negotiations in early autumn. The overall strategy was not to create optimum conventions on nuclear security, but to sign an agreement on notification and assistance before the end of September (Adede, 1987). This objective influenced the content of the conventions. Because the negotiations on some of the contentious issues were difficult and the parties could not agree, significant loopholes were left in the texts. Loopholes meant that some controversial stipulations were not specified as well as they could have been. For example, one of the main ideas of the notification convention is that if a nuclear accident occurs in a certain nation, neighboring nations that are likely to suffer from the accident should be informed as soon as possible, so that they can take remedial action. However, the text does not clearly define what "early notification" is—at what time governments are to be informed about the accident. The agreement only stipulates that information about the accident should be transmitted promptly (Article 2).

The texts were deliberately and systematically watered down in another way as well. Because nations were committed to reaching a quick agreement, many abstained from having their particular points of view included in the conventions. When the negotiations reached a deadlock over an issue, the opposing parties accepted a controversial wording, but took exception to the offending article in the convention. Virtually all active participants (24 actors if the Ukraine and Belorussia are counted) added reservations to the convention texts (see list of reservations in IAEA, 1987).

The numerous loopholes and exceptions may lead observers to conclude that the operational value of the two conventions is limited. The loopholes and exceptions make it uncertain how the conventions will affect the behavior of nations in a real crisis caused by a nuclear accident. From this point of view, the main contribution of the conventions toward strengthening nuclear security might be described as enlightenment; governments were informed, and perhaps educated, about what they should do in the event of a nuclear catastrophe.

But direct operational usability is not the only criterion for measuring the significance of the conventions. The amount of political goodwill and commitment embedded in these conventions should not be underestimated. This is an important factor in its own right. Despite their shortcomings, the conventions are commonly considered to represent a breakthrough in establishing a regime for international nuclear security. When a government signs the convention on assistance, it joins a new kind of multilateral undertaking to provide tangible assistance if a nuclear accident happens in another signatory nation.

The notification convention also breaks new ground. Until this agreement was signed, many nations had been reluctant to inform other nations about their nuclear installations, particularly the military ones. This attitude had been especially strong in the United States. Previously, the U.S. government preferred bilateral agreements with selected nations on matters of nuclear technology and security. The reason was obvious: the competitive relationship that the United States had with the former Soviet Union. Both nations used different technologies in their reactors and other nuclear installations. There was no doubt that the U.S. technology was superior, so the Americans had nothing to gain from an increased understanding of how Soviet nuclear installations functioned.

The situation for the former Soviet Union was just the opposite. It was extremely valuable for the them to have access to better information about Western reactors and incident reports (U.S. Accounting Office, 1985). The technological differences explain why the two nations participated differently in the negotiations of the convention on notification. The former

Soviet Union belonged to the group of nations that was most active in the negotiations on the notification code; the United States was passive. In the end, both countries, together with other states that possess nuclear weapons, accepted the convention on notification.

In fact, both conventions were widely accepted. One year after the conclusion of the Vienna Negotiations, 73 nations had signed the notification convention and 72 nations had signed the convention on assistance. Luxembourg signed the notification convention but not the assistance convention because its government could not accept the terms for reimbursements.

The Vienna Negotiations were, however, significant beyond the stipulations, rules, and procedures contained in the two conventions. The conventions should also be regarded as elements in an emerging international regime on nuclear security. From this perspective, the negotiations represent at least three different kinds of outcomes.

First, the negotiations and their outcome have a symbolic purpose. The conventions gave direction for future work in the IAEA (IAEA, 1986c). It may be that the political goodwill inherent in the conventions strengthened the nuclear-security regime in its early stages.

Second, the Vienna Conventions gave more responsibility to the IAEA, especially to its secretariat. For a long time, the IAEA had tried unsuccessfully to obtain a clear mandate from its members on nuclear security. When the General Conference of the Vienna Negotiations accepted the conventions, the IAEA received such a mandate.

Third, the nuclear-security conventions accelerated and expanded network-building among nations; that is, it institutionalized international contacts between national authorities. The loopholes and exceptions that weakened the conventions could be corrected through additional multilateral negotiations. Alternatively, two nations could clarify the conventions between themselves. Many nations did. A few years after the conventions were signed, several bilateral negotiations were initiated and concluded, including 29 agreements on the exchange of information. One of these agreements was between Sweden and the former Soviet Union on the issue of early notification in the event of a nuclear accident. This is a good example of the significance of network-building.

In the summer of 1986 the Swedish government was eager to come to grips with the issue of nuclear security. Interest in this issue was high because several Swedish provinces had been severely hit by radioactive fallout from Chernobyl. Beginning in October, Sweden was engaged energetically in diplomatic discussions with its closest neighbors on how they should deal with the problem of nuclear accidents with cross-border consequences. The negotiations produced quick results. On October 21, 1986, only a month after the signing of the Vienna Conventions, Sweden signed agreements with

Denmark and Norway on early notification (Avtal, 1986, 1987c). In early 1987, a companion agreement was signed with Finland (Avtal, 1987b). Sweden was also negotiating with the former Soviet Union. These negotiations took much longer than the talks between Sweden and its Nordic neighbors. It was not until December 17, 1987, that the two nations agreed on a bilateral notification agreement (Avtal, 1988). Sweden reached a similar agreement with East Germany in 1989.

It was easier for the Swedish government to come to an agreement with the other Nordic nations than with politically more distant nations like the former Soviet Union. However, the implementation of the Nordic agreement is less important than the implementation of the agreement between Sweden and the former Soviet Union. The reason is that the Soviet-Swedish agreement helped create the kind of network that the Nordic nations had established long ago without the help of a formal treaty.

Like the other bilateral agreements with neighboring countries, the Soviet-Swedish agreement referred to the 1986 Vienna Conventions. It has approximately the same objectives and contains essentially the same stipulations. It also contains a set of guidelines for the implementation of the agreement. These guidelines specify the obligations of both nations and make the treaty truly operational. The area covered by the agreement extends 300 kilometers on either side of the border between the nations. The treaty lists all of the nuclear installations. For example, in the former Soviet Union, the installations in St. Petersburg/Leningrad, Ignalina, and Kola are listed. In Sweden all installations are covered. The treaty also spells out in great detail what information is to be communicated in case of an accident and what procedures are to be used. The guidelines in the Soviet-Swedish agreement also require that the nations exchange information about the normal levels of radiation inside and outside nuclear installations. This information is to be exchanged at yearly meetings of experts. The meetings alternate between the two nations and sometimes are held at the site of a nuclear installation (Riktlinjer, 1989).

Many networks have been created through these meetings. The negotiations on the notification agreement were conducted at a diplomatic level. However, as a result of the implementation of the agreement, the contacts between the nations have filtered down from the ministerial level to the operational level at state agencies, and then down to the management level at the nuclear installations.

Thus, the Soviet-Swedish agreement shows that the implementation of the Vienna Conventions on nuclear safety was more far-reaching than the mere application of their stipulations. In several cases implementation was equivalent to continued negotiations with the purpose of sharpening the commitments embedded in the Vienna Conventions.

Structure

Multilateral negotiations about complex issues are often protracted and time-consuming. For instance, in the negotiations of the General Agreement on Tariffs and Trade (GATT), the Kennedy Round lasted three years. The Tokyo Round went on for six years. These time schedules are by no means exceptional for multilateral negotiations.

The Vienna Negotiations were different. They lasted only four months, and therefore might be thought of as an unequivocal success story. But the negotiations were far from problem-free. It has already been noted that some issues were highly sensitive. The negotiations were sometimes deadlocked and had their difficult moments; at times failure seemed imminent. As seen in a historical perspective, these difficulties were to be expected.

The nuclear-security issues discussed in the Vienna Negotiations were not unfamiliar topics to the IAEA. Since at least 1983, the IAEA Secretariat had tried in vain to have members reach agreement on nuclear security, including the issues of notification and assistance.

Why was it possible to hold serious negotiations on nuclear security in 1986 while the same issues could not be handled in 1983? One answer predominates: Chernobyl. There is no doubt that this great nuclear catastrophe of April 1986 produced a radically new political climate for international cooperation on nuclear security. The Chernobyl accident paved the way for the Vienna Negotiations and for their comparatively successful outcome.

It is easy to point to the Chernobyl accident as an important factor in this respect. It is, however, difficult to specify *how* Chernobyl affected the Vienna Negotiations. To understand this, it is necessary to relate the Chernobyl accident to the structure of the Vienna Negotiations. In Chapter 2, Guy-Olivier Faure and Jeffrey Z. Rubin state that the structure provides "the set of constraints within which the exchange takes place." One example of structural constraint is the institution in which negotiations are carried out. Another type of structural constraint is the international distribution of power. Other aspects of the structure pertain to the inherent qualities of the problem area as such; in this case, the risk of a nuclear accident.

The structure of negotiations on nuclear security changed significantly in the early 1980s. These changes pointed in two different, and indeed, opposite directions. On one hand, there were indications that the likelihood of a nuclear accident was increasing and that the risks connected with nuclear energy were increasing. On the other hand, there were signs indicating that the obstacles in the way of international cooperation among key nations were disappearing. This bidirectional, apparently contradictory, change in structure strongly influenced the Vienna Negotiations and their outcome. They were indeed determining factors.

Nuclear security. Security was a problem from the very beginning of the nuclear-energy industry. Nuclear reactors were developed and operated with more security concerns than installations in most other industries. Until the late 1970s, public confidence in the nuclear industry was, in fact, reasonably high because the public was not told about any incidents that had occurred; they were effectively swept under the carpet. The policy of most governments was to reveal as little as possible to the public about such incidents. This policy worked until 1979.

Then the drama of the Three Mile Island accident unfolded before the news media and eyes of the world. There was also a massive mobilization of experts on nuclear technology. Although they were able to handle the situation, the incident left a strong impression on the public about the possible consequences of a nuclear accident. The incident proved that a reactor catastrophe could actually happen; accidents were no longer imaginary scenarios (Abbots, 1980, 1981).

In the industrialized world, the public reacted strongly to the Three Mile Island incident. The U.S. Office of Technology Assessment (1984) reported that the public attitude toward nuclear energy grew increasingly negative after Three Mile Island. In October 1983 the Commission of the European Communities (CEC) surveyed 9,700 people in member countries to determine their attitudes toward the nuclear industry. The response was equally negative: no less than 38% were so concerned that they considered it highly possible, or at least quite likely, that a bomblike explosion could happen in one of the several hundred reactors in the European Community (EC) nations (CEC, 1983).

As a result, in the early 1980s nuclear security became an important issue in the domestic politics of most industrialized nations. Accordingly governments also became increasingly concerned about nuclear security. They realized that information about nuclear accidents had been insufficient and that what information there was had not been distributed widely enough. But even the most enlightened nations, including the United States, had not released all information that it possessed about nuclear incidents around the world (U.S. Accounting Office, 1985). The data that were available indicated that the problem of nuclear security was so serious that there was a vital need for more information.

In 1984 the United States reported that at least 151 incidents that, in some way, affected the safe operation of nuclear plants had already taken place throughout the world. At least two incidents had been "significant" in a qualified sense (U.S. Accounting Office, 1985). It became increasingly apparent that incidents in reactors and other types of nuclear installations were quite frequent.

One lesson of Three Mile Island was that a nuclear accident could happen under the most favorable conditions, even in a highly developed country with the most sophisticated technology that the nuclear industry had to offer. From this perspective, it was a cause of great concern that the nuclear industry was growing rapidly in developing nations, with their relatively limited capacity to deal with nuclear accidents.

According to the IAEA Secretariat, by June 1984, 306 nuclear reactors were in operation around the world (*Nuclear News Magazine,* 1984). About 5% were located in developing nations, and 224 nuclear reactors were reported to be under construction or on order. Of these, 25 reactors (11%) were planned for developing countries. Had this growth rate continued, about half the reactors in the world would be in developing countries by the year 2000.

Another IAEA study confirmed the growing manifest risks associated with the increasing number of nuclear plants in developing countries. In 1982, the IAEA Secretariat surveyed 56 nations, each of which had at least one nuclear reactor. Forty-four nations reported that if a nuclear accident were to occur, they would have serious difficulties coping without assistance from other nations (IAEA, 1982).

Changing conditions for negotiations on nuclear safety. The Vienna Negotiations followed the Chernobyl accident and the Gorbachev initiative of 1986. When the negotiations got under way the issues were well understood from the very beginning. Along with the texts drafted by the IAEA Secretariat, work undertaken by the Nuclear Energy Agency (NEA) of the Organization for Economic Cooperation and Development (OECD) had helped prepare the way for the negotiations. The NEA's Committee on Nuclear Installations had conducted studies to increase common understanding and consensual knowledge about nuclear-safety problems. For example, the NEA had established an incident notification system. Although it applied only to NEA members, it included about 75% of the nuclear reactors in the world (OECD, 1983-1986).

The nuclear-security regime of the NEA was important for the Vienna Negotiations for several reasons. One was the NEA's efficiency, which was attributable to its restricted and homogeneous membership and the technical competence of its staff. Information from this organization was respected for its reliability. Furthermore, the NEA's reports on nuclear incidents seem to have been relatively comprehensive. Participating nations informed the NEA about the smallest disturbances in the operation of nuclear plants. By 1984, some 450 incidents had been reported. The NEA notification system helped establish the true risks of nuclear-energy production.

The other reason why the NEA regime was important for the Vienna Negotiations concerned the posture of the United States. Before 1986, Washington favored the NEA approach decisively over the IAEA approach as a solution to the nuclear-security problem. In the sophisticated NEA environment, even U.S. agencies could learn something. The limits that the OECD placed on participation in its notification system hindered the dissemination of sensitive information to the former Soviet Union and its allies as these states were not members of the organization. The preference of the United States and other Western nations for the NEA slowed the creation of a nuclear-security regime under the IAEA, but did not stop it. The IAEA had also started to develop an incident-reporting system before 1986. In May 1985 it included Argentina, Belgium, Brazil, Bulgaria, Canada, Czechoslovakia, the Federal Republic of Germany, Finland, France, the German Democratic Republic, Hungary, India, Italy, Japan, the Netherlands, Pakistan, South Korea, Spain, Sweden, Switzerland, the United Kingdom, the United States, the former Soviet Union, and Yugoslavia (U.S. Accounting Office, 1985). The wide coverage of the IAEA system was, however, somewhat misleading because the United States and other Western nations did not actively participate. Furthermore, a network of bilateral agreements on the exchange of information concerning nuclear matters (and sometimes other forms of cooperation) had emerged since the mid-1970s. The growth pattern of this network is shown in Table 5.3.

As may be seen from Table 5.3, the evolution is fairly continuous until 1986, although the number of agreements entered clearly increased in 1981 and 1982. This may perhaps be a delayed effect of the Three Mile Island accident in 1979. In 1987 and 1988 there was an explosive development with 26 new agreements. This is evidently a result of the Vienna Conventions on Notification and Assistance signed in 1986, and ultimately of Chernobyl.

Thus the Vienna Negotiations of 1986 were part of, and at the same time strongly conditioned by, a process of regime-building in the area of nuclear safety that had been going on for at least a decade. This evolution was certainly not unidimensional. It consisted of several different movements that were partly contradictory. There was a competitive relationship between the regional system of nuclear cooperation under the NEA, on one hand, and the emerging global IAEA system, on the other hand. For some great powers, notably the United States, a network of bilateral agreements also represented a feasible alternative for an international regime in the area of nuclear cooperation.

TABLE 5.3 Bilateral Agreements on the Exchange of Nuclear Information

Year	Agreements
1975	0
1976	1
1977	4
1978	4
1979	3
1980	4
1981	7
1982	7
1983	2
1984	4
1985	8
1986	7
1987	16
1988	10
1989	2

SOURCE: IAEA, 1990.

This competitive relationship between bilateral, selectively regional, and comprehensive global nuclear-safety regimes hindered the efforts made within the IAEA in this area. As long as the United States did not favor the IAEA regime, this was not a viable option. The U.S. position was, in turn, dependent on its relationship to the other superpower. The Soviet invasion of Afghanistan in 1979 had considerably chilled the relations between Moscow and Washington. The Reagan administration had made an effort to reactivate the Coordination Committee (CoCom) and the strategic embargo of the former Soviet Union. The early 1980s, therefore, did not represent a favorable environment for a nuclear-security regime that would include increasing exchange of information about nuclear installations and incidents.

In 1985, with the arrival in the former Soviet Union of the Gorbachev leadership, the perestroika revolution, and the new foreign policy that followed, the relationship between the superpowers improved immensely. As a result, one of the main obstacles blocking meaningful negotiations on nuclear security was removed. The full effect was even more far-reaching: The work by the NEA and the bilateral agreements were now partly transformed into structural conditions that were favorable for an IAEA regime. They represented a pool of knowledge and experience that nations could draw from in multilateral negotiations.

The Chernobyl effect. The Chernobyl catastrophe shocked the world. For the second time in less than 10 years, a superpower's nuclear reactors had gone out of control. The impact of Chernobyl was heightened by the earlier accident at Three Mile Island; Chernobyl could not easily be dismissed as a unique event.

Initially, the Soviet government tried to conceal what happened in Chernobyl. But detailed information about the accident was soon disseminated inside and outside the former Soviet Union. Once it was obvious that concealing the accident would not work, the Soviet media instead covered the incident extensively.

The change in Soviet policy toward providing information about Chernobyl was largely due to a radically increased visibility of nuclear accidents. Chernobyl could not have been kept a secret from the world because Western nations continuously measured radiation. These measurements, along with other kinds of analyses, allowed scientists to track and predict the spread of radioactive pollutants.

The alarm over the Chernobyl catastrophe was set off by radiation measurements taken in Finland and Sweden. After hearing the alarm, some nations took countermeasures, such as slaughtering farm animals or destroying contaminated crops ("The Global Fallout," 1986). Others issued instructions for handling vegetables. Such countermeasures influenced public opinion by bringing the consequences of the Chernobyl accident close to home.

The internationalization of the nuclear-security issue had other significant aspects as well. The Western media published pictures of the Chernobyl reactor with the radioactive cloud rising from it. These pictures had been taken from a new Spot satellite operated by a private company (Rönnow, 1988). This was a noteworthy event; the pictures from Spot demonstrated that governments no longer had the exclusive privilege of monitoring from space what was happening on earth. The Spot pictures were publicly available. Their existence and the continued operation of the Spot satellite also meant that no government, in either the East or the West, could control what the public was told about Chernobyl.

Had information control been feasible, it might have been used more extensively, not only in the former Soviet Union but also in Western countries. It was obvious from the beginning that a Chernobyl effect on public opinion was likely to develop into a political threat to the nuclear industry, at least in some Western countries. Therefore, information control for national security reasons was a tempting option. Because information monitoring was not possible in many countries, it became a vital concern for officials in government and private firms connected with the nuclear-power industry to act swiftly to deal with nuclear security. One strategy was to take advantage of the preparatory work done by the IAEA and other organizations on the issues of early notification and assistance and rapidly produce a set of international agreements. Thereby, the need for international action in the area of nuclear security could be satisfied.

Final Observations

One objective of this case study is to examine the properties of the Vienna Negotiations on nuclear security that are typical of international negotiations on environmental issues and those that are special. The Vienna Negotiations had a number of distinct characteristics. However, some of them clearly do not tally with the hypotheses put forward by Faure and Rubin in Chapter 2 on the expected characteristics of international environmental negotiations.

For example, the Vienna Negotiations were not characterized by scientific or technical uncertainty; the issues on the table, as well as the stakes they represented, were not particularly difficult to deal with from the technical point of view. Governments found it relatively easy to identify and pursue their own interests. Although the issue of nuclear security as such certainly retained the quality of technical uncertainty, this complexity was eliminated from the Vienna Negotiations.

Under the circumstances it was not necessary for negotiators to create a new foundation of information to come to grips with issues, or to design appropriate negotiation solutions. On the contrary, the *epistemic community* of international lawyers played a prominent, and probably decisive, role in the negotiations. The base of consensual knowledge holding the epistemic community together was not privileged knowledge, as has often been the case in other international negotiations on environmental matters (see Patrick Széll's analysis of negotiations on ozone-layer depletion in Chapter 3). The essence of international law is to interpret precedents in a consistent way. Therefore, in the epistemic community of international lawyers, there is little strategic value in looking forward with the help of scientific knowledge.

Another way that the negotiations did not conform to expectations was that the outcome did not result in immediate disadvantages with a long wait for the advantages. On the contrary, most of the negative and positive consequences could take place simultaneously, when the conventions were activated after a nuclear accident had occurred. Furthermore, the Vienna Negotiations were not particularly protracted or difficult to handle politically. Although there were strong differences between some nations, this did not delay negotiations. The most notable feature of the Vienna Negotiations was its extraordinarily short duration.

Other qualities of the Vienna Negotiations conformed with what is expected from negotiations on international environmental issues. The outcome of the negotiations, the two conventions on early notification and assistance, represented typical institutionalization of solutions. Furthermore, the Vienna talks should be regarded as a single episode of a longer and diffuse process of regime-building. Faure and Rubin propose that one property of environmental issues in international politics is that they often require new regimes.

The most striking quality of the Vienna Negotiations is, however, their sensitivity to public opinion. This property did not manifest itself openly. The negotiations were clearly controlled by the negotiators and were not immediately affected by demonstrations or other external disturbances. On the contrary, the negotiations seem to have been effectively sequestered. The negotiations were, however, initiated and conducted in the shadow of Chernobyl and the sinister prospect of similar accidents in the future. One common purpose of governments participating in the talks was to demonstrate their political resolve to do something about nuclear security and to calm their constituents.

A recurring theme of the negotiations was the need for more information, as is clear in the following three examples. First, the convention on early notification was established to ensure a sufficient exchange of information between polluters and victims in case of a nuclear accident. Second, the embargo the United States placed on strategic information about nuclear security blocked the IAEA process. The easing of the blockade was required for the negotiations to start as well as a sine qua non for their successful conclusion. Third, and probably most important, the free flow of information, relatively unimpeded by governments in the aftermath of the Chernobyl accident, was crucial for the decisive, although indirect, role played by public opinion in the Vienna Negotiations. Once the pressure of public opinion became apparent, participating governments could no longer afford a failure. Public opinion made it imperative that negotiators not leave Vienna without an agreement on nuclear security. Governments were concerned not only about their own political future, but also about the future of the nuclear industry.

Three Mile Island and Chernobyl had alarmed the public and provided support for the antinuclear movement in several countries. Events in Sweden demonstrated how strong this movement could become. Following the accident at Three Mile Island, the antinuclear movement forced the government to hold a referendum on the future of the nuclear industry in Sweden. As a result, the government initiated a long-term program of denuclearization and Sweden began planning to dismantle its nuclear power plants.

6

Acid-Rain Negotiations
in North America and Europe:
A Study in Contrast

RODERICK W. SHAW

Transboundary air pollution is an excellent example of a relatively new class of environmental problems for which preventive and corrective strategies must be considered not only on a local but on a regional scale. Indeed, these strategies usually involve several nations. The long-range transboundary flow of sulfur and nitrogen oxides, and the resulting regional-scale environmental damage (such as acidification of soil and fresh water and damage to vegetation), has been recognized as an international problem in both Europe and North America. Although there has been extensive scientific research on the problem on both sides of the Atlantic Ocean, international discussions in North America and Europe have pro-

AUTHOR'S NOTE: The author benefited from discussions with Leen Hordijk of the National Institute of Public Health and Environmental Protection, Bilthoven, the Netherlands. Dr. Hordijk is a member of the Dutch delegation to the executive body of the UN-ECE Convention on Long-Range Transboundary Air Pollution.

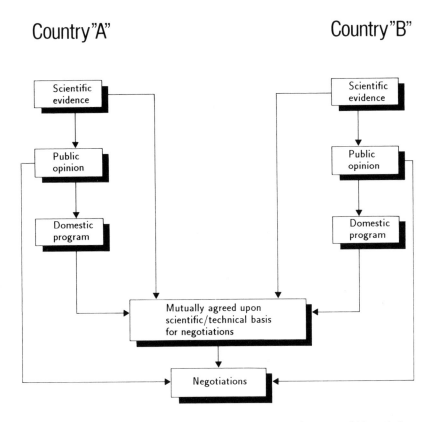

Figure 6.1. The Stages of Activities in International Environmental Negotiation

gressed in different ways. In fact, no real negotiations have taken place between the United States and Canada; in Europe, however, initial protocols to reduce emissions of sulfur and nitrogen oxides (the main precursors of acidic precipitation) have been agreed upon under the United Nations Economic Commission for Europe (UN-ECE) Convention on Long-Range Transboundary Air Pollution. Furthermore, intensive work is taking place under this convention to develop more stringent protocols to reduce emissions further.

Why has progress to reach international agreement taken such different routes in North America and Europe? To analyze the differences, it is useful to break down the process of international negotiations for transboundary air pollution into several stages as shown in Figure 6.1. Although only two countries are represented in the figure, it is applicable to a larger number. The top three pairs of boxes in the figure show the processes that occur, more or less independently, in each country (at least in the initial stages) although there is, of course, an interchange of information among individuals in the two nations. Scientific evidence and public opinion are two essential ingredients within each nation, even if only a domestic program to reduce emissions is to exist (Brydges, 1987). The bottom two boxes depict the stages in which both nations must participate to reach an international agreement.

Following the process shown in Figure 6.1, this chapter reviews briefly the international events in Europe and North America with respect to transboundary air pollution and regional acidification. The first section describes the relatively successful negotiations, and the processes that led up to them, in Europe; the next section deals with the less successful discussions that were transpiring at the same time between the United States and Canada. Finally, the last section compares the events in Europe with those in North America in the light of the attributes of international environmental negotiations described by Guy-Olivier Faure and Jeffrey Z. Rubin in Chapter 2.

Acid Rain Negotiations in Europe

Scientific evidence. The accumulation of scientific evidence about transboundary air pollution and regional acidification in Europe and the ensuing international negotiations have been described thoroughly by Hordijk, Shaw, and Alcamo (1990) and Sand (1987). As in North America, regional-scale acidification first manifested itself in aquatic ecosystems. Since about 1950, the decline of fish populations and even disappearances of whole species have been observed in southern Norway and Sweden. In southern Norway, 1,750 lakes out of a total of 5,000 in a study area of 28,000 square kilometers have lost their entire fish population. This loss has been continuing rapidly; between 1978 and 1983, there was a 30% loss of brown trout and a 12% loss of perch in Norway. Similar damage has been observed in Sweden, where a great percentage of the salmon stock along the western coast has been lost; the roach population has declined in 50% of the lakes in southwestern Sweden (Rosseland, Skogheim, & Sevaldrud, 1986).

The public was first alerted to the problem by the Swedish scientist, Svante Odén; in 1967 he stated that Swedish lakes were acidifying and that damage was becoming visible. His findings were downplayed at first but eventually the Swedish Government took Odén's warnings seriously and placed the topics of the transboundary flow of air pollution and acidification on the agenda of the 1972 United Nations Conference on the Human Environment.

The transboundary flow of air pollution has also been implicated in the decline of European forests. In the 1970s, an outbreak of foliar disease was detected in the Federal Republic of Germany. Since then, forest morbidity and even mortality has been observed in other parts of Europe, notably the Erzgebirge region between northwestern Czech and Slovak Federal Republic (CSFR), southwestern Poland, and southeastern Germany. Nilsson and Duinker (1987) examined the results of a forest-monitoring program carried out by the UN-ECE. In many of the 17 nations included in the survey, the volume of wood in the declining stands was 15% to 20% of the growing stock of exploitable closed forests, and the damaged wood exceeded annual fellings, often by a factor of 5 to 10.

Transboundary air pollution also has been suspected to be a factor in the acidification of groundwaters and in damage to buildings. The latter effect is of particular concern to Europe, which has many buildings of historical significance.

It is one thing, however, to suspect transboundary air pollution as a factor in the damage to certain elements of the environment, and quite another to establish firmly the links between cause and effect. For scientific evidence to play a significant role in international environmental negotiations, it must provide information on cause-effect relationships that is useful to negotiators and, preferably, part of the negotiation process.

Although not all of the controversy has yet been resolved, there is a growing consensus that the cause-effect chain is as follows: acidification of fresh waters is closely linked with the decline and demise of fish stocks. Furthermore, acidification of soil and the effects of ambient air pollutants (especially sulfur dioxide and photochemical oxidants), in addition to drought and insects, are generally accepted as important factors in forest decline. There is a consensus that acidification of water and soil results from the deposition from the atmosphere of sulfur and nitrogen oxides. These two pollutants, in addition to photochemical oxidants, are transported considerable distances through the atmosphere and across national boundaries. The precursors of these pollutants enter the atmosphere through human activities such as the burning of fossil fuels for energy and industrial processes.

In Europe, the accumulation of scientific evidence to support the concept of the cause-effect chain has been mainly international in scope; this has enabled the concept to be accepted as a basis for negotiations. In fact, the scientific research in Europe has been embedded in the negotiation process.

At about the time of the 1972 Stockholm Conference, the Organization for Economic Cooperation and Development (OECD) began a study of the international exchange of air pollutants (mainly sulfur) in Europe. This study concentrated on two efforts: monitoring and modeling. In 1972 the OECD Cooperative Technical Program to Measure the Long-Range Transport of Air Pollution was initiated in 11 nations. It included the monitoring of the concentrations and depositions of specified pollutants and, under the leadership of the Norwegian Meteorological Institute (NMI), the modeling of the transboundary flow of sulfur. The importance of the modeling is that it provided estimates of the international exchange of sulfur, that is, where each nation's emissions of sulfur were being deposited.

Because Eastern Europe and the former Soviet Union contribute significantly to regional-scale air pollution, it soon became evident that an international organization representing all of Europe was needed to provide a forum for further discussion. Such an organization is the UN-ECE. In 1979 the UN-ECE Convention on Long-Range Transboundary Air Pollution was signed by 35 countries. The Cooperative Program for the Monitoring and Evaluation of the Long-Range Transmission of Air Pollutants in Europe (EMEP) took over and expanded the former OECD program. At present, EMEP monitoring consists of more than 90 stations in 24 nations and measures acidity in precipitation and the amount of sulfur in the air. An increasing number of stations have been monitoring nitrogen compounds, and some stations are starting to measure photochemical oxidants. The modeling work also has been expanded to include not only the chemistry of sulfur, but also nitrogen and the photochemistry of oxidants. In addition to the modeling being carried out by the Norwegian Meteorological Institute, designated by the EMEP Meteorological Synthesizing Center West (MSC-West), transboundary exchanges of sulfur also have been estimated by the MSC-East in Moscow. Estimates by the two centers of transboundary exchanges are in general agreement.

The use of this scientific evidence in the European negotiations is explored later in the chapter; it is worth repeating here that its acceptance as a basis for negotiations is due largely to the fact that the international scientific and technical programs have been carried out under the same umbrella as the negotiations, that is, the UN-ECE Convention.

Public opinion. Currently 26 European nations are involved in the negotiations under the UN-ECE Convention, and, as can be expected, there is a wide spectrum of public support within those nations, depending upon the national perception of the urgency of the problem. Even in Sweden, where Odén first sounded the warning about acidification, the public was skeptical. (Initially, Odén's funding was even reduced!) However, since the 1972 Stockholm Conference, during which the fragility of the ecosystems in the Nordic nations was made clear, public concern in this region has been high and citizens have supported their governments' efforts to keep the issue of transboundary air pollution on the international environmental agenda. Public opinion in the Netherlands has followed the example of that in the Nordic nations, possibly because the small geographic size of the Netherlands results in a large fraction of imported pollutants, and also because its extremely high population density and local pollution problems can exacerbate problems from imported pollution.

Public concern in Nordic Europe often has been directed toward the United Kingdom whose power-plant emissions are believed to be transported across the North Sea and deposited in southern Norway and Sweden. (As it turns out, this concern has been somewhat misdirected because modeling calculations indicate that Eastern Germany and Poland are the major contributors to acidic deposition in many parts of southern Scandinavia.) The existence of an identifiable source may have served to alert public opinion not only in Nordic Europe, but also in the United Kingdom, where citizens in the United Kingdom viewed themselves as being unjustly accused.

Opinion in the Federal Republic of Germany, as in the United Kingdom, also was against reducing emissions to safeguard Scandinavian lakes, but this opinion changed in the 1980s when extensive damage was discovered to trees in the Black Forest and in the Harz Mountains. Must damage be discovered at home before public opinion swings in favor of adopting remedial international action?

Because of the character of social and political structures, there was no visible environmental movement during the 1970s and 1980s in Eastern Europe and the former Soviet Union, although the public must have been aware of the region's severe environmental problems. The national policies in those countries emphasized the development of heavy industry, and there was little incentive to operate industries in an environmentally sound way. Following the profound social and political changes that have taken place in these nations since 1989, environmental concerns now are being voiced, but the enormous cleanup costs undoubtedly will need to be addressed during environmental discussions.

Despite the wide divergence of public opinion in Europe on whether or not to take measures to combat transboundary air pollution, significant steps have been taken to reach international agreement on such measures. In addition to the increasing acceptance of the validity of the scientific evidence, the reason for the move toward agreement may be that a group of "green" nations—notably the Nordic nations, the Netherlands, and most recently Germany—have joined forces in the discussions within the UN-ECE.

Domestic programs. Space in this chapter does not permit a detailed description of the national air-pollution programs in all the nations of

Europe; this may be found in a recent report of the United Nations Economic Commission for Europe (ECE, 1990). These measures include specification of maximum concentrations of pollutants in the ambient air, maximum levels of sulfur and lead in fuels, and emission standards for power plants and motor vehicles. Economic measures to reduce pollution include tax breaks for clean motor vehicles and for the use of unleaded gasoline, emission charges and fines, and, most recently, environmental taxes on, for example, the carbon content of fuels. Many of these measures were taken with the abatement of local air pollution in mind but, nevertheless, will reduce transboundary air pollution as well. Specific international measures will be described later.

The large nation-to-nation variation in the strictness of domestic measures reflects the influence of public opinion and the availability of financial resources. The strictest domestic programs tend to be in Western and Nordic Europe. Those in Eastern Europe are less strict because of the low priority given there in the past to environmental concerns. In some European nations in the south, such as Spain and Yugoslavia, environmental policies also are less advanced than in other nations. Groups of nations within Europe, such as those within the European Economic Community (EEC), have attempted to harmonize their national policies with EEC Directives such as those for motor vehicles, municipal waste-incineration plants, and large combustion sources. It should be noted that, although a nation may report its national policies to international bodies such as the ECE, it is difficult to ascertain whether or not these policies are indeed being carried out.

Mutually agreed-upon scientific/technical basis for negotiations within Europe. Under the UN-ECE Convention on Long-Range Transboundary Air Pollution, several technical and scientific activities have been established to support the development of new protocols for the abatement of sulfur and nitrogen emissions within the ECE. In addition to the EMEP activities, there are international cooperative programs on the effects of air pollution on materials (including historic and cultural monuments), forests, and agricultural crops, as well as an international cooperative program to assess and monitor the acidification of lakes and rivers. The purpose of these activities is to document further the damage to the European environment from transboundary air pollution.

An important activity within the convention is the development of "critical loads" and "critical levels," defined as "a quantitative estimate of an exposure to one or more pollutants below which significant harmful effects on specified sensitive elements of the environment do not occur according to present knowledge." (*Loads* refer to deposition; *levels,* to concentrations in the ambient air.) Note the significance of the last four words of the definition; the negotiators are obliged to work with the knowledge that they have at hand. The importance of this activity is that it gives the negotiators environmental goals. "Target" loads and levels will be used in practice rather than critical values (which are based strictly upon scientific considerations). It is expected that the target loads and levels will be based upon critical values that have been modified following negotiations among nations. It is possible, of course, that some nations could negotiate their target values with the ulterior motive of being "free riders," as described by Bergman, Cesar, and Klaassen (1990).

Assuming that agreement can be reached with regard to environmental targets, what would be the best policy to attain them? It was decided within the ECE to consider three sources of information as the scientific/technical basis for negotiations: target loads and levels as described above; the relative contribution by a given source nation to acid deposition in other nations (these are called *source-receptor relationships* and are calculated by the EMEP models); and the relative costs of reducing emissions in different nations. All other factors being equal, it is more cost-effective to reduce emissions in the nations where costs are relatively low.

The EMEP model is capable of estimating the amount of emissions from a given nation that is deposited in other nations of Europe; in other words, who is doing what to whom. This method of assigning responsibility for the deposition in a given receptor region of Europe has been accepted by the nations involved in the negotiations, who provide annual estimates of emissions to the EMEP modelers as input to the calculations of sulfur and nitrogen budgets.

In contrast to the discussions in North America (described below), the use of integrated assessment models, after some opposition (especially from the United Kingdom), has been accepted as a scientific tool in international discussions within the ECE. An integrated assessment model attempts to incorporate all of the processes involved in regional acidification, such as the energy demands resulting in sulfur and nitrogen emissions; emission-control technologies and their costs; atmospheric transfer and deposition; and the effects upon sensitive receptors such as lakes, rivers, and forests. An integrated assessment model should indicate to negotiators the effects, in terms of environmental change and costs of control, of a specific emission policy. Some models, through optimization routines, can help negotiators design emission policies that will help to keep deposition at sensitive receptor points within specified values (for example, target depositions) with the least reduction of European emissions or, alternatively, at the least total European cost.

There are three integrated assessment models in Europe: the ACIDRAIN model developed by Cambridge Decision Analysts in the United Kingdom, the BICRAM model that was developed by the Beijer Institute for Resource Assessment and Management (now the Stockholm Environmental Institute), and the Regional Acidification INformation and Simulation (RAINS) model developed at the International Institute for Applied Systems Analysis (IIASA). The last two models (in particular, the RAINS model) are being used extensively by the Working Group on Abatement Strategies under the ECE Convention to develop new protocols for sulfur and nitrogen emission reductions. These discussions, leading to the development of protocols, are presented in detail in the next section.

In summary, there has been considerable international agreement in Europe on the validity and usefulness of scientific evidence and tools with respect to negotiations on measures to combat transboundary air pollution and regional acidification. This agreement, which was at least partially due to the scientific work that was carried out under the same umbrella as the negotiations, certainly has contributed to the relative success of European negotiations and represents an important difference between events in Europe and in North America.

Negotiations within the UN Economic Commission for Europe. As described by Hordijk et al. (1990), the ECE was the obvious candidate for a forum on transboundary air pollution. Negotiations on the topic began within the ECE in 1977, when Norway, Sweden, and Canada were attempting to reach a widely supported agreement among ECE members to reduce acidifying emissions by a fixed percentage. The Federal Republic of Germany and the United Kingdom were strong opponents; the United Kingdom wanted more research because it was not convinced of the validity of the results of the initial OECD monitoring and modeling study and did not believe that the detrimental results of acid rain had been established. It is interesting that the United Kingdom behaved like the United States during U.S. discussions with Canada.

With two of its member nations (the Federal Republic of Germany and the United Kingdom) opposing measures against acid rain, the European Economic Community adopted the same position. However, Eastern Europe expressed disapproval when the EEC (whose members are in Western Europe) acted officially on behalf of all EEC members, most of whom regarded strict measures more favorably than did the United Kingdom and the Federal Republic of Germany.

These difficulties were eventually overcome, and, in November 1979, the Convention on Long-Range Transboundary Air Pollution was signed by 35 nations, including all European nations, the United States, Canada, and the European Economic Community. It entered into force in March 1983; by early 1989 it had been ratified by 32 signatories. Article 2 of the convention obligated the contracting parties to protect humanity and the environment against air pollution and to endeavor to limit and reduce air pollution, including long-range transboundary air pollution. Article 3 required the contracting parties to develop, without undue delay, policies and strategies to combat the discharge of air pollutants and to engage in additional research and development and exchange of information. Following the signing of the convention, the former OECD monitoring and modeling activities were incorporated into the Cooperative Program for the Monitoring and Evaluation of the Long-Range Transmission of Air Pollutants in Europe, and work began on a sulfur protocol under the convention.

On the 10th anniversary of the 1972 Stockholm Conference on the Human Environment, the signatories to the convention met again in Stockholm at the Conference on Acidification of the Environment. The 1982 conference marked a breakthrough when the Federal Republic of Germany, concerned about forest damage, changed its attitude toward acid-rain controls; a concerted international control program was then brought under the ECE umbrella. At a ministers' meeting in Ottawa, Canada, in March 1984, 10 nations volunteered to reduce emissions of sulfur dioxide by 30% by 1993, relative to 1980 levels. This group of nations was referred to unofficially as the "30 Percent Club." By June 1984 membership in the 30 Percent Club had increased to 18 nations.

With so many signatories to the convention agreeing to voluntary controls, the next step was to draft a sulfur dioxide protocol to the Convention. In July 1985 at Helsinki, Finland, a protocol to reduce sulfur dioxide emissions or transboundary fluxes by at least 30% was signed by 21 nations. Among the nations that did not sign the protocol were two of Europe's largest emitters: Poland and the United Kingdom. The United Kingdom did not sign because, in its opinion, insufficient credit was given in the protocol for past emission reductions, and because of the arbitrary choice of a base year (1980); the latter objection was later overridden in the nitrogen oxide protocol of 1988, to be discussed later. Poland did not sign the protocol because of its lack of technologies and equipment to control emissions.

Although Canada signed the sulfur dioxide protocol, the United States did not. As discussed in the final section of the chapter, by signing the protocol, Canada hoped to put pressure on the United States in the North American discussions, but it was to no avail.

National emission reductions agreed to by the signatories under the sulfur dioxide protocol varied from 30% to 70%. Because some nations did not sign the protocol, and actually have increased their emissions because of economic development, European emissions have decreased by only 15% since 1980 (Hordijk et al., 1990). Calculations with integrated assessment models such as RAINS have indicated that emission reductions greater than those already agreed to under the sulfur dioxide protocol are needed to halt acidification. It also would be more cost-effective to target those emission reductions to the known sensitive areas in Europe, taking into account critical loads, source-receptor relationships established by meteorology, and the relative costs of reducing emissions in one nation versus in another (Shaw, 1989). A successor to the 1985 sulfur dioxide protocol is being developed within the ECE (taking into account the three factors above).

Although the emission reductions resulting from the 1985 sulfur dioxide protocol were quite modest, the protocol set an important precedent in Europe for the use of scientific and technical information to establish international air-pollution agreements.

At the signing of the 1985 sulfur dioxide protocol, an ad hoc group was created to develop an nitrogen oxide reduction protocol. Three years later, in November 1988, an nitrogen oxide protocol was signed in Sofia, Bulgaria. It requires that nitrogen oxide emissions (or transboundary fluxes) not exceed 1987 values by the end of 1994 at the latest. However, nations may choose a year prior to 1987 as their base year. In such a case, the protocol states that the 10-year average annual nitrogen oxide emission (1987-1996) should not exceed the 1987 level. The freedom of choice of a base year (this was provided in response to the objections of the UK with respect to the sulfur dioxide protocol) is compensated by an obligation to an "average standstill."

Work has already begun on a successor to the 1988 nitrogen oxide protocol; as in the case of sulfur dioxide, critical loads may form part of the basis of the new protocol, which is expected to be ready by 1995.

Acid-Rain Negotiations Between the United States and Canada

Scientific evidence. The role that science has played in the development of acid-rain policies in Canada and the United States has been reviewed extensively by Brydges (1987), Milburn-Hopwood (1989), and Schmandt and Roderick (1985). A review of the scientific evidence may also be found in MOI (1983), NAS (1983, 1986), and RMCC (1988). As is often the case, the first evidence came about as a result of unrelated scientific work. In the early 1960s, Harold Harvey of the University of Toronto, and his graduate student, Richard Beamish, failed consistently in their attempts to stock sockeye salmon in the lakes in the Lacloche Mountain area of Ontario, near a large smelter in Sudbury. Discussions with local commercial fishermen revealed that fish stocks had been declining in these lakes for several years. They then examined fishing records maintained by the Ontario Ministry of Natural Resources and discovered that declines in fish stocks had been occurring in areas of Ontario far beyond the Sudbury basin.

Scientific evidence from Scandinavia on the link between acidic precipitation and declining fish stocks lead Harvey and Beamish to determine that acidification might be a significant factor in Ontario as well. Evidence of possible links between regional acidification and fish stocks was also forthcoming from other areas of Canada and the United States. In the early 1980s Walton Watt of the Canada Department of Fisheries and Oceans examined salmon catch records in Nova Scotia rivers for the period between 1935 and 1980. He found that the rivers could be divided into two groups: in the first group the average pH (acidity) of the rivers had not changed appreciably over the past 45 years and fish catches had not changed significantly; in the second group pH values had declined to below 5.0 and salmon catches had plummeted by a factor of 10. The rivers had been chosen carefully to eliminate local influences such as the building of dams and causeways that would pose physical barriers to the fish. Watt's discovery was further evidence of the link between acidification of fresh water and declines in acid-sensitive fish stocks. Interestingly, in the region of Sudbury, Ontario, where declines in fish stocks had been detected by Harvey and Beamish, many of the lakes are now less acidic. This is consistent with the fact that during the same period, the emissions from the Sudbury smelter have decreased by 65% (Environment Canada, 1988). In the Adirondack Mountains of New York, an area known to be sensitive to acidic deposition, declines in brown trout stocks have been attributed to acidification of the lakes.

Unlike Europe, where links generally have been accepted between transboundary air pollution and declines in both sensitive fish populations and forest growth, much of the scientific evidence in North America, at least until recently, has focused upon declines in fish populations. Nevertheless, there is evidence in North America of declines in the sugar maple forests in Quebec and Ontario and damage to forests in the southern Appalachian Mountains in the United States. As is the case in Europe, the long-range transport of air pollution (leading to direct effects on the leaves and needles and indirect effects such as soil impoverishment and toxification) is only one factor in forest decline; others are drought and pests. Despite the multiplicity of factors leading to forest decline, scientific evidence has been accepted more in Europe as a rationale for controlling air pollutants than it has been in North America. Public opinion in Europe has been more supportive of the adoption of corrective measures in the face of scientific uncertainty than it has been in North America.

Although scientific consensus has been established on the link between acidification of fresh water and fish decline in North America, controversy still surrounds the link between emissions of acidic precursors in specific regions of North America and acidification in other areas. Through extensive monitoring programs, it is now well known that precipitation—more acidic by a factor of at least 10 than rainfall in pristine areas unaffected by acidic anthropogenic emissions—is falling over large areas of eastern North America, and that this phenomenon could lead to acidification of fresh waters (MOI, 1983). However, to formulate effective control strategies for transboundary air pollution, knowledge about source-receptor relationships must be accepted and used. Because of the high costs of controlling the precursors of acidic deposition, it is important to control the sources that have the greatest effect upon sensitive receptors. The most practical means of controlling those sources is through the use of computer-based long-range atmospheric transport models. In Europe, the model developed by the Norwegian Meteorological Institute under the aegis of the UN-ECE Convention on Long-Range Transboundary Air Pollution and an integrated model of acidification in Europe—IIASA's RAINS model, which makes use of the NMI model—have been accepted as tools for developing cost-effective emission-reduction strategies against acidic deposition.

No consensus on the usefulness of models exists in North America. Although several atmospheric models have been developed and tested under joint U.S.-Canadian research, no single model has been accepted officially in North America as determining source-receptor relationships useful for developing international control strategies. The United States National Academy of Sciences Report (NAS, 1983) concedes that the occurrence of acid rain in eastern North America appears to be roughly proportional to the average annual emission of sulfur dioxide, but it adds that scientific models describing the movement of acid-forming pollutants over long distances were not yet precise enough to analyze the effects of emission-control strategies.

In using models to develop emission-control strategies, environmental targets must be established, usually by setting strict limits on concentrations or deposition values (which should not be exceeded). As described above, such targets are being developed in Europe under the UN-ECE Convention or Long-Range Transboundary Air Pollution. In North America, within the U.S.-Canada Memorandum of Intent of Transboundary Air Pollution, there was an unsuccessful attempt to develop a deposition target to protect sensitive aquatic ecosystems. Canadian scientists were willing to accept a target loading by wet deposition (precipitation and fog) of 20 kilograms of sulfate per hectare per year. This target was based upon observed lake acidification in about 300 lakes in the Adirondacks in the

United States and in southern Ontario. However, as Riordan (1990) describes, the U.S. scientists viewed the matter of target deposition to be more complex than did the Canadians and felt that target loadings formed a continuum that would determine how many lakes would be at risk from acidification. As a result, no consensus was (or has) been reached between the United States and Canada on environmental targets for acidic deposition.

In summary, the lack of meaningful negotiations on acid rain between the United States and Canada is a result of the different views in each country of the uncertainty surrounding the scientific evidence linking the causes and effects of acid rain. Canadian officials often feel that the economic interests influencing public opinion in the United States have overemphasized the uncertainty as an excuse for delaying expensive action. On the other hand, U.S. officials feel that, to a certain extent, Canadians have ignored the uncertainties and have drawn conclusions from scientific evidence that cannot be supported. In turn, these differing views have influenced public behavior.

Public opinion. Brydges (1987) states that the combination of scientific evidence and public opinion must be strong to prompt action on an environmental issue. If scientific evidence is weak, public opinion (if strong enough) still can bring about action. It was shown earlier that scientific evidence in Europe about the link between acid rain and environmental degradation—although still scientifically uncertain in some areas—in combination with strong public opinion in some countries has brought about international action. In contrast, there is a considerable difference between the United States and Canada when it comes to public opinion. This has been a major factor in the lack of progress in negotiations in North America.

In the opinion of Brydges (1987), the development of public opinion in Canada can be divided into three phases. Before 1972, public opinion supported the control of local air pollution. Between 1972 and 1978, although there were substantial increases in scientific research, public reaction was minimal or even antagonistic toward scientific evidence about acid rain. The lack of response may have been because the public was saturated by "gloom and doom" stories about local air pollution, eutrophication of lakes, pesticides, and internal poisoning from the consumption of mercury-laden fish. Because the link between cause and effect is conceptually tenuous and spatially distant, acid rain is a relatively difficult environmental problem for the public to grasp. The antagonistic reaction to early scientific evidence came from tourist resort operators in the vicinity of the acidified lakes who feared that publicity about the declining fish population would harm their business.

According to Brydges (1987), however, in 1978 public opinion was stirred by a series of articles in Canada's leading newspapers about the relationship between sulfur dioxide emissions (including those from the Sudbury smelter) and acidification of lakes. The articles may have appeared at a point on the public learning curve when the public was becoming sufficiently sensitive to the problem of acid rain. In February 1979 Premier William Davis of the Province of Ontario wrote to Prime Minister Pierre Trudeau of Canada about the need for immediate U.S.-Canadian action on acid precipitation. In 1978 the National Council of Women of Canada called for further research into the problem and an international abatement policy to be reached through bilateral agreement. In 1981 the Canadian Coalition on Acid Rain, supported by more than 50 environmentally interested agencies, was formed as a lobby group to press for control action in the United States. The coalition has been considerably successful in informing the public, government leaders, and businesses on both sides of the border about the problem of acid rain.

The two largest emitters in Canada, the Ontario Hydro Electric Company and the International Nickel Company of Canada (INCO, which operated the Sudbury smelter), have accepted the Ontario government control orders to reduce emissions. Ontario Hydro, a publicly owned utility, is planning to use more washed coal, modify burners, install a small number of scrubbers, and increase the fraction of nuclear power. INCO will reduce daily sulfur dioxide emissions from 6,000 tons (the world's largest point source) to about 1,000 tons by 1994 (Environment Canada, 1988). In 1980, the United Steel Workers of America, representing the workers at INCO, adopted a strong stand in favor of pollution controls at the smelter. In summary, opinion in many public sectors in Canada generally has been in favor of measures to combat acid rain.

In the United States, public opinion has been more divided (Schmandt & Roderick, 1985). The National Clean Air Coalition concedes that, although gaps in scientific knowledge exist, there is enough information about the potential damage from acid rain to compel immediate action. The coalition has attempted to use cost-benefit comparisons, a tool often considered dangerous by many environmentalists. The results of the coalition's analyses, although carefully prepared, have made certain assumptions that have been called into question, such as interstate trading of electricity.

Industry in the United States, including the Electric Power Research Institute, the Edison Electric Power Institute, the National Coal Association, and the American Electric Power Service Company, generally has been cautious about, or even hostile to, the idea of embarking on an acid-rain control program. Some of the arguments hinge on the scientific uncertainty about the problem, and the Electric Power Research Institute even has carried out intensive research on its own. In contrast, the National Coal Association stresses the economic hardships that could ensue from acid-rain control, especially unemployment of coal miners in areas with high-sulfur coal. The United Mine Workers of America supports the position of the National Coal Association. Some U.S. utilities feel that the Canadian complaints about acid rain underlie a plan to increase Canadian penetration into the U.S. power market by Canadian hydroelectric dams and nuclear plants. The Tennessee Valley Authority, a public enterprise, has departed from the position of the other utilities in that it recognizes the acid-rain problem and its regional, national, and international scope.

It appears that the industry's view has strongly influenced Washington legislators and has reinforced the general policy of the administration since 1980 to deregulate industry. Although there is currently a proposal to reduce sulfur dioxide emissions by 10 million tons per year, past bills in the U.S. Congress to reduce emissions have been unsuccessful. U.S. officials publicly have voiced skepticism about the wisdom of embarking too soon without further scientific research. The speech by Fitzhugh Green, associate administrator of the U.S. Environmental Protection Agency, at a conference entitled Pollution Across Borders: Acid Rain—Acid Diplomacy, exemplifies the cautious approach favored by U.S. policymakers in the 1980s (J. E. Carroll, 1984).

Despite the variance of public opinion in North America, domestic and international research has been initiated to control acid rain.

Domestic programs. Both the United States and Canada have a federal form of government in which power is shared between the central government and the state or provincial governments. As Schmandt and Roderick (1985) point out, neither federal government has initiated a domestic policy to control acid rain per se. The United States passed the Clean Air Act in 1970, primarily to improve local air quality. (Of course, the reduction of emissions to improve local air quality also would mean less long-range atmospheric transport of pollutants.) Performance (emission) standards have been imposed for new stationary sources (such as power plants) and light trucks. These detailed strategies for the implementation by individual states of the Clean Air Act include the provision that pollution generated within one state should not interfere with another state's ability to meet national ambient air-quality standards or that state's own air-pollution requirements.

In Canada, legislative power to control sulfur and nitrogen oxides, the precursors of acidic precipitation, rests with the provincial governments rather than with the federal government. The federal government can set emission standards only for pollutants that pose a direct threat to human health, such as lead and mercury, and for pollutants that would cause Canada to violate an international air-pollution agreement. In the latter case, no such agreement has been reached yet between Canada and the United States. Therefore, the Canadian government has concentrated its efforts on encouraging both its provincial governments and the United States government to take action to reduce acid rain. Two provinces with the largest emissions, Ontario and Quebec, have undertaken control programs through existing provincial legislation. More specifically, Ontario has issued nonappealable regulations to two of its major emission sources, INCO and Ontario Hydro. Quebec has issued a control order to reduce emissions at its largest emission source, a smelter at Noranda (Environment Canada, 1988).

In 1984, Canada committed itself to a 50% reduction in sulfur dioxide emissions from its seven easternmost provinces. The negotiations among the federal and provincial governments were assisted by the use of computer models that estimated how the 50% emission reduction should be partitioned among the seven provinces. These models made use of source-receptor links from meteorological models and information on the costs of reducing emissions at various sources. In the end, the negotiated partitioning of emission reductions agreed well with the modeling estimates for Ontario and Quebec and was less than the modeling results for two smaller provinces (Manitoba and New Brunswick) because of political, engineering, and social reasons (T. Brydges, 1990, personal communication). Although the partitioning of emission reductions was achieved through federal and provincial negotiations, the emission reductions will be implemented through provincial legislation.

In summary, the United States and Canada, for different reasons and using different mechanisms, have initiated separate measures that will reduce emissions of the precursors of acidic deposition. However, no integrated U.S.-Canadian control program has been accepted or initiated that takes into account the transboundary source-receptor relationships on a North American basis. Such a program must be negotiated using a mutually acceptable scientific and technical basis. Although there has been a great deal of joint U.S.-Canadian scientific and technical work, the two countries are not in sufficient agreement about the results as a basis of negotiation.

Attempts at a mutually acceptable scientific/technical basis for U.S.-Canadian negotiations. In 1978 the U.S. Congress directed the Department of State to begin negotiations with Canada on an air-quality agreement. Interestingly, this action was spurred by concern in the U.S. Senate about potential environmental damage in Minnesota from a power plant to be built in Atikokan in northwestern Ontario, near the U.S. border. As a result, in October of that year, the Bilateral Research Consultation Group (BRCG) was established to consult on research activities and to exchange information on the long-range transport of air pollutants. The BRCG met twice, once in November 1978 and again in June 1979, and released a statement in July 1979. The statement included a list of principles and practices to be included in formal negotiations between the two countries including transboundary air-pollution control strategies, notification and consultation, technical research and information exchange, and monitoring and evaluation. Two technical reports were also issued by the BRCG in October 1979 and October 1980. These reports represented the most comprehensive assessment of acid rain to date in North America and were important sources of information for policymakers.

Events, however, were soon to overtake the BRCG. In February 1980, the Carter administration announced a program to convert more than 100 oil-fired power stations to coal, in the interest of energy self-sufficiency. The plan failed in Congress, but, despite this setback in U.S.-Canadian relations, negotiations continued and a Memorandum of Intent (MOI) on Transboundary Air Pollution was signed in August 1980. The MOI committed both governments to developing a bilateral agreement on acid precipitation and included arrangements for creating a mutually acceptable scientific and technical information base. Five bilateral work groups were formed to review the scientific information and to present it in a form useful for negotiations: Work Group 1 would assess the effects on aquatic and terrestrial ecosystems, forests, wildlife, and so on; Work Group 2 would review the atmospheric science of monitoring and modeling and especially source-receptor relationships; Work Group 3A would develop control scenarios; Work Group 3B would review the capabilities and costs of control technologies; and Work Group 4 would develop legal and institutional mechanisms for a bilateral agreement.

The progress of the MOI work groups has been well documented in Schmandt and Roderick (1985). The work was divided into three phases. Phase I reports were released in February 1981. At that time, the United States government was transferring power to a new administration and progress became more and more difficult. There were major turnovers in the U.S. memberships of Work Groups 1 and 2. Work Group 1 had three U.S. co-chairs in rapid succession. The lack of continuity on the U.S. side and the increasing divergence of scientific views from both sides slowed progress considerably. (I was a member of Work Group 2, and therefore have first-hand recollection of events.)

Work Group 3A, which was created to develop control scenarios, was relegated to coordinating the activities of the other groups because the development of control scenarios was deemed an inappropriate task for a bilateral group. Work Group 4 never became active. The Phase III (final) reports of Work Groups 1, 2, and 3B were completed considerably behind schedule (in January 1983, November 1982, and June 1982, respectively). There was substantial scientific disagreement between the Canadian and U.S. members of the work groups, a major reason for the delay in the final reports. Some of the disagreements were not resolved before the release of the final reports, especially those in the Work Group 1 report that dealt with aquatic impacts. One of the most significant disagreements concerned the concept of a target loading or deposition to protect freshwater resources. The Canadians accepted an interim target loading of 20 kilograms per hectare per year of wet deposition of sulfate to protect all but the most sensitive of aquatic ecosystems; the U.S. members of Work Group 1 refused, on the basis of uncertain scientific information, to propose any target loading. In Work Group 2, several Canadian members felt that atmospheric models could predict wet sulfate deposition to within a factor of two and could be used to assess the relative merits of various control strategies. The U.S. members, on the other hand, felt that atmospheric models could predict only to within an order of magnitude and could not be used to link sources with receptors. Unlike Work Group 1, which gave separate U.S. and Canadian conclusions, Work Group 2 reported a single set of joint conclusions that were more aligned with U.S. views. The Work Group 3B report contained many mutually agreed-upon conclusions concerning emissions and control technologies.

Upon the completion of the MOI work group reports, Canada suggested that they be reviewed jointly by the Royal Society of Canada and the U.S. Academy of Sciences to overcome the general impression that some views contained in them had been politically biased. However, no agreement on this matter could be reached and reviews were made independently in each country; in the United States by the White House Office of Science and Technology Policy and in Canada by the Royal Society of Canada. There was more agreement in the two peer reviews than there had been among the members of the MOI work groups. The U.S. review noted the problem of scientific uncertainty (which had caused many of the difficulties in the work groups) but stressed that not all of these uncertainties needed to be resolved before taking action to reduce emissions and avoid irreversible damage. Further research then could proceed to reduce the scientific uncertainties. The Canadian peer review concluded that the atmospheric processes were linear when averaged over great enough travel distances and times; a 50% reduction was needed to reduce deposition by 50%. This conclusion was later confirmed in a report from the U.S. National Academy of Sciences (NAS, 1983) and by a report from the U.S. National Acid

Precipitation Assessment Program (NAPAP, 1990). The results of the peer review were delivered to negotiators on both sides.

Following the MOI phase, there has been less emphasis on joint scientific assessment, although there have been joint U.S.-Canadian efforts to evaluate atmospheric models and monitor networks and atmospheric tracer experiments. There have been national reviews, however. In the United States, NAPAP issued an interim report in 1986 and a final report in 1990. The interim NAPAP report was controversial because the summary statements did not always reflect the individual scientific conclusions within the report. In 1986, under its Federal-Provincial Research and Monitoring Coordinating Committee (RMCC), the Canadian government issued several reports by Canadian scientists entitled *Assessment of the State of Knowledge on the Long-Range Transport of Air Pollutants and Acid Deposition* (RMCC, 1988).

Apart from the normal scientific communication among individual scientists, the main intergovernmental exchange of information between the United States and Canada has been the semiannual joint NAPAP/ RMCC meetings and the joint report in April 1987 by the U.S.-Canada Bilateral Advisory and Consultative Group.

In summary, in the first attempt to arrive at a scientific and technical basis for negotiations, the MOI activities in the period between 1980 and 1983, met with only partial success, and official agreement on scientific issues still has not been reached by the United States and Canada.

Negotiations between the United States and Canada. The first formal negotiations between the United States and Canada began in June 1981 when the joint scientific assessment still was being carried out by the MOI work groups. The first meeting consisted mainly of an exchange of ideas and a review of available scientific data.

At the third meeting, in February 1982, Canada submitted a formal proposal for both countries to reduce sulfur dioxide emissions by 50%. The Canadians believed that such an emission reduction would reduce wet sulfate deposition in moderately sensitive lake regions of Canada to less than 20 kilograms per hectare per year, a target loading that the U.S. members of the MOI Work Group 1 had not accepted. In June 1982 the United States rejected Canada's proposal as premature.

At this point, the negotiating process based upon the Memorandum of Intent began to break down. However, as outlined by Milburn-Hopwood (1989), the Canadian proposal formed the basis of a policy initiated in March 1984, whereby the federal government and the seven easternmost provinces agreed to reduce eastern Canadian sulfur dioxide emissions by 50% (from 1980 levels) by 1994. (Federal-provincial negotiations to distribute the 50% emission reduction by province took another four years.)

With the breakdown of the MOI process in March 1985, the Canadian prime minister and U.S. president appointed a special envoy on acid rain from each country to pursue legal and regulatory consultation on pollutants linked to acid rain and to enhance cooperation in research and information exchange. In January 1986, the envoys released their report that concluded that acid rain represents a serious environmental problem in both countries. They also made 12 recommendations to move both countries toward a long-term solution. A bilateral advisory and consultative group, formed in June 1986 and in April 1987, issued a joint report describing the current state of knowledge of acid rain, that is, an update of the MOI reports.

Apart from the normal negotiating process, there have been several top-level contacts between the Canadian prime minister and the U.S. president. These contacts to date have served only to reiterate the general positions of each country—that Canada wishes to initiate action now, while the United States feels that more information is needed.

In summary, negotiations between the United States and Canada have not resulted in a bilateral agreement to reduce emissions leading to acid rain because at least two important ingredients were missing:

(1) While public opinion or the need for action is relatively united in Canada, it is much more divided in the United States.

(2) There is still no mutually acceptable scientific and technical basis for negotiations, mainly because of the large scientific uncertainties. This is a classical scientific dilemma: Which is the greater risk—to act unnecessarily at great expense, or to delay action and risk irreversible and costly damage?

Conclusions: A Comparison of North America and Europe

In Chapter 2, Faure and Rubin argue that international environmental negotiations have a set of distinguishing attributes, features that may be found in other types of negotiations but are more pronounced in environmental disputes. They list 12 such attributes; these will form the basis of the comparison of the acid-rain negotiations in North America and in Europe.

Multiple parties and multiple roles. In the case of North America, two nations were involved in negotiations, one of which (the United States) has 10 times the population and economic power as the other. In Europe, 27 nations were involved. The larger number of countries permitted the formations of influence blocs with common interests, such as the Scandinavian nations and the Netherlands. In fact, although unsuccessful, Canada tried to use the European discussions (both the United States and Canada are members of the UN-ECE) to pressure the United States to move forward on a North American accord on acid rain.

Meaningless boundaries. This attribute generally applies to both North America and Europe: in both regions there is considerable international exchange of acidifying pollutants, except for the more remote regions of Canada, the United States, the United Kingdom, and southern Europe.

Long time frame. This attribute also applies to both North America and Europe. In the United States it has been used as a reason for delaying emission reductions (the time it takes for problems to manifest themselves provides more time to conduct research and devise better control programs) and in Europe and Canada as a reason for *not* delaying emission reductions (corrective actions take a long time before benefits to the environment can be seen).

Scientific and technical uncertainty. As discussed in earlier, the matter of scientific uncertainty has been treated very differently in Europe and in North America, especially in the United States. Uncertainty about cause-effect relationships with respect to aquatic impacts and a lack of confidence in the ability of atmospheric transport models to estimate source-receptor relationships and thereby formulate emission-reduction strategies have prompted the United States to conduct further research (the National Acid Precipitation Assessment Program) and to delay an emission-reduction strategy. However, the United States is now considering a sulfur dioxide emission reduction of 10 million tons per year.

In contrast, Canada decided to use the available scientific evidence from a few freshwater lakes to set a sulfate-deposition target of 20 kilograms per hectare per year and to use the existing atmospheric transport model to partition among the various provinces the planned 50% sulfur dioxide emission reduction in Canada. However, these decisions did not influence the U.S. position.

In Europe, scientific uncertainty has been acknowledged but has been a much less important factor in international negotiations. The general approach has been to use the scientific knowledge at hand, however imperfect. As they become available and are tested, new scientific tools—such as improved versions of the atmospheric model of the Norwegian Meteorological Institute and the critical-load approach for attaining deposition targets—have been used in the UN-ECE discussions aimed at developing new protocols for sulfur and nitrogen reductions. Indeed, embedding the development of a scientific/technical basis for negotiations within the same international agreement as the negotiations themselves, that is, the UN-ECE Convention on Long-Range Transboundary Air Pollution, has increased the acceptability of scientific information.

Power asymmetry. In North America, discussions (they should not be called real negotiations) have taken place between two nations, with the United States having 10 times the population of Canada. Furthermore, although there is a flow of acid precipitation in both directions across the U.S.-Canadian border, it appears that U.S. emissions have a much larger relative impact upon deposition in Canada than vice versa. Because it is the weaker party that is experiencing relatively more import of acid, negotiations are not being conducted between near equals. Furthermore, the relative power of the United States also has made it more difficult for Canada to counter U.S. arguments about scientific uncertainty.

In Europe, 27 nations are involved in the negotiations. Although there is a tremendous range in the size of the nations, from Luxembourg to the Commonwealth of Independent States, there also is an opportunity for smaller nations, such as the Nordic countries and the Netherlands, to form united blocs to increase their influence. This has been used to counter the arguments of large nations such as the United Kingdom that, like the United States, have used scientific uncertainty as a reason for delaying control actions.

Public opinion. As Faure and Rubin point out, negotiators tend to be swayed by public opinion. In the United States, the public is less informed about acid precipitation than it is in Canada and Europe; U.S. negotiators are more influenced by industrial lobby groups such as electric power and coal associations. In Canada, public opinion was so aroused that Canadian negotiators may have been expected to obtain an agreement from the United States in an unrealistically short time, thereby underestimating U.S. reluctance toward the issue.

In Europe, public opinion has been high in the Nordic countries and the Netherlands and later in the Federal Republic of Germany after forest damage from regional air pollution became more evident. The negotiators, especially those from the Nordic countries and the Netherlands, consequently were able to take strong stands at international discussions.

Institutionalization of solutions. In North America, there has been no negotiated settlement to institutionalize solutions, although the United States and Canada exchange information on emission rates, atmospheric concentrations, deposition rates, and modeling activities under joint scientific programs. However, there obviously is no sense of compliance (or lack thereof) implied in this exchange. In other U.S.-Canadian transboundary pollution problems, such as the Trail Smelter case and pollution of the Great Lakes, the International Joint Commission has been given the task of monitoring compliance.

In Europe, although nations have agreed to reduce emissions according to the sulfur dioxide and nitrogen oxide protocols within the UN-ECE Convention, it is not clear how compliance will be monitored other than through the annual national emission reports to the executive body of the convention. It is not clear, furthermore, how lack of compliance will be addressed.

New regimes and rules. There is less of a contrast between North America and Europe with respect to this attribute. Although there is increased awareness on both sides of the Atlantic Ocean that transboundary air pollution is generated by a wasteful use of resources (including energy), there has been no marked shift to a more conservative life-style in either region. Gasoline still is sold at bargain basement prices in North America; cars traveling *legally* at speeds of 200 kilometers per hour are not uncommon on German highways; there is little regard for energy conservation in Eastern Europe, although that may soon change. In short, exhortations of public opinion to negotiators have not been matched by changes in personal life-style. To be fair, however, it should be pointed out that the traditional infrastructure in Europe, with its relatively dense living space and well-developed public transport, means that per capita use of energy in Europe is only one-half that in North America, which is more spread out.

Joint interest. In Europe, negotiators have recognized a joint interest in reducing emissions of acidic pollutants. Because of several relatively small and contiguous nations, emission reductions in a given nation will usually benefit its neighbors, just as emission reductions in the neighboring countries will benefit it. (Exceptions to this are the United Kingdom and southern Europe, which meteorologically are less connected to the rest of Europe.)

Although there also is a joint interest in reducing acid deposition in North America, Canada has not been able to convince the United States of this fact. Much of the Canadian approach stresses the need to reduce deposition in Canada; in fact, emission reductions in the United States would also reduce deposition in sensitive areas such as the Adirondack Mountains in New York.

Negative perceptions of immediate outcomes. As stated by Faure and Rubin, agreement on an environmental problem is likely to increase the constraints imposed on all concerned; there is a price to pay. This fact certainly has been recognized by the coal-producing states in the United States; fear of widespread unemployment in regions with high-sulfur coal have led minors' unions and state governments to lobby against controlling acid precipitation. Interestingly enough, workers at the INCO smelter in Sudbury, Ontario, supported emission controls at their plant, which was at one time the largest single source of sulfur dioxide in the world.

In those nations of Europe that have been pressing for a reduction of acid precipitation, it generally is perceived that, despite the short-term sacrifices involved in controls, long-term benefits will emerge. Thus far, the inconveniences have been rather minor; however, it remains to be seen whether more fundamental changes in life-style—for example, severe restrictions in automobile size, speed, and use—will change public attitude. In Eastern Europe, the sacrifices involved in controlling emissions of acidifying pollutants must be linked with measures needed to increase the general efficiency of the industrial and energy sectors of those nations' economies.

Multiple issues. Because acid precipitation is linked with the power and industrial sectors of the economy, it is obvious that multiple issues are involved. The concern about the plight of unemployed miners in coal-producing states and U.S. fears about Canadian penetration of its electric-power markets, already have been mentioned. In Europe, controlling nitrogen oxide emissions has been opposed by nations that produce mainly small cars because they perceive that catalytic exhaust systems will raise the price of small cars proportionately more than large cars.

Changing actors. In the U.S.-Canadian discussions on acid precipitation (mainly within the joint Memorandum of Intent on Transboundary Air Pollution), the Canadian actors largely had a scientific background; but the dialogue never reached a significant political level. As a result, many issues were scientific in nature; scientific uncertainty was debated at length. However, this debate probably was driven by a hidden agenda of political and economic issues. This was probably to the detriment of the Canadian participants; their scientific background rendered them less capable of dealing with the hidden agenda than their U.S. counterparts, who tended to be drawn from not only scientific but also legal and political spheres.

In Europe, the participants in the debate have been drawn from a wide variety of backgrounds; national delegations to the meetings of the UN-ECE Convention, especially its executive body, are often multidisciplinary. Thus, although changing actors sometimes may represent a problem in the negotiations, under certain conditions they are rather necessary conditions for success.

And, finally, one difference between the situation in North America and that in Europe, not specifically covered in Faure and Rubin's attributes, must be mentioned in closing. Maximum rates of acid deposition in Europe are 10 times those in North America. This fact has had an influence on many of the attributes—*there is no substitute for the sense of urgency.*

7

The Mediterranean:
A New Approach to Marine Pollution

PETER S. THACHER

The 1972 United Nations Conference on the Human Environment (UNCHE) held in Stockholm developed new approaches to marine pollution that changed the way international environmental issues are dealt with and negotiations are conducted. The conference produced the Stockholm Declaration of Principles, which states that "to defend and improve the environment for present and future generations [should be] an imperative goal for mankind . . . to be pursued together with, and in harmony with, the established and fundamental goals of peace and of world-wide economic and social development." In keeping with these principles, the conference participants created the United Nations Environment Program (UNEP) with a mandate to "safeguard and enhance the environment for the benefit of present and future generations of man." General Assembly Resolution 2997, of December 1972, created the four components of UNEP: a 58-member governing council, a small secretariat, a voluntary environment fund, and the Environment Coordination Board.

In 1973 the governing council approved a program to protect the marine environment of the Mediterranean Sea. This program was consistent with the approach of the 1972 Stockholm Conference to prevent damage to the environment rather than react to it after it had occurred.

The Stockholm Declaration of Principles called on nations to "take all possible steps to prevent pollution of the seas by substances that are liable to create hazards to human health, to harm living resources and marine life; to damage amenities or to interfere with other legitimate uses of the sea." This approach elevated marine pollution from a matter of secondary importance in relations among nations on the high seas to one involving many actors and new forms of negotiations, whose goals were without regard to national boundaries.

The UNEP Secretariat and other organizations developed a phased approach to forming regimes that encouraged governments to treat marine-pollution problems in new ways. What had previously been a matter of concern only to states was now open to initiatives by civil servants in the UN system and influenced by nongovernment bodies. At the same time, international attention shifted from concern about exploiting marine resources to safeguarding less-tangible properties and reducing damage, especially in vulnerable areas near the shore.

In the period before Stockholm, nations became concerned about "commons," and accepted that they had duties and rights to protect areas beyond their borders. For example, an international treaty was created to protect Antarctica. Likewise, during the 1960s, nations agreed that other non-sovereign areas also deserved protection: outer space and celestial bodies under the Outer Space Treaty of 1967; and "common heritage" seabed areas beyond national jurisdiction were protected by the principles adopted by the UN General Assembly in 1970.

As international attention shifted from the high seas to coastal and land-based activities, efforts to set up cooperative regimes to deal with marine pollution raised potentially divisive issues of national sovereignty. These issues could have impeded the negotiations, but careful preparations beforehand avoided them. The four decades following the adoption of the 1948 Universal Declaration on Human Rights proved that even in the sensitive area of how a nation treats its citizens, national sovereignty was not impervious to outside pressure, especially from well-organized non-governmental organizations (NGOs) that are active with support from international organizations. This factor, plus agreement at the Stockholm Conference that the Earth's oceans and seas be protected, marked a turning point in the way international environment issues have since been treated.

This chapter describes the role of nonstate organizations during a pre-negotiation phase in the early 1970s when new regimes were formed to protect the marine environment, specifically the adoption in early 1975 of an "Action Plan" for the Mediterranean. The chapter concentrates on the preparations for negotiations, rather than on the negotiations themselves, that led to the 1976 Barcelona Convention and the first of many protocols to follow. Up to this time, international negotiations had been limited to reducing the maritime sources of marine pollution; discussions about the broader and more important issues were limited to nonstate groups and diverse disciplines and special interests that tried to define the problem and identify key issues and actors. Later these groups proposed informal, nonbinding agreements between states, which led to more conventional negotiations and established new laws and norms of conduct.

Many of the characteristics cited by Guy-Olivier Faure and Jeffrey Z. Rubin in Chapter 2 that distinguish international environmental negotiations from other kinds of negotiations apply here. These are discussed in the conclusion of the chapter. But the process of setting the stage for negotiations is different from the negotiations themselves, especially negotiations between disputing nations.

Many of the differing points of view held by coastal nations in the Mediterranean region could be generally characterized as North-South issues. The issues include:

- Whether all nations should be treated equally, or whether some should receive preferential treatment.
- Whether standards should be uniform.
- Whether assistance should be provided as an inducement, and for what purposes.

Before these issues could be discussed, the nature of marine-pollution problems had to be addressed. In doing this, international organizations reduced the scope of subsequent negotiations in a gradual process that encouraged formal negotiations after the ground had been prepared and participants could be confident of their outcome. This approach reduced the issues to those that only nations themselves could resolve. Some issues might have appeared to be procedural, such as who could sign formal treaties for the region, and how a trust fund should be set up, but they were critical issues, and this new approach set important precedents that were later followed in dealing with environmental issues, as in the acceptance of the European Community as a contracting party.

Today the rate of change calls for new ways to organize collective action to decrease risks globally, regionally, nationally, and locally. At the international level, changing conditions threaten to outpace the traditional means by which governments negotiate and agree on action. Protracted negotiations among contending nations, such as the UN Conference on the Law of the Sea (UNCLOS), can be overtaken by financial, technical, and political developments that raise questions about the validity of the agreement. This chapter outlines a process that is different from the path taken by governments in negotiating UNCLOS in 1973.

Mounting concern about marine pollution produced a variety of formulas for action at the Stockholm Conference. Treaty law on marine pollution was advanced by the London Ocean Dumping Convention, a treaty negotiated in preparation for the Stockholm Conference that employed a new formula to speed up the revising of treaties, in light of new scientific understanding, without the need for negotiation and ratification (Contini & Sand, 1972; UNITAR, 1971). Principles on marine pollution that were endorsed at the Stockholm Conference were taken into account by UNCLOS negotiators and embodied in that convention (Thacher, 1973).

The Stockholm Conference also accelerated the use of "soft-law techniques" that built on nonobligatory norm-setting, technical agreements and international standards. While these actions formed the basis for more binding agreements and for formal negotiations, they also reduced the issues to be negotiated, and shifted the work of resolving disputes from formal groups of national representatives to informal meetings of technical experts.

International organizations serving governments developed parallel processes of assessment and management backed up with international support to broaden and encourage participation. This approach was developed during preparations for the Stockholm Conference and first put into practice as the Mediterranean Action Plan, which governments approved in February 1975.

This chapter touches only lightly on the formal treaty route or the use of soft-law techniques. It concentrates on process: the development of a comprehensive approach to cope with marine pollutants, an approach that includes negotiation of a "framework" convention with protocols. Most of the discussions and prenegotiations that shaped this approach were between nongovernment entities who were given new tasks to protect the marine environment.

The experience of forming regimes to deal with marine pollution at the regional level in the early 1970s has since been applied elsewhere, and now involves more than 120 coastal states. It has also been applied to other international environmental problems, such as the depletion of the ozone layer and global warming.

The experience is also relevant to the 1992 UN Conference on Environment and Development, because it provides the first demonstration of the feasibility of a regional agreement on environment and development issues that links poor and rich countries by explicitly recognizing the special needs of developing countries. (Under Article 11 of the 1976 Barcelona Convention (see below), the "Contracting Parties undertake to cooperate in the provision of technical and other possible assistance in fields relating to marine pollution, with priority to be given to the special needs of developing countries in the Mediterranean region.")

Marine Pollution Before the Stockholm Conference

In 1970, as preparations for the Stockholm Conference got under way, marine pollution was on the agenda in many UN organizations. However, international efforts were limited to maritime sources of pollution: that is, release of oil and radioactive wastes from vessels. Three conventions dealt with maritime sources of pollution: the International Convention for the Prevention of Pollution of the Sea by Oil (1954), the Convention on the High Seas (1958), and the Convention on Intervention on the High Seas in Cases of Oil Pollution Casualties (1969).

Several international research programs were also under way: the International Decade of Ocean Exploration (IDOE), the Long-Term Program of Oceanic Research (LEPOR), and the Integrated Global Ocean Station System (IGOSS). But these programs focused mainly on uncovering oceanic resources to exploit, rather than on environmental aspects. A growing issue was whether or not new technology would unleash a mindless scramble to exploit ocean resources for commercial and military purposes. The sustainability of fisheries was already in question, and a few cases of pollution had set off warning signals but the lure of offshore and ocean-floor resources had started a race to expand national sovereignty into the seas.

Faced with mounting concern for the environment, the UN agencies most concerned with these issues set up in 1967 the Joint Group of Experts on the Scientific Aspects of Marine Pollution (GESAMP). GESAMP was different from other groups of experts; it was created by international organizations, rather than by nations, to help them serve governments. It is an interesting example of the influence that international organizations and technical groups can have on negotiations.

GESAMP's definition of *marine pollution,* for example, changed the boundaries for future negotiations and formed the foundation for negotiations that followed. It defined marine pollution as

The introduction by man, directly or indirectly, of substances or energy into the marine environment (including estuaries) resulting in such deleterious effects as harm to living resources, hazards to human health, hindrance to marine activities including fishing, impairment of quality for use of sea water, and reduction of amenities.

By issuing this definition, a group of independent, uninstructed experts, and supporting agencies preempted actions that were traditionally reserved for government negotiators. This definition became a model that set the scope for many environmental negotiations and treaties to follow, notably the Barcelona Convention of 1976 and the Law of the Sea Convention of 1982. For example, the Barcelona Convention defined marine pollution as

> the introduction by man, directly or indirectly, of substances or energy into the marine environment resulting in such deleterious effects as harm to living resources, hazards to human health, hindrance to marine activities including fishing, impairment of quality for use of sea-water, and reduction of amenities.

The Law of the Sea Convention said pollution of the marine environment means

> the introduction by man, directly or indirectly, of substances or energy into the marine environment, including estuaries, which results or is likely to result in such deleterious effects as harm to living resources and marine life, hazards to human health, hindrance to marine activities, including fishing and other legitimate uses of the sea, impairment of quality for use of sea water, and reduction of amenities.

The GESAMP definition was also used in conventions dealing with atmospheric pollution. The Convention on Long-Range Transboundary Air Pollution of 1979 defined *air pollution* as

> the introduction by man, directly or indirectly, of substances or energy into the air resulting in deleterious effects of such a nature as to endanger human health, harm living resources, ecosystems, and material property, and impair or interfere with amenities and other legitimate uses of the environment.

A 1971 summary report by the UN Secretary General to the Economic and Social Council (ECOSOC) cautioned that "pollution is detectably undermining the health of the marine environment and the root cause can be traced to man's activities in an increasingly industrialized and urbanized world" (ECOSOC, 1971). But intergovernmental action to reduce the threat, or even to establish facts on which to judge whether action should be taken, was scattered piecemeal among different institutions: human health issues were discussed at the World Health Organization (WHO), fisheries problems were discussed at the UN Food and Agriculture Organization (FAO), maritime issues were addressed at the International Maritime Consultative Organization (IMCO, now IMO, the International Maritime Organization), and so on.

Thus, from an institutional perspective, the problem of marine pollution was one of excessive compartmentalization; many separate bodies were responsible for pieces of what was essentially a holistic problem. Each effect of pollution in the GESAMP definition had its own constituency, and, although GESAMP provided scientific advice to agencies, there was no means to coordinate all the information. Also, there was no way at the international level to help governments cooperate in reducing pollution, except from ships. This was the role of IMCO.

Marine biologists at the FAO were among the most concerned, but they were limited to dealing with the effects of pollution on fisheries, not on human health. That was the job of the WHO. Physical oceanographers at the International Oceanographic Commission of the UN Education, Science, and Cultural Organization (UNESCO) studied pollution movements by currents. As the public became alarmed by oil spills, such as the Torrey Canyon disaster in 1967, IMCO helped governments prepare maritime agreements on the discharge of oil and petroleum products by tankers. But it was only beginning to consider other hazardous products shipped on merchant vessels. The World Meteorological Organization (WMO) was looking into atmospheric transfer of pollutants to the oceans. The International Atomic Energy Agency (IAEA) set up the only international laboratory for improving the measurement of marine pollutants; its work, however, was limited to radioactive materials.

In 1971 a new round of negotiations on the Law of the Sea was being planned to discuss marine pollution, and IMCO was working on a new convention on shipboard pollution. However, the issues underlying marine pollution were not well defined and the dialogue between different disciplines and sectors had barely begun. There was no international body that could compare the effects of crude oil spilled on the high seas or on coastal rocks with less visible but more insidious pollutants, such as the mercury released in Minimata in 1959, or Itai-Itai, the PCB poisoning of Kyushu in 1968. Other questions needed answers. For instance, were effects on "living resources" more or less important than effects on human health or on the tourist industry? Issues of ownership of deep-sea nodules and the rights of "innocent passage" seemed irrelevant to the public concern that the Mediterranean might be dead or dying. Even the line between national and international jurisdiction was a problem; exaggerated concern over sovereignty limited international cooperation on marine pollution to areas beyond the three-mile limit.

Little wonder then that the Stockholm Conference was thought of as an opportunity to pull together a wide variety of research and other activities scattered throughout the UN system and beyond.

Preparing for the Stockholm Conference

In November 1970, two months before beginning his job as secretary general of the Stockholm Conference, Maurice Strong met informally with delegations in New York. Strong recognized the advantages of taking action before the conference, when there was a sufficient basis to do so. He suggested that there was already an adequate intellectual-conceptual basis on which to negotiate a convention on ocean dumping before the conference started. By identifying areas of consensus and gaps in knowledge, he suggested, an action plan at the Stockholm Conference could list the main issues and indicate how to proceed.

Three months later in Geneva, Strong suggested to the intergovernmental preparatory committee for the Stockholm Conference that an Intergovernmental Working Group on Marine Pollution (IWGMP) be set up to "lay out a comprehensive program and strategy—a master plan—by which governments can move progressively to protect the oceans and to take some of the urgent first steps in implementation of this plan" (CESI, 1971).

Article 25 of the 1958 Convention on the High Seas asked all nations to "cooperate with competent international organizations in taking measures for the prevention of pollution of the seas or air space above, resulting from any activities with radioactive materials or other harmful agents." With this as a basis, Strong proposed that the "master plan would derive largely from work already underway throughout the UN system" and made clear that most of the actions called for should be taken within national jurisdiction by nations, especially those bordering on "more or less landlocked seas." The preparatory committee agreed, and the IWGMP was established.

At IWGMP's first meeting in London in June 1971, Strong said that most of the biosphere on which all life depends lies beyond the protection of any nation or group of nations. He called for a "comprehensive plan which will lay out the framework for future action" to protect the marine environment as a whole. He cited the importance of land-based activities and suggested that "regional action is the practical approach for problems such as enclosed and semi-enclosed seas and other bodies of water whose health is the common concern of a number of nations."

At this meeting hosted by IMCO, the UNCHE Secretariat presented a list of marine pollutants ranked according to the severity of their impact in the four categories defined by GESAMP: harm to living resources, hazards to human health, hindrance to maritime activity, and reduction of amenities (IWGMP, 1972). These were listed in a matrix showing the principal sources of each category of pollutant. This presentation made it clear that the most damaging marine pollutants were produced on land and reached the oceans through rivers, continental runoff, or atmospheric transfer. The long-term cumulative effects of this widespread insidious pollution were more serious but less visible than pollution caused by oil tankers running aground. Until this meeting, land-based pollution was not considered for international control.

This meeting was also the first opportunity for 10 northern and southern Mediterranean coastal nations (Algeria, Cyprus, Egypt, France, Italy, Malta, Morocco, Spain, Turkey, and Yugoslavia) to discuss a regional approach to identifying and controlling pollutants entering the Mediterranean. Growing awareness that no nation bordering a semienclosed sea could protect itself put a premium on identifying the sources and routes of the pollutants and on developing a cooperative approach to a common problem in which costs and benefits could be shared.

But given the cultural and economic differences among these nations, despite their common history, disagreements arose over other marine issues, such as navigation rights. The cradle of Western civilization was now characterized by ancient coastal settlements with mushrooming populations and was faced with all of the pollution problems that come from squeezing industrial, transportation, urbanization, agricultural, and other human systems into narrow coastal strips (except along the southeastern desert shore) between the sea and mountains.

Oil spills and beach closures had led to piecemeal and limited measures to address maritime safety, oil spills, and pollutants that worried the fisheries community. Italy had convened an International Conference on Oil Pollution of the Sea (Rome, 1968) followed by another on Protection of the Sea (Milan, 1969). The 1970 FAO conference in Rome on Marine Pollution and Its Effects on Living Resources and Fishing dealt with local marine pollution, and produced dozens of recommendations addressing the problems faced by fisheries. Significantly, FAO was urged to "bring all these recommendations immediately to the attention of the UN at its Conference on the Human Environment" (FAO, 1971). Despite its ad hoc status, the UNCHE Secretariat was given a mandate to coordinate different agencies working on marine pollution.

It became evident that little reliable information was available about marine pollutants except those that could easily be seen, like tar balls on beaches. Tar and oil kept tourists away, but beaches were being closed for other reasons, principally the risk of typhoid and infectious hepatitis.

Public attention was on these symptoms, especially when public health and amenities were at risk near large coastal settlements or tourist areas. While governmental attention was fixed on interstate interests on the high seas, the public saw the preparations for the Stockholm Conference as more responsive to their concerns.

As is customary at meetings such as the IWGMP meeting in London, participants sat behind signs identifying them as government representatives rather than as individual experts. But it was obvious that two kinds of government participants were present. Those negotiating what would become the convention on ocean dumping came from ministries of external affairs and carried formal instructions. Those interested in the comprehensive action plan for Stockholm came from technical departments or scientific institutions concerned with fisheries, maritime, health, tourism, or other disciplines and were able to operate more or less freely, on the basis of their experience. As usual, scientists—whether from national delegations or from international agencies—joined together and shared a common outlook on the need for research that, in some cases, was more welcomed by their international colleagues than by their own nation's policymakers. The contrast between the formal negotiations among diplomats and the discussions among technical experts encouraged the secretariat to think of a phased approach. Such an approach would improve the knowledge base and form technical agreements to establish norms that might influence national actions and prepare the way for treaty negotiations or customary law.

Throughout the Stockholm preparatory process, developing nations expressed concern that their plans for industrial development would be set back by the environmental concerns of rich nations, especially those that were the biggest polluters. Developing nations were handicapped by not knowing whether marine pollution and other environmental problems required the attention and scarce resources they needed for economic growth. These ideological disputes provided little basis for negotiation. Several factors—the uneven distribution of expertise and laboratories along the shores of the Mediterranean, political tensions, and suspicion of other nations' motives—hindered cooperation among nations. The need for a phased approach and a catalytic mechanism was apparent in the IWGMP and in other preparatory meetings for the Stockholm Conference and influenced the design of the mechanism recommended there, UNEP (Thacher, 1990b).

Other divergent interests emerged during this period, interests that characterized other environmental issues and had less to do with national differences than with sector differences, often within the same government. These interests became apparent in the widely differing views expressed by marine biologists, oceanographers, health experts, economists, lawyers, agronomists, and engineers. While those responsible for maritime interests were on the defensive because of oil spills and tar balls that threatened tourism revenues, fishery representatives wanted to blame declining catches on pollution rather than on overfishing. Public health officials were concerned with different types of pollutants and knew what their problems were. But they were powerless to get funds to fix municipal sewerage systems. Many domestic groups saw in the UNCHE Secretariat an opportunity to promote action at the international level that might pressure their own governments to support local needs. This strategy was not new; national ministries have often used international agencies to lobby for more money at home. Marine pollution and other environmental issues now made it possible for local authorities to use the same tactic.

As the date for the Stockholm Conference approached, the UNCHE Secretariat came to regard the pollution issue as potentially useful for gaining political leverage, and for highlighting the value of analysis as a way of identifying the most appropriate sources of pollution to be attacked cost-effectively. Much of this thinking was based on earlier analytical work on the effects of radiation that linked health effects to dosage, pathways, and original sources. This kind of scientific analysis had been conducted by the UN Scientific Committee on the Effects of Atomic Radiation (UNSCEAR) since the 1950s.

The need to identify the flows, pathways, and sources opened the door, conceptually, to viewing pollutants as "warning signals" that, with proper analysis, might lead to corrective actions at the source. This could improve system efficiency, ultimately leading to improved industrial processes and reducing wastes, rather than investing in their capture and recycling. In the principal paper on Pollutants of International Concern (United Nations, 1972), the UNCHE secretariat suggested that governments might view pollutants as *resources*: "A substance may be considered a pollutant simply because it is in the wrong place, at the wrong time, and in the wrong quantity." For marine pollution, it meant finding critical valves far upstream and on dry sovereign land that deserve more international attention than tankers on the high seas.

But an outright attack along these lines risked offending nations preoccupied with their sovereign rights and would be too complex for the delegations normally sent to international negotiations. This appraisal by the secretariat reinforced the idea of a phased approach in which international organizations would play an active role, relying on expert working groups and technical experts to prepare the way. Ultimately, formal negotiation would be needed to resolve policy issues, especially the problem of reducing land-based sources of pollution. Meanwhile, the attention in the IWGMP was on what could be accomplished, like a convention on ocean dumping, while improving the knowledge base for negotiations and resolving as many issues beforehand as possible on technical grounds.

Based on the advice of three IWGMP sessions held in 1971-1972, the secretariat recommended to delegates at the Stockholm Conference a comprehensive approach to rank marine pollutants according to their impact, regardless of their source, and to tackle the sources at sea and on land, with whatever legal regime, domestic or international, that was applicable. The setting that the secretariat proposed for all recommendations adopted at Stockholm was a framework for environmental action based on three interconnected functions that should be part of any action plan. The functions were:

- Assessment: Improving understanding and reducing uncertainty to provide a rational basis for action.
- Management: New policies, practices, and agreements, both formal treaties and political and technical agreements at the international level, that make a difference by influencing national practices and encouraging changes in human behavior.
- Support: Strengthening financial, institutional, and human resources to ensure that all key actors, including Third-World nations, have the means to contribute to agreed actions and share in their obligations and benefits.

The actual action plan that governments approved at the Stockholm Conference, and subsequently in the UN General Assembly, consisted of 109 recommendations that had been dealt with by sector and subject area, and redistributed according to function into three components: the global environmental assessment program (known as Earthwatch), environmental management activities, and supporting measures (United Nations, 1973).

Terms such as *action plan* and *comprehensive* have since acquired more distinct meanings, but when they were used in the 1970s in relation to marine pollution their meanings were specific. *Action plan* implied an understanding that a plan, once approved, should lead to specific actions by identified parties in a specified time. Like "International Decades," many so-called action plans since have amounted to little more than unfulfilled gestures, sometimes because the agreements were unrealistic, often because the parties did not provide resources to support the actions. Because of this experience any action plan today is viewed with skepticism unless it contains specific and credible support. This contributes to the popularity of framework conventions and associated protocols that combine generalities with contractual obligations.

In the context of the Mediterranean Action Plan, *comprehensive* acquired meanings related to geography, scope, and institutional and financial means. Geographic boundaries were defined by the problem to account for biological and oceanographic factors, as well as jurisdiction. Coastal nations, for example, belonged to three different UN Regional Economic Commissions and different interstate bodies like the Organization for Economic Cooperation and Development and the Organization of African Unity, but they were all in the same watershed.

The scope was broad enough to include all activities that affect the area of concern, not only the physical sources of pollution but also human activities harming the area. This included national policies inside the region and financial and trade flows from outside the region in some of the economic studies now under way (Batisse, 1990).

Each of the three functional elements of the Stockholm framework—assessment, management, and support—were addressed in the plan. Institutional and financial means were specified by which to carry out activities that were agreed on.

Even before UNEP came into being in January 1973, a broad framework existed for drawing up a regional plan for the Mediterranean. Many of the recommendations came from actors in the UN system and other groups. Governments were in charge, of course, for it was up to them to approve the recommendations. But a whole new approach had been shaped by a temporary secretariat even before the negotiations between governments had begun. The stage was set for action, including parallel scientific research and actual negotiations.

First Steps by UNEP After the Stockholm Conference

At its first meeting in early 1973 the UNEP Governing Council asked the executive director to stimulate regional agreements with a policy objective "to detect and prevent serious threats to the health of the oceans through controlling both ocean-based and land-based sources of pollution." A year later, the council decided that "in view of the many activities of numerous other agencies in this field, UNEP should concentrate on the coordination of these activities and on the protection of the marine environment," with priority given to "regional activities . . . in the Mediterranean." These decisions were based on the recommendations of the UNEP Executive Director.

The job of drawing up a comprehensive action plan for the Mediterranean was assigned by UNEP's headquarters, which was being established in Nairobi, to its European office in Geneva. Initially, UNEP concentrated on the assessment function to diagnose the problem, trends, and risks, and find the sources of significant problems. It had to find out was the "Med dead," as Jacques Cousteau asserted, or merely "sick."

Since government approval was required for any action plan, governments had to be involved in its design. But they could not be given a commanding role until the plan was ready to be presented for their approval. To accomplish this, UNEP worked closely with the agencies that had helped shape the Stockholm Action Plan, drawing on their scientific, health-related, and legal expertise to draft material in many different disciplines. UNEP consulted informally with government experts, rather than negotiating with governmental representatives.

UNEP's role of catalyst and coordinator, backed up by a voluntary fund and good working relationships around the Mediterranean, allowed it to collaborate with the organizations that were involved: FAO and its General Fisheries Council for the Mediterranean (GFCM), the International Oceanographic Commission (IOC), UNESCO, IMCO, the IAEA, the Economic Commission for Europe (ECE), WHO, WMO, and the UN Development Program (UNDP). The easy communications that had been established between civil servants in the UN system and their counterparts at the national level helped UNEP, especially when political conditions prevented groups from certain nations from directly communicating with one another.

Particularly striking during this period were the contributions from organizations outside the UN system. Some, like the International Council of Scientific Unions (ICSU) and the International Union for the Conservation of Nature (IUCN), were well-established international nongovernment organizations that had close ties to the UN system. Other organizations were participating in international meetings that brought together public and private groups, including industrial groups, that would later be associated with the regional plan. These included municipal and other local leaders whose perception of marine-pollution problems often differed from the views of governments, especially the views expressed by diplomats and lawyers. Help also came from outside the region. The International Council for Exploration of the Seas (ICES) in Copenhagen provided technical knowledge based on years of experience of designing monitoring programs in northern waters.

The contributions of nongovernment organizations were particularly striking, however, within the region, where they were active in ways that supported the plan that the UNEP Secretariat was trying to develop. The work of Pacem in Maribus, municipal leaders, parliamentarians, fishermen, and scientists are particularly noteworthy and are examined here.

Pacem in Maribus. In mid-1971 the International Ocean Institute convened the second Pacem in Maribus conference in Malta. Participants at this conference considered a provocative proposal, drawn up by Elizabeth Mann Borghese, to control Mediterranean pollution. Her idea was opposed by government officials as premature; several of the key governments signaled that they found ongoing activities sufficient, France and Italy were already tackling oil pollution, and Spain was dealing with dumping. But the discussions at the conference were useful and informative.

After the Stockholm Conference, the Pacem in Maribus conference held in Split, Yugoslavia, considered scientific reports on sea pollution dealing with conditions, trends, and methodologies; fishery problems; tourism; oil; industry and coastal aspects; and legal, strategic, and institutional considerations. The conclusions reached at these meetings did not lead directly to action, but they helped define the agenda and the plan that UNEP was developing. They also brought together several important participants.

At these meetings, participants got to know each other and, under agreeable and informal conditions, were able to discuss issues, especially North-South controversies, that might be difficult to deal with in formal, public meetings. Such personal relationships later helped UNEP stimulate government policy to support the plan it had developed.

Municipal leaders. The UN General Assembly had adopted a resolution in 1971 on "town twinning as a means of international cooperation" (United Nations, 1971). In June 1973 the United Towns Organization, representing 132 Mediterranean towns and cities, met in Beirut to adopt the "Charter of Beirut." The charter said that "the pollution of the seas and their shores, which has reached a level of gravity unknown in the history of humanity, especially threatens the Mediterranean Sea," and urged governments to act quickly. Developing countries agreed that antipollution measures were "an investment in the future," but their concerns about the relationship between environment and development were clear. The charter continued, "Preservation of the sea is inseparable from its development." Oil pollution was frequently mentioned, but many viewed municipal waste as a more urgent problem. Urbanization throughout coastal areas was accelerating faster than could be coped with by national funding. There were also signs of a growing interest in autonomy, such as in Barcelona, Corsica, and parts of Yugoslavia. In these circumstances, local leaders wanting to put pressure on federal ministries found international meetings and organizations useful.

Parliamentarians and fishermen. Another assembly of influential domestic leaders was convened by the Inter-Parliamentary Union (IPU), in Rome in March 1974. The session discussed Mediterranean pollution, in particular oil pollution, and the need to ratify existing IMCO conventions. An earlier document, Review of the State of Marine Pollution in the Mediterranean Sea, had been presented to the General Fisheries Council for the Mediterranean. The scope of this report exceeded the concerns of fisheries, because it included pollutants whose effects were on human health or amenities, and presented different kinds of problems in various parts of the Mediterranean (Haas, 1990).

In 1974 FAO consultations produced a set of guidelines for drafting a framework convention to protect the Mediterranean against pollution. But differing perceptions by northern and southern nations made the issue too sensitive for the FAO to handle. The matter was turned over to UNEP within its more comprehensive mandate.

Scientists. The clearest example of the role played by international and nongovernment organizations in preparing a Mediterranean Action Plan concerned the assessment portion of the plan. In the assessment, scientists in the region described the research and monitoring activities that were needed to produce information that they thought their governments needed to manage the area better. To organize the assessment, UNEP turned to three organizations: IOC/UNESCO, GFCM, and the International Commission for Scientific Exploration of the Mediterranean (ICSEM). UNEP chose these organizations because they coordinated the work of scientists from three disciplines. The IOC had launched the Cooperative Investigations of the Mediterranean (CIM), which involved primarily physical oceanographers. The GFCM had, for many years, brought together marine biologists concerned with fisheries. The ICSEM supported a variety of research projects in the area and shared the IAEA's International Laboratory of Marine Radioactivity.

At a workshop in Monaco in September 1974 scientists were asked to survey the work under way in the region and identify the specific scientific tasks—and how to carry them out—that would produce the information to help their governments understand important environmental trends. This information, UNEP hoped, would be taken into account in national plans and decisions that affected the region.

The chairman of the workshop was Stjepan Keckes, a distinguished scientist from Yugoslavia. He later said that this was the first meeting at which scientists from the region were asked their opinions on the priorities for research. Until then, research priorities were largely dictated by the authorities of the major powers. Only these nations had vessels capable of carrying out research in open seas. These nations tied their support to priorities that suited their interests, like underwater seismic properties, that often had little to do with local concerns.

The workshop noted that pollution in the coastal zone was higher than in open waters. Scientists linked this pollution to predominantly land-based sources and the circulatory currents that concentrate pollutants along the coast. The workshop concluded that human health, amenities, and coastal ecosystems were at risk. The risk was heightened by concentrations of populations along the coasts, particularly during tourist season.

The main problems along the coast were caused by a lack of treatment facilities for sewage and industrial waste. This situation caused pollution problems: high biological oxygen demand, eutrophication, heavy metals, pesticides and other chlorinated hydrocarbons, oils, and pathogenic organisms. A central finding of the workshop was that the "present lack of knowledge of ecosystems was a serious problem in the evaluation of pollution" (UNESCO, 1974).

The work that was under way was found to be "limited by the specific aims and terms of reference of the various international organizations," and lacking regional coordination. The workshop tackled the question of priorities for synoptic surveys of distribution, and concentration of pollutants "as part of a future comprehensive program for the Mediterranean." Given the heterogeneous quality of the sea, with uneven distribution of industry, population, agriculture, and other "special features," the scientists agreed to concentrate their work on the following pollutants, but did not agree on their order of priority: oil and petroleum hydrocarbons; mercury and heavy metals; chlorinated hydrocarbons (PCBs and total DDT); and components of domestic sewage.

While such surveys provided the rationale for designing a monitoring program, studies of the effects of pollutants were needed to assess their impact. Methodological problems were studied along with how best to coordinate a system that would rely on national institutions backed up by training and other forms of support. The workshop concluded that seven pilot projects were needed:

(1) Baseline studies and monitoring of oil and petroleum hydrocarbons in marine waters.
(2) Baseline studies and monitoring of metals, particularly mercury and cadmium, in marine organisms.
(3) Baseline studies and monitoring of DDT, PCBs, and other chlorinated hydrocarbons in marine organisms.
(4) Research on the effects of pollutants on marine organisms and their populations.
(5) Research on the effects of pollutants on marine communities and ecosystems.
(6) Problems of coastal transport of pollutants.
(7) Control of coastal water quality.

UNEP then commissioned Keckes and a scientific officer from the ECE to conduct an on-the-spot survey of scientific institutions to determine whether they could carry out the seven pilot projects in the region. The study found that the institutions could undertake the pilot projects if they were given equipment, training, and maintenance support. UNEP would provide the necessary support if asked, and if governments set the assessment process, along with other parts of the proposed comprehensive plan, in motion. Because UNEP's ability to support the work depended on its voluntary fund, it was in a position to place conditions for its use.

Through meetings such as these, a comprehensive plan of the sort envisaged at the Stockholm Conference gradually took shape in 1974 and Spain agreed to host a meeting in Barcelona in January 1975. UNEP's objectives for the meeting were (United Nations, 1974):

To prepare an action plan identifying actions that should and could be started immediately without waiting for the signature of conventions and protocols.

To initiate a change in the way of thinking of the riparian countries with respect to the establishment of development styles based on cooperation and optimal use of the resources of the Mediterranean while ensuring their preservation for future generations and to this effect agreeing on the broad outlines of various elements of long-term plans for action and setting the procedures to reach final agreement on various elements of this plan.

To include in the action plan detailed guidance for the final preparation of the framework convention and one or two protocols for signature at a plenipotentiary conference to be convened in September or October, 1975.

To indicate clearly further actions required to reach agreement on other protocols.

To consider ways and means of assisting research and monitoring centers in developing countries through technical assistance and training to bring them up to the level which allows them to participate fully in the execution of the coordinated programs on research and monitoring.

During this period frequent consultations were held with governments, but no attempt was made to solicit formal reactions to the content of the plan. This was left to informal consultations (Thacher, 1977).

Barcelona I: The Action Plan Is Approved

The important moment for UNEP's draft action plan occurred on January 28, 1975, with the opening of the first Intergovernmental Meeting on the Protection of the Mediterranean. The invited nations, which border the Mediterranean between the Straits of Gibraltar and the Dardanelles, were presented with four papers describing the proposed activities:

(1) *Integrated Planning of the Development and Management of the Resources of the Mediterranean Basin.* This paper called for studies of the styles of development that would use the wealth of the region without causing damage to the environment. It covered a broad range of topics such as the use of salt lagoons, parks, solar energy, abatement of agricultural runoff, tourism, treated sewage, and waste-water recycling. UNDP identified international development activities that were planned or under way in the region, and their potential effects on the environment.

(2) *A Coordinated Program for Research, Monitoring, and Exchange of Information and Assessment of the State of Pollution and of Protection Measures.* This paper was based on the results of the Monaco workshop and the survey. It suggested steps for setting up cooperative programs among national laboratories backed by international agencies. It focused on standardizing methodologies for sampling and analysis to ensure compatibility, and technical assistance and training to improve the skills in developing nations.

(3) *A Framework Convention and Related Protocols With Their Technical Annexes for the Protection of the Mediterranean Environment.* This paper was based largely on the May 1974 FAO consultations on a framework convention and identified possible additional protocols (with drafts of two) on land-based sources of pollution, dumping, pollution from ships, cooperation in emergencies, seabed pollution, research, and monitoring.

(4) *Institutional and Financial Implications of the Plan of Action.* This paper presented UNEP's views on implementing the action plan.

By the time the Barcelona meeting began, it was clear that the earlier meetings had helped participants from around the Mediterranean understand their common problems. The earlier meetings had contributed to the ease (despite conditions of near hostility between nations at both ends of that sea) with which governments and nongovernment organizations collaborated. Since many participants in the earlier meetings were now members of national delegations, there was a feeling of confidence about the prospects for a positive outcome, despite the complexity and variety of issues.

Well-prepared substantive contributions by international civil servants helped nations to agree. The FAO and IMCO presented the initial drafts for both the Barcelona Framework Convention and the Protocol on Cooperation in the Event of Emergencies. The Protocol on Dumping was presented by the representative of Spain (UNEP, 1975). Also worth noting was the role of a senior IMCO official, Jean de Quequiner, who traveled extensively in the eastern basin to explore how to set up an international contingency center to serve nations that would cooperate with each other as long as they did not have to communicate with each other directly. This was the origin of the present Regional Marine Pollution Emergency Center (REMPEC) in Malta.

Given the political problems that existed from one end of the Mediterranean to the other, luck was also needed to prevent political disputes from delaying agreement. The Mediterranean Action Plan was approved after only seven days, on February 4, 1975. The final report of the meeting reflected satisfaction with the roles played by international organizations, particularly the preparatory work by the FAO on a draft framework convention, and the work of the IMCO on the draft protocol on cooperation in combating oil spills.

In the final report, the executive director of UNEP was requested to:

> Convene working groups of governmental legal and technical experts as required, with the eventual collaboration of other international organizations concerned, to put into definitive form the draft legal instruments enumerated, with a view to their adoption by a conference of plenipotentiaries. These working groups should take due account of the debates of the Barcelona meeting, without prejudice to the codification and elaboration of the law of the sea by the United Nations Conference on the Law of the Sea.
>
> Convene such a conference of plenipotentiaries, to invite to this conference the coastal states of the Mediterranean region as well as observers in accordance with United Nations practice, and to provide the necessary support for the preparation and completion of the conference.
>
> Convene as soon as practicable, working groups of governmental experts to prepare additional protocols, taking into account the work of the present meeting.

Twelve months later, in February 1976, the Barcelona Convention and its first two associated protocols were signed. They came into force two years later. Continuing confidence in the preparatory work by UNEP was shown in the charge to the executive director, at the conclusion of the 1976 Barcelona meeting, "to continue the preparatory work for a draft protocol for the Protection of the Mediterranean Sea Against Pollution From Land-Based Sources" (in Resolution 2 on interim arrangements).

At an Intergovernmental Review Meeting on the Mediterranean Action Plan in Monaco in January 1978, governments agreed that human activities on land were "the most significant sources of pollution in the Mediterranean Basin." The meeting recommended that nations continue their work on the protocol and requested UNEP to "assist the states in this task by providing as complete technical data on land-based pollutants as possible" (Kuwabara, 1984). The Athens Protocol for the Protection of the Mediterranean Sea Against Pollution From Land-Based Sources was signed in May 1980. The

Protocol Concerning Mediterranean Specially Protected Areas was signed in April 1982 in Geneva. Both protocols have since come into force.

Today, periodic meetings of the parties guide treaty activities, with support from the UNEP Secretariat in Athens and a widespread network of regional and national centers. The gradual shift of emphasis from assessment to reducing pollutant flows, especially with the agreement to tackle land-based sources, required more funds. The initial funds from UNEP and UNDP covered only technical assistance and other forms of support to meet the North-South imbalances in the region and put together modest research and monitoring programs. But the Athens protocol required more money for the developing countries to tackle land-based problems at the source.

In effect, the Athens Protocol converted the "undertaking" of the Barcelona Convention into more binding obligations. Article 10 of the Athens Protocol says:

> The Parties shall, directly or with the assistance of competent regional or other international organizations or bilaterally, cooperate with a view to formulating and, as far as possible, implementing programs of assistance to developing countries, particularly in the fields of science, education, and technology, with a view to preventing pollution from land-based sources and its harmful effects in the marine environment.
>
> Technical assistance would include, in particular, the training of scientific and technical personnel, as well as the acquisition, utilization, and production by those countries of appropriate equipment on advantageous terms to be agreed upon among the parties concerned.

While larger resources within the region were being mobilized, support from organizations outside the region was also needed. In 1988 the World Bank launched the Environmental Program for the Mediterranean (EPM), the "single largest environmental initiative to date in the World Bank" (World Bank, 1988). This program, funded jointly with the European Investment Bank (EIB), has since launched the Mediterranean Environmental Technical Assistance Program (METAP). It defines policy measures and identifies and prepares investment projects and activities in four areas: integrated water-resource management, solid-waste and hazardous-waste management, prevention and control of marine pollution from oil and chemicals, and coastal-zone management (World Bank, 1990).

Looking Back

The functional framework approved at the Stockholm Conference—assessment, management, and support—continues to be useful for analyzing the roles played by the actors who shaped the action plan adopted at the Barcelona Conference in 1975 and who are still active more than 15 years later.

UNEP and the other agencies in the UN system were the architects of the Mediterranean Action Plan, but the plan would not have been approved as fast as it was, nor would the new regime have been set in motion as speedily, without strong substantive and political support from many nongovernment bodies in what has been described as *epistemic communities* consisting of a variety of actors, such as scientists, municipal leaders, nongovernment organizations, and parliamentary groups (Haas, 1990).

In keeping with the initial focus on the assessment parts of the action plan, the scientific groups strongly influenced the priorities for the Mediterranean Action Plan Coordinated Pollution Monitoring and Research Program (MEDPOL) proposals. After the proposals were approved at Barcelona, UNEP and its collaborators set up networks of institutions and provided them with equipment and training. Today more than 120 institutions study marine pollution throughout the region. This work started immediately after Barcelona I, that is, well before the convention and two protocols were negotiated and signed at Barcelona II a year later in 1976. Later, MEDPOL products provided critical support during the negotiation of the 1980 land-based protocol (Kuwabara, 1984).

While parts of the UN system were important in the assessment and management processes, nongovernment organizations played lesser roles in management activities until some of the main elements were put in place by the Barcelona Framework Convention and its protocols, and the Integrated Planning chapter, with its principal components, the Blue Plan and the Priority Action Program (Grenon & Batisse, 1989).

Similarly, nongovernment organizations had little hand compared to IMCO's role in establishing the Regional Oil-Spill Combatting Center in Malta. However, the IUCN played a supporting role during negotiations of the 1982 Geneva Protocol Concerning Mediterranean Specially Protected Areas, and the setting up of a regional center in Tunis.

The support function, especially providing the funds to encourage national action, was the responsibility of governments and international organizations associated with the UN. Initially, it was the UNEP's catalytic responsibility to provide resources to develop the action plan and support activities until the Barcelona Convention came into effect and a formal funding arrangement could be worked out. Afterward, UNEP and the UNDP played supporting roles while nations gradually built up the trust fund set up under the convention. As mentioned above, the World Bank and European Investment Bank have provided additional funds for expenses in recent years.

However, the role of nongovernment organizations in building public awareness, an important component of the support function, was a critical element in the speedy implementation of the Mediterranean Action Plan.

Concluding Observations

Governments have certainly not become marginal actors in dealing with international environmental problems, but the role of nongovernmental actors, both international and local, is growing, especially in determining whether human actions will benefit or harm the oceans and other parts of the environment. Nongovernmental organizations that were earlier viewed as onlookers have now moved into the negotiating room and are active participants, even if not seated at the table during negotiations.

Faced with the complexity of the issues and their economic, social, and political implications, the Mediterranean Action Plan was designed to encourage nations to start its implementation gradually. It provided inducements, including financial ones, during the preliminary phases to encourage nations, especially developing nations, to participate long before treaty obligations entered into effect or started making funds available.

The idea of holding meetings of experts rather than formal negotiating sessions is sound. In addition to providing a neutral setting for North-South discussions, meetings of experts allow specialists from developing countries to attend meetings on issues their governments might not normally feel are worth the expense. These meetings resolve many issues on which differences are essentially based on ignorance. They help nations preempt unnecessary disputes between themselves.

Given the breadth of issues involved, the legal content of formal agreements required inputs from experts far removed from ministries of external affairs. Several meetings convened by UNEP brought together members of national delegations who rarely worked with each other at home. In one case, the meeting was delayed so that members of a large national delegation could be introduced to each other. It was an example of an international catalytic effect on the national scale.

Another example of the catalytic role of international organizations was the provision for studies by international organizations working together to synthesize sectoral information about national actions and emissions, especially during the negotiations on the land-based protocol. Since all this information was provided to the agencies by national sectoral ministries, it might be assumed that similar material would be available to governments. In fact, it was rarely assembled at the national level. International civil servants who analyzed and provided this consolidated information to governments increased their leverage during negotiations.

A difficulty mentioned by Faure and Rubin in Chapter 2 is that of evaluating environmental problems over long periods. International agreements like the 1975 Mediterranean Action Plan and formal treaties like the 1976 Barcelona Convention can be evaluated in terms of whether or not they are ratified and lead to national regulations and administrative actions that might not otherwise be taken. However, it is difficult to attribute causal links in either the natural or social sciences, and particularly between them. Therefore, it is unlikely that physical evidence, such as declining levels of pollution over a long period of time, will soon be linked to international agreements. One can say with confidence that the Mediterranean Action Plan has produced better assessments than were available before, and that a good start has been made in developing information about trends in the levels of certain pollutants. Quantitative relationships between pollution levels in recreational waters and human health repercussions is the work of epidemiologists, which may help to set national standards. However, to be able to attribute changes in pollution to international agreements, economic incentives, or tighter emission standards requires baseline data and longer data sets than are currently available.

Public opinion and the news media played important roles during the negotiations over the Mediterranean Action Plan. Public opinion and the media supported more aggressive stands on environmental protection than most governments were initially prepared to give. National representatives tried to avoid public criticism, such as by outspoken public figures like Cousteau. While the secretariat maintained links to international media agencies like Reuters and Agence-France Presse, there were times, especially in the two intergovernmental meetings in Barcelona, when the absence of close media attention was welcomed. Given the state of hostility between some nations, close coverage and news photos of apparently friendly contacts between representatives of these nations could have caused security problems. In the case of one coastal nation that, at the time, lacked diplomatic status with the host government, special arrangements had to be made by UNEP with municipal authorities to provide protection against acts of terrorism.

Perhaps the most important experience was the role played by international organizations in reducing the burden on nations to negotiate. Many issues that customarily must be resolved in protracted negotiations were prepared with balance and objectivity and fed into the interstate process in ways that reduced contention, or sharpened the problem to policy choices that only governments could properly resolve. Similarly, good

staff work by international technocrats has long been practiced in some of
the agencies of the UN system in fields such as telecommunications, postal
matters, meteorology, and civil aviation. As for marine pollution, Article
25 of the 1958 High Seas Convention had opened the door to active roles
by "competent international organizations," at least with regard to "radioactive materials or other harmful agents." But the nonmaritime sources
had not been addressed, because of a lack of knowledge and the concern
for national sovereignty.

Speaking in 1974, UNEP Executive Director Strong said:

> Preservation of the marine environment, its life-sustaining functions, and its
> living resources are not getting the priority attention they deserve and require in
> the larger interest of the whole human community. In the scramble for the oceans,
> someone must speak for the environment. Governments have given this role to
> the United Nations Environment Program.

After asking the question, "How do we find our way towards a new order
in the oceans?" he cited UNEP's role as a catalyst, not a new oceans
agency, and said UNEP's "unique function" is to provide the framework
that makes possible the "mobilization and coordination of various mechanisms to form a system for management of the ocean as an ecological
whole."

"Thus," he concluded, "it is imperative that the voiceless environment
of the oceans and their living resources be represented, and UNEP takes
its responsibilities in this respect very seriously indeed."

8

The Rhine:
A Study of Inland Water Negotiations

CHRISTOPHE DUPONT

From south to north, the Rhine flows through Switzerland, France, Germany, and the Netherlands. These four nations and Luxembourg, which is connected to the Rhine by the Moselle River, share an interest in protecting the Rhine. For decades, their main concern had been transportation on the river, so they set up a commission to control it. Later, the nations became concerned about protecting the Rhine's environment and reducing the industrial pollution and waste water discharged into the river.

As the nations learned more about the pollution problem, they realized that neither unilateral action nor bilateral agreements would be enough to tackle the pollution problem. They also realized that just as all riparian nations were responsible for polluting the river, they were responsible for correcting the problem. However, none of the nations was willing to give up its sovereignty and allow a powerful supranational body to make decisions for it about the Rhine.

Regional, multilateral negotiations seemed the most appropriate way to handle the problem, because all five nations realized that among themselves there were both conflicting and joint interests, and a common desire to find mutually acceptable solutions. The appropriate format for these negotiations was conference diplomacy—frequent contacts between and formal meetings of representatives.

Such a format could be provided by a commission that would act on behalf of its members. The commission would be a forum for collective decision making and would provide information, technical expertise, administrative support, and other services. Thus the International Commission for the Protection of the Rhine Against Pollution (ICPR) was set up in 1950. Although it cannot negotiate by itself, the ICPR has proved to be the nexus in a well-developed and successful network of negotiations that have produced several international conventions.

This chapter analyzes the main features of these negotiations, concentrating on those that took place in the 1980s, as concrete examples of international environmental negotiations. The first section summarizes the background of the ICPR. The next section details the process and strategies. The third describes the type, framework, and substance of the Rhine negotiations. The fourth section identifies specific features of the negotiations.

Background of the ICPR

The Rhine is Europe's most important river, and has historical, political, and cultural significance. As it flows through four countries, it passes densely populated cities, industrial areas, and rich agricultural land. Every day, chemical plants, potash and coal mines, paper mills, and municipal waste systems discharge large amounts of toxic substances, such as chloride, mercury, and cadmium, into the Rhine. More than 100 toxic substances have been identified in the river. Every country through which the river flows contributes to its pollution, although the extent of pollution varies from country to country. One may legitimately speak of collective responsibility for polluting the Rhine.

All five nations that are members of the ICPR benefit from the Rhine. How they benefit depends on the way in which they use the river. The Rhine provides drinking water, shipping, fishing, leisure and recreation activities, and ecological resources. The various uses of the Rhine have to be planned and coordinated carefully to avoid conflict among its users.

The degree of responsibility for polluting the river, and the amount of enjoyment from its benefits, differs from nation to nation. Concern for pollution is strongest in the downstream nations, especially the Netherlands. Yet an event such as the Sandoz accident in November 1986 shows that no nation along the river is immune from pollution problems. When the riparian nations realized they were collectively responsible for the Rhine's problems, they decided to coordinate their individual water-protection policies. Eventually, they established the ICPR.

The ICPR now has six members: the four riparian nations, Luxembourg, and, since 1976, the European Community (EC). From its headquarters in Koblenz, Germany, the ICPR operates under the authority of its member nations. Decisions are usually made at annual meetings of member governments' ministers in charge of the environment or foreign affairs. The ICPR has its own secretariat that draws up proposals, coordinates plans and recommendations, and provides secretarial and technical assistance for such things as meetings of preparatory working groups and discussions among experts. There are 25 working groups or subgroups made up of specialists from government ministries and enforcement authorities.

All proposals must be approved at an annual meeting or a ministerial conference at which ministries may commit their governments, subject to later ratification. The annual meeting usually is attended by the heads of government departments concerned with environmental problems or foreign affairs. A coordinating group of high-ranking civil servants ensures that decisions are implemented and acts as a clearinghouse for the working groups and the annual meeting.

The ICPR has been responsible for a number of declarations of intent and conventions. The following chronology lists its accomplishments and indicates the scope of the ICPR's negotiations:

1950: ICPR established.

1963: Signing of the Bern Convention gives ICPR official status.

1972: First ministerial conference. It decides to tackle chloride pollution caused by potash mines in Alsace, France.

1973: Proposal to stock salt residues permanently on French soil rejected by France. ICPR agrees to study alternatives.

1976: EC joins ICPR as contracting party. Members sign Bonn Convention on chemical pollution and the chloride problem. France agrees to a two-phased program on the chloride problem with time limits and partial joint financing.

1977-1983: Tension increases as France is slow to ratify convention. The Netherlands temporarily recalls its ambassador to France.

1983: France ratifies a modified convention; tension eases.

1983-1986: Negotiations take place on measures to reduce chemical pollution and the chloride problem.

1986: The Sandoz accident; negotiations follow immediately. France issues declaration of intent on chloride problem.

1987: First phase of French program begins; aims at reducing chloride by 20 kilograms per second. Members decide to create the Action Plan for the Rhine to deal with pollution problems; the Action Plan aims at ridding pollution by the year 2000.

1988: Ministerial conference on the Action Plan and the chloride problem.

1989-1990: Negotiations continue on the Action Plan and chloride programs.

The Rhine negotiations are typical of many international environmental negotiations, and they closely fit within the framework for analysis described by Guy-Olivier Faure and Jeffrey Z. Rubin in Chapter 2. In this chapter, the more salient features of the negotiations process and observed strategies of actors are identified. This is complemented by an analysis of the characteristics of the negotiations, either as illustrations of the general framework relating to environmental negotiations or as original dimensions of these negotiations.

Process and Strategies

The results from the various negotiations on the Rhine have been—and still are—produced by working out agreements between the riparian states. These agreements—which may take various forms such as an international convention, declarations of intent, or an exchange of letters—are the results of proposals and discussions that culminate in the formal acceptance of an international instrument by the concerned states. Subsequently, this instrument is brought before the legal authorities of these states for ratification. To understand the process, one must define and delineate the roles of the various actors.

Central to the process is the ICPR, which acts as an intergovernmental body. Decisions are made during the course of annual or extraordinary meetings at which commission members are represented by ministers who are granted authority from their governments. In recalling the institutional setup of the European Community, a sharp distinction must be made between the ICPR, which acts as a decision-making power at the ministerial level, and the secretariat and the working groups to which certain specific tasks are assigned.

In reviewing the record of the past 10 or 20 years, especially during the more recent period, it is evident that the ministers utilize the ICPR for two purposes: as a forum to make joint decisions about "mature" issues, such as setting goals and deadlines, creating and designing funding for future tasks or projects, determining types of measures and whether they will be taken individually or collectively, and implementing control and monitoring mechanisms; and as a forum to exchange views as well as debate and discuss pending issues and new problems as they arise. A major feature of the negotiating process in this respect is the discontinuous timing of events and decisions as opposed to a continuous, quasi-permanent activity.

In contrast, the time structure is linked closely to the recurring, almost day-to-day activities of the technical bodies or subbodies set up by the ministerial conference. Many of the working groups are specialized in specific areas and meet frequently. Examples of working groups include coordinating groups or subgroups (the so-called K groups such as inventory groups, groups on morphology, biology and hydrology, and diffuse sources), the working group on chemicals (B), the working group on chlorides (C), the legal working group (D), the working group on thermic aspects (T, including the mathematical model, Tm), and various other groups (P, particularly on warning systems, methods of analysis, and so on). These groups generally are chaired by a high official from one of the five concerned states and are made up of officials and experts from the various national administrations. They also increasingly are assisted by officials of the secretariat of the ICPR.

Apart from verifying the time structures that apply to the different levels of the decision-making process, another important feature of the process is the intertwining of technical and political dimensions. The general principle of a pollution-free Rhine has led—and continues to lead—the actors to agree on a common recognition of the nature of the problem and the need to cooperate toward a betterment of the situation. When considering more specific technical details and operations, issues tend to emerge and develop as a local interest. Interest at a local level leads to a tentative identification of the causes of the problem and a search for a solution through intergovernmental and traditional channels, including day-to-day contact with various levels of experts, administrators, or subdiplomats (for example, through the lower or technical echelons of the local embassies).

Administrative offices and agencies of the various states involved as well as interested third parties (such as private and business interests, pressure groups, and the media) take up the issue internally, engaging in complex exchanges of views—which sometimes may be close to being conflictual—among different administrations or agencies, between government, regional, or local authorities, or between public and private interests. There is, thus, an exchange of analyses and proposals, which are then transferred to coordinating or ad hoc groups by the higher echelons of the administrative or governmental body. However, it can be disputed whether or not to depict this sometimes lengthy process as negotiation; the process seemingly would better be described as intraorganizational prepositioning or prenegotiation.

Next comes the exploration and testing phase. This involves the individuals and groups at the interstate level. For example, proposals are submitted to the appropriate channels in individual nations, gradually leading to technical reformulations or, in many cases, to the traditional play of diplomatic influence. Whenever a technical issue is involved, working groups at the ICPR join the process to help assemble data on comparative bases, narrow differences, and begin to draft or redraft proposals. Thus, gradually the issue normally finds its way to the higher levels of the ICPR where conference diplomacy then develops (Kaufmann, 1988, 1989; Lang, 1989; Plantey, 1980).

To illustrate better the fluidity of this multistage process as well as the complex interplay of influences between internal and external actors, it may be helpful to examine the levels of the functional and political dimensions concerning the chloride problem. France proposed to its partners—who agreed as part of a compromise to speed up ratification of the Bonn Convention—that the French government would submit alternative plans to dispose of salt residues to reduce direct discharge into the Rhine. The French minister in charge of this environmental problem appointed a group of four experts to examine various schemes.[1] The experts then were to report back to the ICPR for feedback. At the same time, the French administration decided to test a plan involving the transportation of certain quantities of salt residues by means of railway to the North Sea. To design these plans and implement a preliminary test—including the March 1988 discharge of 700 tons of salt residue at Dunkirk—involved the complex interplay of influences between internal and external actors. From an international perspective, this led to contacts between the Dutch (and also Belgian) and French authorities; letters were exchanged at the diplomatic level between May and July 1988, and the plan subsequently was abandoned.

Many other examples of the multistage process could be mentioned, for example, the process dealing with the Sandoz accident at Schweizerhalle on November 1, 1986, and the subsequent setting up of monitoring measures and instruments. These examples illustrate the combination of influences, actors, and decision-making procedures that enter into the negotiating process and involve varying technical and political levels.

Within the process it is interesting to note the importance, not uncommon in conference diplomacy, of submitting draft resolutions or agreements to delegations that are invited to propose alternative reformulations or reservations. This provides some degree of flexibility as well as the possibility to draw a line between what is and is not negotiable at this particular juncture.

A final point is that the process as it has evolved so far has been centered at the ICPR as the crucial negotiation mechanism. As new problems gradually are added to the agenda (such as, accidents and thermic pollution) and commitments are made more precise and binding, the role played by experts and working groups may expand. This expanding role gives rise to different positions among the member nations. Since 1986, however, the secretariat has been reinforced and new tasks have been assigned to it. In several cases, the secretariat has been given a direct role in carrying out various tasks and assignments.

Strategies in these negotiations have been marked by sharp differences between the member states. The major factor that has influenced strategies has been the degree of importance that each actor has ascribed to the various issues. Thus the Netherlands—the downstream territory—has attempted to increase awareness by the other states of its vital need for a fair degree of pollution-free water. In so doing, it has constantly insisted that effective measures be adopted by the upstream states. To strengthen this strategy, it has applied diplomatic pressure and promised to contribute to the expenditures involved. The Netherlands also has shown some flexibility by agreeing to alternative plans to reduce pollution that were less stringent in terms of time and cost than initially planned. Thus some objectives were traded off in favor of rapid implementation. The Dutch strategies have been influenced by attempts to make the role of the ICPR more autonomous and less dependent on traditional diplomacy. Its strategy has been to enlarge the scope of agreements and to make the agreements more stringent (for example, imposing stricter requirements regarding the classification and maximum discharge limits of toxic substances, demanding more stringent monitoring and control measures, and forcing shorter time limits).

In a similar situation, France and the Federal Republic of Germany have tried to combine agreement on broad lines of policies with a more pragmatic and gradual treatment of the issues. France mainly was concerned with not appearing as the main contributor of pollution from salt; thus the strategy was an attempt, on one hand, to broaden the issue (that is, not isolate the salt problem from other forms of pollution such as toxic substances) and, on the other hand, to gain time to consider the economic aspects of the problem (competitiveness of the potash mines). With its industrial complex—particularly in the Ruhr Valley—involved in the problem, the Federal Republic of Germany had a somewhat similar preoccupation. However, Germany's position has been made more complex by several outstanding factors such as the role of regional authorities (Länder) and the increasing political strength of the environmental movement (the Greens). Germany needs pure water for many uses and therefore has followed a strategy of making agreements stringent (for example, in respect to the chloride problem), but at the same time it has been somewhat reluctant to enforce strong and detailed requirements (communication of data, implementation of international monitoring systems, and so on).

Switzerland's strategy has changed dramatically after the 1986 Sandoz accident. Following the accident, the Swiss delegation has become much more involved in water negotiations. Swiss participation has been marked by a reluctance to permit international surveillance and constraints. In relation to the EC delegation, its major interest is to obtain some form of parallelism on measures (directives) decided by the Community for the 12 member countries and the policies agreed on by the ICPR members.

The differences in the stakes involved always have been well perceived and understood by the various delegations. Important as they were, however, several factors have helped members to reach some gradual solutions. Except for Switzerland, the other ICPR members are part of the EC. It would have been difficult for them to ignore this affiliation; many EC issues become linked sooner or later by the systematic use of trade-offs between issues, costs and benefits, and the time structure of decisions and actions. Another favorable factor has been a common awareness of the problem and the recognition of the need for some form of solidarity. Close diplomatic relationships, a constructive climate, a large degree of cooperative spirit, and a commonality of perceptions, methods, and purposes on the part of technicians and experts also have contributed to soften distributive strategies and give prominence to more cooperative ones.

General Features of the Negotiations

Multiple parties and multiple roles. The format of the negotiations is conference diplomacy. First, each nation's bureaucracies and experts study the issues. Then, preliminary conclusions are usually submitted to the other parties to identify positions and to try to reconcile differences through traditional diplomatic channels. The ICPR helps in this process; its annual meeting and ministerial conferences are the forums for consensual decisions.

The negotiation process is more complex than this description may suggest, however. Working parties and meetings of experts can intervene and often change official positions. Negotiations between a nation's central government and local authorities also play an important role. For example, the local authorities in Alsace pressured the French government to change its position on stocking salt residues in France. External bodies and organizations—such as the United Nations Economic Commission for Europe, the Organization for Economic Cooperation and Development, the Council of Europe, and the Intergovernmental Commission of the North Sea—have also affected negotiations.

Multiple issues. Negotiations have dealt with many issues ranging from far-reaching principles to specific technical points. The following items, abstracted from the agenda of the ninth ministerial conference of the ICPR, illustrates how extensive the range of issues can be: the Action Plan for the Rhine, safety of industrial plants, disposal of communal waste water, chlorides, thermic problems, transparency of data, procedures for speeding up implementation of decisions, accidents and compensation for damages, and pollution of the North Sea.

Meaningless boundaries. The parties that have negotiated pollution issues and related problems have regarded the Rhine as an entity that transcends national borders. The trend is toward accepting a positive sum game, implying formulas to share costs and benefits. Such formulas are not easy to formulate and implement. Typically in river-environment problems, downstream nations are more vulnerable than upstream nations. An example of what may be called the solidarity principle has been to accept cost-sharing for investments that were required to reduce pollution.

Scientific and technical uncertainty. Although negotiators have benefited from more information about the causes of pollution and the benefits and efficiency of antipollution measures, experts are still uncertain about some technical and economic issues, including:

- The full impact of schemes to dispose of salt residues.
- The thermic effect of nuclear plants along the Rhine.
- The toxicity levels of certain substances.
- The relevance of measurement methods.
- The costs and the value of the discount rates used to measure future expenditures.

Power asymmetry. All ICPR members are interdependent, but not to the same extent. Also, constraints are not equal among members. These two factors account for asymmetries in the way nations deal with one another. The balance of power has, to some extent, been influenced by moral suasion exerted against some parties by the nature, urgency, or intensity of problems. For example, France was pressured to do something about its potash mines; Switzerland was pressured over the Sandoz accident; the Federal Republic of Germany was pressured about cataloging and measuring toxic substances.

Joint interest. This has proved to be a powerful influence on reinforcing political will to find mutually acceptable solutions. Joint interest has motivated individuals to avoid unilateral action and to seek collective solutions.

Negative perceptions of immediate outcomes. The Action Plan to restore the Rhine to its pollution-free condition by the year 2000 requires costly investments and expenditures in the short term. Equally sensitive are the changes that are required in technologies, production plans, and existing regulations. The decision to issue new regulations is also a sensitive matter.

The nature of the pollution problem imposes constraints on some nations or regions but not on others. This situation may result in negative perceptions. The immediate costs are borne by some parties, but the common benefits are long term. Such a situation was successfully negotiated in the French-Dutch proposal on chlorides, which was subsequently agreed to by all parties. It required that prepayments be shared by all, regardless of where the expenditures were made.

Long time frames. The problems of the Rhine require long-term solutions. The institutional cooperation that has existed for 40 years is proof of this. Current plans should guarantee continued cooperation until the year 2000. Governments have also compromised on their time preferences.

Changing actors. The main actors are governments. Within the government structure, new actors, such as administrative bodies and experts, have gradually taken part as the scope of interventions has been enlarged and as requirements have been increased.

Public opinion. The pollution of the Rhine has generated a great deal of public interest, either to find solutions or to protect vested interests. The ingredients of public opinion mentioned in Chapter 2—amplification, the role of constituents, and the dual roles of negotiators who risk appearing soft in the eyes of their constituents and hard in the eyes of other negotiatiors—apply here.

Institutionalization of solutions. The chronology of ICPR activities supports the point that solutions are institutionalized. ICPR negotiations have resulted in several conventions: the Bonn Convention of 1976, which was modified in 1983; the Thermic Convention; the Action Plan. The way the ICPR functions also signifies a great deal of institutionalization. Including the EC as a contracting party has increased institutionalization and has created new issues, such as how to comply with decisions made in two forums: at the level of the nation and that of the Community.

New regimes and rules. One major success of Rhine negotiations has been an increased awareness of the pollution problems and the need to solve them collectively. This awareness has gradually changed the behavior of nations, which, in turn, has produced a reinforcing effect. The "tragedy of the commons" has developed closer cooperation among parties, despite their differing opinions and the tensions that have resulted. Eventually, the result has been new *soft* or *hard* rules.

Distinctive Characteristics of Rhine Negotiations

The Rhine negotiations exhibit a number of distinctive characteristics, which are examined in this section.

Appropriateness and structure of the ICPR framework. Confronted with the issue of the pollution of the Rhine, the governments of five nations supplemented their traditional diplomatic contacts by setting up the ICPR. This organization has been useful as a permanent secretariat and advisory body. Its statutes have been designed to match the minimum amount of cooperation that members are willing to accept. The working groups, coordination committees, annual meetings, and ministerial conferences make up the framework for members to collect information, reconcile differences, exert pressure for recommendations and programs, and monitor implementation. As its members gain expertise, their awareness increases and their teamwork improves. Collective understanding and learning has developed over the years.

At present, joint decision making and national sovereignty seem to fit together well. However, future problems may arise over how the framework can be modified to permit more constraints and regulations. Some nations, in particular the Netherlands, favor formulas to reinforce implementation, but other nations have resisted such institutional change. For the practitioner and the analyst alike, the questions are: What is the proper amount of controls and regulations in such an international framework? How institutionally flexible should these rules be? How can a particular balance that is satisfactory at one time become dynamic, that is, be adaptable to changing conditions? What changes should be made?

"Maturity" and external factors. ICPR members have gradually become aware, in varying degrees, of the need for collective action as environmental issues have become politically important. External events unrelated to the Rhine, such as the nuclear accident at Chernobyl, and events that were directly related, such as the Sandoz accident, have brought the process a maturity that has greatly increased cooperation in negotiations.

A gradual instead of an all-or-nothing approach. Realistic gradualism or pragmatism is the negotiating approach that has prevailed in Rhine negotiations, particularly since 1986. This approach replaced an all-or-nothing approach, and it prevented differences from becoming real conflicts, as happened in the late 1970s. The danger of deadlocks in negotiations is that they induce negative perceptions, errors in attribution, and self-justifying arguments. The compromise agreement on chloride pollution did not fully satisfy the objectives of all parties, but it did allow them to take immediate action.

Alliance diplomacy. The Rhine negotiations demonstrate that in any multilateral negotiation, strategic or tactical alliances are always present. When alliances are tactical, they may be opportunistic and, therefore, unstable. Shifts are often observed. An example of a tactical alliance in the Rhine negotiations is the French-Dutch alliance on alternative solutions to the chloride problem. A few years before the alliance, the two governments were antagonistic toward each other over the problem. Another example is the tactical alliance among the riparian nations to pressure Switzerland to assume responsibility for the Sandoz accident.

Linkages. The multiple issues that are characteristic of Rhine negotiations and the responsibilities and priorities related to these issues have required ICPR members to find linkages to reach agreement. France has subtly and consistently alluded to the Rhine problem as being global: that progress on one issue could lead to progress on another. Another consideration, although more difficult to pinpoint, is how cooperation on Rhine issues relates to overall economic cooperation, especially for nations that are members of the EC.

Sharing costs and benefits. Any attempt to reduce pollution involves costs and benefits. Finding appropriate formulas to identify costs and benefits is a major part of environmental negotiations, and is important to arriving at a balanced agreement. Sharing costs and benefits points to the systemic nature of environmental negotiations, which encompass political, economic, technical, ecological, and psychological factors that are interrelated in ways that negotiators must identify and control.

The role of experts. During negotiations, technical experts are needed to identify and rank toxic substances, determine what levels are acceptable, decide on the location and timing of measurements, and so on. However, discussions among experts tend to resemble real negotiations when the problem-solving discussions include the experts' policy preferences.

It is sometimes difficult to separate scientific problem-solving activities from policy discussions. Therefore, practitioners must ask themselves to what extent experts should be allowed to intervene in negotiations. A related point is to determine the appropriate sequence—parallel, serial, or other—of events and sessions, and how to receive feedback from them.

The complexity of the network of actors. Practitioners and analysts need to know more about how negotiators are controlled by instructions from the capital. Network analysis of this kind is important for this type of negotiation. Understanding the complex interplay of influences—direct or indirect, and internal or external—on each negotiating party is a key consideration. The Rhine negotiations contain many instances of the use of power strategies in this regard.

Controlling the process. It is difficult to know which kind of process is best for this type of negotiation. Is it more productive to agree on principles first, and then draw up policy guidelines, action programs, and binding agreements based on the principles? Or, is it better to give priority to actions, even at the microlevel, that then accumulate increasingly wider agreements and global policies? The questions are raised, although the Rhine experience does not provide any clear answers.

Concluding Remarks

The Rhine negotiations provide a good example of how international environmental negotiations have developed. It is a 40-year-old story in which many negotiated outcomes have found concrete, practical application.

On balance it is also a success story, which is another reason for using these negotiations as a case study (based on work begun by Willem Mastenbroek in Amsterdam).[2] Ruchay (1990) concluded that the success of the Rhine negotiations can be attributed to several "critical success factors," including a declared political will; the pressure of public opinion; open access to information; contributions to pollution by all parties; joint factual base, comparative surveys, and joint monitoring of agreements; and high level of expertise and decision-making procedures.

Overall success in the negotiations, however, does not mean that all issues have been totally or easily solved. As awareness of the complexity of the stakes increases with time along with the need for higher standards and more interstate solidarity, new issues will crop up continuously and lead to fresh negotiations. That some of these issues are not yet ripe for a solution is underscored by the difficulties in the December 1990 negotiations between city authorities in Rotterdam and the management of the Alsace potash mines. In contrast, recent negotiations between the city of Rotterdam and the Swiss firm Sandoz on the same topic—the outflow of heavy-metal substances from factories to the Rotterdam harbor—have resulted in an agreement.

Notes

1. This expert group, led by two high civil servants, Mr. Delmas and Mr. Gautrat, submitted to the French government two comprehensive reports (in 1987 and 1988) in which they compared the advantages and drawbacks of several alternative schemes dealing with the chloride problem. These reports were transmitted to the other members of ICPR as a basis for further discussion. The reports were part of the conference documentation and were restricted to limited circulation.

2. Mastenbroek wrote a case describing the negotiations that took place regarding the question of control of toxic substances. This case is currently used as a basis for simulations in several training fora in the Netherlands as well as in certain universities, notably in France.

9

The Sahel

MICHAEL MORTIMORE

Environmental degradation in the Sahel—specifically, the loss of soil productivity, the reduction of biomass in natural ecosystems, and the decline of farm production—is widely perceived as a problem that requires an international response. However, the diffuse nature and the scientific uncertainty of the problem, together with a preference for institutional responses, have kept the Sahel off the agendas of international environmental negotiations until recently.

The Sahel Defined

No generally accepted geographical definition of the word *Sahel* exists. The name is derived from the Arabic word for "borderland," in this case, the land bordering on the Sahara Desert. Two geopolitical definitions are available: one with exclusive usage, the other with inclusive usage.

The more exclusive use of Sahel refers to the nine member states of the Comité Permanent Inter-Etats de Lutte Contre la Sècheresse dans le Sahel (CILSS). Except for Cape Verde, the Gambia, and Guinea-Bissau, these countries were part of France's colonial empire, from which they inherited the French language, systems of government, and the CFA franc. Political and economic ties to France are still close.

The more inclusive use of Sahel refers to the 22 countries that qualify for financial and technical support from the United Nations Sudano-Sahelian Office (UNSO), whose mandate extends into East Africa and includes countries having quite small dryland areas.

Another definition, this one used by the International Union for the Conservation of Nature and Natural Resources (IUCN, 1988), includes 11 countries. Definitions of the Sahel that are based on groups of nations may be justified by geopolitical realities, such as the nations' eligibility for aid and membership in international organizations. But these definitions bear little relation to the ecological realities, because even these definitions are subject to alternative technical interpretations.

The definition preferred in this chapter is derived from the bioclimatic zones used by the United Nations Environment Program (UNEP), which identifies semiarid and dry subhumid zones. These zones provide an ecological definition of the Sahel. It is readily apparent from Figure 9.1 that several countries included in the geopolitical definitions of the Sahel contain large areas outside this ecological zone. For practical reasons, this discussion is confined to West Africa.

The Problem Defined

The absence of a universally accepted definition of the Sahel arises from the fact that, since 1973, this region has been conceived largely as a problem, whose nature is not self-evident. The Sahelian problem has many perceived dimensions, including:

- Decreased mean annual rainfall by up to 35% since 1965 (Boulier & Jouve, 1988).
- Diminishing surface water resources, such as Lake Chad (Kindler, Warshall, Arnould, Hutchinson, & Varady, 1989), and groundwater.
- Persistent droughts (Mortimore, 1989a).
- Diminished biomass in the natural ecosystems caused by agricultural clearance, woodcutting, and reduced rainfall (Gorse & Steeds, 1985).
- Overstocked natural rangelands.
- Degradation of cultivated soils, caused by shortened fallows and insufficient fertilizer (Gregoire, 1980).
- Frequent outbreaks of pests, especially locusts and grasshoppers (SAS, 1990).

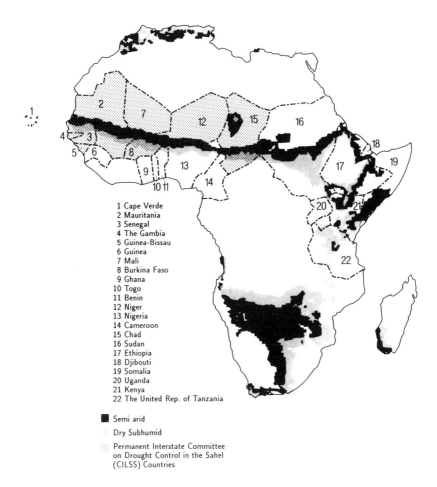

Figure 9.1. Map of the Sahel

- Diminished production of food staples and self-sufficiency; periodic food crises (IUCN, 1988).
- Population growth at rates faster than the expected growth of primary production or employment in the secondary or tertiary sectors (Gorse & Steeds, 1985; IUCN, 1988).
- Persistent poverty, as indicated by a low average life expectancy, undersupply of basic needs, and periodic, widespread hunger.
- Increased dependency on foreign aid (OECD, 1988).

The items in this list are subject to significant qualification, if not controversy. There is universal agreement that there is a problem, but there is no consensus on the core of the problem. Neither can the environment be easily isolated from its social, economic, and political components.

What is happening to the environment of the Sahel? Since the drought cycles of the early 1970s and early 1980s, scientific opinion about the problem has changed significantly. Some observers were quick to point to a socioeconomic crisis triggered by the droughts. This crisis has its roots in structural causes, such as market incorporation, colonial export agriculture, the domination of the state, and the collapse of social organization. Others saw the problem as resource mismanagement in the farming and livestock-production systems, caused by population growth and technological stagnation. More recently, as the evidence for secular change in rainfall has become more conclusive, the rationale and adaptive capabilities of indigenous systems of resource management have received broader recognition (Boulier & Jouve, 1988; Mortimore, 1989a). Interest has shifted from grand theory toward applied empiricism.

At the heart of the controversy are the causes—nature and rate of degradation of the land—meaning biomass decline, soil erosion, and physical or nutrient degradation. A recent study of the evidence available in northern Nigeria (Mortimore, 1989b) concluded that evidence cannot support the consensual view of widespread degradation. This view, though extremely influential, remains without a conclusive empirical basis. The neglect, over several decades, of longitudinal studies of changes in land use and in vegetation, of surface and groundwater, and of the status of soil fertility is responsible for this situation. Several longitudinal studies are in progress in West Africa.

Meanwhile, the rate of desertification, or dryland degradation, is also the subject of conflicting claims. Its definition (proposed by UNEP in 1977) has been greatly criticized and recently revised. It is likely to be revised again before too long. The term *desertification,* along with the doomsday scenarios of popular writers, is becoming discredited (Nelson, 1988; Odingo, 1990; Warren & Agnew, 1988).

The causes of dryland degradation are controversial and need to be examined. The assumption that overstocked rangeland causes dryland degradation is being questioned, and indigenous strategies for stocking species are being reinterpreted in rational terms (Sandford, 1984). The impact of population growth on farming, which is often thought to be intrinsically degradational, in certain conditions, may induce intensification (Mortimore, in press). Woodland management on small farm holdings may yield higher volumes of timber under a stable, woody biomass than natural woodland yields (Cline-Cole et al., 1990). Without doubt, the popular views on runaway degradation in dryland Africa (Eckholm & Brown, 1977; Grainger, 1982; Timberlake, 1985) need to be examined critically before they are used to justify spending more public money and changing policies.

The fundamental contradiction implicit in the literature concerns the relative culpability of exogenous (climatic) causes and endogenous (management) causes. Given the current knowledge about climatic change (Farmer & Wigley, 1985), the answer can no longer be assumed. Environmental negotiations can only influence the outcome if endogenous factors are to blame. There is wide agreement, however, that production systems are under pressure from increased monetization of the economy, increased centralization of political administration, and economic policies that are urban-biased (Gorse & Steeds, 1985).

Environmental degradation is neither pollution nor, necessarily, destruction. The reversibility of desertification processes is controversial. Unless the soil profile has been removed, improved rainfall or management may make it possible to restore biological productivity partially or totally. This resilience has been widely demonstrated in field observations, and contradicts the often-quoted concept of fragile ecosystems—a concept that requires a proper definition and more qualified use than it is usually given.

Scientific uncertainty is not unusual in environmental issues that are the subject of international negotiations. What is perhaps unique to the Sahelian case is that the uncertainty has extended from the causes to the assessment of the degradation of the environment.

A Transnational Problem

Land degradation is traditionally the responsibility of the individual farm manager or, where access rights are shared, of the landholding community, subject to incentives, penalties, and restrictions imposed by the state. What are the special characteristics of the Sahel that justify a transnational approach to identifying the problem and its solution? Is it a legitimate subject for international negotiations? Apart from the long-standing links between France and French-speaking West Africa, the following factors are reasons for a transnational approach to the problem.

Common natural processes. All Sahelian nations are influenced by the same regional weather systems. These include the dry, continental air mass in the Northern Hemisphere winter, together with its accompanying harmattan (dust haze) and the moist maritime (rain-bearing) air in summer. It seems logical, then, that nations share objectives for managing resources and priorities for scientific and technical research.

Resource constraints. Two of the most important reasons for adopting a transnational approach to the Sahelian environment are the poverty of the French-speaking Sahelian nations and their dependence on financial and technical assistance from outside the region. Nigeria, on the other hand, with its larger and more diversified oil-based economy, has tended to "go it alone" in assessing and managing dryland degradation.

Spillover effects of dryland management. If the Burkinabe, or the Nigerians, choose to degrade their environment, it is a national problem. If what they do affects their neighbors, it is a regional problem. If the degradation affects climate, it could become a global problem. Models of atmospheric circulation systems have indicated that there may be links between the removal of vegetation and reduced rainfall. Until these connections are refuted, the possibility that land use affects rainfall in the region has to be taken seriously.

Impact of droughts. Because international borders are permeable, food-supply crises cause refugees, livestock, and food grains to move across borders. Because some countries are landlocked, and relief food supplies have to pass through other countries, which may have poor transportation systems, cooperation among nations in the region is vital.

Proposed regional solutions. Although it has not been implemented, a transnational greenbelt for the Sahel was proposed after the droughts of the 1970s. Also proposed was a plan for regional livestock production. This plan was based on setting up special zones for breeding and fattening cattle. More appropriate and, it is to be hoped, more feasible responses to the problems of environmental management are expected in the future.

Transborder interdependency. The nations of West Africa do not exist in isolation. Changes in the parity of currency, tariffs, or taxes in one country have repercussions in neighboring states. The distortions that may result provide strong arguments for a transnational regime to oversee the management of the environment in the region.

Actors and Conflicting Interests

For the purposes of this examination of the Sahel, the following actors and interests have been identified as potential participants in environmental negotiations.

Smallholders. Smallholders who farm and graze animals are unaware of the ongoing debate. In the past, their perceptions have been regarded as unhelpful to scientific studies of the problem. Smallholders are accustomed to authoritarian, nondemocratic governments. If the imposition of government is seen as burdensome, smallholders avoid the issue, rather than resist. Although community participation is sometimes written into project plans, it may still be implemented as education that is forced on recalcitrant farmers, rather than as a way of involving them in diagnosing problems, identifying goals, and designing and managing projects.

Socioeconomic differences among smallholders affect their goals and benefits. Farmers and livestock producers who are more affluent—and who have better access to land, livestock, and labor—may have different views from poorer farmers whose main aim is the short-term survival of their families. Sustainable technologies for managing resources are not cheap.

Entrepreneurs. Among the domestic groups, the commercial elite partly controls the import trade on which the national economy depends for new and replacement technology. Entrepreneurs control the food markets, own and speculate in land, and influence government. The accumulative logic of their economic system contradicts the redistributive goals of some poverty programs and donors. These entrepreneurs are moving increasingly into agriculture or livestock because, as in Nigeria, they can make a profit. And as they become more involved in agriculture, increasingly, they have direct relevance to the conservation of resources.

Bureaucracies. Bureaucracies, staffed by technical and administrative professionals, are insulated from the public they "serve." Government departments—forestry, agriculture, veterinary services, water resources—may be preoccupied with maintaining infrastructures, staff levels, and project commitments with inadequate budgets. Scientific information may be sparse, and the capability of departments to review policies and to carry out cost-benefit analyses may be limited. Their effectiveness is further weakened by over-centralization, inadequate professional cadres, and conflicts between professional and private goals. However, they occupy the critical middle ground between smallholder resource managers and policymakers.

Research organizations. Technical and professional information comes from domestic and international sources. Research in domestic universities or institutes may be underfunded or understaffed. Its impact on environmental management in the drylands has yet to meet expectations.

However, information from international research institutes and foreign consultants dominate government policy and practice in environmental fields. The result is a weak integration among governments, their own research establishments, and the public. This contrasts with the experience of developed market economies.

Governments. A recent study by the Organization for Economic Cooperation and Development (OECD, 1988) argues that governments in the Sahel have become remote from their people.

> Today's Sahelian state has taken over the reigns of power from the colonial rulers and is the progeny of an alien tradition. The modern state has set for itself the ambitious objective of building a nation and modernizing the economy. In view of its origins and the action it has taken, the state has become detached from the population, and the population does not identify with the state. Sahelian populations are unorganized, incapable of making themselves heard, and there is no genuine opposition anywhere in the region. A rift has formed between the power base and the population.

One further observation may be added: whether military or elected, a government may be more concerned with ensuring its own survival than with pursuing long-term environmental objectives. In a volatile political environment, the absence of a consensus on national objectives undermines the effectiveness of governments in practical fields.

Aid interests. In the Sahelian environment, aid interests include the following:

- Food suppliers, whose interests have been linked with obtaining commercial import contracts.
- Bilateral and multilateral donors—governments, agencies (such as USAID), the World Bank, the International Development Agency, and the European Community—whose priorities vary and whose influence on policy is exerted through technical advice, project selection, and a semipermanent presence in the region.
- Nongovernmental organizations, which proliferate in certain nations. There are 80 foreign organizations in Mali, for example (OECD, 1988, p. 236). Their traditional emphasis on small-scale projects is now increasingly orthodox, and it is arguable that they have been more successful than big donors.

Potentially, aid interests have a considerable influence on environmental negotiations, for several reasons: there are so many of them; the economies in the Sahel seem unable to increase their self-sufficiency and reduce their dependency on aid; nations are certain that aid will always be needed to implement major environmental programs.

International organizations. International organizations have a high profile. The UN system, which supports projects and provides technical and policy advice directly to governments, includes UNEP, the United Nations Sudano-Sahelian Office (UNSO), the Economic Commission for Africa (ECA), the Food and Agriculture Organization (FAO), the United Nations Development Program (UNDP), and the United Nations Educational, Scientific, and Cultural Organization (UNESCO).

Other organizations include the Economic Community of West African States (ECOWAS) and the Organization of African Unity (OAU). Given the regional nature of the environmental problem as it is usually perceived and the weaknesses of individual governments, one of these organizations must assume a third-party role during environmental negotiations to initiate multilateral action, gain the support of the international community, and mobilize funds.

Other actors may appear when a coherent thrust toward a new environmental regime begins to threaten (or benefit) additional interests. The important point is that, in the past, only the governments, aid interests, international organizations, and possibly research organizations were likely to be present at the negotiation table. The Sahelian environment is assured of international interest, but the weak links between those who make the decisions and those who will be asked to implement them should cause concern. And conspicuous by its absence is the public. Notwithstanding a broadening and deepening of interest in environmental issues, the government still expects to set the agenda. There is no Green vote in the Sahel yet.

The art of government has to reconcile extremely powerful conflicting interests in the absence of a consensus about major national objectives that can temper such interests. Environmental management is no longer a noncontroversial subject. Improved management regimes inevitably impinge on established interests and exacerbate conflict between them. For a government to embark on international negotiations, whose outcome may alter individual behavior and the balance of interest, it needs to be sure of its ground.

The Institutional Response

Largely untroubled by uncertainties of definition, semantics, and diagnostics, governments and international interests perceive the degradation of the environment in the Sahel as a regional problem that requires a concerted international response. This perception is founded on the premise, accepted by UNEP since 1977, that the new technologies needed to deal with the problem already exist. This premise has not been examined critically. But the premise makes the task primarily one of mobilizing resources and generating the necessary "political will" (an expression frequently used by technical advisers) to provide an institutional climate conducive to technological change. A recent statement from the FAO (Knowles & Pratt, 1990) cautions against expecting too much from available technologies in arid environments, and says that in Africa (and Asia), "technology is powerless to control degradation within prevailing sociopolitical and organizational environments."

The multinational response has been expressed in institutional forms. This section examines several institutions and shows that their commitment to environmental objectives is wide-ranging. The institutions are ECOWAS; the commissions involved with developing and managing river basins; and UNEP, UNSO, and the African Ministerial Conference on the Environment (AMCEN).

ECOWAS. Like its forerunners (mostly customs unions among French-speaking nations), ECOWAS was designed to overcome the economic disadvantages stemming from the political fragmentation of West Africa (Ezenwe, 1984). ECOWAS included both the French-speaking and the English-speaking countries in a new community, created in 1975, with broad objectives of liberalizing trade, reducing restrictions on the flows of people and capital, harmonizing policies, and conducting joint projects.

So far, ECOWAS has failed to fulfill the expectations of its founders (Robson, 1985). Economic liberalization threatens to polarize the more powerful members, such as Nigeria, and the less powerful members, such as the nations of the Sahel. Relevant to the Sahelian question, for example, is Nigeria's refusal to accept unrestricted migration from farther north, even when the migration is caused by a drought. The resources committed by member nations for joint activity have been inadequate, and the commitment of individual nations seems to vary. Progress toward unity among the former colonial powers in Europe does not seem to have diminished the fear of Nigerian domination among French-speaking West African countries.

More relevant to the question of environmental management is that ECOWAS was founded on the neoclassical economic development theory that dominated economic planning in West Africa in the first decade after independence. Its concept of development and the logic of its market-oriented strategy have not been revised to reflect the current concern about sustainable development, or the negative impact of changes in rainfall (and other external events) on the economic potential of its member nations. ECOWAS was conceived in terms of interactive national economies, so its instruments may not always be appropriate to the particular environmental problem in the Sahel. The problem is both subnational, that is, affecting parts of member nations, and transnational.

River basin development and management commissions. In the past, West Africa's major rivers were sometimes used to demarcate colonial boundaries. The concept of integrated river basin planning (Barbour, Faniran, & Oguntoyinbo, 1974), and access to the large amounts of capital needed to release the irrigation and electricity-generating potential of these rivers, led to setting up commissions to plan, develop, and manage these river basins. The commissions are:

• The Niger River Commission, set up in 1963. The commission has concerned itself mainly with navigation agreements and studies.
• The Lake Chad Basin Commission (LCBC), set up in 1964. The commission deals with sharing irrigation water and research for development.
• The Organization for the Development of the Senegal River replaced, in 1972, the *Organisation des États Riverains de Sénégal.* It is concerned with irrigation and the construction of dams.

These organizations were formed before the debate began about how major hydrological changes affect ecosystems, land use, and human communities. But it was found that the expected economic benefits of large-scale irrigation, which requires costly capital investment, did not always occur. A river basin authority that is heavily committed to making such investments is not qualified to be either a social or ecological watchdog of its own activities.

The LCBC exemplifies some of the problems. The agreement that set up the commission entitles each nation to a "reasonable and equitable share" of water from Lake Chad, provided it does not disrupt co-riparian development. Early on, Nigeria obtained an agreement, when the level of the lake was high, to irrigate up to 100,000 hectares of land. Financed by Nigerian oil revenues, the South Chad Irrigation Project (SCIP) began operations in the 1970s. Unfortunately, expectations of water availability were based on consultants' studies that failed to warn of the possibility of falling lake levels on the scale that actually occurred after 1972. The huge pumping station that lifts water from the lake had to suspend irrigation from 1984 to 1988 when the level of the lake fell below the intake (Kolawole, 1987). The SCIP may never catch up on its developmental schedule or achieve its original target. The social and economic impact of removing such large quantities of scarce water from other users has not been assessed.

The LCBC also is required to coordinate national development proposals in the basin, to undertake joint projects and research, to regulate navigation, and to settle disputes. But so far, the commission has lacked the resources to have much of an effect. Meanwhile, the reported environmental deterioration in the Chad Basin, along with reduced rainfall, compels the commission to reorient its objectives from development to conservation. A recent study recommended that the commission change its policies to reflect such a focus. The study also recommended projects to combat environmental degradation and proposed some new tasks for the commission (Kindler et al., 1989). Whether or not the commission changes its objectives is important for the future of environmental negotiations being conducted through institutions elsewhere in the region.

UNEP, UNSO, and the AMCEN. The Desertification Control Program Activity Center (DCPAC) of UNEP has a mandate to implement the Plan of Action to Combat Desertification (PACD), which was approved at the United Nations Conference on Desertification in 1977. In a sense, this conference was an international environmental negotiation. It resulted from a resolution by the UN General Assembly that expressed concern at the impact of the Sahelian drought of the early 1970s. However, none of the 28 resolutions agreed to had any binding effect on member nations. Most of the resolutions recommended action at a national level, but some multinational action was also proposed.

The DCPAC lacked the financial resources to implement its worldwide mandate, because international resources did not come through on the scale needed. Of the $2.4 billion needed over a 20-year period, only about 25% was available, according to a review (Mabbutt, 1987). It said: "A review of achievements under the PACD makes for generally disappointing reading."

One function of the DCPAC is to assist governments in preparing national antidesertification plans. Implementing these plans is another matter. Increased awareness of the "threat of desertification" is claimed to be a positive achievement, but it is questionable whether awareness has been bought at the price of scientific objectivity (Odingo, 1990).

UNEP supports UNSO, the mandate of which is limited to 22 African nations, and which enjoys access to UNDP's resources. Each year it spends $25 million to $30 million on projects in dryland agriculture, rangeland management, afforestation, soil protection, dune stabilization, and water resources development.

UNEP took a major role in initiating AMCEN. At its first meeting in December 1985, the conference adopted the Cairo Program for African

Cooperation (UNEP, 1985). This program (AMCEN, n.d.) was based on the African Priority Program for Economic Recovery (APPER), adopted by the OAU in 1985, and the Program of Action for African Economic Recovery and Development (PAAERD), which was adopted by the UN General Assembly in 1986.

The point of these elaborately titled initiatives was to establish African self-reliance in tackling Africa's problems. Thus the environment has become enmeshed in the broader economic context of indebtedness, poverty, and dependency. But the nature of these linkages has never been clearly stated, except at the broadest hypothetical level. Like desertification processes, it is assumed that everybody knows what the linkages are.

The AMCEN has a secretariat at UNEP in Nairobi, a Technical Regional Environment Group, an Inter-Agency Working Group, and a specially assigned UNEP task force to facilitate its work. Below these are four subject committees, including one for deserts and arid lands, and eight professional, technical, and training networks, including one on environmental monitoring. Five networks were in operation in 1988. In addition, AMCEN sponsors a regional coordinating unit for each network, a management and planning group, selected national coordinating institutions, and member institutions.

This intricate structure has been elaborated since 1985. Some may question whether the activity that AMCEN has generated so far justifies its existence. A recent reassessment of the effectiveness of AMCEN's operational and organizational structures found many areas of under-achievement and many constraints (AMCEN, 1989). In particular, networks and committees have been ineffective and governments have not committed the resources expected. In view of the previous experience of the DCPAC in trying to mobilize resources, one may ask how AMCEN justifies its optimism at a time of economic crisis throughout the continent.

The only area of practical, rather than diplomatic or bureaucratic, activity is the Pilot Project scheme. This scheme aims at setting up 150 farming and 30 pastoral projects in villages in its member nations. The projects hope to demonstrate sustainable development using traditional techniques of farming and livestock husbandry, supplemented by appropriate technologies. So far, about 30 projects are reported to be in progress. The objectives and assumptions of the scheme do not appear to have been made explicit, nor have they been published in detail.

CILSS and the *Club du Sahel*

The Sahel conforms to the principle that environmental management is carried out under a regime of rules, penalties, and inducements. Precolonial management regimes evolved under conditions of lower population densities and greater self-sufficiency than today, and were irreversibly changed during the colonial period. The changes are intensifying under current conditions. A new regime is needed in the Sahel, but what form that regime should take is not clear.

The institutions mentioned above have had little impact on environmental management regimes. This is because international action, as far as the allocation of resources has been concerned, has focused on specific projects. Its impact on regimes, which are usually the province of governments, has been essentially hortatory.

The experience of the *CILSS dans le Sahel* appears to differ significantly. Three aspects are worth noting. First is the intense interaction among a relatively small number of nations. Second is the strength of the North-South partnership, which intimately involves the donors (*Club du Sahel*). Third is the emergence of genuine multilateral negotiations on specific issues that have a direct impact on environmental management, namely, the Ségou Encounter (or Roundtable) and the Food Aid Charter.

CILSS was set up in response to the food crises caused by the droughts in the early 1970s. In September 1973, the heads of six former French colonies—Burkina Faso, Chad, Mali, Mauritania, Niger, and Senegal—formed the CILSS to coordinate emergency actions against the drought (Somerville, 1986). The membership was later extended to include the Gambia (December 1973), Cape Verde (1976), and, oddly, Guinea-Bissau (1986). An application from Nigeria was rejected.

Early proposals focused on measures that attempted to find technical solutions to the spread of desertification, against a background of emergency food aid, widespread loss of livestock, and economic disruption. A list of 123 projects (the Ouagadougou Program) in the areas of agriculture, forestry, livestock, and water resources was adopted. Under donor pressure, an early cost estimate of $3 billion was reduced to $1 billion.

The OECD initiated the formation of the *Club du Sahel* (originally *Club des Amis du Sahel*) to unite donors with Sahelian states in a loosely structured organization to promote the goals of the CILSS. In spite of the horror engendered in the minds of Europeans by the 1972-1974 food crises in the Sahel, only 28 of the CILSS's projects had secured funding by December 1975. The Club needed to overcome initial misgivings among member states about CILSS's objectives (Somerville, 1986). The Club's objectives were to communicate Sahelian needs to the international community; to promote financial support of developmental priorities; and to coordinate donor support for CILSS projects. Membership is open to all Sahel states as well as any government or institution with an interest in the development of the Sahel. Regular participants include 12 bilateral and

8 multilateral donor groups, and include prominent West European and North American interests.

The CILSS differs from other regional integration schemes in the following important ways: the formation of the CILSS and the club were precipitated by a major historical event—the Sahelian famine; CILSS activity has focused on the rural, least-developed sector rather than on industrialization and trade objectives; and rather than attempting to reduce the influence of external forces, the Sahel's dependency on the world economy, which is admitted, has put it in close alignment with donor interests.

Nevertheless, the CILSS started down a road familiar to other regional integration schemes. It has its own bureaucracy at Ouagadougou, Burkina Faso; national committees; specialized institutions including the AGRHYMET (Centre for Agro-Meteorological and Hydrological Research) at Niamey, Niger, and the Sahel Institute for Technological Research; projects organized by sector including dryland and irrigated agriculture, village and pastoral hydraulics, livestock, fisheries, human resources, ecology and forestry, price-marketing-storage, and transportation infrastructure; and special programs.

The number of projects in the *First Generation Program,* written by CILSS staff for donor consumption, grew to 714. According to the OECD, aid to the Sahel increased from $196.5 million in 1971 to $1.105 billion in 1978 and $1.513 billion in 1982 (Somerville, 1986, p. 179). However, support, which was extended to only 60% of the first-generation projects, was spread unevenly across the sectors, and tended to favor financially attractive projects and donor interests rather than Sahelian needs. According to Somerville (1986, p. 200), "More and more, development in the Sahel is shifting from a North-South cooperative blueprint for action to one in which CILSS responds to donor ideas about development."

By the early 1980s, a review of the CILSS's priorities became essential for economic and administrative reasons (USAID, 1989a). Despite massive investments in development, economic conditions in the Sahel continued to deteriorate. Grain imports increased steadily from 1974 to 1982, terms of trade fell from 1979 to 1982, and aid represented an average of 17% of the GNP in 1982. Donors were dissatisfied with the CILSS's project planning, management, and integration of its regional objectives with national development plans. Individual members were "going it alone." In 1985, therefore, the functions of the CILSS were redefined to exclude project design and implementation and to emphasize policy analysis and advice. This must have altered the balance in favor of bilateral aid negotiations and the influence of individual donors, such as the USAID.

The Sahel futures study (OECD, 1988), conducted by a group of commissioned intellectuals between 1985 and 1987, reflects the new orientation of the CILSS and the Club. This study projects a "present trends scenario" of economic stagnation, increasing dependency, and environmental degradation over the next 25 years—factors that point to the potential for a future disaster. This scenario is considered unacceptable. Instead, the study calls for a restructuring of the internal relationships of the Sahelian systems, which so far have changed very little. The restructuring is driven by the concept of a "redynamized nongovernmental sector," including strengthened local communities, and supported by sensitive assistance from local and foreign NGOs (OECD, 1988, pp. 211-214). Such communities potentially will increase their responsibilities in managing natural resources, an area in which the state's role often has been both weak and misdirected and should be reduced.

The CILSS has come a long way since its inception in 1973. Its experience can be divided into three learning phases (Shaikh, 1990). In the first phase, early attempts to find technical solutions to stop desertification processes demonstrated the need to involve the peoples concerned, and to promote appropriate technologies. In the second phase, technical solutions were unsuccessful, so it became necessary to establish legal, political, and socioeconomic conditions for sustainable rural production systems. In the third and present phase, there is a consensus on two points: macroeconomic development depends on dynamic rural systems of production; and these systems are directly undermined by environmental degradation.

Could such a painful and expensive learning process have been abbreviated? Possibly, if the CILSS had received better advice from the donor community, made better use of scientific research on Sahelian systems of primary production, or commissioned relevant research on indigenous management systems. This redirection from technical interventionism toward the creation of better management regimes is relevant to international environmental negotiations. At the level of technical intervention, the role of negotiations is mainly restricted to allocating resources (aid). At the level of regime amelioration, the scope of negotiations is broadened to incorporate economic and legal institutions or policies, and donor support.

In May 1989 the CILSS and the Club sponsored the Ségou Roundtable, a regional encounter on the management of local natural resources in the Sahel. The purpose of the roundtable was to emphasize the need for dynamic and sustainable systems of rural production (OECD/CILSS, 1989; USAID, 1989b). For the first time, member states applied a multilateral negotiating mode toward the objective of ameliorating environmental management regimes.

Among the potential actors, representatives of rural organizations were selected to take their place at the negotiating table with CILSS government representatives and donors. Because it originated from the perceived failures of the first-generation "project decade" and reflected the need to shift "popular participation" from rhetoric to reality, the Ségou Roundtable was forced to find a way of creating a viable negotiating partner out of the sleeping rural constituency. This was achieved by employing independent consultants to find, interview, select, and prepare the representatives of rural and women's organizations (OECD/CILSS, 1989, pp. 179-186).

In order to find representatives, rural organizations had to be defined and listed; their diverse experiences were systematically researched. In addition to technical and economic criteria, the organizations were evaluated on the basis of their structure, cultural content, objectives, and strategic choices and uses of local resources. A female consultant was charged with finding women representatives. The consultants recommended 36 candidates (including 9 women) who spoke French fluently and were likely to make a positive contribution to the encounter. The candidates were then trained in presenting their practical experiences. According to USAID (1989b, p. 5):

> The majority of representatives of rural organizations were not poor farmers. Often they were local organizers, association leaders, and/or organization founders. If not typical of traditional village leadership, they were representative of the new class of rural leadership which is likely to grow as decentralized local management becomes a reality. Understanding the "sociology" of this emerging group of rural intermediaries will be an important part of understanding future relationships between rural populations, central authorities, and international partners (both governmental and nongovernmental).

The objectives of the roundtable may be summarized as follows: (1) to promote popular participation in sustainable development (a) in project definition, selection, and implementation, (b) in partnership with governments and donors, and (c) through decentralization, which would encourage local initiatives and management; (2) to disseminate appropriate technology for the management of public and private lands; and (3) to share learned experiences in ways of modifying production to achieve a new "socioecological balance."

From the negotiating-process perspective, the Ségou Roundtable had three parts. First, during the 18 months of preparation, in which rural representatives were selected and trained, teams visited every country to develop the agenda, secure political approval, and prepare documentation. This included 4 "main" and 12 "supporting" studies as well as several national reports on desertification control and popular participation policies.

Second, the roundtable concentrated on the themes of rural participation, environmental preservation, and the transformation of production systems. These themes were discussed by the working groups, each of which included government representatives, donors, and rural participants. The records of the discussions (OECD/CILSS, 1989) indicate that the exchanges were characterized by considerable diversity and that the rural representatives were able to articulate their thoughts without becoming intimidated by the international nature of the meeting. Also, there was an

> absence of clearly demarcated positions between the three "partners" who attended. Rural representatives showed the greatest overall consistency in the issues they raised, but the relative importance of a given issue (such as decentralization, for example) varied according to individual circumstances. There was no clear-cut "government" or "donor" position. Individuals appear to have relied on their own experience and insights rather than on negotiating positions. (USAID, 1989b, p. 10)

Third, the discussions were synthesized into the Ségou Declaration, a final document that represents the negotiated outcome of the roundtable. This declaration embodies eight principles, which are believed to create the conditions necessary for sustainable natural-resource management in the Sahel. These principles—"landmarks for concerted action"—may be summarized as follows:

(1) Ecological rehabilitation must restore degraded land. The land must be recapitalized, by mobilizing local resources and participation, external aid, economic incentives, and technical support. In this way, productivity will improve and land conservation can take place.

(2) Local-level natural resource management must share responsibility with local communities. There is already a variety of rural organizations; they must be given legal recognition and autonomy, and appropriate techniques of resource management must be distributed to them.

(3) Decentralized management must increase efficiency. Governments and donors alike should decentralize their responsibilities to communities and prepare them for shouldering such responsibilities; ground rules for this partnership must be established.

(4) Land tenure reform must protect local investments. Legislative solutions must be found for the lack of security for land investments, and flexible ways should be found to combine modern and customary land law.

(5) Local credit and savings institutions must increase local investment. Credit and savings systems based on mutual trust should be encouraged as well as ways to link mutual trust with the formal banking system.

(6) The participation of women must be encouraged. Ecological degradation (such as the scarcity of wood fuel) and the migration of men out of degraded areas fundamentally have altered women's responsibilities and social position.

Training should be directed toward women and ways should be found to reduce their work load and diversify their incomes.

(7) Information, training, and experience sharing are part of the process. People are eager to learn from successes and failures. A communications policy should be developed to promote an organized sharing of experience; management and leadership training also is necessary.

(8) Population and development must be controlled. Population policies should "strike a balance between the population growth rate, economic growth, and the desired level of social development," and birth control should be made available (the N'Djamena Plan of Action).

The status of the Ségou Declaration differs in several important respects from the negotiated outcomes of more orthodox environmental negotiations. First, as the terms *encounter* and *roundtable* imply, representatives had no intention of negotiating an international treaty. Neither the separate governments nor the three interest groups represented at the meeting came with prepared negotiating positions. (Paradoxically, it was the least experienced of these groups—the representatives of rural organizations—who showed the greatest consistency in the issues they raised.)

Second, the declaration commands no binding force. Its conclusion

wishes the Sahelian governments to consider the frame of reference outlined at Ségou and to work within that framework whenever appropriate; calls upon [governments and donors] to nurture the spirit of Ségou by organizing three-sided coordination meetings so that concrete action can be taken . . . ; requests the CILSS and the *Club du Sahel* to take guidance from the Ségou landmarks. (OECD/CILSS, 1989, p. 78)

Third, the constituencies of the three negotiating partners—the CILSS governments, the donors, and the rural populations—remain internally heterogeneous. Given that rural participants in the encounter had to be "stage-managed," the representatives of rural organizations in particular cannot be held accountable to their interest groups.

Nevertheless, it would be hasty to dismiss the Ségou Roundtable as only a learning experience or a public relations exercise, having no greater significance than the results of an average technical or academic meeting. First, a consensus of intent and priorities was reached by three very different interest groups and was expressed in a negotiated and specific text. Second, the CILSS-Club partnership is committed and possesses the resources to maintain the momentum of the Ségou Roundtable, both at the analytical level and through intergovernmental relations. Third, given the top-down tradition of rural development interventions in the past, the

Ségou gesture toward meaningful rural participation may well turn into an unstoppable trend. Whether or not there is a fundamental change in the regime of natural-resource management—with everything that such a change implies for the political economy of the environment—remains to be seen.

A second example of a negotiated agreement concerns food aid, a prominent issue in Sahelian affairs since 1974. Under the auspices of the *Club du Sahel* and the CILSS, a series of research seminars on cereals policies was held at Nouakchott (1979), Minelo (1986), and Lomé (1989). The conference at Lomé included coastal West African countries. The seminar participants recognized that regional trade fell short of expectations, notwithstanding the interdependence of different ecological zones in West Africa, and that the alternative for the Sahel was increased dependency on food imported from outside the region. The Lomé seminar advocated that Sahelian and coastal countries coordinate policies. Bilateral discussions were reported to be taking place between Nigeria and Niger (Snrech, 1990).

Even when properly administered, food aid has its limitations: late delivery, unsuitable foods, a destabilizing effect on local food markets, and encouraging preferences for food whose delivery cannot be sustained. At worst, food aid can be abused when it is used to secure commercial import contracts and gain political objectives.

Food aid from outside the region was the subject of a Food Aid Charter that was negotiated and ratified by Sahelian heads of state at Bissau in February 1990 (Josserand & LeClerq, 1990). Representatives of foreign governments and their commercial suppliers took part in the negotiations, which, reportedly, were prolonged:

> The U.S. representative recognized that "every word, every sentence of the charter has been discussed by the Department of Agriculture, and it took months to reach agreement on the text." The French representative also admitted that "the dialogue with exporters and the ministries concerned was more polite but just as difficult." (Josserand & Leclerq, 1990, p. 7)

The Food Aid Charter applies the general principles of the FAO and the International Wheat Agreement (1980) to the specific West African situation. The charter calls for closer cooperation between donors and beneficiaries, the exchange of information and evaluations, discussions on the nature of aid and its distribution, and joint evaluations of the annual harvest. Between the lines of the charter may be found the weakness of the recipient governments that created the need for a greatly improved food aid administration.

These examples show that CILSS is moving increasingly into regime amelioration in fields that are relevant to environmental management, whether or not these negotiations turn out to be effective. The North-South structure of the CILSS-*Club du Sahel* negotiating process, as well as the Club (France in particular) assuming a third-party negotiating position, seems to have played a key role in getting this far. Aid dependency will not disappear quickly, even in the foreseeable future, and donor activity is already as much a part of the environmental regime as local institutions. This fact is not, of course, confined to West Africa.

Concluding Comments

Four points arise from the examination of the environmental problem in the Sahel and the responses to the problem.

The first point is that there is no clear consensus about the nature of the environmental problem from which an agenda for environmental negotiations may be derived. This statement may appear to conflict with the proliferation of research programs in the Sahel since the 1970s. The more prominent programs include the International Crop Research Institute for the Semi-Arid Tropics (at Niamey), the agro-meteorological AGRHYMET program (also at Niamey), and the recent initiative (the Sahara and Sahel Observatory). This last program has a mandate to address longitudinal change and, supposedly, has socioeconomic as well as technical objectives.

Response to exogenous environmental change is as important as limiting endogenous processes. That is, the normal outcome of negotiations—a text that imposes restrictions on the behavior of signatory nations—may only encompass a part of the Sahelian problem. It is not surprising, therefore, that the most successful moves thus far have concerned activities related to regime amelioration that can be circumscribed by a "normal negotiating model," namely, donor activity (the Ségou Roundtable) and the Food Aid Charter.

The second point is a question: How much time do we have? Customarily, international environmental negotiations and the public are informed, however inaccurately, by projections of the impact of environmentally unfriendly behavior. No such timetable can be constructed for the Sahel, for the following reasons:

- There are too many variables: social, economic, political, and environmental.
- The interactions among some variables are extremely complex.
- Some variables, in particular the growth rate of the population, lie beyond the scope of environmental negotiations.

Indeed, a "present-trends scenario" has been rejected by the OECD in a study of the future of the Sahel (OECD, 1988), on both methodological and philosophical grounds. The answer to the question, "How much time do we have?" will be determined, in part, by the adaptive resourcefulness of the Sahelian peoples, in whose hands their own future largely lies.

The third point concerns the relationship between the environment and "development." The belief that environmental conservation is an added cost on development in Third-World countries must now be regarded as outmoded, where systems of primary production are concerned. For these systems, the resource is the environment. Redefining *development* as *sustainability* mainly comes down to abandoning the five-year-plan concept of development for a medium or longer term horizon. Such a horizon is usually important in African systems of primary production anyway, in view of the need to pass on to one's heirs a viable farm or livestock holding. Development that is sustainable or friendly to the environment focuses on long-term technologies and management practices. It also recognizes that using profit as the sole principle of resource management is inappropriate.

A fourth point concerns the impact of environmental conservation on national sovereignty. Sahelian nations have already compromised their economic sovereignty by becoming chronically dependent on foreign aid. However, the need for regime amelioration, in the cause of providing the conditions necessary for improved environmental management, and the internationalization of moves toward such new regimes, ultimately adds issues such as land tenure, pricing, and taxation policy to the agenda for international negotiation. These issues had traditionally been regarded as national concerns. However, the more the environment is thought of as an international interest, the greater the likelihood that a nation will have to accept limits on its sovereignty. This idea is not confined to the Sahel. But there, the principle has some poignancy, because land degradation concerns national territory per se.

The environment is in no sense marginal to the lives of Sahelians. It is embedded in their political and economic lives. To an extent perhaps not found elsewhere, the environment of the Sahel harbors not only a potential, but also a threat to the continuity of society. So far, the threat has been contained by autonomous and richly diversified adaptive behavior. To place the matter on the agenda for international negotiations should not weaken such social resources.

10

Biological Conservation and Biological Diversity

JOHN TEMPLE LANG

Wildlife conservation agreements are the oldest type of environmental treaties. The first were essentially bilateral agreements on the exploitation of single-species resources, such as fish and marine mammals. Later the conservation of exploited populations, including multispecies populations of waterfowl, became important. More recently, several multilateral treaties have been concluded to conserve wildlife habitats and species over wide areas even though they were not being commercially exploited.

Three important treaties that provide insights into the characteristics of international biological conservation negotiations are the Ramsar Convention on Wetlands of International Importance Especially as Waterfowl Habitat, the Bonn Convention on Conservation of Migratory Species, and the Washington Convention on International Trade in Endangered Species (CITES).

The Ramsar Convention, 1971. This was the first worldwide conservation treaty and the first to deal only with habitat. The treaty conserves

AUTHOR'S NOTE: Opinions expressed are purely personal.

migratory quarry species (waterfowl) and wetlands that are being threatened by drainage and pollution. Under the treaty, each party agreed to promote "wise use" of all wetlands, to protect at least one wetland of "international importance," and to promote research on wetlands. The negotiations consisted of meetings at which nations were persuaded to agree to a draft written by the International Waterfowl Research Bureau (IWRB, 1972).

This is a successful convention, if judged by the large number of parties, the large number of wetlands listed for conservation, and the total area of the wetlands protected. Parties have subsequently listed many more than the minimum number of wetlands. The convention is successful because it was promoted by the International Union for the Conservation of Nature and Natural Resources (IUCN) and the IWRB. These organizations created lists of areas of "international importance" and pressured nations to conserve these areas. The convention has been managed mainly by scientists, not by administrators.

The convention has been criticized for being weak and imposing too few legal obligations. However, the minimal obligations probably encouraged some nations to join. Also, the criteria of "international importance" became an implied moral and political obligation to conserve all wetlands meeting the criteria, instead of being merely a requirement to conserve some of the wetlands that were listed.

Another criticism of the convention centered on its having too few non-European participants. As a result, it did not protect waterfowl in the tropics and the Southern Hemisphere. The lack of an effective secretariat was also regarded as a weakness, but one that was overcome by the IUCN and the IWRB. Although the convention failed to require parties to meet regularly, parties did hold meetings. One important weakness in the convention remains: the lack of money to encourage developing nations to join the convention and to help them fulfill its aims.

An examination of the Ramsar Convention leads to two conclusions. First, for a biological conservation treaty to be successful, its implementation should be left to scientists rather than to administrators. Also, a secretariat or some other independent body should actively promote it, and scientific representatives of the parties and potential parties should meet regularly to discuss improving its operation.

Second, the effectiveness of a biological conservation treaty does not depend on the institutions associated with it or on the obligations included in it. This is especially true with treaties that conserve habitats. Precise legal obligations are not easy to write for this type of treaty. What really matters is what is accomplished in the areas that need to be conserved.

The Bonn Convention. This convention was first suggested at the UN Conference on the Human Environment in Stockholm in 1972. It was promoted by the Federal Republic of Germany on the basis of a draft prepared by the IUCN. It was signed in 1979 and came into force in 1983.

The convention protects species in danger of extinction by imposing obligations on the states where the species live. The convention also promotes supplementary agreements between the range states of species that are wholly or partly migratory, and that are listed as needing conservation. For species in Appendix I of the convention, nations must "endeavor" to take a wide variety of measures to protect the species' habitats. There are so far no supplementary range-state agreements to conserve species in Appendix II, although four agreements—on bats, small cetaceans, the white stork (*Ciconia ciconia*), and migratory waterfowl—are being drafted.

The convention has a number of drawbacks. First, there is no effective body to promote it and no clear policy on how such a body should operate. Second, the wide scope and obligations of the convention make setting priorities essential. The key word *endeavor* greatly weakens the obligations for Appendix I species. Third, the convention includes too many complex administrative provisions.

An examination of the Bonn Convention suggests that little is gained by broad obligations that cover a variety of situations, if parties are required only to "endeavor" to do something. If a treaty is to be implemented by supplementary agreements, the responsibility for drafting and promoting the agreements must be given to a body capable of doing its job in a reasonable time.

Three lessons can be learned from this treaty. First, overly elaborate administrative provisions achieve very little. Second, a treaty may be too comprehensive to be effective. Third, a treaty intended to be global does not necessarily obtain worldwide acceptance if it is drafted primarily by nations from one region.

The Washington Convention. This convention resulted from a call by the IUCN for a treaty on trade in threatened species. The treaty came into force in 1975, and had 101 parties by February 1989. It prohibits international trade in species threatened with extinction (Appendix I of the convention) except in exceptional circumstances for noncommercial purposes and for which export and import licenses are required (Favre, 1989). Less-strict controls apply to species that may become threatened unless trade is regulated; for them, import permits are not required. The treaty aims at limiting exports of Appendix II species to levels that will not harm their chances of survival.

CITES is flexible enough to control trade no more than the conservation status of the species in question requires. It also allows different populations of the same species to be treated differently. The criteria for identifying species threatened with extinction allow all species in a genus to be treated alike if most are threatened and if it is difficult to distinguish between them. Imports from nations that are not parties to the convention are permitted only if the importers produce the documentation required by CITES. Reservations are permitted when a nation ratifies the treaty, and when an appendix is added. Some reservations, notably those by Japan, have seriously affected the convention.

Commercial interests have strongly opposed some measures taken under CITES, but exporting as well as importing nations realize that trade needs to be regulated if it is to continue on a sound basis.

Lyster (1985) says that CITES "on the whole, is better enforced than many treaties." It is effective because its secretariat supervises the permit system and its parties meet regularly. Above all, it is effective because of the obligation to trade with nonparties on the same basis as parties, which, in effect, required nonparties to ratify the convention. In addition, each party's management and scientific authorities cooperate directly with the corresponding bodies in other parties to ensure enforcement and to reduce cheating. The success of CITES is also due to supervision of the wildlife trade by IUCN, and to strenuous lobbying and criticism by nongovernment organizations.

The increasing length and complexity of the lists of species in the convention's appendices has made enforcement difficult, and has led to strong demands for "reverse listing," that is, permitting trade only in a relatively small number of species. The obligation on parties to import from nonparties solely on the terms of the convention not only forced nonparties to ratify the convention, but also compelled them to carry out their obligations. CITES, therefore, solved the problem of the reluctant negotiating nation; nations wanted to maintain their export trade as far as CITES would permit, so their commercial interests forced them to join.

The problem of nations that are reluctant to join a treaty is not as easy to solve in conservation treaties not concerned with trade. But the story of CITES illustrates how vital it is to solve the problem, and it also shows that the solution chosen is compatible with the General Agreement on Tariffs and Trade (GATT).

Types of Negotiations

There are four types of treaty negotiation. The first is the traditional form of conservation treaty negotiation, intended to provide participants with a fair share of a resource and to prevent overexploitation of a resource. The parties have a common interest in ensuring that long-term exploitation remains possible, and in preventing nations that do not participate in the negotiations from sharing in the benefits of the exploitation. The participants, however, have competing interests over how the crop—or, in fisheries, the allowable catch—should be divided.

The second type of negotiation concerns joint measures to counteract a threat to a common stock other than by overexploitation, such as by pollution. In this type of negotiation, the parties share a common interest in preventing or minimizing the threat, and need to cooperate to make their action effective.

A third type of negotiation, essentially altruistic, involves conservation of a species or habitat that is not currently being exploited. The participants may have to cooperate for the solution to be effectively implemented, or to share the cost. Public opinion, usually expressed by conservation groups, often provides the pressure. The aim of the negotiators is to achieve results efficiently at the minimum cost.

A fourth type of negotiation aims at ensuring a sustainable yield and at regulating international trade in products obtained from a natural resource. The difficulty of identifying the source of products traded makes complex arrangements necessary. Each nation's resource can be effectively conserved and exploited only if the resources of other nations are treated in the same way. For example, under current proposals to regulate trade in tropical timber, nations would be allowed to trade in timber that comes only from nations that manage their forests on a sustained-yield basis. But if traders in a participating nation use fraudulent evidence of origin to trade in products from a nonparticipating nation, the regime would likely become ineffective. This problem existed in the trading of elephant ivory.

Aspects of Negotiations on Biological Conservation

This section examines several aspects of biological conservation negotiations: the reasons nations negotiate, the ongoing nature of the negotiations, the importance of an independent scientific body, the role of nongovernment organizations, and the problem of reluctant participants.

The reasons nations negotiate. Nations have numerous reasons for entering into negotiations on conservation. The reasons affect the characteristics of the negotiations and the behavior of the nations during the negotiations.

In practice, nations often take part in conservation negotiations because of pressure from internal public opinion and from other nations; to promote

economic interests concerned with the resources that are the subject of the
negotiations; or for altruistic reasons. Because of the moral element in
conservation, it may be difficult for a nation to refuse to negotiate.
Therefore, in a negotiation, some important nations may not be enthusias-
tic about conservation measures. Obviously, this hidden reluctance of key
actors influences the development of the negotiation process.

Conservation measures produce various effects:

- They allow a nation to influence the behavior of citizens in other nations on
  their territories and in international waters. A nation usually could not have
  this influence without a treaty.
- They put pressure on nations that have taken no conservation measures, or
  have taken inadequate measures.
- They ensure that the measures taken by one nation are not wasted or offset by
  the action or inaction of other nations.
- They bring about international cooperation, which is often essential for effective action at the national level, and they help coordinate conservation measures throughout a distribution range or migration route of a species or
  population.

The nature of the negotiations and the negotiating strategies used will
be influenced by the purpose of the treaty itself and the problems it is
intended to solve. Problems include destruction of habitats caused by
overutilization or by free riders, extractive exploitation, or pollution.

The ongoing nature of the negotiations. In practice, many biological
conservation negotiations are ongoing or intermittent. Changing circumstances or improved scientific knowledge require that parties meet again
and again to consider whether further or different action is needed. For
example, census data may indicate that measures already taken are inadequate or excessive; new problems may arise; and new scientific knowledge
may indicate that modified measures are more effective or less costly.

Obligations written into conservation treaties are often expressed in
general terms, sometimes merely exhortatory. They may be obligations to
achieve results that are imprecisely described rather than obligations to
adopt specific measures. Such general obligations, to be effective, often
have to be elaborated, clarified, or supplemented by interpretations of key
phrases. This was the technique used to elaborate the phrase of "international importance" in the Ramsar Convention.

Further discussions may be needed for parties to agree on how to apply
general obligations to inventories, such as lists of important habitats. In
such discussions, scientific arguments will be combined with arguments

by nations that are reluctant to spend money or to offend the feelings of local residents.

Framework treaties that set up organs and provide for an exchange of information require further negotiations on supplementary protocols to put scientific information into practice. Supplementary agreements have been used in the Bonn Convention and in the Barcelona Convention on the Mediterranean.

Supplementary negotiations also occur if a treaty provides for regular meetings of the parties to discuss progress and problems. Such meetings put pressure on reluctant nations and may become ad hoc negotiations on particular issues. The line between pressure to enforce obligations and discussions to clarify imprecise obligations is not, in such situations, a clear one.

Negotiations may also be ongoing because a party may change its mind. For example, nations may want to extend the obligations of the initial treaty. Also, they may want to lift reservations that they originally made, agree to stricter interpretations or criteria, or add areas to be conserved.

If the initial treaty contains only general principles rather than clear directives, research may be needed to determine what the principles require in practice. Research may also be used to persuade reluctant nations to accept obligations that might have been unacceptable if the implications had been clearly stated at the start.

The implementation of treaties has to be monitored, and parties have to discuss what to do when areas suddenly become threatened. Progressive implementation is sometimes required in habitat conservation, especially if nations cannot totally meet their treaty obligations on the day that the treaty comes into force. Habitats that are not threatened may not need conservation measures immediately. Acquisition, if required, cannot be accomplished overnight, and management plans take time to prepare.

Another reason why negotiations are ongoing is that if a treaty says that an obligation is fulfilled only if a protected area is important enough (such as in World Heritage Convention sites and national parks), an assessment is needed to determine if the proposed sites meet the requirements. These assessments may require negotiation about enlarging or improving the areas.

Negotiations may also be ongoing because issues arise that were not foreseen by the scientists or drafters of the initial treaty. The issues may not be resolved by the original treaty, or they may have been considered too detailed to be dealt with in the initial treaty.

Biological treaties usually provide for an exchange of information on such matters as the management of stocks or populations to be conserved. The information is used to assess the adequacy or success of measures taken and to identify new problems. Data on exploitation levels must be discussed and verified. Nations may trust each other if the treaty operates smoothly. If it does not, additional means of verification may be needed.

Controversies about whether obligations have been carried out fully, or about the consequences of an action or inaction, are partly or wholly scientific issues. They are not suitable for resolution by a court and are, therefore, likely to be left for scientists to discuss.

In general, the atmosphere in conservation negotiations—especially in negotiations with "altruistic" objectives rather than those concerned with competitive exploitation of an inadequate resource—is one of cooperation. Cooperation promotes ongoing negotiations and allows parties to regard them as a way to solve problems.

Finally, when a broadly worded framework convention has been adopted without a plan of action or statement of what should be done next, further discussions are needed to set priorities.

The importance of an independent scientific body. Biological conservation treaties need an independent scientific body to supervise and promote the application and enforcement of the treaty. Such a body can identify what supplementary measures are required, develop plans, collect and distribute scientific and economic information, and update lists of species and habitats that require conservation. A scientific body can provide technical advice to parties and potential parties, thereby making the treaty more effective. Even regular meetings of the parties are not a satisfactory substitute for a body that is independent enough to call attention to and criticize nations for failing to implement a treaty.

An independent body is particularly important for the success of multilateral treaties covering a variety of species and habitats. Only an independent body can have a useful and effective role as an arbiter and enforcer. Lyster (1985) repeatedly calls for such a body, and attributes the failure of some conventions to the absence of any organization capable of such a role. The European Community's (EC) directive and resolution on conservation of migratory birds, like the EC's other environmental measures, have depended on the role of the Commission of the European Communities (Temple Lang, 1982, 1990).

The role of nongovernment organizations. Another feature of biological conservation treaties and negotiations is the role of nongovernment organizations. These may be international, such as the International Union for the Conservation of Nature and Natural Resources, the Worldwide Fund for Nature (formerly the World Wildlife Fund), the International Council for Bird Preservation, and the International Waterfowl Research Bureau.

They also may be national bodies with significant international interests and activities, such as, in the United Kingdom, the Royal Society for the Protection of Birds.

These bodies vary in size, influence, motivation, professionalism, and effectiveness. They also vary in technique. Some are actively aggressive, and others are weighty and "respectable." The more influential bodies fulfill important functions. They urge governments to initiate negotiations for new treaties, and to ratify treaties that have been signed. They prepare useful drafts of new treaties on the basis of which negotiations take place. They provide continuing pressure for better implementation and enforcement of treaties, especially if they attend meetings of the parties.

The problem of reluctant participants. All nations that are on the migration routes or in the distribution ranges of a species to be conserved, or that are involved in the trade to be regulated, must take part in the negotiations. If one nation does not take part, the efforts of the other nations may be wasted. Participants may see that the nonparticipating nation is receiving a free benefit, and decide not to continue to negotiate. However, even when persuaded to become a party, a reluctant nation may continue to cause difficulties.

One strategy to deal with the problem of nonparticipating nations is to write a treaty in such a way that it is strict enough to be useful, but not so strict that it makes nonparticipants unwilling to ratify it. Once the nation becomes a party, negotiating techniques may lead it to accept stricter obligations. These techniques include making the initial obligations minimal but progressively increasing their strictness; allowing the reluctant nation to opt out of obligations that it finds unacceptable; and drafting obligations to produce results, but not forcing parties to use a particular means to achieve them.

A nation can opt out of obligations considered too strict in several ways: by ratifying the treaty with reservations; by not becoming a party to a stricter protocol to the treaty; or by refusing, under the objection procedure, to be bound by decisions of the parties. This last tactic has in an interesting way influenced the implementation of the International Convention for the Regulation of Whaling. Because some nations opted out of the conservation decisions, the United States passed legislation authorizing sanctions against nations whose activities reduce the effectiveness of the International Whaling Commission's conservation measures. As world environmental problems become increasingly serious, national sanctions are likely to become increasingly necessary unless nations agree to more effective treaty procedures. The problem with sanctions in a conservation treaty is that denying a party the privileges of the treaty is unlikely to be a serious enough sanction. The need for effective means of preventing nations from benefiting from treaties without paying their share is one of the most important problems facing international law today.

Characteristics of Biological Conservation Negotiations

A study of several conventions (Lyster, 1985) points out that biological conservation negotiations usually have characteristics that together make them different from other types of negotiations and, to a lesser extent, from other environmental negotiations. The most important of these characteristics pertain to subject matter and the desired results; moral aspects; actors; cost-benefit issues and the negotiation process; negotiating alliances; and treaty-drafting, obligations, and compliance.

Subject matter and the desired results. Biological conservation negotiations are frequently about resources that are common to several states, whether or not the resources are exploited. They are often about new or increasingly serious issues; problems caused by the increased pressures of human population or habitat destruction, increased exploitation, new pollutants, or destructive technologies. Biological conservation negotiations often treat scientific problems that are difficult to understand because of their ecological complexity or because there has not been time for scientists to study them. Many problems require multidisciplinary solutions, and, in many cases, the answers are not known.

The success or failure of conservation measures, in principle, is capable of being measured over time. If the necessary funds and techniques are available, scientists can measure the decline or increase of the population to be conserved or the development of the area of a habitat to be protected. It is, however, not easy to measure habitat quality or genetic diversity. Both the strength of the scientific theories and the success or failure of the measures taken may be capable, in practice, of being measured only by quantitative statistical methods.

The need to conserve habitats and the inability of the "beneficiaries" (the species and habitats that are being conserved) to protect their own interests mean that mere enactment of rules is not enough. Negotiations need to bring about practical, often physical, measures that may be more effective and more valuable than rules, as well as more acceptable to the people in the area. These measures usually require money and the work of either a governmental conservation body or a private conservation organization. The nations whose biological conservation policies are most effective are those with the best nature conservation authorities, not those with the best-drafted legislation.

If there is inadequate information or uncertainty about scientific data or the validity of conclusions, negotiators must decide how cautious the measures should be (the "precautionary principle") and how much they should cost—not only in financial terms, but also in terms of the inconvenience they would cause and the regulations that would be required. Negotiators who are reluctant to agree to far-reaching conservation measures make extensive, often exaggerated use of any scientific uncertainty, especially when the costs of conservation measures are likely to be substantial to their national authorities or industrial interests.

Comprehensive biological treaties that are concerned with conserving more than one species must contain lists of species to be protected. The lists make the general obligations that are set out in the text concrete and specific. The lists may themselves be the subject of negotiations, and the scientific appropriateness of the lists may have an important bearing on the merits and effectiveness of the treaty as a whole. Revision of such lists is an important method of improving or adapting the treaty, and can usually be done without a formal treaty-amendment process. Lists that negotiators agree on initially are not always satisfactory, as they often result from compromises.

Most biological conservation measures either depend on or are concerned directly with effective conservation of the habitat or ecosystem in which the species exist. Significant influences on habitats may need to be controlled. Habitat conservation usually demands, at least in the medium and long term, integrated approaches to ecosystems. Any serious negotiation about habitat conservation needs to include the following elements:

- A statement of the objectives to be achieved or the general obligations undertaken.
- Criteria for identifying or selecting the sites subject to habitat conservation measures.
- Identification of the areas in question.
- An agreement on the nature of the conservation measures needed for each area identified.

Criteria do not need to be worked out in the negotiations for the treaty itself, provided that there is a way to have them written and adopted. Measures of different kinds and degrees of strictness may be needed in different areas, depending on the ecological threats in each area.

Treaties that deal with habitat conservation usually contain obligations that cover the results to be achieved without specifying the means for achieving them. It is up to scientists to identify the areas and determine the measures needed to conserve them effectively. A spirit of cooperation normally develops between scientists that helps them to reach agreements.

In theory, the same process and elements are needed in habitats outside nature reserves and national parks that are subject to habitat conservation obligations. No satisfactory formulas have yet been found for defining treaty obligations to protect habitats outside specifically protected areas. The formulas used in the Bonn Convention and in the EC directive on bird conservation are broad and imprecise.

Moral aspects. A growing number of nations regard conserving endangered species and biological diversity as a moral duty. Prompted by humanity's enlightened, long-term self-interest, nations feel morally bound to save part of the common heritage. This duty implies that all nations have a right to take whatever conservation actions they want without other nations objecting. For example, it is now generally accepted that nations that are not party to the Convention on International Trade in Endangered Species or the Vienna Convention on the Protection of the Ozone Layer cannot object, under GATT or other agreements, to restrictions on their exports of, for example, endangered species if they trade with nations that are parties to the treaties. In effect, nations can legally be made to suffer economic loss if they do not participate in a treaty. However, to avoid resentment and accusations of colonialism, negotiators and nongovernment organizations should not expect developing nations to bear a disproportionate share of the cost of conservation.

Actors. The actors in biological conservation negotiations include indigenous peoples, conservation bodies, the news media, scientific bodies, and local, regional, and national authorities. Biological conservation measures often demand special consideration for indigenous peoples who have traditionally exploited a species or whose use of land has not been compatible with conservation. This problem needs to be solved for moral reasons and because the cooperation of indigenous peoples is essential for effective conservation. Their knowledge is often valuable to scientists, and their way of life may be compatible with conservation.

The "beneficiaries" of biological conservation measures—wildlife—cannot represent themselves, negotiate, lobby, or sue. Therefore, conservation bodies that act on their behalf play an important role, especially if they are present at the negotiations and scientific discussions, or if they collect information that governments do not collect.

The news media and media-influenced public opinion can be significant actors in negotiations. The moral element in biological conservation and the arguments for conservation enable nongovernment groups to campaign actively and get publicity when they do. The issues in conservation negotiations are publicly known. Conservation-minded governments use the media to pressure reluctant nations during negotiations. As a result, reluctant delegations may have to explain their positions and face hostile criticism. Public interest, a feature of environmental negotiations, is particularly apparent in biological conservation negotiations, and puts significant pressure on reluctant governments to accept conservation measures. Media attention and public pressure are heightened if the issues were initially raised, as they often are, by nongovernment organizations, or if public opinion is stronger or more convinced than scientific opinion.

Because of the close relationships between policy, enforceability, and science, biological conservation treaties can be satisfactorily negotiated and drafted only by multidisciplinary teams that include lawyers and scientists. Both groups should understand as much as possible about the other's disciplines. Delegations sometimes include scientists who represent government conservation bodies and representatives of government bodies whose activities cause conservation problems. Technical and other problems may be solved by bilateral discussions between the technical experts of delegations who understand what measures are objectively needed. There may be differences of opinion within delegations, and alliances may form between like-minded people in different delegations.

Because many biological conservation measures depend on physical-planning measures, land-use policies, nature reserves, and management plans, the role of local, regional, and national authorities is important. A nation or federation may negotiate a treaty, but its implementation and success may depend on the actions of local or regional authorities. This dependence can cause legal complications in federations and similar bodies (Temple Lang, 1986, 1987). Local and regional authorities must receive clear explanations of treaties and be consulted about them.

Cost-benefit issues and the negotiating process. In principle, conservation should benefit all parties. In practice, neither the costs nor the benefits are shared equally among nations. Bargaining, therefore, tends to be about short-term costs and long-term gains, serious inequalities of costs and benefits, and substantial differences in the structural features of nations. A large part of some negotiations are also concerned with how extensive and strict the obligations should be, in particular when the negotiations are based on a draft prepared by a conservation body like the IUCN or the IWRB.

Negotiators have to achieve, within their own negotiating positions, a balance between costs and benefits. In multilateral negotiations this process becomes a search, often in informal discussions, for a formula appropriate to all, rather than an effort to reduce costs and increase benefits vis-à-vis other parties. In some multilateral negotiations, the costs of implementing measures are moderate and evenly distributed between parties. In others, a party's obligations are partly under its control; that is, parties may have a discretion to determine how far they will go to carry out the aims of the treaty. Sometimes, as in the case of tropical forests, the world benefits from their conservation, but the costs fall on only a few nations, the ones in which the forests are found. It is essential for the success of a biological conservation treaty that the nations in which the main populations or habitats exist are persuaded to ratify the treaty.

The great variety of species and issues in biological conservation often cause policy problems that are neither totally legal nor totally scientific, and that often involve compromises between legitimate objectives. For example, customs officials may not always be able to distinguish between species that are endangered and species that are not. Is it realistic to expect customs officials to know the difference?

When the resources to be conserved are exploited, negotiations must try to bring about a sustainable yield. This often means reducing short-term overexploitation, either by outside commercial interests (who then form an anticonservation lobby) or by local people whose interests are not always fully represented by their government. Ongoing management for a sustainable yield can be based only on scientific advice, not on pressure from lobbyists.

Negotiating alliances. Small nations in negotiations often form alliances, which can be very effective, especially if they use the news media for publicity.

Treaty-drafting, obligations, and compliance. After negotiators have agreed on what criteria they will use to identify areas, species, or populations in need of conservation, they must compile lists of the areas or populations that meet the criteria. Well-prepared lists provide a basis for assessing how well governments have carried out their obligations. The lists also allow parties to negotiate the precise, concrete, and practical results of the obligations. Supplementary lists are especially useful if there is no list in the treaty itself, or if a list is an illogical compromise of various lists drawn up to meet different criteria. Efforts to achieve consistency on the basis of lists that are not themselves consistent, cause a great deal of trouble.

When questions arise over whether a party has fulfilled its treaty obligations, the aim of a formal or informal settlement is different in biological conservation treaties from other kinds of treaties. There is no question of compensation, because the damage cannot be measured precisely in money, and cannot be paid to the "beneficiaries." The aim of a settlement process in this case is to persuade the nation at fault to fulfill its obligations. Persuasion, rather than judicial or arbitral procedure, is required. Persuasion works best if the negotiators on both sides are scientists.

Some of the older multilateral biological conservation treaties are ambiguous, but recent treaties are more precise and legally binding (Lyster, 1985; Temple Lang, 1982, 1990). The older treaties may have been the best possible at the time, but they should not be used as precedents. A biological conservation treaty is useful only if it results in measures that would otherwise not have been taken. Areas that are already protected are usually not better protected by additional commitments. Scientists are less likely to forget this than diplomats. This means, among other things, that complicated procedures should not be established for applying weak obligations.

A treaty imposing modest obligations that are 100% fulfilled may be more satisfactory for lawyers than a treaty imposing strict obligations that are incompletely fulfilled. The effect of both treaties on populations and habitats may be the same. However, the stricter treaty can be used in ongoing negotiations: the less-strict treaty cannot.

The most effective treaties are not necessarily the most precisely drafted treaties. Provided that the treaty is the subject of ongoing discussion, and that the drafting is not fundamentally flawed by obligations only to "endeavor" to do something, an imprecisely worded treaty may be a reasonably satisfactory basis for valuable activity. The best treaties are those that are most effectively acted on.

Some biological conservation treaties are not well drafted because drafters realized that a genuine desire to collaborate was more valuable than arguments over inconveniently strict obligations. The drafters are often aware that they are writing a new kind of treaty, and that no nation can solve all problems in one document.

The trend toward obligations to conserve habitats and communities of species is a wise and necessary one. No species can be conserved without its habitat, and habitat destruction or deterioration will destroy a species more surely than most forms of exploitation or pollution. Only habitat-conservation obligations form the basis for an ecosystem approach.

Without a doubt, biological conservation treaties are becoming more complex. Effective conservation of habitats is more complicated than conserving single species. Managing threatened resources for sustainable yield, if the resulting products are traded internationally, is far more complex than banning products. Provision and management of funds under treaties are always complicated; but provision of funds to poor countries may become an essential element in worldwide conservation treaties, and may be the only way to solve problems when the costs and benefits of conservation are not equally shared. Funds may be essential to persuade developing countries to accept obligations that they may feel they cannot easily afford.

Biological conservation treaties often have, in effect, more than one class of party: some nations undertake all treaty obligations, others undertake the minimum or none at all. To force reluctant nations not to become free riders, it might be useful to divide parties into full- or first-class parties (that is, nations that have accepted all the additional protocols or supplementary obligations added to the basic treaty) and second-class parties. This distinction might be merely a matter of nomenclature, or it might also involve loss of rights under the treaty. The political effect of losing first-class status might be a way of getting reluctant nations to ratify a protocol. Many conservation treaties operate partly by making it embarrassing for nations to remain outside them. As far as possible, biological conservation treaties should include measures to be taken against nations that do not fulfill their obligations under the treaties, or that fail to accept necessary but additional obligations. If the treaties themselves do not provide these sanctions or loss of rights, other parties will take unilateral measures to put pressure on uncooperative nations.

If sanctions are imposed in accordance with a treaty, the obligations need to be precise so that there is little doubt when an obligation has not been met. Some important obligations, such as those on habitat conservation, do not seem to be precise enough. Some obligations are precise and clear once the scientific facts are known, others are so imprecise that their implications are not clear even when the facts are fully available. Some provisions in conservation treaties have not been designed to be justiciable. They are intended to be applied by scientists rather than by lawyers. Provided that the preconditions (such as regular meetings or an independent body to enforce the treaty) are fulfilled, that approach can be successful. But that cannot in itself solve the problem of the reluctant nation.

Special Features of Biological Negotiations

Biological conservation negotiations contain, to a greater or lesser extent, the characteristics of other environmental negotiations identified by Guy-Olivier Faure and Jeffrey Z. Rubin in Chapter 2. However, bilateral and multilateral biological conservation negotiations and initial and posttreaty negotiations that are ongoing differ in some respects. This section examines the special attributes of biological conservation negotiations.

Multiple parties and multiple roles. A striking feature of biological negotiations is the involvement of international conservation bodies that may produce a draft treaty, act as technical advisers, and perform as arbitrators in resolving difficulties in negotiations, without ever becoming parties to the treaty.

Meaningless boundaries. Unless political boundaries follow natural features such as mountains or straits, they are irrelevant to biological conservation except insofar as they limit the enforcement activities of parties to a treaty. This situation creates the free rider problem. It requires nations to cooperate with each other, especially over the conservation of migratory species or populations.

Long time frame. The time for biological conservation solutions to take effect is not as long as in other types of negotiations, such as climate change or pollution. In some negotiations to protect threatened species or ecosystems, quick action may be needed to prevent the species from becoming extinct or the habitat from disappearing. Conservation measures may involve stopping exploitation for a short period to allow a population or resource to increase to a certain level before it can again be exploited. Also, in the area of biological diversity, negotiators to some extent have to trade short-term costs for long-term gains and must think in terms of the time it will take to do this intelligently.

Scientific and technical uncertainty. This often exists in biological conservation negotiations. The precautionary principle is particularly important in biological negotiations, because of the risk that species may disappear if adequate precautions are not taken in time.

Power asymmetry. This exists only in some negotiations, usually for geographical reasons similar to those that create asymmetry in pollution negotiations. For example, one nation may be destroying the summer breeding area of a migratory population that, in winter, is harvested in another nation. Or, overfishing by large-scale methods may threaten the livelihood of an isolated community using less-destructive methods. In such cases the source of power is the degree of control a nation has over the fate of an endangered species. But asymmetry of power does not seem to be a general property of negotiations on biological diversity.

Public opinion. This is an important factor in some negotiations, in particular if the species needing conservation is popular with the public. Public opinion strengthens the influence of nongovernment conservation bodies and of international conservation organizations and puts pressure on reluctant nations. However, it is harder to mobilize public opinion for ecosystems than for species.

Institutionalization of solutions. Multilateral negotiations almost always require regular meetings of the parties, and usually produce more effective measures if there is an independent, scientific, secretariat-type body to monitor, improve, and administer the regime. In bilateral fishery arrangements, regular meetings of scientists may achieve similar results. All ongoing negotiations are a form of institutionalization.

New regimes and rules. In biological conservation, as with all environmental matters, what matters is what gets done, not what a treaty says.

Joint interests. There is a joint interest in conserving biological resources, even those that are not exploited. However, this interest may not be obvious to people who are only interested in money.

Negative perceptions of immediate outcomes. Most biological conservation measures cause a short-term inconvenience or loss of profit. But a greater obstacle may be in convincing people of the importance of conserving species or ecosystems.

Multiple issues. The number and variety of issues in biological conservation negotiations varies greatly. Negotiations about joint exploitation of a fishery may only be concerned with assessing and sharing the total allowable catch. But negotiations about conserving small whales may be concerned with their being accidentally caught in fishing nets, poisoned by pollutants, prevented from breeding, or deprived of food by overfishing. If the whale population is exploited, it may be necessary to consider the socioeconomic effects of a ban on whaling in certain communities. All negotiations on the conservation of habitats are likely to raise numerous other issues.

Changing actors. In biological conservation negotiations, the actors should change little as the negotiations progress. Each expert needs to be involved throughout, because ongoing negotiations are primarily technical.

11

The Law of the Sea Conference:
Lessons for Negotiations
to Control Global Warming

JAMES K. SEBENIUS

Ongoing and future negotiations to control global warming parallel the earlier United Nations-sponsored Law of the Sea (LOS) negotiations in many important respects. Obviously, both the oceans and the atmosphere are global resources. Moreover, when the General Assembly authorized the 1992 United Nations Conference on Environment and Development (UNCED), whose mandate includes global issues such as climate

AUTHOR'S NOTE: This work has benefited from the ideas and helpful comments generously offered by Lance Antrim, Arthur Applbaum, Sorin Bodea, Albert Carnesale, Abram Chayes, William Clark, Robert Dorfman, Tommy T. B. Koh, Henry Lee, Marc Levy, Ronald Mitchell, Bradford Morse, Howard Raiffa, Elliot Richardson, Jeffrey Rubin, Eugene Skolnikoff, Lawrence Susskind, John Swing, Peter Thacher, and Shirley Williams, as well as members of the Negotiation Roundtable at Harvard and the Salzburg Environmental Initiative. This chapter draws freely on previous work (Sebenius, 1984; 1991a) and incorporates by reference the relevant bibliographic citations contained therein.

change, it forged a direct personal link to the LOS experience by choosing T. T. B. "Tommy" Koh as chairman of the Preparatory Commission. Koh, who later became Singapore's ambassador to the United States, was president of the LOS Conference during its final decisive sessions. Designed to come together with the 1992 UNCED Conference were the deliberations of the Intergovernmental Negotiating Committee (INC) on climate change, which began in 1991 and were also sponsored by the UN General Assembly. Given current and future diplomatic activities dealing with global climate change, it becomes more important to explore the deeper implications of the intensive and precedential LOS experience for negotiated responses to the prospect of greenhouse warming.

On the positive side, contrary to the predictions of many knowledgeable observers, a broadly acceptable LOS Conference—an international "constitution for the oceans"—resulted from this mammoth effort despite technical complexity, uncertainty, and ideological division. It is quite possible that something similar to the present convention would have been ratified by the United States if completed during the Nixon, Ford, or Carter administrations. The twelve year negotiation process and the resulting LOS treaty have reduced much of the ocean conflict that was burgeoning at the outset of the negotiations. Claims of extended territorial jurisdiction into the ocean—a prime U.S. motivation for participating in the LOS Conference—have been largely moderated, while hot conflicts have diminished such as the "cod war" between the United Kingdom and Iceland (which involved not only gunfire but Iceland's threat to expel a NATO base). Rights to fish, offshore oil, deep seabed minerals (the "common heritage of mankind"), and other resources have been clarified; agreements were reached on rules for the protection of the marine environment along with the conduct of marine scientific research. The conference itself made several innovations, from negotiations by a "single text" process to novel roles for conference officers to unique structure and voting systems for an international seabed authority. Given these factors—and that the atmosphere, like the oceans, is a "global" resource—there have been calls from some quarters, notably at the 1988 Toronto Conference on the Changing Atmosphere, for a loosely analogous, comprehensive Law of the Atmosphere to address global warming (Zaelke & Cameron, 1990).

By contrast, many view the Law of the Sea as precisely the wrong way to negotiate a convention. As British UN Ambassador Sir Crispin Tickell noted, "There are many . . . who would like to look forward to a Law of the Atmosphere on the same lines as the Law of the Sea. To them I counsel caution." More bluntly, United Nations Environment Program (UNEP) Executive Director Mostafa Tolba declared, "With an eye toward the frustrations and difficulties in the elaboration of the Law of the Sea, I don't want to see UNEP take on a 'Mission Impossible' " (Tolba, 1989). The process was conducted at a level of detail that arguably should have been unthinkable in a treaty framework; moreover, 20 years after its inception, the result has yet to enter into force. For those who hold these views, if there is a lesson to be learned from the Law of the Sea as an example of how to negotiate a convention, especially with respect to the possibility of a comprehensive Law of the Atmosphere, it is simple and resounding: "Don't!"

Faced with these sharply conflicting views of the implications of the LOS experience for climate-change negotiations, therefore, this chapter seeks more nuanced answers to the question, What lessons does the Law of the Sea contain for possible global action on climate change? Rather than join the substantive controversy over global warming and judge the scientific or economic underpinnings of the issue, however, this essay simply takes as a point of departure—for purposes of analysis—the currently intense political concerns about climate change and addresses present and future diplomatic efforts to fashion a collective response.

Law of the Sea and Climate-Change Negotiations: Critical Similarities and Consequential Differences

Critical Similarities

The range of vital interests at stake makes quick negotiations with decisive results unlikely. Both the Law of the Sea and the climate-change negotiations affect major national interests of many countries, virtually guaranteeing the time-consuming nature of any meaningful negotiations. In the case of the Law of the Sea talks, vital interests at stake included definition of the territorial sea, fishing rights, oil on the outer continental shelves, submarine passage under straits, naval and maritime mobility, overflight of international and territorial waters, marine pollution, scientific research, manganese nodules, and other deep-sea resources.

Climate change also covers a number of separate issue-areas. New rules to deal comprehensively with the greenhouse effect could greatly alter a range of crucial national activities for many countries. In conventional scenarios, slightly less than half of the expected warming from emissions during the 1980s comes from energy-related activities (coal, petroleum, and natural gas), with nonenergy industrial activities (mainly chlorofluorocarbons, CFCs) delivering about a quarter or less depending on the effects of the Montreal Protocol, and land-use activities (deforestation, rice cultivation, fertilization, and so on) causing the rest. About 55% of the expected contribution to warming from emissions during this period is due to carbon dioxide, with CFCs (24%), methane (15%), and nitrous oxides delivering the rest. About half of the expected warming will reflect population growth and about half will reflect growth in per capita demand. Some 40% of the expected warming now comes from activities in the developing nations, a figure that may rise to 60% by the end of the 21st century. (These proportions are reversed, of course, for the developed world.) Thus issues of both economic growth for the industrial nations and economic development in the Third World will be critical as possible responses to global warming are fashioned.

It is widely assumed that negotiators will seek to hammer out an overall or nation-by-nation schedule of emission reductions, such as the 20% decrease in carbon dioxide by the year 2005 that was discussed by 68 nations during the November 1989 Ministerial Conference on Atmospheric Pollution and Climate Change held in Noordwijk, the Netherlands (*Noordwijk Declaration,* 1989). Yet, any such simple target will face overwhelming complexities. In part, as Michael Grubb of the Royal Institute of International Affairs has argued cogently, this derives from the great variation in the energy economies of different nations. Carbon emissions per unit of gross national product vary internationally by a factor of more than 10. Sizable international differences in population, level of development, fuel mix, amount and kind of energy reserves (from high-carbon coal to low-carbon natural gas to no-carbon hydro), and industrial and transportation patterns add up to a powerful case for the complexity and difficulty of reaching negotiated targets. In short, to seek equal absolute or percentage reductions (à la Montreal) or efficiency targets or similar benchmarks will entail inequities and frustrations. Grubb (1990) concludes that the notion of "all the countries of the world sitting around a table and agreeing on who should reduce by how much . . . like the Montreal Protocol writ large [is an] illusion best dispersed before it leads us irretrievably down a blind alley." By late 1990, the nations of the European Community had committed themselves to a *collective* greenhouse stabilization target. Yet within a year, negotiations to establish *individual* country targets consistent with reaching the collective EC target had failed—and attention turned from targets per se to energy taxes that increased with carbon content.

Given the high level of public concern about the greenhouse issue, many environmental advocates expect quick negotiations adopting decisive, sustained actions to mitigate greenhouse gas emissions. By late 1990, the optimistic view was supported by the significant number of industrial countries that unilaterally or in small groups had committed themselves to greenhouse gas stabilization or reduction targets (although there is a long road between target and result). These included the European Community, the European Free Trade Agreement nations, Japan, Canada, Australia, and others. Yet, powerful economic and political actors will face potential restrictions and will seek to delay, avoid, and shift abatement costs. Even more than the 12-year Law of the Sea process, climate-change negotiations could impinge seriously on a range of vital activities and should be expected to be an enduring feature of the diplomatic landscape.

Genuine mutual dependence gives real leverage to all sides and implies the centrality of North-South issues. In any large-scale climate-change negotiation, as was the case with the Law of the Sea, developing nations (the South) will have a major influence on something that many developed nations (the North) want or genuinely fear. Despite an air of greater pragmatism at the UN today than was the case in the 1970s, this may lead to Southern insistence on an agenda derived from principles of the New International Economic Order (NIEO), including significant wealth redistribution, greater participation for less developed countries (LDC) in the world economy, and greater Third-World control over global institutions and resources. Already, United Nations General Assembly debates and early sessions of the preparatory commissions for the 1992 negotiations on environment and development have included NIEO-like LDC demands for technology transfer and large resource commitments from the industrial world.

To develop the parallel with climate talks, it is instructive to review the source of LDC leverage in the LOS negotiations. Major maritime establishments, especially in the former Soviet Union and the United States, were powerfully motivated in the 1960s by the desire to stop so-called jurisdictional creep or the tendency for territorial claims to expand and cast an ever-widening net of restrictions on submarine, ship, and aircraft mobility in what had traditionally been the high seas. Developing nations in South America, along with those bordering critical straits (such as Gibraltar, Malacca, Singapore, and Bab el Mandeb), had asserted many such claims during the 1950s and 1960s and could have continued this expansionist territorial trend. As a result, previously routine maritime activities could have been increasingly curtailed, could have required politically costly confrontations, or could have led to endless renegotiations with coastal or straits states (resembling base rights negotiations). Thus the developing world influenced something of high value to the maritime powers.

Emboldened by this genuine maritime interdependence, many developing nations effectively pressed for a seabed regime modeled on NIEO precepts. This real LDC leverage meant that the maritime powers could not reject NIEO demands without cost and just walk away.[1] This perceived vulnerability to LDC coastal state power kept the United States and other maritime powers at the LOS bargaining table for years, but ideological disagreements ultimately spurred a rejection of the treaty.

The long-term success of global climate-change negotiations is impossible without the cooperation of the developing world. Greenhouse gases in the atmosphere now are mainly due to developed nations. With projected population and economic growth in the developing world, however, the source of the greenhouse problem will shift rapidly over time, especially if India and China choose the least expensive development paths that rely on their vast coal resources. China, for example, now plans to expand its coal consumption fivefold by 2020, a result that would add nearly 50% to current worldwide carbon emissions (Grubb, 1990). Anti-global warming steps agreed to and accepted by the developed world alone could be heavily offset over time by inaction in the developing nations; by 2050, projected warming without developing nation cooperation would be 40% higher than with it (Lashoff & Tirpak, 1989).

Thus, the developed world cannot solve the climate problem in the long run without the cooperation of the LDCs.[2] In the case of the CFC negotiations, developing nations' concerns played a significant role in the Vienna/Montreal process. Many LDCs concurred with the 1985 Vienna Framework Convention with its hortatory language about their concerns, but were disappointed with the final Montreal result that contained only general undertakings on funding for ozone-friendly technology for the developing world. India, China, and Brazil—all potentially significant future CFC producers—did not initially sign the Montreal Protocol. They were especially irritated by the Bush administration's decision—ultimately reversed after a firestorm of international environmental protest—against contributing to a fund intended to assist LDCs in this area. Only after substantial and far more specific undertakings were made in London during the June 1990 meetings, did key LDC representatives agree to urge their governments to sign a strengthened protocol.

Although it has been moderated considerably since the 1970s, the underlying ideological template, present in both the LOS and Vienna/Montreal negotiations, is that of the New International Economic Order. It is quite possible that either or both of the INC framework/protocol processes and the 1992 conference could end up focusing mainly on generalized North-South concerns expressed in well-worn NIEO terms. The risk, to be assessed later in more detail, is that the attempted use of real Southern leverage on behalf of NIEO precepts might meet Northern intransigence based on antipathy to the underlying ideology. Any progress on climate issues per se could be blocked as a result. Further, Northern opponents of climate-change action may well use the actual or alleged NIEO-like character of a proposed regime as a basis for political opposition to a greenhouse convention.

Like the Law of the Sea, therefore, the range and depth of the vital national interests involved combined with the real interdependence means that climate-change talks contain the ingredients for an inescapable, long-term engagement with the prospect of North-South clashes. As will be discussed, creative steps are essential for meeting legitimate interests while reducing the risk that such an engagement will result in endless delay and damaging ideological confrontation.

Consequential Differences

A "convention of expansion" versus a "convention of limitation." Perhaps the most important difference between the Law of the Sea and significant climate-change negotiations is the fundamental nature of each enterprise. Much of the LOS accord granted or legitimated a series of previously tenuous new claims to resources by many states. For example, the United States solidified its claim to the rich resources contained in more than 2.2 million additional square miles of ocean space off its coastlines. Mankind in general, with special provisions for developing nations, developed a mechanism to share in any eventual benefits of completely new and physically vast resources of the deep seabed. Devising an LOS convention of expansion involved the relatively easy problem of how to divide an expanding pie.[3] By contrast, climate-change negotiations probably will focus on developing convention(s) of limitation, of shared sacrifice, and of painful transfers and compensation—requiring curtailments in energy use, more expensive LDC development paths, changes in agricultural patterns, cessation of currently profitable deforestation, and other such activities. To the extent that climate-change negotiations are perceived as allocating sacrifices, they fundamentally will be more difficult than the LOS problem of allocating "new" resources. Of course, to the extent that the participants focus on the joint gains relative to preventing a feared climate disaster, the process will be that much easier. And some groups that will benefit directly—such as the vendors of renewable, cleaner, more efficient energy and the technologies that make such energy use possible—may join environmental advocates as vocal proponents of a greenhouse control regime.

The "common heritage of mankind" was not a true global commons. Though the atmosphere is widely and correctly recognized as a global "commons," such status is analytically distinct from what many people see as a similarity to deep seabed resources—which the UN General Assembly unanimously declared as the "common heritage of mankind." This declaration concerned collective property rights to manganese nodules. By contrast, the global atmosphere is a true commons because any greenhouse gas emissions from a single country eventually will mix and adversely affect the entire world.[4] True commons resources contain economic disincentives for individual initiatives to curb emissions (Hardin, 1968). This results from the fact that the full costs of efforts to mitigate harmful emissions by one state can be borne fully by that state—while the benefits of such actions are diffused throughout the global community. Moreover, any benefits of actions that would slow the present rate of growth of greenhouse gases would be felt only decades hence by the inhabitants of a future world. Thus, facing full costs of abatement today but enjoying only a fraction of any future benefits, individual entities lack powerful incentives to cease emitting.[5] Moreover, an abatement agreement can be frustrated by the inherent commons characteristic of the climate problem that allows those who do nothing to take a "free ride" on any costly actions others might take to mitigate the problem.

The LOS negotiations addressed immediate problems and conflicts, not future uncertain ones. While global climate change threatens a rise in sea level, crop pattern alterations, increased variability and severity of weather conditions, and a host of other consequences decades hence, most of these harms are subject to considerable scientific uncertainty about their timing, magnitude, and distribution across countries and regions. Indeed, for both genuine and cynical reasons, some observers even claim to see future winners as well as losers from global warming (such as milder winters in Massachusetts and Siberia, expanded areas of cropland in currently cold climates), a stance that could greatly complicate negotiations on costly mitigation measures.

By contrast, LOS negotiators faced a range of pressing problems as well as future concerns. Lyndon Johnson warned about an imminent "race to grab and hold the lands under the high seas"; other observers made dire predictions of the "biggest smash and grab" of (ocean) territory since the great powers carved up Africa in the late 19th century. Seaward territorial claims had proliferated; conflicts over fishing rights had frequently turned violent; ownership of oil under continental shelves was disputed; legal duties and liability provisions were muddled around ocean environmental disasters such as the breakup of the *Amoco Cadiz*; and a range of other problems proliferated. As Henry Kissinger (1975) apocalyptically warned, "The current [LOS] negotiation may thus be the world's last chance. . . . The breakdown of the current negotiation . . . will lead to unrestrained military and commercial rivalry and mounting political turmoil." Further, in addressing these ocean problems, LOS delegates could build on centuries of legal development, with a relatively small part of their task requiring entirely new legal regimes. By contrast, climate-change negotiators mainly face a distant, uncertain threat requiring entirely new legal rules and standards of behavior.

Climate-change issues are far more publicly salient. A primary difference from the LOS problems that favors action on climate change concerns the public salience of the issues and the magnitude of potential ecodisasters that threaten without a decisive collective response. In general, the Law of the Sea negotiations were quite obscure. By contrast, public concern about environmental issues in general, and global-warming issues in particular, is very high, and the demand for action could grow enormously. Actual and potential public concern, as drawn on and even shaped by activist negotiators, can be a major resource in pressuring governments toward international accommodation.

As difficult as the Law of the Sea negotiations proved to be and as mixed as their results, a comprehensive collective action on climate change would appear to face far higher obstacles: as a convention of limitation and restriction versus a convention of expansion, as a "true" global commons with the associated problems of incentives and free riding, and as a response to distant uncertain problems rather than to an immediate, tangible set of problems.

Lessons From the Law of the Sea Process

Some lessons from the Law of the Sea process, although valuable, are obvious: the importance of personalities, relationships, trust, mutual respect, and understanding of others' perceptions and real interests; the need to convert the negotiation process from blame-casting and ideological clash to joint problem solving; the value of focusing on future common interests as opposed to present conflicting ones; the critical importance of rules of procedure; the crucial effect of the choice of conference officers; and so on. Moreover, the specific processes, practices, and inventions of the conference and their evolution offer some useful lessons. Beyond these items, valuable lessons for climate negotiations derive from the LOS Conference itself, its global and comprehensive character, as well as the complexity and detail involved; from the formation of the Seabeds Committee in 1967, to the UN General Assembly's authorization in 1970 to start LOS negotiations in 1973, and to their conclusion in 1982. It is well worth investigating the causes behind this lengthy process. The balance of this chapter suggests and elaborates a dozen specific lessons from this and other aspects of the LOS experience for climate-change negotiators.

A broad agenda, universal participation, consensus, and the package deal. Several related factors contributed to the length of the LOS Conference. These included the sheer scope of the agenda, the large number of participating states, the vital importance of many of the issues to the national interests of the participants, the substantive and bargaining interrelationships among the various agenda items together with the objective of a single convention, the fact that the conference was progressively advancing international law and agreement rather than merely codifying existing practice, the degree of specificity and detail of the negotiations, the sometimes cumbersome and obstructionist tendencies of a "group" system in which like-minded states coalesced and acted in unison, the frequent difficulty that national bureaucracies had in LOS-related decision making, the novel nature of the Enterprise, and the requirements of expertise and technical knowledge.

However, taken together in this context, four cornerstones of the LOS process virtually guaranteed its duration and easily could do the same if adopted for global-warming negotiations. These included: (1) virtually universal participation; (2) a powerful set of rules and understandings aimed at taking all decisions by consensus (if at all possible); (3) a comprehensive agenda; and (4) the agreement to seek a single convention that would constitute a "package deal" (Evensen, 1986; Koh & Jayakumar, 1985).

Lesson 1. It would be a very time-consuming mistake for climate-change negotiators to create a universally inclusive process with respect to both issues and participants, together with the requirements of consensus on an overall package deal. As with the LOS process, the ultimate results would be held hostage to the most reluctant party on the most difficult issue.

A broad convention versus a framework convention and specific protocols. An understandable reaction to this aspect of the LOS experience has been the decision to seek a general framework convention on climate change followed by more specific and independent protocols. While ideally retaining the virtues of universal participation and consensus, these protocols on various subjects would not be lashed together in an enormous and unwieldy negotiating bundle; in a sense this negotiating vision is analogous to the LOS process but *minus* the comprehensive agenda linked into a package deal. To strive for a framework followed by manageable protocols has attractive negotiating features, but it was the failure of precisely this approach—of independent packages—in earlier LOS conferences (in 1958 and 1960) that led indirectly to the comprehensive package approach of the UN Conference on Law of the Sea III (UNCLOS III).

Lesson 2. Expect highly selective adherence to independent "mini-conventions" or "protocols" on separate issues.

By 1958 the International Law Commission had suggested a negotiating structure for the Law of the Sea Conference with four separate conventions, concerning different issues such as the breadth of the territorial sea and the extent of the continental margin. With respect to the comprehensive agenda that came to mark the 1973 LOS Conference, President Koh observed:

> The intention was for the present conference to adopt a single convention of wide acceptance promoting international stability. A disadvantage of adopting several conventions is that states will choose to adhere only to those which seem advantageous and not to others, leaving the door open to disagreement and confrontations.

Lesson 3. Expect great pressure to combine issues rather than negotiate separate protocols as is intended in the INC and UNECD talks.

Following the 1958 and 1960 LOS experiences, two separate negotiations were attempted; until linked, each proved fruitless. With deep seabed resources being declared as the "common heritage of mankind," the Seabeds Committee undertook a negotiation on the regime for seabed mining. Developing countries wanted this convention to offer meaningful participation in deep seabed mining and the sharing of its benefits. Yet the developed countries whose companies potentially possessed the technology, the capital, and the managerial capacity ultimately to mine the seabed saw no reason to be forthcoming, and these negotiations went nowhere. At about the same time, the United States, the former Soviet Union, and other maritime powers— greatly concerned about the increasing numbers of claims by coastal, straits, island, and archipelagic states to territory in the oceans—strenuously sought to organize a set of negotiations that would lead to a halt of such "creeping jurisdiction." In effect, the maritime powers were asking coastal states to cease an activity (claiming additional ocean territory) that was valuable to the coastal states, but without compensation. Not surprisingly, these discussions concerning limits on seaward territorial expansion in the ocean yielded little result. It was ultimately the linkage of these two issues, "navigation" and "nodules" in a bargaining sense, that was at the heart of the comprehensive LOS Conference negotiations.

The LOS negotiations were certainly the products of large-scale "horse-trading" among different interests, but there were also widely shared interests, such as concern about radioactive contamination of the ocean and other environmental threats. Yet, as the negotiations evolved, those shared interests were not nearly strong enough to ensure the treaty. Indeed, noting the intense desire of many developed countries for environmental provisions with some force, certain developing countries—for both genuine reasons and tactical reasons—negotiated as if they did not want nor were able to afford even unrelated environmental provisions, unless the developed world made concessions.

With respect to climate-change negotiations, it is easy to imagine that separate protocols calling on different groups to undertake painful and costly measures will be rejected in a similar way unless they can be packaged in ways that offer sufficient joint gains to all. Since any action on climate change will involve shared and parallel sacrifice, it is probably only by linking issues such as technological assistance and various forms of compensation, financial or in kind, that many countries will be induced to join.

Lesson 4. Within the structure and procedures of the climate-change and related environmental negotiations, seek to link issues into packages that promise that sufficient joint gain is attractive to a large number of parties—yet that are not so broadly comprehensive as to risk excessive complexity and delay.

It is generally preferable to deal with issues on their separate substantive merits as much as possible, yet be alert to potential linkages to break impasses. This suggests a conference design with independent working/negotiating groups with a higher level body seeking to integrate the groups and facilitate valuable "trades."

The LOS experience suggests mutually beneficial "manageable packages" of protocols under a framework climate convention, and the same logic could be extended cautiously to other issues in the context of the 1992 Conference on Environment and Development. For example, desertification and soil erosion issues may be more pressing than greenhouse questions to key developing countries. Many developed countries that are unwilling to make what could be characterized as "bribes" to induce developing country participation may be more willing to be forthcoming on these regional issues in the context of a larger agreement that promises global climate benefits.

One of the most effective long-term steps that developing countries could take to combat global warming (as well as a host of other environmental issues) is a significantly stepped-up population control program.[6] Unlike, say, energy-use restrictions, this course of action helps rather than hinders economic development objectives. For cash-strapped LDCs, relatively modest developed country aid in this dimension could considerably enhance domestic population-control efforts. Unfortunately, population issues were not on the agendas of either the INC process or the 1992 UN Conference on Environment and Development.

Lesson 5. Link with caution. It can be extraordinarily difficult to "un-package" issues once they have been combined for bargaining purposes.

In the most prominent example from the LOS experience that illustrates this point, the United States was generally in favor of the navigational portions of the LOS treaty, but had problems with the concessions demanded on a seabed regime. The United States exerted strenuous efforts to unlink or separate these topics into manageable packages, but to no avail. The package deal was too strong in the minds of many delegates, and ultimately the convention contained both elements.

Outside scientific information and models. One unusual element of the LOS experience consisted of the influence of a computer model of deep ocean mining that was developed at the Massachusetts Institute of Technology (Sebenius, 1981). Largely as a result of its sponsorship, process, and other credible features, the MIT model came to be widely accepted in the face of tremendous uncertainty felt by the delegates about the engineering and economic aspects of deep seabed mining. A critical point in the negotiations occurred during a Saturday morning workshop—held outside the UN premises, under the auspices of Quaker and Methodist nongovernmental organizations (NGOs)—in which developed and developing country delegates were able to meet and extensively query the MIT team that had built and revised the model.

Over time, the delegates made frequent use of the model for learning about and inventing new options. In some cases, delegates even used the model's analysis as a political excuse to move from frozen positions. Similar roles were played by analyses offered by the U.S. Office of the Geographer in the State Department and by senior scientists from the U.S. Geological Survey on technically complex issues of continental shelves and boundary delimitations.

Analogous experiences leading to the Montreal Protocol on the protection of the ozone layer occurred at a series of informal, off-the-record workshops where diplomats and politically active participants in the negotiations gathered with scientific experts (Benedick, 1991). These informal events greatly increased scientific awareness and mutual understanding, improved relationships, and directed the process toward a successful treaty.

Lesson 6. Despite its potential abuse, outside scientific information—when it is objective and is accessible to all participants—can move a complex and deadlocked negotiation, even one that is highly politicized and ideologically controversial, toward mutual cooperation. Low-profile forums in which scientists and diplomats can interact can be very useful.

Unexpected dynamics. In conventions that involve many delegates handling many issues, leverage is diffused, procedural elements have unexpected consequences, and different groups and people become decisive in ways that need careful analysis. For example, the requirement that any action by the LOS Conference receive two thirds of the vote gave potential blocking power to any group larger than a third of the conference membership—even though consensus largely characterized conference decision making. At the beginning of the negotiations it was scarcely expected that the "landlocked and geographically disadvantaged states" would constitute such a blocking group as an artifact of this rule, but the results gave this unlikely group considerable sway over a range of issues.

Likewise, some of the most potent spoilers in the Law of the Sea process were those mineral-producing nations that felt threatened by the potential emergence of a competing seabed-mining industry. In particular, cobalt producer Zaire, nickel producers such as Cuba and Canada, and copper producers from Latin America and Africa become adroit at using treaty procedures and bloc politics to impose burdensome restrictions on a future seabed-mining regime. In general, one should expect the "politics of blocs"—both familiar and unanticipated—in such international conferences. There was an emergence not only of the traditional UN geographic groups such as the Asians, the Latins, and the Group of 77, but also of groups of states, for example, with wide continental margins that acted in concert and coordinated their strategies.

In large-scale climate-change negotiations, one might expect to see many such new groupings emerge around such common characteristics as states with large coal reserves (India, China), states generating a sizable fraction of their electricity through nuclear power (France, the Commonwealth of Independent States), energy-efficient states (Japan), island or low-lying states vulnerable to sea-level rise (Bangladesh, the Seychelles, the Maldives), as well as those that genuinely or cynically might act as if they would benefit from global warming (Argentina, the Commonwealth of Independent States). The positive aspect of such emergence is a clear articulation of their interests. A negative characteristic may be the tendency toward rigidity and obstructionist tactics.

The central role of various individuals and nations was even more difficult to anticipate. For example, in one of the crucial conference issues—how to divide any profits from an ultimate seabed-mining operation—the final agreement was struck between representatives of Pakistan,

Singapore, Mauritius, Argentina, and the United States. This was hardly a coalition that might have been expected on an a priori basis.

Lesson 7. Excessively detailed prior strategizing may be futile since it is very difficult to predict the negotiating dynamics of mega-conferences with widespread participation and agendas of broad scope.

Lessons From the U.S. Rejection of the LOS Treaty

One of the more significant aspects of the LOS experience was its blunt rejection by the United States; a careful analysis suggests lessons that transcend the actions of a conservative U.S. administration. To draw meaningful lessons for climate-change negotiations from the U.S. rejection of the LOS treaty requires a clear understanding of the rationale for the U.S. action by focusing on the dominant issues: navigation and ocean resources. As U.S. Ambassador Elliot Richardson explained, "Although the convention has . . . dealt with issues ranging all the way from piracy to vessel source pollution, its participants understood from the outset that the accommodation of navigational and resource issues must be at the core of any eventual single 'package deal' " (Richardson, 1980).

When an announced absolute requirement of maritime nations on one issue (mobility rights) is linked with an apparently flexible position on an issue of keen importance to developing nations (nodule mining), it should not be surprising that concessions on the latter issue are the currency with which the former demand is bought, most likely at a high price. This proposition is exemplified by the negotiating progression through the Nixon, Ford, and Carter years leading to the acceptance of the parallel system for manganese nodule mining.

In particular, the original "navigation for nodules" proposition no longer offered the lure of joint gain to the Reagan administration. U.S. interests had shifted to place a relatively heavier emphasis on seabed access and in particular a much greater negative weight on precedential aspects of the seabed regime. The alternatives to a negotiated agreement—assertion of customary law with the threat of force in the background, along with the "mini-treaty" option for nodule mining—looked far more tolerable than earlier assessment had held. "Paying dear" (with seabeds) for "something cheap" (navigation) looked like a bad bargain (Sebenius, 1984).

Blocking coalitions.[7] It is sobering to recall how the LOS treaty's burdens on seabed mining—for all intents and purposes a nonexistent industry—engendered tenacious and ultimately effective opposition, for both economic and ideological reasons. In the early days of the LOS process, U.S. industrialists supported a universal treaty as the only feasible means of ensuring them the needed 20 to 30 years of secure tenure over the vast ocean mine sites required by the technology (and their bankers). Yet as the seabed regime became more elaborate—with what prospective seabed miners judged to be onerous financial requirements, technology transfer provisions, production limitations, and a complex international regulatory bureaucracy—the industry grew increasingly strident in its opposition. As the UN treaty evolved, the industry began to support an alternative involving a much smaller group of countries—the so-called minitreaty option—and lobbied for it very actively in Congress, along with the broader U.S. mining and business communities and the administration.

Yet the raw economic self-interest of the seabed miners is an insufficient focus. The most effective vehicle found by the seabed-mining industry to oppose the LOS treaty was the great discomfort of many participants about the governance precedents involved in the entire exercise. *Wall Street Journal* editorialists, observers of the LOS process in conservative think tanks, and others were preoccupied with the UN's (earlier and unanimous) declaration that seabed resources were the "common heritage of mankind." Prior U.S. agreement with that principle, while dismissed by many at the time of UN resolution as bland, innocuous, and largely meaningless, turned out to have a dramatic effect both during the LOS negotiations themselves and subsequently toward energizing opposition to the treaty.

In response to such objections and to problems in the evolving seabed regime, the negotiation strategy of the United States can be understood as a detailed effort to generate a system that, while burdensome, was commercially workable. Ultimately, U.S. negotiators acceded to provisions that "gave" ideological declarations (on technology transfer, seabed production limits, and financial payments) to the developing world and cloaked commercially workable substantive provisions in quite visible trappings of the New International Economic Order. Close analysis, for example, of the technology transfer provisions of the LOS treaty suggests that it would be almost impossible to invoke them, and that the international community would obtain this technology by other, nonforcible means. The production limits were negotiated on the basis of technically complex formulas that generally ensured that they would pose no real constraint. The financial terms of contracts, if anything, are more flexible and efficient at sharing risks than most mining contracts negotiated for land-based contracts or oil leases. Enormous U.S. negotiating effort was expended in obtaining these substantive outcomes. Yet, an approach that in effect placed a relatively pragmatic system behind a Third-World facade proved decisive in energizing opposing ideological coalitions. (For an extended analysis of these assertions, see Sebenius, 1984.)

In a time when population policy, social issues, and the proper role of public authority are hotly contested in the United States, climate-change negotiations may well engender powerful blocking coalitions based on these ideological or precedential considerations. For example, while very real issues of efficiency and mission surrounded the sustained U.S. attacks on UNESCO, a sizable ideological component animates this U.S. policy. Likewise, if the shape, coloration, character, and language negotiated as part of a climate-change convention invoke images such as central command, heavy-handed international bureaucracy, forcible technology transfer, blame-casting ideological declarations, guilt-based wealth transfers, and the like, the results of any such negotiations run substantial risk of being overturned for these reasons.

Lesson 8. In an age of media-driven symbolic politics, be careful not to energize opponents by a negotiating strategy that appears to make major ideological concessions in return for pragmatic fine print.

Subjects for negotiation should be chosen carefully with an eye toward the potential blocking coalitions that may be energized by international action. After all, the LOS treaty was scuttled in the United States and other important industrial nations by the economic and ideological concerns of an industry segment (seabed mining) that did not even exist. With respect to the ozone process, the 1990 *Economic Report of the President* estimates the U.S. costs of compliance with the Montreal accord at $3.7 billion—one measure, since reduced, of the costs that motivate skeptical policymakers and corporations to oppose the treaty (U.S. Council of Economic Advisors, 1990). Despite periodic public concern over the ozone layer, the Montreal treaty was effectively delayed for several years by these groups until the scientific consensus shifted. The same report cites the costs of an anti-greenhouse measure to cut carbon dioxide emissions by 20% at between $800 billion and $3.6 trillion (Manne & Richels, 1990; for a contrasting view, see Williams, 1989). If these figures are even remotely accurate, they suggest that those concerned by large-scale greenhouse control (such as policy skeptics, coal and oil companies, automakers) would have an economic motivation for opposition—regardless of the level of environmental benefits—literally hundreds of times stronger than that of the CFC industry.

One of the greatest mistakes that might be made by a comprehensive climate-change convention would be to energize and unify a large set of otherwise independent potentially opposing interests. An unlikely but illustrative domestic parallel may be found in Michael Pertschuk's stewardship of the formerly sleepy Federal Trade Commission (FTC) in the late 1970s. The FTC had launched a number of rule-making efforts directly affecting a range of small-business interests in the United States, from funeral homes and used car dealers to optometrists and others. Further, the FTC decided to challenge the issue of "kidvid," or children's television advertising, that not only threatened major media advertising revenues, but also smacked of First Amendment restrictions. In effect, by energizing and unifying an enormous coalition of large and small businesses and media companies—many of whom formerly had been bitter rivals in Washington politics—the FTC engendered a firestorm of protest, had its budget and authority slashed, and was shut down for some time. In part, Pertschuk's legacy was a far more unified and politically effective business community. A comprehensive Law of the Atmosphere, replete with across-the-board regulations that affect several potentially powerful interests, would run the grave risk of energizing and unifying otherwise independent forces—targeted oil companies, coal-mining interests, or automobile-manufacturing firms, as well as various agricultural concerns—let alone the full range of human activities that result in greenhouse gases.

Lesson 9. Those concerned with organizing effective international action to combat global warming should carefully anticipate having to deal with the potential blocking coalitions that it in turn may create—for both economic and ideological reasons.

Beyond converting opponents by irresistible science and appealing to shared interests, careful procedural and substantive choice can sometimes prevent their formation at the outset (Sebenius, 1991). Opponents sometimes may be swayed by providing selective incentives, by linking issues as "side payments," by demonstrating how a new control regime really would be in their interest, or by inventing new options that sidestep specific objections. Opponents sometimes may be isolated and overwhelmed by political pressure, divided and conquered, lulled, or simply outmaneuvered.

In this connection, recall that the climate negotiations have aimed at producing a general "framework" convention, followed by specific "protocols." As such, the choice of which specific issues or protocols to pursue, singly, in combination, or in sequence (for example, transportation, energy, tropical forestry) will heavily determine which interests will arise to oppose action. Protocols have been suggested, seemingly without much explicit analysis of their implications for negotiating success, on a virtually endless number of potential subjects (such as targets for reducing national greenhouse gas or carbon emissions, credits for providing carbon "sinks," automotive transportation, industrial energy use, tropical forestry, agricultural practices, sea-level rise, technology transfer, international funds to aid LDCs, population growth, a carbon tax, tradable emission permits, and methane controls). A good way to guarantee an endless negotiating impasse would be to handle all or many of the above mentioned protocols in a comprehensive Law of the Atmosphere package to be agreed upon by consensus. Despite potential joint gains from trades across disparate issues, and economic efficiency considerations, a comprehensive climate-change convention might well energize and unify a large set of otherwise separate opposing interests. To avoid creating a potent unified opposing coalition, one option is to proceed sequentially with protocols. Greenhouse control advocates might first pick "easy" subjects—protocols directed at greenhouse contributors that are politically weak, morally suspect, and concentrated in countries with a strong Green movement—to generate momentum, with strategically chosen later protocols building on early successes.

Another preventive approach to the problem of domestic blocking entities would be the early negotiations of a protocol specifying a baseline date after which anti-greenhouse measures taken by individual nations would be credited against the requirements of a later international agreement (Moomaw, 1990). With such an agreed-upon date in place, states could promptly undertake unilateral or small-group initiatives to reduce greenhouse emissions in the confidence that these measures would count toward the reductions required by an ultimate regime. Such a baseline year agreement could help to neutralize a major delaying tactic of domestic opponents of anti-greenhouse measures who argue that individual action without an overall international agreement is unwarranted or foolish.

However, enough nations and environmental organizations have already supported anti-greenhouse action that it may be unnecessary to wait for the conclusion of a framework convention to begin taking steps to prevent global warming. Former UNEP Deputy Executive Director Peter Thacher has argued against the conventional wisdom of waiting for a negotiated framework convention as a "first step," to be followed by specific protocols. Instead, in line with the Mediterranean and Ozone Action Plans, he suggests that as many nations as are now willing should agree first on a greenhouse "action plan" that contains no formal obligations, but offers the willing sponsors a coordinated vehicle within which to commence valuable research, monitoring, and assessment programs, as well as offers developing countries needed assistance to participate in technical and negotiating forums. Such voluntary actions would support and may well expedite the conventional framework/protocol negotiation (Thacher, 1990a).

A slightly "harder" option has been suggested by Abram Chayes in an analogy to the launching of the International Monetary Fund (Chayes,

1990). By creating a postwar "transition" period during which IMF treaty members could simply "maintain" various forbidden restrictions (e.g., on currency convertibility) until they voluntarily relinquished them, the institutional apparatus could be developed, professional staffs and reporting practices established, and general momentum built toward the result that ultimately was widely accepted. Applied to the greenhouse case, this approach would permit further collection of detailed statistics on global emissions, facilitate technical assistance to environmental agencies (especially in the developing world), permit the development and empirical validation of more specific performance criteria, and help develop a technically competent and credible monitoring and compliance capability.

The actions discussed thus far have had the potential to overcome potential opposition to a greenhouse treaty. Yet, return to the possibility of an ideologically driven impasse. Beyond exhortations to shared interest and attention to special developing country needs, a number of specific measures could help avoid recreating a sterile North-South clash in a climate context. First, well-publicized regional workshops prior to the negotiations—presented by regional scientists and policymakers and focused on possible local impacts—could help spread the conviction that this is a common threat from a shared problem. Joint developing-developed country research likewise could be encouraged. During the negotiations, similar informal workshops, perhaps presented by nongovernmental organizations on neutral ground, could be helpful. Second, conference leadership could avoid structuring the issues and work groups in a way that makes latent North-South clashes more salient. Examples include assigning preparation of negotiating drafts to groups with mixed memberships; likewise, designating protocols or negotiating groups as dealing solely with, say, technology transfer, carries higher risk of polarization than considering such issues together with others. Third, conference leadership could make extensive use of broadly constituted advisory groups—composed of business and other interests—to understand concerns, anticipate emerging problems, correct misapprehensions, and communicate about the issues and evolving negotiating responses. Not only could the two-way communication be useful in such settings, but cross-cutting coalitions might form (such as industries that want to sell energy-efficient equipment combining with Green advocacy groups and LDCs to press governments for more resources).

Finally, ideological blockage may be diminished by the development of a new ideological template. Until recently, many international negotiations were hobbled by the ideological clash between East and West. With this ideological conflict receding into the past, new creative solutions are becoming possible in areas from trade to human rights and arms control.

At a minimum, this new conception need not shoehorn countries with vastly different climate interests—from coal-rich developing countries such as China and India to sub-Saharan Africa to the Second World of Eastern Europe to Norway and the United States—into catchall categories such as "North" and "South." The most promising candidates to date are the principles of "sustainable development"—an insistence on development that meets the needs of the present without compromising the ability of future generations to meet their own needs—articulated by the Brundtland Commission in *Our Common Future* (World Commission, 1987). Although in need of clearer definition, these widely discussed principles call for tight links between environment and development, and offer some hope of reframing the climate negotiations in terms distinct from "old" North-South conceptions.

Effects of the passage of time on reaching agreements. Had the treaty that ultimately resulted from the LOS Conference been concluded earlier, it would have stood a better (though by no means a certain) chance of acceptance by the United States. This has led some observers to endorse the Wall Street adage that the passage of "time is the enemy of 'doable' deals" for international accords. In other words, when the confluence of issues and personalities permits the conclusion of a complex and significant agreement, even on a less than fully comprehensive basis, action should be taken before these underlying conditions (inevitably) shift.

For example, imagine that a tax on carbon emissions were agreed on, but initially set at a low enough level—for example, to collect resources for an international environmental fund—so its relatively diffuse impact did not trigger the same concentrated opposition that more targeted protocols could arouse. Later with the structure in place, the levels might be increased gradually, if the state of the science merited it and broad-based support existed for such a move. In virtually any case, getting the structure in place along with a ratchet mechanism for tightening the standards seems preferable to holding out for a more stringent regime at the outset.

Indeed, a review of the history of the ozone negotiations suggests the potential value of the advice to proceed step-by-step, rather than to seek a comprehensive accord like the LOS treaty. When an agreement to set CFC limits proved unreachable in 1985, the United States and others pressed for the Vienna Framework Convention that collectively legitimated the problem, set in motion joint efforts to monitor, coordinate, and exchange data, and envisioned the later negotiation of more specific "protocols."[8] (This is another in line with the "softer" options discussed above.) In 1987, after scientific consensus on the problem had solidified and industry opposition was largely neutralized, the Montreal Protocol embodied an agreement to cut chlorofluorocarbon production and use by 50% by the year 2000. Many environmental activists harshly criticized these agreed-upon targets as inadequate. Yet negotiators at the time felt that the 50% cut was the maximum that then could be negotiated, and that to press for more would have resulted in deadlock.

More importantly, as part of the institutional arrangements set up by the Montreal Protocol were provisions that facilitated a review of the agreed limits in the face of new evidence (or, effectively, with shifts in public opinion). In effect, these provisions functioned as a "ratchet," whereby the 50% cut served as a base; later findings stimulated treaty parties to tighten the limits. This treaty model of settling for relatively modest restrictions on which early agreement can be reached, together with arrangements that facilitate reconsideration, may well be emulated in the climate context. As UNEP's Tolba recently put it, "By aiming in 1987 for what we could get the nations to sign . . . we acquired a flexible instrument for action. If we had reached too far at Montreal, we would almost certainly have come away empty-handed. . . . [The] protocol that seemed modest to some . . . is proving to be quite a radical instrument" (Tolba, 1989). This assessment was borne out by the 1990 London negotiations that converted a 50% reduction into a virtual CFC ban (Browne, 1990).

Yet there is a danger with partial agreements, as exemplified by the 1963 Partial Nuclear Test Ban Treaty. Some observers have criticized these accords as stopping too soon and bleeding off the intense public pressure for change—when, arguably, a comprehensive test-ban treaty was then attainable with intensified negotiating efforts. By addressing the concerns about strontium 90 from atmospheric testing in the food chain (mother's milk in particular), according to this argument, the broader dangers of nuclear testing were not addressed and a more valuable opportunity was squandered. Rather than acting as a stepping stone to a larger accord, the Partial Nuclear Test Ban Treaty became a stopping place.

One might also draw an analogy to the U.S. Gramm-Rudman anti-deficit law, which eerily resembles a climate framework convention in that it contains targets and timetables but leaves specific agreement on budget cuts and tax increases for later. As such, this law served for years as an expedient political solution—at a time of intense public deficit concern— allowing executive and legislative officials to declare the problem solved and to return to budgetary chicanery. It is quite possible that the significant number of unilaterally adopted greenhouse gas control targets or a very weak framework convention that was politically touted as the solution to global warming could have analogous effects.

It is important, therefore, to be aware of the two different risks associated with the passage of time. To sea-law advocates, dragging out the LOS negotiations in search of a comprehensive accord paved the way for a new administration with a contrary view to scupper the treaty. By contrast, settling too quickly on partial, expedient measures may reduce the pressure for more genuinely effective accords.

With respect to climate-change negotiations, in particular, it is quite likely that public concern will be cyclic, in part as a result of natural variations in climate as well as unrelated environmental events (such as medical waste on beaches and the *Exxon Valdez*). Arguably, a naturally occurring period of climatic calm, including milder summers and normal rainfall, will lead to a reduction in public concern and pressure for action. Moreover, scientific understanding will change over time. These prospects argue for more limited agreements with analogs to the ratchet mechanism in the Montreal Protocol—that would be activated if, and as, more stringent action appears warranted. Such agreements could constitute a "rolling process of intermediate or self-adjusting agreements that respond quickly to growing scientific understanding" (Mathews, 1989). And an even more fundamentally adaptive institution might be envisioned, better matching the rapidly changing science and politics of this issue. Yet the overall point seems clear: the hazards of blocking coalitions, as discussed above with respect to the U.S. rejection of the LOS treaty and the experience of the ozone negotiations, likewise suggest a stepping-stone approach.

Lesson 10. Better an earlier, more modest treaty with provisions to expedite reviews of the specifics, if attainable, than the uncertain prospect of a more sweeping instrument down the road.

Alternatives to negotiated agreement and the dangers of free riders. Perhaps the most obvious lesson from the LOS experience for climate-change negotiators is the role of alternatives to negotiated agreement. In the encompassing atmosphere of large-scale international negotiations, it is sometimes easy to lose sight of the fact that each state ultimately will assess the value of a possible agreement relative to the best no-agreement alternative—and will choose that alternative if, rightly or not, it is judged preferable to that state's full set of interests. In the longer run, of course, the inherent interdependence between North and South on greenhouse issues means that a "Northern-only" alternative is not viable over time; it will be essential to have the cooperation of at least certain critical "Southern" states like China, India, Brazil, Mexico, and Indonesia. Yet, just as a mining minitreaty appeared to offer advantages over the LOS seabed regime to the Reagan administration, so may a smaller scale climate accord (perhaps as a stepping stone to a more universal arrangement; this possibility will be elaborated later). Moreover, the "commons quality" of the atmosphere—that all nations could benefit from actions to mitigate warming, while the costs of the actions may be narrowly concentrated—offers a powerful economic incentive to "free ride" the treaty, since nonadherents could share fully the later benefits of reductions by others without bearing the costs themselves.

Lesson 11. To enhance the prospect of sufficient adherence to a climate convention, substantial negotiating attention is required to design an instrument that over time is preferable—in terms of the perceived interests of a wide group of states—to the inherently attractive alternatives to negotiated agreement.

Some observers admit the theoretical correctness of this observation about the attractiveness of free riding but minimize or ignore its practical consequences for climate accords. Yet, a major example from the Law of the Sea that, as indicated above, was not even a true "commons problem" perhaps unexpectedly illustrates the very real dangers of free riding the actions of others. A somewhat cynical interpretation of the U.S. strategy, once the LOS treaty was negotiated, would be of a choice to free ride the benefits of the treaty (the navigation and other provisions), while rejecting the costs involved (the seabed-mining provisions).

Lesson 12. Anticipate and provide for the likelihood of free riders.

Climate-change agreements contain far more evident incentives for free riding than the Law of the Sea agreement since the uncertain future benefits of actions to mitigate emissions accrue to signatories and nonsignatories alike, although the costs would be borne by specific, identifiable interests in the near term. While the U.S. rejection of the LOS treaty underlines the potential seriousness of free riding, the question arises concerning the appropriate responses. Briefly, care should be taken to make joining a regime and adhering to it preferable to the alternatives—by a combination of moral suasion, tangible benefits for signatories perhaps in the realms of financial and technical assistance or preferences with respect to trade or debt, along with sanctions for those remaining outside the agreement (for example, bad publicity, financial or trade penalties). Special attention should be given to adherence by states that are major greenhouse gas contributors. Finally, to avoid setting in motion events that might cause a negotiated regime to unravel, some free riding should be anticipated and should not be overly discouraging to adherents.

A Promising Option: The Small-Scale (Expanding) Agreement

In spite of the previous suggestions for successful climate negotiations, the complexities of a universal process, either in a stand-alone framework/

protocol context or as part of a larger conference, may threaten endless delay or impasse. In such cases, an alternative possibility will likely become more salient.[9] Suppose that a smaller group of nations, probably certain industrialized states with potent domestic interests keenly concerned with anti-greenhouse measures, were to negotiate among themselves a reduction regime, which could take on various forms—including timetables and targets, either voluntary or mandated. Presumably the core group of any such smaller scale negotiations would include major contributors to the greenhouse problem in which there was substantial and urgent domestic sentiment for action. A natural starting core would be the 12 nations of the European Community, the six member states of the European Free Trade Association, plus Japan, Australia, and Canada—all of which by late 1990 had unilaterally or collectively adopted greenhouse gas stabilization or reduction targets. At present, the OECD countries account for approximately 45% of carbon emissions; with the addition of the Commonwealth of Independent States and Eastern Europe, the total would rise to 71% (Manne & Richels, 1990).

It would likely prove far easier to achieve agreement among such a group than to achieve a global accord as a function of the smaller number of states involved as well as their greater economic and political homogeneity. Existing institutions (such as the UN Economic Commission for Europe or the OECD) might facilitate the process. And while there clearly would be substantial negotiating difficulties involved, this smaller scale process could avoid the protracted, inconclusive North-South clash that might characterize a larger forum.

To be effective in the longer term, of course, a smaller scale agreement would have to be expanded later to include key developing countries such as China, India, Brazil, Indonesia, and Mexico (as well as additional developed nations, especially in Eastern Europe). In this sense, an agreement explicitly designed for an increasing number of adherents has strong parallels to agreements that "ratchet" to become increasingly stringent.

The design of the smaller negotiations could anticipate and facilitate such an expansion in several ways. First, the smaller agreement should seek to follow the negotiation of a widely accepted framework convention on climate, such that the general problem is legitimated and accepted to the largest possible extent.

Second, the smaller scale agreement should be cast not so much as an alternative to the global process over protocols but as a complement to it—in which those nations that evidently have caused the present greenhouse gas problem so far are those who are taking early action to mitigate emissions. This would give the smaller group that had agreed to cuts a higher moral standing in soliciting later reductions from others.

Third, the smaller scale group should structure its accord with the explicit expectation of collectively negotiating incentives, likely tailored to special circumstances, for key developing nations to join the accord. For example, the smaller group might agree to tax its members on their carbon emissions. All or part of those tax proceeds could be used to gain the acquiescence of key countries to anti-greenhouse measures. Rather than attempt ad hoc negotiations by its members with such other countries, the smaller group could create an entity that itself would carry out these negotiations. Such negotiations between the smaller treaty group and, say, China, could set a schedule of emission targets and offer China significant incentives to reach them. Or it could address a range of China's special concerns—environmental and other—in return for less climate-damaging development (such as assistance with greater exploration for Chinese natural gas reserves and Chinese agreements to use CFC substitutes in refrigeration and to undertake more greenhouse-friendly coal development, perhaps by the transfer of more efficient electrical-generating equipment). Critically, the character of such "customized" small-group Chinese negotiations—as well as with others such as India and Brazil—should be more conducive to environmentally desirable results than would generalized North-South clashes in a full-scale UN conference.

Fourth, as the group of adherents to the smaller convention grew, it might choose, in addition to such incentives, to impose a tax on products imported into their member countries from nonadherents, perhaps based on the direct or indirect carbon content of those products. The carrot (of providing individually tailored, negotiated incentives for nonadherents to join) and the stick (of raising such a "carbon-fence" around the anti-greenhouse group) together might lead to more countries jointly taking measures to prevent climate change. Evidently, a price to be discussed, anticipated, and (reluctantly) accepted by the smaller group would be a substantial number of free-riding countries. With a large enough group of adherents, however, the smaller group agreement could still be preferable to no agreement at all.

Ironically, though several developing countries have joined the Montreal Protocol, it is quite possible after the fact to interpret this experience as strongly analogous to the smaller scale convention just discussed. While carried out in the context of a widely accepted framework (the Vienna Convention), the relatively small number of key CFC-producing countries ultimately acceded to the CFC reductions in the Montreal Protocol. However, important LDCs (India, China, Brazil) did not go along with 1990. India, for example, demanded $2 billion—an amount related to its cost of using more ozone-friendly technology in the future—as its price to join the 1987 protocol (Stone, 1990). In 1990, a number of developed nations agreed to provide such assistance up to $240 million. This proved sufficiently attractive to representatives of states such as India and China, and they indicated willingness to join. Yet, crucially, as a result of the smaller scale 1987 Montreal Protocol, more significant ozone-protection measures got under way—well before the full resolution of important issues such as financial aid and technology transfer to the developing world.[10] In retrospect, especially given the sharply heightened scientific evidence on ozone depletion since 1990, these early actions appear to be of particular benefit.

It is important to note that the provisions in the Montreal Protocol for LDC financial and technical assistance, while favoring such actions in general terms, did not contain very specific commitments. Taking this frustrating experience as a lesson, LDC activists (such as India, Brazil, and China) will likely press for far more specificity in a larger climate conference, possibly at the framework stage. Clearly these questions must be addressed; equally clearly, requiring their resolution before any climate action is undertaken could be a recipe for considerable delay. The experience of Montreal as a de facto smaller scale convention may give rise to a more explicit minitreaty in a larger climate context.

Notes

1. Analogously, NIEO demands became much more salient after the first oil embargo, when the price to the developed world of ignoring them appeared to be deprivation of vital energy resources.

2. This does not, of course, mean that action by developed countries themselves would be useless; it could help mitigate the problem and buy valuable time to fashion other responses.

3. There were, of course, limitations on various activities (for example, coastal state seaward territorial claims, marine scientific research) negotiated in the LOS context. Not surprisingly, they were among the most difficult aspects of the conference.

4. There were true commons LOS issues, such as the marine environment and the depletion of fish stocks, but they were far less important in a negotiating sense than navigation and seabed resource issues.

5. The greenhouse gas stabilization and reduction targets adopted to date by individual countries and groups of countries stands in contrast to this simple "commons logic"—perhaps illustrating the power of domestic political forces and the moral aspects of the greenhouse issue as seen by many people. Viewing states as monolithic, strategically rational actors in this context may be misleading.

6. See Ehrlich and Ehrlich (1990). Even if the United States did not go along with such a proposal, the amount of money required at the margin to increase the effectiveness of population programs is relatively small enough that contributions of other nations could be very effective.

7. The phrase *blocking coalition* is used in a looser sense than is common in a well-structured (e.g., parliamentary) context. For traditional discussions of these concepts see Luce and Raiffa (1957) or Riker (1962). Think of a *winning coalition* as defined only with

respect to a set of policy measures from the point of view of the particular actor or actors; such coalitions consist of sufficient numbers of adherents to render the policy effective (again from the point of view of the specific actor or actors). Blocking coalitions, then, are those opposing interests that could prevent a winning coalition from coming into existence or being sustained. The term *actor* should be contextually obvious and can include states, domestic interests, and transnational groupings of either as appropriate.

8. Indeed, the negotiations that led to the Vienna Convention began in 1981, four years after UNEP had formulated a World Plan of Action on the Ozone Layer (Chapter 3 this volume; Thacher, 1990a).

9. The idea of a smaller scale agreement was considerably discussed and developed in the discussions of the Harvard Negotiation Roundtable during 1989-1990. For a perceptive discussion of other such alternatives, see Grubb, 1990.

10. The experience of the Convention on Long-Range Transboundary Air Pollution, in which groups of expanding size acceded to the later sulfur and nitrogen oxides protocols, is also generally in accord with this small-scale approach. For a summary, see Jackson (1990).

Part III

ANALYSIS

The case studies in Part 2 were guided by the analytical framework presented in Chapter 2. They describe the negotiation processes in detail—how the issues are defined, who participates, how the process evolves, what structural elements influence the negotiations, and what factors characterize the outcome. This description certainly has value in its own right.

If we are to draw lessons from history to assist future environmental negotiations, we need to ask additional questions. These are integrative questions that seek to find the common threads among diverse cases. What are the general characteristics of environmental negotiations? How do the 12 attributes of environmental negotiations postulated in Chapter 2 fare in these cases? How are environmental negotiations significantly different from other types of international negotiations?

One basic lesson learned from the case studies is that lessons are hard to learn. Most case studies give witness to the complexity of environmental issues and their dynamic nature as more scientific knowledge is developed concerning environmental problems. The Law of the Sea case study presented in Chapter 11, in particular, points to some of these difficulties, but also demonstrates that lessons learned from one negotiation may be useful for the conduct of another.

The evaluation of the case studies presented in Part 3 is conducted along several dimensions. First, in Chapter 12 Richard Elliot Benedick provides the perspective of a practitioner, a professional diplomat with extensive experience participating in environmental negotiations. Oran R. Young analyzes options for practical policy recommendations on the role of international organizations in Chapter 13. A central part of his assessment pertains to one of the grand themes evoked in the UN Conference on Environment and Development process: problems related to the allocation of work and collaboration between different international organizations. Next, I. William Zartman's lessons for analysis and practice identifies ideas for further research on environmental negotiations, in Chapter 14. A central message of this chapter is that effective policy recommendations to future negotiators must be based on a better knowledge of the particular character of environmental negotiations. In Chapter 15, Jeffrey Z. Rubin treats mediation in international environmental disputes, and he assesses the role of third-party intervention. Rubin's chapter identifies practical ways by which a third party can facilitate the process of environmental negotiations at different stages. Finally, in Chapter 16, Gunnar Sjöstedt and Bertram I. Spector summarize the analytical assessment of the cases by bringing forward several policy recommendations, the requirements for decision support, and suggestions for further research.

12

Perspectives of a Negotiation Practitioner

RICHARD ELLIOT BENEDICK

Politics," noted a British peer during 1988 debates over the Montreal Ozone Protocol in the House of Lords, "is the art of taking good decisions on insufficient evidence" (UK House of Lords, 1988). For the negotiator of modern international environmental agreements, this observation assumes the quality of a maxim.

Environmental problems in the past have tended to be local in nature and relatively limited in scope. In recent years, however, a different type of ecological threat has begun to move to the top of foreign policy agendas. Such issues as greenhouse warming, depletion of the stratospheric ozone layer, transboundary air pollution, destruction of forests, extinction of plant and animal species, pollution of oceans, and spreading desertification represent a new generation of environmental dangers.

These new dangers share several characteristics that inescapably influence the approach to diplomatic solutions. They are slow and long term in developing. Because of the long time frame, their consequences may be essentially irreversible if countermeasures are delayed for too long. They generally originate from manifold causes. Localized actions are revealed to have unanticipated regional or even global consequences. The offending activities are inextricably linked to the perceived imperatives of modern societies and economies, whether it is the need for rapidly growing populations in the Third World to decimate surrounding forests for firewood or the life-styles in wealthy countries that demand powerful and luxurious (and energy inefficient) personal vehicles.

And the new generation of international environmental issues is characterized, above all, by a high degree of scientific uncertainty. Precisely because the impacts are so long term and the interaction of events and responses so intricate, the scientists cannot usually point with certainty to a given outcome. The mechanism by which acid precipitation can damage forests, the amount of sea-level rise caused by a given average global temperature increase, the point at which logging renders a tropical forest inviable, the consequences to the food chain of extinction of a particular insect or fish or plant—none of these portentous questions, nor many similar ones, can yet be answered with precision.

Indeed, our very awareness of the new environmental dangers is due to research at the frontiers of modern science, often dependent on advanced and enormously complex computer modeling, highly sophisticated theoretical chemistry and physics, and measurements of minute changes in our environment by satellites and other arcane means. The concepts are not obvious: using a perfume spray in Paris releases chlorofluorocarbons (CFCs) that accumulate in the stratosphere and thereby contribute to skin cancer deaths half a world distant and decades in the future.

Although the dangers are long term and the science uncertain, the costs of mitigating measures occur in the short run. Entrenched economic interests, preoccupied with short-term profits and sensitive to the vagaries of financial markets, resist changing traditional ways of doing business. Political leaders, with an eye to near-term elections, may be reluctant to impose regulations and economic dislocations that can cause unemployment or consumer dissatisfaction. There is a not unnatural tendency to postpone decisions when the costs seem obvious and the benefits questionable.

Challenges to Diplomacy

Whereas past environmental problems were generally addressed through national legislation, unilateral measures, or occasional international treaties, the global issues present unique challenges to traditional international law and diplomacy. The scope for disagreements or conflict among nations due to environmental threats is real and growing. Some have already been the subject of negotiations; others are latent.

At a regional or subregional level, the conflicts tend to be South-South or North-North in nature. As water for irrigation and cities comes under increasing pressure from growing populations, the damming or diversion of water from shared rivers by upstream states has major conflict potential (Egypt-Sudan-Ethiopia, Israel-Jordan, Turkey-Iraq). Rivers can also be contaminated by chemical spills that affect several nations, as illustrated by the necessity for negotiations among countries sharing the Rhine. Environmental refugees due to drought or flooding can contribute to strains between nations if the numbers are perceived to be unmanageable. Transboundary air pollution was a source of contention and long negotiations between Canada and the United States (acid rain), and among nations of northern Europe (Convention on Long-Range Transboundary Air Pollution). The Chernobyl nuclear accident affected many European countries and led to new international agreements under the International Atomic Energy Agency (IAEA).

Environmental conflicts involving countries of North and South can arise from industrial accidents (Bhopal) or from exports from the North of toxic chemicals or hazardous wastes. But it is the new global issues, which affect the well-being of the entire planet, that bring the greatest potential for confrontation between the wealthy countries of the North, with their energy-intensive industry and consumer demand, and the poorer South, with huge and rapidly growing populations that aspire to the same life-styles.

Even if the industrialized countries eliminate CFCs, for example, their efforts to protect the ozone layer will be overwhelmed if developing nations increase use of these chemicals to satisfy the refrigeration needs of their populations. Similarly, reductions in carbon dioxide emissions in the North will be in vain if China, India, and other populous countries expand their burning of coal and oil to meet the energy requirements of their growing economies. And the industrialized nations have no direct control over the rate of tropical deforestation in Malaysia, Indonesia, or Brazil, which contributes both to the greenhouse effect and to the extinction of biological diversity.

These planetary issues can be resolved only if the wealthier countries acknowledge a responsibility to aid the South by compensating for the costs of adopting environmentally benign policies and by furnishing the relevant technology on fair terms. A beginning has been made in this direction in the 1990 London amendment to the landmark Montreal Protocol on protecting the ozone layer, which established the first-ever global environmental fund (UNEP, 1990b).

When governments face up to these new environmental challenges, they find that the traditional tools of national policy and diplomacy are blunted.

Neither military nor economic power can be effectively applied because the origins of the danger are so widely dispersed. The nature of these issues requires an unprecedented degree of international cooperation—in coordinating research, in monitoring trends, in harmonizing measures and regulations. No single nation, or group of nations, however powerful, can solve these problems. And since local decisions and activities can affect the entire planet, the solutions may be difficult to reconcile with historical conceptions of national sovereignty.

In effect, one can regard contemporary environmental negotiations as the reflection of a modern society coping with new and dangerous uncertainties. Policymakers and diplomats confront the task of striking a balance between short-term costs and long-term but uncertain risks. Premature actions based on incomplete data and possibly erroneous scientific theories could impose unnecessary economic dislocations. But waiting for better evidence carries risks of larger and possibly irreversible future damage and the need for even costlier countermeasures.

Environmental negotiations of the type described in this volume must reconcile complex and interconnected national interests and considerations—political, economic, commercial, technological, and scientific. In a sense, the negotiators are designing international insurance policies: cooperative preventive actions among sovereign states. There are few formulas or guiding principles from other types of negotiations. Instead, there is a premium on innovation, flexibility, and pragmatic solutions.

Actors: The Diversity of Modern Society

The immediate parties to international environmental negotiations are, of course, the *executive branches of governments*. However, reflecting the complexity of the issues, many different ministries may be involved in setting a national position. These could include, besides the obvious ministries of foreign affairs and environment, departments responsible for science and technology, industry, finance, trade, defense, foreign aid, planning, energy, agriculture, transport, and others. At least 18 different U.S. departments and agencies participated in preparations for the negotiations leading to the Montreal Protocol on ozone-layer protection.

As these ministries have different constituencies and interests, there are likely to be considerable internal conflicts and negotiations before a national delegation can even advance a firm position to the outside world. In the interagency process, one government department will generally assume the lead role; in the case of the United States, there is a statutory responsibility under the Clean Air Act for the Department of State to take the lead in negotiations involving the atmosphere (Clean Air Act, 1977). Many of the concerned ministries may also insist on being represented at the international negotiations, which can lead to excessively large national delegations.

Governments of developing countries often face special problems in participating in environmental negotiations. A major question for many poorer nations is the cost involved in despatching delegations to spend one to four weeks at an expensive world city such as Geneva or New York. This problem is compounded by the increasing frequency of environmental conferences; on the subject of climate change alone there were at least a dozen international meetings scheduled for the first half of 1991.

Realizing the importance of assuring adequate representation from the South, the industrialized nations are increasingly setting up special funds, financed by voluntary contributions, to pay for travel and related costs of representatives from developing countries. The logistical problems can be formidable, however, especially communications: getting invitations, funds, and appropriately translated documents out to remote capitals in time to plan and prepare for complicated negotiations. It is not surprising that frequently the turnout from the South is disappointing.

Apart from this issue is the question of technical expertise within a given government on what may be a particularly esoteric set of topics. Experts on meteorology or atmospheric chemistry may be in short supply or cannot be spared from their domestic responsibilities. On the other hand, there is no shortage in the South of skilled generalists, diplomats expert in the ways of the United Nations. Thus, for example, the opening round of the Intergovernmental Negotiating Committee on a Framework Convention on Climate Change, meeting in Chantilly, VA, in February 1991, was dominated by endless procedural matters raised by developing-country diplomats sent from their UN missions in New York. Two weeks of discussion managed to avoid any sustained consideration of the substance of greenhouse warming.

In addition to the executive branch, national *legislatures* also play an increasingly important role in international environmental negotiations. Parliamentary hearings are an especially useful forum for airing scientific theories and exploring conflicting economic and social interests. Parliamentarians will often follow the international negotiations closely and have been known to attend or send staff members as observers. During the course of intergovernmental negotiations, hearings may be held at which executive branch officials are questioned critically on progress made and difficulties encountered.

Beginning in 1974 when the first scientific hypotheses appeared on the threat to the stratospheric ozone layer, the U.S. Congress had a major influence in stimulating awareness of the problem and in promoting an international response; the volumes of reports of hearings held by numerous Congressional committees would fill several shelves. In the Federal Republic of Germany, a special multiparty select committee of the Bundestag (Enquete-Kommission) invited domestic and foreign experts to testify on the ozone and climate-change issues over a period of months, producing an impressive volume that was later translated into several languages and distributed widely (Deutscher Bundestag, 1988). Deliberations in the British House of Lords during the summer of 1988 were instrumental in triggering a major change in the government's attitude that transformed the United Kingdom into a leader in international efforts to protect the global atmosphere. The European Parliament in Strasbourg and national parliaments in Canada, the Netherlands, and the Nordic countries (Denmark, Finland, Norway, and Sweden) have also been among those particularly active in influencing international environmental negotiations.

Finally, new mechanisms have arisen linking parliamentarians of North and South on environmental issues, providing forums for mutual education, exchange of information, and coordinated lobbying on specific issues such as climate change or biological diversity. These bodies range from subcommittees of a large, formal, and traditional institution (the Interparliamentary Union) to smaller groups (Parliamentarians for Global Action) to informal ad hoc networks or conferences. All of these are serving to bring national parliaments and parliamentarians closer to the actual process of intergovernmental environmental negotiations than ever before.

Multilateral organizations generally play a crucial role in the new environmental diplomacy. An international secretariat is essential for the logistical tasks of convening meetings, developing or commissioning background documentation, and providing translation and similar activities. The secretariat provides a continuity for negotiations that may stretch through numerous sessions over a period of years, during which there may be considerable turnover among government negotiators. The secretariat also services the bureau, a small group of individuals elected by the negotiating parties, that presides over plenary sessions and working groups, and that will often meet before the formal negotiating sessions to define the issues, plan agendas, and agree on appropriate documentation.

But a multilateral organization can also go beyond a secretariat function, important as that may be. The organization can play a critical catalyzing and mediating role, mobilizing pertinent data, sponsoring scientific studies, informing world public opinion, defining issues, and developing agendas. Typifying this expanded role were the United Nations Economic Commission for Europe (ECE) during negotiations for the 1979 Convention on Long-Range Transboundary Air Pollution, the United

Nations Environment Program (UNEP) in the negotiation of the 1985 Vienna Convention and the 1987 Montreal Protocol on protecting the ozone layer, and the IAEA during the deliberations leading to accords on nuclear-reactor safety. The ECE and UNEP kept issues alive at times when many participating governments might have preferred the negotiations to languish (see Chapter 5).

In the case of ozone protection, it was UNEP—inviting, cajoling, and pressuring sometimes reluctant or disinterested governments to the bargaining table—that enabled the treaty to become a truly global accord (see Chapter 3). Indeed, during the ozone negotiations as well as those leading up to the 1989 Basel Convention on the Control of Transboundary Movements of Hazardous Wastes and Their Disposal, UNEP Executive Director Mostafa Tolba played a central personal role: he risked taking personal positions, he initiated ideas and advanced concerns that might otherwise have been overlooked, and he in effect made UNEP a subtle advocate for governments and populations not represented at the formal negotiation (see Chapter 4).

UN bodies frequently have a credibility and authority, especially vis-à-vis developing or newly independent countries, that can be crucial in guiding complex negotiations to a successful conclusion. The effectiveness of UN agencies can be marred, however, if they permit extraneous political issues—which are more appropriately debated in the UN General Assembly—to intrude on the scientific, economic, and technical substance.

An outstanding characteristic of modern environmental negotiations is the critical role played by the *scientific community*. To ensure the success of the negotiation, it is essential to build an international scientific consensus that can agree on basic parameters and narrow the ranges of uncertainty. In recent years, as demonstrated by their work on the ozone-layer and global-warming issues, an international network of cooperating scientists and scientific institutions has developed as a major new actor on the scene. They have been aided in this process by the catalyzing efforts of such institutions as UNEP, the World Meteorological Organization (WMO), and the International Council of Scientific Unions (ICSU).

In effect, there now exists a community of scientists from many nations, committed to scientific objectivity and welcoming cooperative research, transcending the narrow political or commercial interests of sovereign states. This development profoundly affected the ozone negotiations, operating to counterbalance the industrial lobby. It is having an equally important influence on the climate negotiations that began in February 1991 in Washington, D.C., following two years of intense scientific work under the Intergovernmental Panel on Climate Change. In this process, the scientists come out of the familiar ambience of their laboratories and collaborate closely with key government officials, assuming a new responsibility for the implications of their findings for policy options. It is important not only that governments provide adequate financing for such scientific research, but that they heed the resultant findings.

Science, however, can be another area of potential North-South tension. While a handful of developing countries have first-rate scientific establishments, and brilliant scientists in particular fields can be found everywhere, it must be admitted that the preponderance of scientific research on environmentally related subjects is concentrated in the North. This is accentuated by the panoply of instrumentology and capital investment required for the monitoring and analysis that goes with modern study of the environment: supercomputers, satellites, sophisticated laboratories.

Very few scientists from developing countries were involved in the international exercises accompanying the ozone negotiations. Special efforts were undertaken to involve more in the Intergovernmental Panel on Climate Change. Looking ahead, a persistent theme from Third-World diplomats is the need to build into future environmental treaties provisions for training, technical assistance, and scientific capacity building in developing countries, to permit them to function as more equal partners in this domain.

Industry and industrial associations are traditional participants in many environmental negotiations because of the commercial and economic implications of the outcome. The overwhelming majority of observer delegates from the nongovernmental sector during the ozone negotiations were industry representatives rather than environmental groups. In some cases, corporate officials were even part of national delegations, with all that implies in terms of influence over governmental positions (Benedick, 1991). Although most industry representatives traditionally come from industrialized nations, by the Second Meeting of Parties to the Montreal Protocol in 1990 there were also entrepreneurs present from several developing countries, a possible harbinger of the future.

Industry groups are invariably sophisticated and well organized, particularly in their public relations and lobbying efforts, to which they can devote considerably more resources than their environmental critics. During the ozone negotiations, however, some of the slick publicity backfired and industry lost valuable credibility when distortions were exposed by Green groups and scientists.

Although industrial emissions, effluents, and waste products are generally the root of an environmental problem, industry is also a major part of the solution. Initially, many industrialists resist changing traditional ways of doing business; they tend to underestimate the seriousness of an environmental problem and exaggerate the costs of remedial actions. But if regulatory policies can provide the market with the appropriate signals, the vast financial, intellectual, and technical resources of the private sector can be stimulated to undertake the needed research and development of environmentally benign products and technologies.

Environmental organizations and citizens' groups are a relatively new major actor. Such groups in the North have traditionally been active on the local scene in mobilizing public opinion and lobbying governments for regulatory or remedial action. These organizations have increasingly expanded their horizons to include the global environmental issues. And new environmental groups have arisen in many countries in the South (and in Eastern Europe) in recent years, often with technical and financial assistance from similar organizations in the North.

Environmental organizations have become more sophisticated in their methods, frequently sponsoring scientific or policy research and legal activities; examples of such groups include the Worldwide Fund for Nature (WWF), World Resources Institute, Environmental Defense Fund, and Natural Resources Defense Council (NRDC) in the United States, and the Institute for European Environmental Policy in Bonn and London. Other groups, such as Greenpeace and Friends of the Earth, specialize in consumer boycotts to put pressure on recalcitrant companies and public demonstrations to attract media attention.

Many of these organizations now also demand a seat at the table in international environmental negotiations—or at least in the back of the room as observers, with the accompanying right to deliver statements, circulate papers, lobby delegates, and hold press conferences that are often a dissonant leitmotif to the official deliberations.

An often overlooked legacy of the ozone negotiations has been the development, beginning roughly in 1988, of an international network of environmental groups that coordinates activities and develops common positions to influence negotiations. Although only a handful of such organizations—all American—attended the 1987 meeting that resulted in the Montreal Protocol, by 1989, representatives of 93 environmental and citizens' groups from 27 countries met in London and issued a joint statement aimed at persuading governments to strengthen the treaty (Benedick, 1991). The same network is participating actively in the climate negotiations.

As the South has become more actively involved, some developing-country delegations have expressed resentment at the presence and activities of environmental groups in intergovernmental deliberations. There is some sentiment that these groups are self-selected, elitist, and primarily projections of industrialized nations. (This is somewhat ironic, as environmental organizations from the North are usually much more critical of their own governments than they are of those in the South.) At the same time, citizens' groups from developing countries themselves are no more popular, as they are often regarded as creations of sister organizations in the North and in any case overly critical of their own national policies. Developing countries were successful, for example, in excluding nongovernmental observers from most deliberations of the intergovernmental executive committee established to oversee the new multilateral fund established under the Montreal Protocol.

After a treaty is signed by governments, private organizations can undertake a watchdog role, monitoring compliance of companies and nations with the treaty's requirements and sounding the alarm when transgressions are discovered. The WWF's Traffic Program plays a central role in uncovering violations of the 1973 Convention on International Trade in Endangered Species of Wild Fauna and Flora (Chapter 10). Similarly, in 1990 Friends of the Earth and NRDC publicized misleading consumer product labeling by chemical companies that was inconsistent with the spirit of the Montreal Protocol.

Environmental negotiations are often significantly influenced by the *mass media,* in particular the press and television. The environment has become front-page news and cover-story material. In nearly all of the subjects covered in this volume, the media have played a critical role in interpreting data, educating public opinion, and changing attitudes of governments.

Closely related to this is the role of *consumers and voters.* One should never underestimate the power of an aroused public opinion. Between 1975 and 1977, for example, the U.S. market for CFC-propelled aerosol sprays declined by two-thirds, *before* any government regulation was instituted—the result of tens of millions of individual consumer decisions, based on what they had seen in the media, not to purchase such products. Similarly, more than a decade later, consumer boycotts in the United Kingdom forced British producers to eliminate CFC-aerosol sprays even though this was not yet mandated by the Montreal Protocol.

Finally, a new actor with potential influence on environmental negotiations is the *religious community.* Symbolic of a growing concern among spiritual leaders over new environmental threats to future generations was the Global Forum on Environment and Development convened by President Mikhail Gorbachev in Moscow in January 1990. This meeting attracted more than 1,000 participants, including leaders from all major— and many minor—religions from around the world. Interest in this initiative from spiritual communities in the South was a significant new feature. It can be expected that these new actors will reinforce the efforts of secular environmental groups in pressuring governments to act in concert against threats to nature.

Structure of Negotiations

A major factor influencing multilateral environmental negotiations is the trade-off between *national sovereignty and international interdependence*. The scope of the problems being addressed often means that substantial cooperation among many nations is essential.

This raises questions of possibly having to subordinate to common will decisions traditionally considered an attribute of national sovereignty. Not surprisingly, the largest and wealthiest nations—which are invariably called upon to foot the bill—bridle at the prospect of being outvoted on critical issues by a multitude of states pursuing their own self-interest.

In a few international agreements—including the World Bank, International Monetary Fund, and International Maritime Organization—some form of weighted voting was instituted to reflect the interests of major stakeholders. The original version of the 1987 Montreal Protocol included a voting formula skewed in favor of the largest producers and consumers of CFCs—all industrialized countries. By 1990, however, a powerful and insistent coalition of developing nations overturned this decision mechanism and replaced it with a system requiring parallel majorities among parties of both North and South (UNEP, 1990b). It can be anticipated that, in future environmental negotiations, North-South balance will be the order of the day in treaty-voting and decision-making provisions.

A significant new influence on the structure of negotiations is the *state of the science.* The importance of scientific consensus on what is happening or what is likely to happen is a persistent theme in these negotiations— and this consensus must not rest on scientists from a single nation or small group, however competent they may be, but must include representatives of the broader international community, including the South. The pre-negotiation deliberations of the Intergovernmental Panel on Climate Change (IPCC) epitomized this new aspect.

Science can affect the negotiation through several routes: by establishing a factual data base (as in the Rhine River deliberations, Chapter 8); by theoretical modeling of possible future consequences (such as ozone-layer depletion, climate change, and the IIASA RAINS model for transboundary air pollution in Europe); and by monitoring and measuring new developments (the 1986 Chernobyl nuclear accident and the 1988 Ozone Trends Panel Report). The parties to the ozone negotiations called on scientists during the actual negotiations in early 1987 to convene a special ad hoc meeting to test on their models the impacts of the various policy options being debated; the resultant findings proved crucial in moving governments toward a consensus on stronger controls over CFCs. For the climate-convention negotiations, which began in 1991, the IPCC has been extended as a parallel ongoing process—a mechanism for continuing dialogue between the diplomatic negotiators and the scientific community.

Economic constraints are another major factor in these negotiations. The conflicts can be real and potentially painful: trade, investment, profits, and jobs are at stake. In negotiating food aid to the Sahel, for example, the parties had to consider the immediate humanitarian needs, the implications for food self-sufficiency in recipient countries, and the interests of suppliers in donor countries (Chapter 9). In U.S.-Canadian negotiations over acid rain, the impact of sulfur dioxide controls on coal miners and depressed industries in the American Midwest were a real factor (Chapter 6). Banning international trade in ivory under CITES had serious implications for small industry in Hong Kong and elsewhere. In the Montreal Protocol negotiations, the demand of American industry for a "level playing field" vis-à-vis their powerful competitors in the European Community, which had previously gained commercial advantage from unilateral U.S. action against CFCs, had an important influence on the U.S. negotiating position.

In the new global environmental negotiations, developing countries are particularly sensitive about being forced to undertake obligations on behalf of environmental protection that could interfere with their economic growth. With a rising proportion of the world's population—already more than 80%—concentrated in the South, potential future emissions and effluents from the developing world under prevailing technologies could swamp any reductions undertaken by the industrialized North.

Developing nations stoutly maintain, however, that the industrialized countries have grown wealthy while, albeit inadvertently, polluting the global commons with greenhouse gases and toxic wastes; therefore, it is the responsibility of the North to pay for restoring the balances of nature on which future life on Earth may well depend. In the short run, the top priority in the South is to reduce poverty and raise standards of living, and if this means burning coal or cutting down tropical forests, with uncertain and probably adverse implications for the future, so be it. Developing-country representatives insist that the only alternative to this course is for the South to be enabled, through new and additional financial assistance and technology transfer, to leapfrog over the polluting phase of the industrial-energy-agricultural revolution that began in the 18th century.

Economic factors thus translate into significant pressures on negotiators from important constituencies, including political leaders, industry, labor, and relevant government ministries.

The structure of negotiations is also affected by several elements of a technical or logistical nature. *Breadth of participation* can be particularly critical to international environmental negotiations. The importance of participation by poorer developing countries has been recognized by establishing special funds in the ozone-layer and climate negotiations to finance the travel and related costs of their representatives. An additional factor, noted earlier, is the growing presence of observers from interest groups and other constituencies—industry, Greens, academics, parliamentarians; the 1990 London Meeting of Parties to the Montreal Protocol established another "first" in its accreditation of an Australian youth delegation, whose 17-year-old representative addressed the assembled ministers of state on their responsibility to the next and future generations (UNEP, 1990b).

The aspect of negotiating in a goldfish bowl of nongovernmental scrutiny affects the *number and type of meetings.* Full-scale plenary meetings, attended by scores of official delegations and dozens of nongovernmental observers, tend to be reserved for exhortatory speeches that set out extreme positions. The real business of negotiating takes place in smaller working groups, ad hoc constellations of delegates, and informal contacts among individuals in the corridors. The importance in this process of the "bureau" (elected chair and vice-chair of the negotiations) and key delegation heads and secretariat members (such as UNEP Executive Director Tolba in the Montreal Protocol and Basel Convention deliberations) cannot be overestimated.

Working groups, which focus on particular subtopics within the broad negotiating subject, tend to be scheduled, large, and rather formal in structure. Because of this, there is growing pressure from nongovernmental organizations to be permitted to "observe" these meetings as well. To the extent this occurs, there will be an increasing premium on smaller ad hoc meetings, closed to public scrutiny, where the negotiators can trade ideas and offer hypothetical trade-offs without making headlines before the objective is attained. An unusual example of secrecy in a large group occurred at the 1990 London Meeting of Parties to the Montreal Protocol, when delegation heads of nearly 100 countries—many of them ministers— met at a critical stage in closed session without advisers from their own delegations (Benedick, 1991).

The proliferation of negotiations has engendered a counterreaction from the South, which feels constrained by a lack of personnel to cover adequately the growing number of time-consuming meetings abroad. During the 1990 preparatory committee meeting for the 1992 UN Conference on Environment and Development, and again at the 1991 opening of negotiations on a climate convention, developing-country delegations insisted that no intersessional working group meetings be permitted. As explained privately by many delegates, this prohibition was at least partly motivated by a desire that all parties be present at all meetings, and a distrust of deals being struck in the absence of some players.

This was in sharp contrast to the Montreal Protocol process, and could prove to be a constraining factor that could considerably prolong the negotiations. At the same time, however, it is difficult to prevent contacts between groups of countries outside the formal negotiating structure; indeed, the Chinese government itself convened a meeting of developing nation environment ministers in Beijing on the eve of the June 1991 climate negotiation. It also remains to be seen whether the chairs of these negotiations might not at some point seek permission to convene informal and unofficial meetings of "friends of the chairs" to try to avoid roadblocks that are seemingly impassable in a larger meeting.

Related to this factor is the issue of *size of delegation.* There is a tendency, particularly among large and wealthy countries with diverse and conflicting constituencies (the United States is the prime example), for delegations to grow in size. They may come to number 20 or more individuals, many of whom perform little function other than monitoring whether the principal actors stray from the party line. Large numbers tend to be unwieldy, absorb excessive time merely for internal coordination, and raise questions of delegation discipline, unauthorized contacts with other delegations, and leaks to the press (which may serve to undermine an official position). On the other hand, when a country's delegation is too small, there may be gaps in expertise required on complex environmental subjects and an inability to be represented at parallel working-group meetings. This can be particularly poignant for small and poor nations, and may be compensated for by informal cooperative arrangements whereby responsibilities are shared and feedback pooled among two or more small national delegations.

A further structural consideration is the *time factor.* The point at which new elements are introduced into a negotiation may have a critical influence on its outcome. When Canada, the Nordic countries, and the United States attempted to insert a control protocol into the deliberations that culminated in the 1985 Vienna Convention for the Protection of the Ozone Layer, the effort foundered in the face of strong opposition from the European Community, Japan, and the former Soviet Union; it was only some 30 months later at Montreal that the parties were able to agree on actual control measures.

Another aspect of timing is linked to the state of the science. Negotiations on Rhine River chemical spills, the Chernobyl disaster, and transboundary air pollution were all responses to environmental damages that had already occurred. In contrast, as represented by the ozone-layer and climate-change negotiations, there is a growing recognition among governments that negotiations on controls may need to begin before there is unmistakable evidence of damage.

Finally, setting a firm closure date for the achievement of a treaty adds a critical element to a negotiating process. When the ozone-protocol negotiators, at their February 1987 meeting in Vienna, fixed the final negotiating session for September of that same year in Montreal, they increased the pressure on recalcitrant parties and removed any lingering doubts as to the seriousness of the intention to impose an international control regime over CFCs. A variant of this time pressure is present at a final negotiating session, when the travel schedules of busy ministers may preclude extending the meeting and impose an additional imperative for compromise.

Negotiating Strategy

A nation's strategy in these negotiations can comprise an array of diplomatic and related activities. This was exemplified by the U.S. strategy in the 1986-1987 ozone negotiations. The United States faced formidable opposition to stringent controls over CFCs, comprising the international chemical industry and allied industrial sectors (plastics, motor vehicles, appliances, food, electronics, and others), as well as governments that accounted for two thirds of the world's CFC production: the 12-member European Community, Japan, and the former Soviet Union. Few knowledgeable observers predicted at the time that a meaningful international treaty could be achieved.

Under these circumstances, the U.S. Department of State designed a diplomatic strategy even before the formal negotiations began (Benedick, 1991). The United States made extensive use of U.S. embassies in more than 60 countries, providing them with detailed analyses of the issues and the rationale for U.S. positions. The department stimulated an ongoing dialogue and exchange of views with host governments, most of which in the beginning were indifferent or even hostile to the idea of a protocol. There was particularly close coordination with such like-minded governments as Canada, Finland, the Federal Republic of Germany, the Netherlands, New Zealand, Norway, and Sweden.

U.S. embassy efforts on the ozone issue were complemented by parallel political activities, including high-level contacts of the secretary of state and the administrator of the Environmental Protection Agency with their counterparts from other countries, in which the seriousness of the U.S. position was underscored. A U.S. initiative placed ozone protection as a priority issue at the June 1987 Group of Seven Economic Summit meeting.

It is fair to say that bilateral diplomatic contacts were an essential prerequisite to a successful multilateral outcome. Discussions among governments during the intervals between formal negotiating sessions

contribute significantly to understanding national positions and their underlying rationale and concerns, and hence to influencing a convergence.
Much progress is therefore "invisible": what becomes apparent at the
negotiating session is often less a product of that meeting than a result of
the painstaking groundwork that had occurred, on a bilateral basis, in the
weeks or months preceding. If one delays contact until the actual negotiating session, positions may be set and therefore much harder to influence.

In addition, U.S. officials directly reached out to foreign constituencies—including the general public—by creative use of the media, press
conferences, speeches, television, and radio. To this end, they also encouraged U.S. environmentalists to establish contacts with their colleagues
overseas, in an attempt to counterbalance the influence of the chemical
industry on certain European governments.

An important element of the diplomatic strategy was its reliance on
scientific data and the avoidance of ideological arguments or exaggerated
rhetoric that could damage credibility. Of particular significance to the
successful outcome were offers of bilateral scientific cooperation with the
former Soviet Union and Japan: leading U.S. atmospheric scientists established close working relationships and shared the latest findings with their
colleagues from countries whose governments had been initially among
the strongest opponents of a CFC-control protocol.

In contacts with foreign governments, U.S. ideas were advanced as
illustrative approaches rather than firm positions. U.S. officials were
intentionally vague about details of their proposals, referring more to
general principles and ranges of actions. The U.S. position was thus
allowed to evolve in give-and-take discussions with other governments—
all, however, within the general parameters of the original U.S. objectives.

In these discussions, U.S. negotiators continually probed for the real
interests behind stated positions. An important example of this occurred
during the final round in 1987, when unyielding Soviet resistance to the
1986 reference year for controlled output levels, which had by then been
accepted by all other parties as essential to prevent enormous expansion
of CFC production, threatened the negotiations with a stalemate. The U.S.
delegation head discovered that the Soviet insistence was linked to domestic legal constraints of a five-year plan, ending in 1990, that provided for
a modest increase in CFCs to levels still far below those of the Western
producers. With this knowledge, it was simple to design a "grandfather
clause" for the protocol that would effectively apply only to the former
Soviet Union and that was so restrictively formulated that the potential
impact on CFC emissions would be minimal.

Through their diplomatic strategy, U.S. negotiators were able to gain
the confidence of many governments that had been originally disinterested

in the ozone issue, as well as some that had even opposed controls. The flexibility of the U.S. approach was a persuasive indicator of the reasonableness of its underlying position. In the course of the ozone negotiations, more and more countries gradually endorsed the structure and the contents of the draft protocol that the U.S. delegation had put on the table at the very opening session.

Many of these principles have been applied to other environmental issues and negotiations, as illustrated in Part II of this book. A noteworthy recent development in strategy is the increasing use of formal declarations by ministers, or even heads of state, at specially convened conferences, as a means of maintaining political momentum on an issue and influencing future negotiations. Examples include the 1988 Sophia Declaration of environment ministers on reducing nitrogen oxide emissions, the 1989 declaration of heads of government at the Hague relating to the global-warming threat, and the emphasis at the 1990 Group of Seven Economic Summit on the preservation of forests.

Finally, negotiation leadership may also be attained by undertaking preemptive actions: imposition of controls unilaterally or by a small group of nations, in advance of a broader international agreement. Such action (as in the case of the U.S. 1977 ban on CFC aerosols) enhances the credibility of a country in promoting broader controls: it demonstrates willingness to take the first step. Although there may be some fear that domestic industry could suffer a competitive setback by such unilateral action, it is equally plausible that it could prove a long-term boon by stimulating investment in new technologies.

Consideration of preemptive protective measures in advance of international negotiations may prove particularly important to the climate-change issue. The industrialized countries, whose past and continuing use of fossil fuels are the prime cause of the greenhouse effect, could only gain in credibility vis-à-vis the South if they undertake serious measures to reduce their own carbon dioxide emissions before asking developing countries to at least limit emissions of greenhouse gases. Such measures would bring other advantages as well: They would buy time by delaying or reducing adverse environmental impacts of global warming, stimulate new technology, and legitimize change by undercutting the validity of arguments for delay. As of this writing, more than 20 industrialized countries have declared a willingness to impose targets to stabilize and reduce carbon dioxide emissions, but these pledges have not yet been formalized in an international "mini-accord."

A persistent theme of the discussion so far has been the potential for North-South confrontation over international agreements to protect the global environment. The complexity of modern environmental issues argues, however, against the future effectiveness of the type of bloc politics that has characterized many UN deliberations of the past.

Certainly it is increasingly difficult for any country or group to dominate the proceedings. Leadership—as manifested by the United States on the ozone issue or by the Nordic countries and the Federal Republic of Germany on the 1985 sulfur emissions protocol to the Convention on Long-Range Transboundary Air Pollution—is critical, but the system rewards persistent persuasion rather than power plays. Environmental negotiations are frequently characterized by shifting alliances on different sub-issues, reflecting varying priorities and domestic influences among the parties. Traditional North-South differences may become blurred.

For instance, in the 1991 climate-convention negotiations, there were clear differences among several categories of developing nations comprising the so-called Group of 77 (a traditional developing-country bloc in United Nations forums that actually comprises more than 100 nations). National attitudes and positions toward the necessity for actions to reduce carbon dioxide emissions from fossil fuels or to limit cutting of tropical forests varied considerably. At one extreme were the OPEC oil producers, led by Saudi Arabia and Venezuela, that opposed possible international restraints on their major asset. Countries with a rapidly growing industrial sector, such as China, India, and Mexico, also strongly resisted limits to use of traditional fossil energy to fuel their development. Forest-rich countries such as Brazil, Malaysia, and Indonesia were mistrustful of what they perceived as international interference to limit exploitation of their national patrimony.

On the other hand, a new alliance *within* the Group of 77 emerged during the climate negotiations of 1991: the Association of Small Island States (AOSIS), comprising more than 25 countries of the Pacific and Caribbean whose very existence could be threatened by rising sea levels induced by greenhouse warming; the formal adherence to this group in June 1991 of Singapore, no mean economic power, caused heads to turn at the Geneva session. Several countries in Africa and elsewhere, concerned about expanding drought and desertification, were also inclined to support stronger measures against greenhouse gases. Thus the traditional voting bloc of the Group of 77 was riven by dissension during the climate negotiations because of clearly differing national considerations. This led to many hours of internal caucuses of the Group of 77, during which the larger negotiating process came to a standstill.

Negotiators from the industrialized countries are more accustomed to dealing with differences among their national positions. Here again, however, economic or political power may be difficult to wield. For example, at the 1990 Second Meeting of the Parties to the Montreal Protocol in

London, it was interesting to observe how a coalition of smaller industrialized countries—Norway, Sweden, Finland, New Zealand, and Australia—whose economic stake in production was insignificant, was nevertheless able to prevail over the United States, Japan, and the European Community to achieve a surprising strengthening of proposed controls over methyl chloroform (Benedick, 1991).

The opening of negotiations for a climate convention in Chantilly, VA, in February 1991 epitomized a different type of negotiating strategy, practiced primarily by representatives from developing nations. Many delegates were more familiar with the North-South political and economic rhetoric of the UN General Assembly in New York than with the complex scientific theories of the climate-change issue. To this factor was added real concerns over the implications for national sovereignty and economic growth of potential wide-ranging obligations that might be imposed under a climate treaty.

Hence, the strategy was to delay substantive discussion by means of procedural tactics. For two weeks, delegates argued over the formation, composition, and mandate of the working groups that would be essential to hammer out a treaty text. Many delegates from industrialized countries, who had arrived with specific proposals, expressed frustration as the Group of 77 was unable to agree within itself on candidates for leadership of the working groups. Other delegations, led by India, Brazil, and Mexico, attempted to define the mandates and terms of reference of the working groups in such precise and limiting language that their outcome would be virtually predetermined. This met predictable opposition from the North and the result was a long stalemate.

It was not until well into the second negotiating round, in Geneva, June 1991, that the leadership of working groups was finally agreed upon, with representation appropriately divided among the various regional interests—including the new alliance of small island states. However, the intervening time had in fact been well-used: more than 20 countries—including many from the South—presented specific draft treaty language in Geneva, and the stage was set for serious and substantive debate. Every negotiation must clearly find its own pace, assuming the parties are serious about arriving at an outcome.

The Process of Negotiation

The scientific uncertainties and the complexity of the issues—the interrelationships between environmental, commercial, scientific, and technological factors—will inevitably condition the negotiating process. An important lesson from many of the environmental negotiations described in this volume is the usefulness of separating an issue into more manageable components rather than trying to design an ideal and comprehensive treaty at one stroke. Attempting to solve all aspects of a complex problem within one framework can prove to be a formula for delay; the perfect becomes the enemy of the good. Instead, it may be desirable to work for a step-by-step consensus—incremental agreements that can be reviewed and revised as negotiations progress.

A useful element in this process can be informal fact-finding meetings that constitute a prenegotiation phase. Such meetings can comprise bilateral contacts among governments or larger workshops that involve not only government officials but also scientists, academics, and representatives of industry and environmental organizations. Participants usually attend in their personal capacities and not as members of national delegations with established positions. One of the most highly developed examples of a prenegotiation process was the Intergovernmental Panel on Climate Change, which assembled hundreds of participants from within and outside governments for dozens of workshops over a two-year period preceding the formal opening of negotiations on a climate convention in 1991, and which has been extended in an advisory function to the negotiators (WMO, 1990).

A major purpose of such forums is to explore options and encourage creativity in an informal setting. Informal meetings are more conducive to breaking barriers to communication than are the structured intergovernmental negotiations. The aura of informality encourages posing hypothetical questions and advancing unorthodox answers. An additional benefit is that the more collegial atmosphere can aid negotiators in developing personal rapport and working relationships that may prove useful when the formal negotiations are under way.

When the governments convene, the stakes become higher. As pointed out earlier, a useful technique for disaggregating a complex problem and achieving incremental agreements is the establishment of small working groups. In contrast to the large plenary session, such behind-the-scenes working groups share some of the informality of the prenegotiation workshops. Participants are not bound by traditional diplomatic etiquette. Most important, they can discuss more freely in the absence of observers from interest groups.

Another device that promotes a gradual convergence of views is the use of a consolidated negotiating text that is not associated with any of the protagonists but rather with a neutral party, such as the chair or the secretariat. There is a tremendous efficiency in concentrating debates on a single text rather than having multiple, mutually exclusive drafts in circulation. Such a text will reflect, within square brackets and paragraph by paragraph, the divergent positions of countries.

The negotiations for the Montreal Protocol opened chaotically with several conflicting proposals on the table. The convergence over the next two negotiating rounds of a growing number of countries on a single text provided an essential focus to the deliberations. This draft protocol never had formal status, however, until it was signed by governments on the final day in Montreal. Because it was designated as "the Executive Director's text," government representatives were not committed to any part of it at any interim stage in its development. This flexibility left opportunities open for trade-offs and adjustments at later phases of the negotiating process.

Many negotiations also illustrate the importance of coalition-building— reaching out to an ever-widening group of like-minded governments in an attempt to build momentum toward consensus. Ways were found, often with the assistance of a multilateral agency that enjoyed credibility with all parties, to encourage countries to recognize their interest in participating.

It is also important to prevent the formation of a blocking coalition—a group sufficiently powerful to prevent an agreement. The Group of 77 can represent such a potent force. But, as pointed out earlier, there may be conflicting interests within this group, and alliances can be forged across traditional North-South boundaries. Similarly, as the ozone negotiations demonstrated, the European Community's opposition to strong chemical controls was gradually undermined by diplomatic efforts of the United States with governments within the EC, such as Belgium, Denmark, the Federal Republic of Germany, and the Netherlands. And the 1990 ozone negotiation in London showed how adroit diplomacy by a group of smaller industrialized countries successfully overcame opposition of major economic powers.

Negotiators at the front line must also deal regularly with their authorities at home, particularly in a situation in which there are evolving treaty texts and new proposals from other parties. Modern telecommunications— telephone, fax, and, for confidential messages, embassy cables—substantially facilitate this process. In some countries, however, where such facilities are unreliable, negotiators may remain uninstructed from their supervisors and hence unable to demonstrate flexibility. Similar problems may occur because of problems of obtaining or transmitting precise translations of an English operating text. Finally, and perhaps most importantly, interagency disagreements in the capital can severely constrain the negotiating flexibility of the diplomat abroad.

An aspect of modern diplomacy that is of growing importance is the interaction of negotiators with the media. Press conferences and television interviews during a negotiation can be used by government representatives to reassure domestic constituencies, to float ideas unofficially, or to apply pressure on opponents. Nongovernmental observers—environmental groups as well as industry—also turn to the media to amplify their positions and influence the negotiators.

Finally, the time sequence of a negotiation, illustrated clearly in the example of the Vienna Conventions on nuclear security, is an important consideration. Negotiators must be sensitive to the rhythm of the process, the evolution of consensus. Positions crystallize, participants waver, government policies subtly change. There are almost predictable points at which stalemate and failure seem imminent. Bringing a negotiation back from the abyss tests the quality and skills of the bureau and the secretariat: the creative use of recesses, informal working parties of key protagonists, reformulations of critical texts.

The end-game strategy involves a delicate balancing by the negotiators of the optimal and the attainable. Sheer stamina is not a factor to be ignored. The final hours of an important negotiation, when so much is at stake and the pressures can become unbearable, often occur after days of long night sessions.

The Outcome of Negotiations: Some Personal Observations

The nature of modern environmental issues raises some particular questions concerning the outcome of negotiations. Mitigating a global danger such as ozone-layer depletion or climate change requires virtually universal participation to be truly effective. At some point, however, negotiators must determine whether to go ahead with a less than optimal number of signatories or to delay the process to obtain wider agreement. They must assess the benefits—substantive and psychological—of a formal agreement involving fewer nations against the potential of nonparties undermining the treaty's impact as free riders or pollution havens.

In the case of the Montreal Protocol, the negotiators decided that the most urgent priority was to get the CFC regulations into international law, even without global participation. The primary consideration was that at least the major actors—in this case the European Community, the United States, Japan, and the former Soviet Union—should join. This was, in a sense, a preemptive action by the principal current producers of CFCs in the North, buying time and establishing credibility vis-à-vis potential future producers of the South. Only 24 nations actually signed the protocol in September 1987. By mid-1991, however, 70 governments had ratified, including China, a previous holdout; this represented nearly 100% of global

CFC production and well more than 90% of consumption (Benedick, 1991). Although India, the remaining large potential major producer and consumer of CFCs, had still not acceded, the political momentum, bolstered by changes in the protocol in June 1990 providing explicitly for financial aid and technology transfer, was expected to attract the remaining holdouts.

Another element of a successful outcome is the effective use of the market mechanism to provide signals and incentives to industry to invest in the research and development necessary to achieve environmentally desirable solutions. In effect, the rules of the market can be altered to influence the research agenda, stimulate competition, and reward the right kind of technological innovation.

Negotiators of environmental treaties involving controls—for example, dealing with hazardous materials, sulfur dioxide, or CFC emissions, pollution of the Rhine or of regional seas—must decide whether to link such controls with the best available technology (BAT) or whether to mandate technology-forcing targets. BAT clauses in effect ratify the status quo; the Montreal Protocol negotiators decided this was an insufficient response to the threat to the ozone layer, and established target dates for a phasedown of CFCs *before* alternatives were developed.

This philosophy was reflected in a statement in 1990 by German Environment Minister Klaus Toepfer: "I am absolutely convinced that if you give a clear-cut timetable, it will stimulate industry to come up with substitutes. But if more time is allowed, I really believe they will take more time" (Frankel, 1990). The international chemical industry long claimed that it would be impossible to find practicable substitutes for CFCs. Only in 1986, when the prospects of internationally agreed controls became serious, did they resume, after a several-year hiatus, serious research into substitutes. And within the first year after the Montreal Protocol was signed, the initial research results made a total phaseout of these chemicals a practicable goal.

Industrial planners abhor uncertainty, particularly involving regulatory obligations. Prolonged negotiations or ambiguous targets contribute to such uncertainty. Thus in some situations it may be both technically practicable and environmentally desirable to establish goals beyond BAT to stimulate innovation. If a treaty's requirements are unrealistic, however, they may provoke substantial economic dislocations, massive resistance by industry in the courts, noncompliance and evasion, and offshore pollution havens. This can be a delicate balance to achieve: ostensibly weaker controls can be more conducive to stimulating solutions than a seemingly optimal regulation that in actuality unleashes a storm of resistance that delays the changes desired.

Increasingly important elements of the outcome are treaty provisions for monitoring compliance, sanctions against nonparties and parties in noncompliance, and adjudication of disputes. Full reporting of data and accessibility to such data by parties *and* the interested public are essential for determining compliance. Yet, in the case of the Montreal Protocol, some European countries successfully argued against open reporting on grounds of business confidentiality (Benedick, 1991). If data are accessible, or if noncompliance is technically visible, it can be expected that environmental groups will serve as informal watchdogs. The CITES agreement established a wide network to monitor trade in endangered species (Sand, 1990). Political pressure—whether exercised through bilateral diplomacy, a meeting of parties, or a UN agency—can also play a role.

The Montreal Protocol imposed trade restrictions against nonparties to limit profits for free riders. Such restrictions, linked explicitly to protection of the health of living species or the conservation of natural resources, were determined at the time to be compatible with the General Agreement on Tariffs and Trade (GATT, Article XX).

Finally, the scientific uncertainties and the increasingly preventive objectives of modern environmental negotiations dictate a pragmatic and flexible approach. Under these circumstances, there are distinct advantages to interim solutions or framework conventions such as the Barcelona Convention on regional seas (Chapter 7), the Vienna Convention on the ozone layer, or the climate-change convention now under negotiation (Chapter 11). Such a treaty, even when it falls short of imposing strict environmental regulations, can set up a structure that facilitates a more stringent legal regime in the future. It can influence the political context, maintaining the momentum for further action. Provisions that coordinate and focus international research and monitoring efforts and promote reporting and exchange of data can formalize the scientific input and establish the basis for future consensus on hard actions (Sand, 1990).

An environmental treaty can also be designed to allow parties to assume obligations gradually. This is especially important in securing the agreement of developing nations to controls on substances that contribute to their economic growth, and was the rationale behind the grace-period provisions of the Montreal Protocol.

In conclusion, the experience of a negotiator in environmental diplomacy reveals that, in many respects, nations are entering uncharted waters. Even though the new threats are global and require an unprecedented degree of international cooperation and harmonization, nation-states remain, perhaps not unnaturally, preoccupied with traditional attributes of sovereignty.

In the North, there is a concern that donor countries not commit themselves to open-ended new obligations for financial assistance or technology transfer over which they have no control. In the South, there is often a mistrust of the motivations of the North, a pervasive anxiety about being relegated indefinitely to a condition of "underdevelopment," and a jealous guarding of relatively recently acquired sovereign rights over their own natural resources. Yet there is general agreement that the wealthier countries must assume the lion's share of responsibility and that the South's concern about equity and fairness is justified. It is the negotiators' task to translate these principles into reasonable commitments.

Perhaps the outstanding feature of this new diplomatic challenge is the prominence of science and scientists, as has been noted in many contexts above. The transparency of environmental negotiations and the roles of many nontraditional actors—citizens' groups, industry, specialized agencies, the media, legislators, religious leaders—are other important factors that the practitioner must take into account. The use of informal workshops and meetings in the negotiating process represents an innovative accommodation to this situation.

The experience in recent years suggests that it is difficult even for major powers to resist the unremitting pull toward a political agreement that is bolstered by scientific consensus of a serious risk—even if the scientific evidence is incomplete. There is only so far a delegation can carry dogmatic rhetoric, inflexible positions, or delaying tactics when there is a growing momentum for action among a critical mass of the other negotiating parties. Particularly in the area of the environment, where ethical considerations are increasingly emphasized, the power of moral suasion should not be underestimated.

Looking back, the Montreal Protocol may be a paradigm for a new negotiating approach mandated by threats to the global environment. The treaty contained explicit procedures to facilitate its adaptation to evolving conditions. Moreover, any such revisions would be based upon regularly scheduled periodic reassessments of the changing science, of environmental impacts, of economic factors, and of technological advances—a process that came to involve the mobilization of hundreds of international experts in a path-breaking and innovative exercise (UNEP, 1989b).

Most negotiations of the past have been undertaken in order to set an international decision in concrete. In contrast, the Montreal Protocol points the way toward a new concept, in which the negotiators deliberately avoid a static solution and design a dynamic and flexible instrument capable of responding to changing circumstances. Thus the experience of the ozone treaty may offer hope that it is possible for sovereign nations to agree on cooperative and costly actions even in the face of scientific uncertainty and remote threats—utilizing the skills of negotiation in the longer term perspective of stewardship of the planet.

13

Perspectives on International Organizations

ORAN R. YOUNG

Any effort to understand the place of intergovernmental organizations (IGOs) in international environmental negotiations must begin with the observation that negotiations of this type ordinarily focus on the (re)formation of institutional arrangements or regimes intended to regulate the behavior of members of international society (including the activities of individuals and firms operating under their jurisdiction) whose actions would otherwise produce harmful environmental effects extending beyond their jurisdictional boundaries. To comprehend the role of international organizations in these negotiations, therefore, we must direct our attention toward institutional bargaining—that is, bargaining that occurs when several autonomous parties seek to reach agreement on the terms of the networks of rights and rules expected to govern their subsequent interactions in a given issue area. This contrasts with the process of bargaining over single-shot or self-contained issues of the type envisioned in most formal models of bargaining (Young, 1975, 1989b).

To set the stage for a consideration of the place of international organizations in institutional bargaining related to the (re)formation of environmental regimes, some preliminary definitions and illustrations are in order. *Regimes* are social practices based on constellations of rights and rules that govern interactions among the occupants of recognizable roles defined with reference to more or less distinct issue areas (Keohane, 1989; Krasner, 1983; Young, 1989a). While they vary greatly in terms of membership, functional scope, geographical domain, complexity, degree of formalization, and stage of development, all regimes are properly understood as social institutions. By contrast, *organizations* are physical entities possessing offices, personnel, equipment, budgets, and individual legal "personalities." They play important roles in implementing and administering the provisions of many, though by no means all, international regimes. Studies of the interplay between institutions and organizations constitute a central concern for those interested in governance at the international level (Rosenau, 1991; Young, 1989a).

The United Nations Environment Program (UNEP) is an organization; some examples of international regimes include the environmental protection arrangements for the Mediterranean Basin set forth in the 1976 Barcelona Convention for the Protection of the Mediterranean Sea Against Pollution and Its Related Protocols (Chapter 7), as well as the environmental protection arrangements for stratospheric ozone formalized in the 1985 Vienna Convention for the Protection of the Ozone Layer together with the 1987 Montreal Protocol on Substances That Deplete the Ozone Layer, as amended in 1990 (Chapter 3). The Economic Commission for Europe (ECE) is an organization; the 1979 Geneva Convention on Long-Range Transboundary Air Pollution, coupled with its 1985 and 1988 protocols on sulfur emissions and nitrogen oxide emissions (Chapter 6), lays out the terms for an international regime. Similar observations are in order about the relationship between the International Commission for the Protection of the Rhine Against Pollution (ICPR) and the Rhine River regime articulated in the provisions of the 1976 Bonn Convention on the protection of the Rhine River against chemical pollution and against chloride pollution as well as in the terms of the 1987 Rhine Action Plan (Chapter 8).

In international environmental negotiations, international organizations figure prominently in two distinct capacities. Organizations like UNEP, the ECE, and the ICPR can and often do become instruments of regime formation. Such agencies play significant roles in the institutional bargaining processes that produce constitutional contracts that give rise to environmental regimes.[1] Those engaged in institutional bargaining, by contrast, often foresee a need for organizations to implement and administer the provisions of the international regimes they create. As a result, the character of the organizations to be established in connection with environmental regimes regularly becomes a prominent agenda item during institutional bargaining processes. Some organizations—UNEP is a striking example—figure in both capacities, initially serving as instruments of regime formation and subsequently advancing to assume roles in the administration of the regimes they helped to form. For purposes of this analysis, these themes can be labeled "international organizations as instruments" and "international organizations as objects," respectively, and are addressed below.

International Organizations as Instruments

We live in an era of rapid growth in the number and variety of intergovernmental organizations (Archer, 1983). In part, this is a reflection of rising levels of interdependence in international affairs and the resulting need for organizations to manage the complex webs of interdependencies linking the members of international society (Keohane & Nye, 1989). So, too, is it a product of the emergence during the postwar period of a worldview that highlights the benefits expected to be accrued to individual members of international society from intensive interactions with others while de-emphasizing the dangers of foreign entanglements and the attractions of autarky. Under the circumstances, there is no shortage of international organizations capable of playing active roles in international environmental negotiations.

A choice of organizations. A variety of international organizations can and do become actively involved in environmental negotiations. Multipurpose organizations, like the ECE and the Organization for Economic Cooperation and Development (OECD), assume leading roles in some environmental negotiations; organizations whose mandate is limited to environmental issues, like UNEP, take on these roles in other cases. Even among environmental organizations, there is an important distinction between those focused on a single issue and those whose concerns extend to a broad spectrum of environmental issues. Whereas the ICPR has played a key role in devising the terms of the Rhine River regime, for example, UNEP has emerged as an important player in developing regimes to control regional pollution, protect the ozone layer, regulate transboundary shipments of hazardous wastes, and, most recently, deal with climate change.

Participation in environmental negotiations often involves a number of international organizations. To develop the Mediterranean Action Plan in the 1970s, several organizations joined forces, including UNEP, the Food and Agriculture Organization (FAO), the International Maritime Consultative Organization (now simply the International Maritime Organization or IMO), the International Atomic Energy Agency (IAEA), the World Meteorological Organization (WMO), and the World Health Organization (WHO). Similarly, in the ongoing effort to form an international regime to cope with climate change, UNEP and the WMO are working together to structure and facilitate the forces of institutional bargaining. Among other things, these alliances can give rise to new organizational arrangements, such as the Joint Group of Experts on the Scientific Aspects of Marine Pollution (GESAMP) in the Mediterranean case and the joint UNEP/WMO Intergovernmental Panel on Climate Change (IPCC) in the climate-change case.

Why have international organizations chosen to become involved in environmental negotiations? Some organizations are endowed with legal or constitutional mandates that give them strong claims to participate in any negotiations taking place in a more or less well-defined issue area. It would be awkward, for instance, to proceed with negotiations relating to the issues of high-seas fisheries without the participation of the FAO. The same is true with negotiations on atomic energy in the absence of IAEA as a significant player. In other cases, the choice is determined by the suitability or fit between an organization's membership, functional scope, or geographic reach and the nature of the issues under consideration. This accounts, for example, for the choice of the ECE in contrast to the European Community (EC), the OECD, or the Conference on Security and Cooperation in Europe (CSCE) as the organizer of the negotiations leading to the 1979 Geneva Convention on Long-Range Transboundary Air Pollution. The membership of the EC was too narrow while the OECD's membership was too broad, and the CSCE had not yet emerged as an effectual organization. Similar remarks are in order about the choice of UNEP over the OECD in the negotiations leading to the 1989 Basel Convention on the Control of Transboundary Movements of Hazardous Wastes and Their Disposal (Chapter 4). Because relations between developed and developing countries became a central issues in the negotiations, UNEP was better situated than the OECD to operate as an instrument of regime formation in this area.

Frequently, however, the choice of organizations to become active players in environmental negotiations involves political considerations as well. Prior to 1986, for example, the United States and some of its allies preferred the OECD's Nuclear Energy Agency (NEA) over the IAEA as an arena for negotiations on nuclear security not only because of its technical sophistication but also because the countries involved in this agency's work were politically compatible (Chapter 5). The members of the Antarctic Club have long maintained that the Antarctic Treaty Consultative Meetings (ATCMs) are more suitable than various United Nations organs as a forum for efforts to work out additional elements of the Antarctic Treaty System. However, it is no secret that the Antarctic Consultative Parties strongly prefer the ATCMs in part, at least, because this forum maximizes their control over the negotiating process and blunts efforts to apply the doctrine of the "common heritage of mankind" to Antarctic activities. Similar observations are in order about the roles of the United Nations Conference on Trade and Development (UNCTAD), the World Bank, and the United Nations Development Program (UNDP). Whereas many developing countries prefer UNCTAD because it tends to mirror their views on North-South issues, developed countries are far more comfortable with the World Bank where they can exert greater influence. These conflicting preferences have strengthened the role of UNDP in some environmental negotiations because this organization has endeavored, with some success in the eyes of many observers, to steer a middle course between the preferences of the developing countries and those of the developed countries.[2]

One of the more striking developments of the past two decades in the realm of international environmental affairs is the emergence of UNEP as a prominent and effectual player in international environmental negotiations. Given the modest political and material resources at its disposal, UNEP has had remarkable success in launching the Regional Seas Program, promoting the ozone-protection regime, and sponsoring negotiations on transboundary movements of hazardous wastes. What accounts for this success? It seems clear that a combination of endogenous factors and exogenous factors has facilitated the work of UNEP. The organization has achieved a reputation not only for technical competence but also for strong leadership. At the same time, UNEP has followed a strategy of bringing science to bear and stressing the technical aspects of marine pollution, ozone depletion, and hazardous wastes. This strategy has served UNEP well, in part at least because the nations involved in these negotiations have found it expedient to downplay the political dimensions of the issues at stake.

Will UNEP be able to play an equally central role as we strive to come to terms with global environmental issues, like climate change and the loss of biological diversity? There is no doubt that UNEP possesses the technical competence to participate in negotiations on these matters.[3] Yet it will be much more difficult to de-emphasize the underlying socioeconomic and political issues at stake in negotiations over climate change and biodiversity (Benedick, 1991). Coping with climate change may require drastic alterations in our thinking about economic growth; coming to terms with the loss of biodiversity also could necessitate actions that seem highly intrusive to nations, such as Brazil, that possess large tracts of moist tropical forests. In both cases, negotiators will be faced with profound questions concerning the relationship between environment and development as well as the relations between developing countries and advanced industrial nations. Under the circumstances, the relatively apolitical approach successfully adopted by UNEP to deal with regional seas or ozone depletion is not likely to prove tenable as a way of handling issues like climate change and biodiversity. This is surely one of the lessons to be drawn from the controversy surrounding Resolution 44/228, which the UN General Assembly passed in December 1989 to set forth the terms of reference for the 1992 United Nations Conference on Environment and Development (UNCED). This is not to say that UNEP's role in international environmental negotiations will now vanish. But it does seem clear that we are entering a new phase in the effort to devise and implement international environmental regimes—a phase that requires some degree of political motivation.

Roles for international organizations. What specific roles do international organizations play when they become involved in institutional bargaining on environmental issues? It is customary in many quarters to stress the technocratic or apolitical nature of these roles. This is certainly understandable as a form of deference to states long regarded as the primary, if not exclusive, members of international society and that exhibit a pronounced tendency to react negatively to perceived encroachments on their primacy in international affairs. Nonetheless, as we move further into an era of complex interdependence, it becomes increasingly apparent that international organizations cannot and will not confine themselves to purely technical roles. Nowhere is this more evident than in the realm of international environmental affairs.

International organizations (together with nongovernmental organizations in many instances) frequently play a catalytic role in environmental issues, influencing the way the issues are conceptualized or framed and acting to propel them toward the top of the international policy agenda. In capitalizing on the momentum generated by the 1972 United Nations Conferences on the Human Environment (UNCHE), for example, UNEP has had remarkable success in advancing one issue after another to the top of the international agenda. In cases like the Regional Seas Program, moreover, the organization has contributed substantially to the fund of intellectual capital available to those engaged in environmental negotiations (for example, by contributing to the development of the concept of an ecological region). On a similar note, international organizations can and often do keep international environmental issues alive during periods when one or more of the major states have reasons to downplay them.

Particularly instructive in this regard is the role played by the IPCC—a joint enterprise of UNEP and WMO—in countering efforts on the part of some nations (including the United States) to slow the pace of international negotiations on climate change (Sebenius, 1990; Skolnikoff, 1990).

Increasingly, international organizations also have assumed a coordinating role in environmental negotiations. Because environmental issues involve many other concerns, efforts to form environmental regimes typically touch on the interests of several functionally oriented agencies. At the international level alone, for example, those agencies concerned with Mediterranean pollution during the 1960s and 1970s included IMCO, the FAO, the United Nations Educational, Scientific, and Cultural Organization (UNESCO), the WMO, the WHO, the IAEA, and—following its establishment in 1973—UNEP. Under the circumstances, it is easy to grasp the significance of GESAMP's role as a coordinator. And part of the genius of UNEP's effort in the period immediately preceding the signing of the 1976 Barcelona Convention surely lies in the organization's ability to coordinate the activities of a host of interested agencies.

More and more, international organizations have become a source of leadership in environmental negotiations, a development that makes it appropriate to refer to them as the architects of the institutional arrangements emerging from these negotiations. Partly, this is a matter of developing negotiating texts on key issues. While there is nothing new about this source of influence, international organizations now are increasingly active in formulating negotiating texts, often prior to the initiation of formal negotiations. What this means is that organizations such as UNEP can exercise considerable influence over the course of environmental negotiations, even when they are not key players during the negotiation phase itself. Add to this the fact that individuals acting in the name of international organizations, like Maurice Strong and Mostafa Tolba at UNEP or Hans Blix at the IAEA, have become influential leaders in environmental negotiations. And the nature of the roles played by these leaders is by no means limited to purely technical considerations. Regardless of whether observers view the results as good, bad, or indifferent, it is difficult to avoid the conclusion that international organizations now find themselves in the thick of environmental negotiations. No account of specific negotiations is likely to make sense today without considering the roles played by these organizations.

On the other hand, international organizations, like states, may emerge on occasion as obstacles to the negotiation and implementation of environmental regimes. Institutional arrangements espoused by some actors may either impinge on the interests of particular organizations or require an assessment of the principal forces that conflict with the premises on which existing organizations operate. It is sometimes said, for instance, that the World Bank has been part of the problem rather than the solution in efforts to reconcile the demands of development and environmental protection in the Third World. This is because the World Bank has relied on a theory of economic development that fails to account properly for the value of standing stocks of natural resources and that does not accord adequate weight to environmental externalities, like the loss of biodiversity caused by the destruction of tropical forests (Repetto, 1989). Whatever the merits of this case, there is no reason to assume that the influence of international organizations on environmental negotiations always will be constructive. Like states, these organizations have interests that may or may not provide them with incentives to occupy a place in the vanguard when coping with specific transboundary environmental issues.

Some observers have suggested that organizations loom larger in some phases of the negotiating process than in others. Specifically, the idea has surfaced that international organizations are more central to the pre-negotiation phase and the implementation phase than they are to the actual bargaining phase. There is some merit to this idea. The experience of UNEP leaves little doubt that international organizations can and often do exercise considerable influence over the formulation of environmental issues before negotiations actually get under way. Depending upon the character of the regimes formed, organizations may be critical to the implementation or administration of the mechanisms established. Even so, it would be a mistake to overlook the growing importance of international organizations during the course of institutional bargaining on the provisions of environmental regimes per se. We have reached the stage where it seems fair to conclude that if international organizations were not available to participate in institutional bargaining, they would have to be invented.

The effectiveness of international organizations. How effective are international organizations as instruments of regime formation with regard to environmental issues? The evidence in this volume and elsewhere suggests, not surprisingly, that the record in this area is mixed. For the most part, UNEP has been a success story. Much the same can be said of the role of the ECE with regard to transboundary air pollution and of the IMO in the case of the regime established under the terms of the 1973-1978 Convention for the Prevention of Pollution from Ships (MARPOL). The same is true of the International Union for the Conservation of Nature and Natural Resources (IUCN)—a hybrid between a nongovernmental organization and an intergovernmental organization—in connection with biological conservation regimes (Chapter 10), like the arrangements for trade in endangered species set up under the 1973 Washington Convention on International Trade in Endangered Species (CITES).

In other cases, international organizations have been less successful. The OECD encountered significant limits in dealing both with nuclear security and with transboundary movements of hazardous wastes. In the immediate aftermath of the Chernobyl accident, the IAEA may well have set its sights too low in pushing for the adoption of the 1986 Vienna Conventions on notification and assistance in the event of a nuclear accident. The FAO has participated in establishing several international regimes dealing with fisheries, but, once in place, the regimes themselves have not proved particularly effective. Somewhat similar observations are applicable regarding the role of UNCTAD in establishing commodity regimes to regulate international trade in primary products, such as tin, coffee, sugar, and wheat. Beyond this, there are hints that international organizations can become overactive participants in environmental negotiations. In some cases, they have exacerbated the collective action problems associated with such negotiations, rather than helped to solve them, or have pushed for arrangements that seem attractive on paper but that are unlikely to prove workable. While the evidence is far from clear-cut, such problems may have occurred in the negotiation of some of the biological conservation regimes.

What accounts for variations in the effectiveness of international organizations as players in environmental negotiations? The answer to this question undoubtedly relies on a combination of exogenous and endogenous factors. In the case of ozone depletion, for example, UNEP benefited from strong public interest, the development of a relatively high degree of consensus among scientists on the issue, and the emergence of the necessary political will among the participating states. Yet it is undeniable that UNEP also was able to capitalize on the reputation for efficacy it had developed through previous activities, such as the Regional Seas Program. Also, Tolba, UNEP's Executive Director, played a highly skillful leadership role, particularly in the crucial negotiations eventuating in the 1987 Montreal Protocol on Substances That Deplete the Ozone Layer. Similar observations appear regarding the regime for transboundary movements of hazardous wastes articulated in the 1989 Basel Convention. What is needed, in effect, is a convergence of exogenous and endogenous factors that maximize the effectiveness of international organizations in environmental negotiations.

Will convergences of this type occur regularly in the future and, in particular, can we expect them to occur in conjunction with the emerging issues of global environmental change, such as climate change and biodiversity? There is no basis to assume that such convergences will occur. As the

1989 United Nations debate on UNCED suggests, these issues may become too important and too politicized to be handled by an organization like UNEP, no matter how technically competent it seems. The issues themselves, such as the responsibility of states for environmental destruction occurring within their jurisdictions or the obligations of developed countries to assist developing countries in dealing with their environmental problems, may raise questions that can only be resolved at the highest political levels. Yet it would be inappropriate to form bleak conclusions about the probable roles of international organizations as instruments of environmental regime formation. Just as the 1972 United Nations Conference on the Human Environment set in motion a train of events that facilitated the work of UNEP during the 1970s and 1980s, the United Nations Conference on Environment and Development may propel organizations such as UNEP, WMO, or other international agencies to the forefront in coming to terms with issues of global environmental change during the 1990s. This suggests that the roles played by international organizations in specific environmental negotiations are closely linked to broader political developments. Depending on the extent that these larger trends are favorable, international organizations may emerge as key players in a variety of environmental negotiations during the next decade.

International Organizations as Objects

Up to this point, we have examined the roles international organizations play in negotiations that give rise to environmental regimes, without paying much attention to the nature of the specific issues at stake. It is now appropriate to shift gears and address some questions relating to efforts during the course of environmental negotiations to design international organizations intended to implement or administer the provisions of environmental regimes. In other words, it is time to move from a discussion of organizations as instruments to an examination of organizations as objects. As it happens, the cases in this volume have made interesting observations about the creation of international organizations as products of the institutional bargaining resulting in the formation of environmental regimes.

The demand for organizations. At what point are organizations needed to implement or administer the provisions of international regimes dealing with environmental matters? While this is a complex subject, it is clear at the outset that some regimes are capable of operating successfully with little or no assistance from organizations and that regimes vary considerably in these terms. The core regime for Antarctica established under the terms of the Antarctic Treaty of 1959 has no administrative apparatus. The complementary regime for living resources created under the terms of the 1980 Convention on the Conservation of Antarctic Marine Living Resources (CCAMLR) is administered by a commission assisted by a scientific committee and supported by a secretariat. Although the regime for whales set up under the 1946 International Convention for the Regulation of Whaling features standing organizations of some significance, the international regime for the conservation of polar bears relies entirely upon administrative mechanisms operating within the participating states. The same is true of the regime for the protection of stratospheric ozone. While it made perfect sense to rely on national governments to administer the provisions of the 1987 Montreal Protocol, the administration of the compensation fund established under the 1990 London amendments will be entrusted to an international organizational mechanism known as the Executive Committee.

This said, the cases in this volume suggest the value of differentiating among a number of functions that may justify the creation of organizations to administer the provisions of environmental regimes. The need to gather and disseminate information—a category that encompasses but is not restricted to research—seems to constitute an undeniable, albeit circumscribed, basis on which to build the case for establishing organizations in conjunction with international regimes. Without an available source of credible information, how could the International Whaling Commission set quotas for harvests or establish moratoria, the World Heritage Committee make decisions about sites to be included on the World Heritage List, or the biennial CITES Conferences reach conclusions regarding the placement of species in Appendices I and II? But not even this argument is ironclad. The core Antarctic Treaty regime has functioned well without an apparatus of its own for gathering and disseminating information.[4] Much the same is true of the polar bear regime and the regime for North Pacific fur seals (though the latter arrangement collapsed in the 1980s because of other reasons).

Similar comments can be made about other functions that seem to require an administrative apparatus, such as authoritative decision making, raising and disbursing revenues, handling transfer payments (including technology transfers), managing buffer stocks, eliciting compliance, resolving disputes, and evaluating outcomes. Given the way in which the regimes in question are structured, it seems natural to turn to organizations to handle such tasks as deciding whether Antarctic marine living resources are sufficiently abundant to allow commercial harvest, managing economic returns and rents accruing from deep seabed mining, managing the compensation fund for developing countries endeavoring to phase out their use of chlorofluorocarbons (CFCs), and certifying compliance with the rules pertaining to the peaceful uses of atomic energy. Imaginative negotiators, however, can and often do succeed in devising ways to perform those tasks that eliminate or minimize the need to create new international organizations. For example, the across-the-board reductions in the production and consumption of CFCs, mandated under the terms of the Montreal Protocol, will be carried out under the supervision of national administrative agencies operating within each participating country. National administrators can take responsibility for implementing common rules within their own jurisdictions, as in the case of polar bears, without any need for an international organization to oversee the administration of a regime. And the mutual inspection provisions of the 1959 Antarctic Treaty offer an ingenious device for ensuring compliance without creating a specialized organization to handle this function.

While the establishment of organizations is certainly justifiable in connection with some international environmental regimes, therefore, it is worth emphasizing the extent to which ingenious negotiators can devise institutional arrangements that operate effectively in the absence of organizations to administer their provisions. There is a sense, moreover, that the burden of proof rests on those who advocate the creation of international organizations in conjunction with environmental regimes. All organizations are costly to operate, whether we measure these costs in straightforward monetary terms or in terms of intangible consequences like opportunities lost as a result of bureaucratization or the inefficiencies resulting from co-optation by special interests. It follows that where it is possible to eliminate or minimize reliance on organizations without sacrificing effectiveness, the case against the creation of new international organizations is compelling. On the other hand, in the case in which there are trade-offs between the usefulness of organizations in the pursuit of effectiveness and the costs associated with the operation of these organizations, a clear-sighted analysis is needed to make appropriate decisions. In some instances, the parties to institutional bargaining on international environmental regimes will have conflicting preferences in regard to these trade-offs. But in many cases, the problem is more a matter of a need for analysis to arrive at well-reasoned conclusions about the character of suitable organizations than a matter of bargaining to resolve conflicts of interests.

Types of organizations. To conclude that some sort of organization is needed to administer the provisions of an international regime does not resolve the issues at stake. On the contrary, such a decision is a gateway to several additional sets of considerations. To begin with, there is the question of whether to create an independent organization to administer a new regime, to piggyback on an existing organization created initially for some other purpose, or to form a coalition with others for the purpose of sharing administrative mechanisms among several distinct regimes. The CITES regime, for instance, delegates many administrative chores to UNEP, which, in turn, has handed them over to IUCN and the Worldwide Fund for Nature (WWF). Although not formally a component of the international whaling regime, the Bureau of Whaling Statistics is able to handle some tasks relating to the collection and dissemination of information about whaling. Similar comments are in order about the role of the IAEA in administering the provisions of the 1986 Vienna Conventions dealing with notification and assistance in the event of nuclear accidents.

Although we live in an era of rapid growth in the ranks of international organizations, there is much to be said for taking seriously the ideas of piggybacking on existing organizations or sharing organizational arrangements among regimes. The downside of this approach is that the resultant arrangements cannot be tailor-made to fit the needs of particular regimes. In some cases, this may seem a significant drawback. But those negotiating the terms of environmental regimes are well aware of the fact that it is difficult today to fund international organizations in a secure fashion. A diversified portfolio of functions may contribute to the financial stability of any organizations they establish. Here again, conflicts of interest may emerge among the participants in institutional bargaining relating to the formation of international environmental regimes. More often than not, however, this issue is likely to become a topic for joint problem solving as participants seek to devise administrative mechanisms capable of handling tasks effectively, while minimizing the financial contributions required from the members of the resultant regimes (Walton & McKersie, 1965).

It is also apparent that the nature of the organizations needed will be closely tied to the character of the regimes or institutional arrangements they are intended to serve. Any regime calling for authoritative decisions about catch quotas or harvesting limits, the inclusion of species on protected lists, measures to protect migratory routes, and the like will require a sophisticated capability to make scientific judgments about the population dynamics of individual species (not to mention other species with whom they interact) and also for monitoring the results of these decisions over time. A regime that relies on command-and-control regulations, such as the arrangements governing sulfur and nitrogen oxide emissions under the 1979 Geneva Convention, calls for different administrative capabilities than a regime that makes use of incentive systems, such as transferable fishing permits or permits for the emission of various pollutants. Regimes that contemplate the raising or distribution of revenues, such as the ozone compensation fund or the revenue-generating provisions of the proposed Convention for the Regulation of Antarctic Mineral Resource Activities (CRAMRA), require administrative mechanisms that are not needed where there are no issues pertaining to revenues. Even more dramatically, the Enterprise, envisioned as an operating authority under the deep seabed mining provisions set forth in Part XI of the 1982 Law of the Sea Conference, would differ profoundly from the International Seabed Authority (ISA), envisioned as an agency with regulatory authority but without the capacity to engage in its own mining operations.

Unlike the issues addressed in the preceding paragraphs, it is easy to imagine the emergence of conflicts of interest regarding the nature of the organizations to be established in conjunction with environmental regimes. This follows directly from the fact that such matters are closely tied to the underlying character of the regimes themselves. For example, given the clash between the United States and the Group of 77 over the fundamental character of a regime for deep seabed mining, it comes as no surprise that it was ultimately impossible to reach an agreement on organizational details pertaining to the International Seabed Authority and the Enterprise. Much the same can be said of the sharp differences that have surfaced regarding the administrative machinery envisioned in CRAMRA. Because organizations are material entities that can be envisioned relatively easily in concrete terms, it is to be expected that those participating in negotiations aimed at creating environmental regimes will bargain particularly hard over the character of the organizations set up to implement and administer the institutional arrangements they create.

Avoiding perennial problems. Although the establishment of organizations may be unavoidable, any move to set them up triggers concern about a set of classic problems just as relevant to international environmental regimes as they are to any other social institutions. These problems include paralysis, underfunding, co-optation, intrusiveness, and bureaucratization. There are no magic solutions to these problems. But those engaged in institutional bargaining at the international level would do well to foresee the relevance of such problems to the specific situations they are confronting and take steps in advance to mitigate their impact.

The problems of paralysis and underfunding are twin dangers that emerge again and again in connection with international organizations. Paralysis typically occurs when those setting up an organization insist on a decision-making procedure requiring unanimity. In this way, they are assured the power to veto actions they dislike even after the organization is up and running. Interestingly, we have already seen examples of imaginative ways to alleviate this problem in conjunction with international environmental regimes. One constructive device is to rely on a majority-decision rule with a provision for a limited veto, as in the case of CRAMRA, or a provision allowing individual members to opt out of specific decisions, as in the case of the whaling regime and CITES. Another is to combine a majority rule with some form of weighted voting, as in the case of the International Monetary Fund (IMF). In some instances, the problem of underfunding is at least as serious as the danger of paralysis in limiting the effectiveness of international organizations. Proving particularly debilitating in this regard is the common tendency of member states to refuse to grant international organizations a means of generating their own revenues, compelling them to rely exclusively on dues or voluntary contributions from individual members. Yet the development of environmental regimes offers some particularly attractive options for mitigating this problem. It is an interesting idea to allow organizations, acting in the name of humanity's common heritage, to collect economic royalties or rents, as envisioned in the cases of the International Seabed Authority and the commission to be created under CRAMRA. So also is the idea of allowing organizations to collect revenues through the sale of permits for the harvest of renewable resources or the emission of various effluents.

Just as relevant is the danger of co-optation or the capture of administrative agencies by special interests, though perhaps less familiar at the international level than at the national level. The developing countries have long complained about the capacity of affluent countries in general and the United States in particular to control IMF decisions. For its part, the United States has taken a similar view of the role of the Group of 77 in UNCTAD and this group's role in ISA activities. The Antarctic Treaty Consultative Parties claim that any move to bring the Antarctic Treaty System under the umbrella of the United Nations would play into the hands of the special interests of the developing countries. Many environmentalists have asserted that mining interests would be able to exercise undue influence over the behavior of the organizational mechanisms (especially the regulatory committees) envisioned under CRAMRA. No doubt, there is an element of truth to some of these charges; few organizations are immune to pressure from special interests. But the danger here is that steps taken to minimize the problem of co-optation, such as insisting on unanimity as a decision rule, run the risk of exacerbating other classic problems, like paralysis.

Intrusiveness and bureaucratization also are problems well known to those who have studied the behavior of administrative agencies at the national level. The administration of complex regimes requires the promulgation of implementing regulations. In turn, regulations are apt to become bones of contention among those who charge that they are not being implemented in a manner consonant with the intent of a regime's creators as well as among those who argue that the resultant red tape constitutes an inefficient and unjust burden on actors whose activities they regulate. While there is no final solution to such problems, experience in the domestic realm suggests lessons that are worth learning when creating organizations to administer international environmental regimes. In contrast to command-and-control regulations, for example, systems relying on transferable use rights leave more room for discretionary action and encourage efficiency by allowing subjects to meet requirements in the least expensive manner. Similarly, devices designed to maximize transparency as a way of ensuring compliance reduce the need for intrusive monitoring and avoid inconclusive arguments regarding the extent to which subjects have or have not complied with applicable rules in specific situations.

It is hoped that those responsible for negotiating the terms of international environmental regimes will give systematic thought to alleviating these perennial problems. There is no guarantee that the resultant negotiations will be trouble free; it is not difficult to foresee conflicts of interest regarding such matters. Those who fear co-optation are likely to push for unanimity as the applicable decision rule, whereas those more concerned about paralysis will favor some form of majority rule. Negotiators representing capitalist countries are apt to be more resistant to arrangements based on command-and-control regulation than those who come from socialist countries. And those concerned about the deadening effects of bureaucratic red tape are likely to resist efforts to provide international organizations with sizable revenue sources that they can control on their own. There are no correct answers to such differences of opinion. Negotiations are therefore apt to reflect the mixed-motive character long familiar to students of bargaining (Schelling, 1960). Yet we should not conclude that the search for solutions to these perennial problems of administration offers no opportunities for imaginative and mutually beneficial problem solving. In fact, this is an area in which there is considerable scope for inventiveness on the part of those who think about institutional design coupled with leadership efforts of those who participate directly in institutional bargaining concerning international environmental regimes (Young, 1991).

Conclusion

We live in an era of rising international interdependencies that promote a growing need for institutions to manage human activities that would otherwise produce harmful impacts. Nowhere is this more apparent than in the realm of issues relating to natural resources and the environment. In this connection, the anarchical character of international society will appear as an obstacle to progress. But this is not the only perspective from which to approach issues linked to the management of environmental interdependencies. The absence of a central government at the international level does not rule out the prospect of creating international environmental regimes and the organizations needed to implement and administer them. Equally important, the absence of an entrenched central government makes it possible to avoid the problem of establishing new arrangements in the face of parochial opposition from interests entrenched in existing organizations. The cases in this volume make it abundantly clear that the resultant opportunities have produced considerable activity regarding the development of international environmental regimes. While recent initiatives in this realm vary greatly in terms of their effectiveness and desirability, there are good reasons for a sense of cautious optimism among students of international environmental affairs (Sand, 1990).

At the same time, new challenges are arising that may soon make the issues of the recent past seem elementary. The advent of an era of global environmental changes is particularly striking in this regard. Some of these changes, like the greenhouse effect, may well require fundamental alterations in the way we think about economic growth and may force us to confront North-South issues as they arise in discussions of environment and development in forums such as UNCED (Grubb, 1989). Other issues like biological diversity will raise complex questions concerning international stakes in activities occurring largely inside the borders of individual states and the justifiability of various forms of intervention from outsiders. While there is great potential for conflicts of interest over such matters, there are also opportunities for international cooperation that could provide a basis for the establishment of important new international institutions and the organizations needed to implement and administer them. To the extent that such opportunities become available in the foreseeable future, it will be essential to draw lessons from the experience of the recent past. In this way, we can examine what does and does not work when it comes to the institutions and organizations capable of solving large-scale environmental problems. Only through conducting such analyses can we learn from our experiences and prepare ourselves to deal constructively with the challenges ahead.

Notes

1. While we often associate constitutional contracts with formal statements of the provisions of regimes in treaties or conventions, the concept applies as well to informal practices centered on unwritten networks of rights and rules. Many regimes encompass both formal and informal elements (see Buchanan, 1975).

2. This is not to say that UNDP has been particularly well managed or effective in its major undertakings. There is, in fact, considerable controversy regarding UNDP's performance.

3. This does not mean that UNEP's internal management has been particularly efficient. There are those who maintain that UNEP has succeeded in a number of its undertakings despite weak or inefficient management.

4. This situation has undoubtedly contributed to the development of a significant role for the Scientific Committee on Antarctic Research (SCAR), which belongs to the International Council of Scientific Unions (ICSU) and has no formal link to the Antarctic Treaty System.

14

Lessons for Analysis and Practice

I. WILLIAM ZARTMAN

Practitioners and analysts alike are interested in the same question: How is it done when it is done well, and why when it is not? The "it" in both cases is an outcome to environmental negotiations. For practitioners, the challenge is to create an outcome; for analysts, to explain one. Both can combine efforts to make the outcome better; the analyst by identifying the determinants and ingredients that go into the creation of results, and the practitioner by putting those lessons to work. "Better," of course, may have different criteria; it may refer to any party's individual interests or to the combined interests of all the parties. Again, the challenge for both practitioner and analyst is to combine these two criteria into one standard, conceiving and providing both the largest pie possible and also the largest shares of it for each party—a Pareto-optimal outcome.

Before examining the different ways of answering the questions at hand, one preliminary doubt must be laid to rest. Some practitioners and even a few analysts consider environmental negotiations to be a case in problem solving rather than in negotiation, as suggested, for example, by Peter S. Thacher in Chapter 7. What is involved is seen simply as a policy life cycle (Winsemius, 1990) in which the adversary is not some other party but the problem itself, and the appropriate problem-solving phases include recognition, formulation, implementation, and control. The process then would be more appropriately one of information gathering: identifying and alerting attention to the problem, finding the solution and convincing others of it, and then pinpointing the technicalities of enactment and verification (MacNiell et al., 1991). During the process, there is, or should be, no conflict; what conflict does exist is the result of ignorance and can be overcome through research and education.

The view is partially correct but incomplete. The process of working out environmental solutions does assume many characteristics associated with a policy cycle—catastrophe, research, and effectiveness versus efficiency as criteria for a solution in principle and implementation in detail. Technical solutions are necessary, but they are not sufficient; analysis based on education, problem solving, and discovery eschews conflict rather than explains and confronts it.

Conflict is inherent in the existence of environmental problems, and negotiation—the process of combining conflicting points of view into a single decision—is the dynamic way in which problem solving takes place. Conflict is simply an incompatibility between two conditions or positions, not necessarily a violent manifestation of that incompatibility. Environmental conflict can be conceptualized in two different ways as a basis for negotiation. The first way considers the problem as the adversary and seeks to negotiate, as in a game against nature. To find a real solution necessitates compromise or integration between the problem and the ideal outcome in which the needs of each side—the demands of the problem and the demands of the parties—are met in compatible ways. It recognizes that to end wars or solve environmental problems means handling conflicting interests in ways that avoid violence, or—to maintain the spirit of Clausewitz— that negotiation is a mere continuation of policy by nonviolent means.

The second way recognizes that the existence of a problem is prima facie evidence that some parties benefit from it and have a vested interest in its continuation; problem solving then is not merely discovery and education, but dealing with motivated, interested conflict inherent in both the problem and its solution. More than just a matter of creating awareness through consciousness-raising, the challenge is one of negotiating new solutions with an interest-based opposition. Negotiations analysts often have proposed the problem-solving approach as the best way of overcoming conflict (Jean Monnet once said, "Get the parties together on one side of the table and the problem on the other"), but that is not enough. Inherent in the conflict with nature is conflict among the interests of different parties; inherent in problem solving is a need for conflict management. It is hard to strike a deal with a problem. Environmental problem solving needs to address the means and motivations for bringing parties to the point where they can recognize problems, seek solutions, and resolve differences with other, conversely motivated, parties.

Structures

Negotiating theory identifies ripe moments for compromise or agreement. Such moments are characterized by two key elements: a mutually painful stalemate and a recent or impending catastrophe. Other elements necessary to the existence of a ripe moment include valid representatives and a way out (Kriesberg 1991; Hampson & Mandell, 1990; Zartman, 1989). Structural analysis ties the explanation of negotiated outcomes to the distribution of capabilities and interests among the parties prior to the negotiations (Zartman, 1991). The importance of the key elements lies in the fact that they dramatically signal the inability of either party to prevail or to facilitate its way out of the conflict in which it is locked, and at the same time they signal the worsening consequences for both sides if that conflict continues its present course. Stalemate and catastrophe also provide the most immediate key to the question of why environmental negotiations take place.

In environmental matters, the inability of a party to find a unilateral solution to the problem often is thrown into public headlines through a catastrophe, real or impending. Rising public concern is the next most immediate key to initiating environmental negotiations, and catastrophe triggers public concern. But it also triggers scientific inquiry and debate, one of the three necessary—but alone insufficient—keys to opening negotiations.

There is scarcely a case in this collection that does not contain the three keys: a catastrophe-marking stalemate, authoritative representatives, and a plausible solution. The Three Mile Island and Chernobyl accidents, the Torrey Canyon mishap, the Sandoz incident, the discovery of the effects of CFCs on the ozone layer, the result of the British Antarctic survey of 1985, the Sahel droughts of the early 1970s and then again in the early 1980s, chemical-waste dumpings in West Africa, acid-rain effects in Europe (contrasted with the lower perceptibility of effects in North America), all triggered a critical awareness on the part of authoritative decision makers as well as their publics. The result was not to eliminate conflict; in a sense, it was to create it. Some of the former opponents to action now became its proponents, negotiating now among themselves and with their former adversaries to find a way out of the predicament highlighted by the catastrophe.

The lesson seems to be so pervasive that one is forced to ask whether in problem solving as in conflict resolution, it is necessary to wait for the horse to be stolen before the gate is locked. Not surprisingly to readers of *Romeo and Juliet,* the answer seems to be affirmative. Preemptive problem solving is rare and often lacks the drive and urgency of negotiation in the wake of catastrophe. Preemptive bargains tend to be more of an inadequate compromise, since opposition interests have not yet been split and converted by the consciousness-raising event. However, as Shakespeare's readers also know, catastrophe is expensive and runs the danger of triggering a response too late, since it is a substantial down payment on the very events the bargain is designed to prevent. Catastrophes are hard to fake, and interested parties can only hope that the galvanizing event will be a Three Mile Island rather than a Chernobyl, shocking but in the end nonfatal. The result is that the start of negotiation is usually linked to a stalemate reinforced by a catastrophe, the degree of conversion being proportional and the magnitude of compromise inversely proportional to the size of the catastrophe.

Process

Negotiation is best performed when the parties involved jointly identify and agree on a formula that defines the problem in a resolvable way, and then translate the principles of the formula into specific details for implementation. That formula-detail process is made possible when prepared by thorough and often cooperative diagnosis or prenegotiation at the outset (Zartman & Berman, 1982). Environmental negotiations are an admirable illustration of this three-phased process. The scientific preparation provides the diagnosis of the problem, the nature of the process is optimally a matter of crystallizing a formula rather than of merely trading concessions from fixed positions, and the elaboration of details is given coherence and direction as a result of the formula.

Diagnosis or prenegotiation involves two clusters of six components: determination of risks and costs, requirement, and support; and participants, bridges, and agenda, which leads directly into the next phase of formulation (Stein, 1989). The importance of scientific study on environmental questions bears most directly on the first elements, highlighting the degree of risks and costs in both nonaction and various forms of action. The evolving nature of continuing scientific inquiry into environmental questions marks environmental negotiations from the start as a crystallizing process, characterized by skepticism without fixed positions and a search for solutions without clear adversaries.

Formulation is characteristically a trial-and-error process, and in the case of environmental problems it is a looser process than usual. The element of precedence is generally absent, the nature of the problem itself is multiplicious and unfocused, and solutions are ill fitting and scientifically uncertain. As a result, the regimes or formulas—the sets of rules and expectations defining the problem and governing the solution—are temporary, evolving, and continuously expandable and perfectible rather than overarching and deductive as an optimal formula should be.

As a result, formulation becomes an incremental process at the core of environmental negotiations, in which many parts are put together by trial and error until a comfortable and agreeable formula is found. Definitions often are avoided initially in favor of lists of covered activities, which only later are joined under a definitional umbrella. Component areas of attention are isolated and cobbled together to form the scope of the agreement.

A package is constructed out of a small core coalition of key interests, and then the agreement is expanded to the greatest extent possible. More often even than in other multilateral negotiations, environmental problem solving involves a complex management process set in motion by a conference leadership that orchestrates partial competing interests of parties. Commitments are outlined and then strengthened; environmental negotiations have characteristically begun with statements of intent, codes of conduct, or differential obligations, exceptions, and reservations, which then gradually are turned into binding obligations; private watch groups that monitor behavior replace signatories' engagements or international organizational constraints, until new norms have been introduced far enough to constitute informal international law.

There is no model or method for this process, although there are strategies that the parties employ. Also a procedural sequence, as outlined by Gunnar Sjöstedt in Chapter 5 gives a certain order to the parties' efforts at devising a formula: philosophical or plenary thoughts, sectoral interest-related positions, and horse-trading resolutions. The inchoate nature of the subject, problem, and solution all indicate an ad hoc trial-and-error means of crafting a formula that necessarily is only temporary. Thus, at the end of the process as at its beginning, instability is a creative characteristic of environmental negotiations; the temporary formula should be constructed so that it calls for its own improvement and moves the process along—or, like the Sinai disengagement agreements of 1974-1975, that it "falls forward" as a temporary solution that, constructively, cannot last in its momentary form.

A few examples of the formulas adopted will illustrate both the process and the outcome. In the 1985 Vienna Convention for the Protection of the Ozone Layer, the formula was "a loose framework agreement in exchange for research and a commitment to a workshop and a future conference," exchanging looseness now for a chance to gather evidence and revise later, and bridging the positions of the "declaration of intent" and the "total ban" camps. Then the 1987 Montreal Protocol on Substances That Deplete the Ozone Layer embodied the formula, "variable production and consumption cutbacks in exchange for individual exceptions and derogations." Thereafter the Helsinki Declaration of 1989 was based on "intent to total phaseouts in exchange for information and funding," again tightening the general obligations but at the cost of inducements, not exceptions. In yet another reworking of the Convention, the London Amendments of 1990 comprised "obligatory phaseouts in exchange for financial incentives." Over the period, the process of formulation involved tightening the obligations and broadening the coverage in exchange for particular incentives rather than exceptions.

Even in the absence of a process that moves through an evolving form of the formula, other cases still embody a basic formula. The Ramsar Convention on Wetlands of 1972 (Chapter 10) was based on "conservation of one wetland of international importance in exchange for commitment to research," again providing a compromise agreement between a hard camp and a soft camp that was designed to "fall forward" when the impact of research and of the commitment to sites of "international importance" became evident. The Bonn Convention on Migratory Species of 1979 produced a less effective compromise: "broad, strict protection in exchange for a mere 'endeavor,' " so that the loose operative verb undermined the overly constraining coverage. The Washington Convention on International Trade of Endangered Species of 1975, on the other hand, was based on the formula of "limitations in exchange for legal trade within those limits," again with a possibility of "falling forward" by moving from a focus on prohibited species to one on a smaller number of permitted species. Similarly, the 1989 Basel Convention on the Control of Transboundary Movements of Hazardous Wastes and Their Disposal was based on a different type of formula of "reduced generation of export, managed disposal, and importers' bans," as a compromise between hard and soft camps (Chapter 4). Like the Ramsar Convention, the Basel Convention started an incremental process by establishing a floor on efforts (and unlike the Bonn Convention, which tried to establish a leaky ceiling). Like the Washington Convention, the Basel Convention extended its participant coverage, thereby covering nonparties as well as parties in its restrictions (but not its benefits), forcing nonparties to ratify in order to stay in the trade.

One other aspect apart from incrementalism that characterizes and complicates the process of environmental negotiation is the difficulty in finding clear trade-offs. Trade-offs are the essence of formula-building and of negotiation in general; they provide the means of creating a positive-sum agreement, both by constituting elements evaluated differently by the parties and by incorporating additional payments to enlarge the pie (Homans, 1961; Nash, 1950). Numerous, clear, graduated, available divisions within the potential stakes facilitate trade-offs. Such characteristics are hard to find in environmental issues. The problem is that potential items for trade-offs are as ill defined as the issues themselves and are differentiated by time as well as nature and size. Time-related payoffs are unusually difficult to compare and equate, not only because discount rates fluctuate wildly but also because delayed payments can change in value or even can be evaded (see Chapter 11).

The cases show that there is a very limited range of available trade-offs, generally falling into one of three categories. The first is the exception category: parties often agree to a regulation, even a stringent one as in the ozone, Rhine, and hazardous wastes agreements, at the price of claiming exceptions for themselves at the end of the agreement. While this has the advantage of establishing a principle, it considerably weakens its effectiveness. A second category is sounder: trade of breadth for depth in regulation. Many are the cases where a regime began with a relatively strict coverage of a comparatively small number of items, often implemented through a small number of steep steps. The opposite approach is a relatively broad coverage through loose restrictions or gentle steps. The problem with the first is that it can lead to incoherence and imperceptible results, whereas the weakness of the second is that it invites generalized resistance and tends to "fall backward" to less, rather than more, extensive effectiveness, as the Bonn Convention on Migratory Species shows.

The third type of trade-off is the reverse of the first: trading restrictions for inducements. Many environmental negotiations have turned to compensation as a way of establishing trade-offs across the North-South divide. Indeed, the entire structure of the 1992 United Nations Conference on Environment and Development (UNCED) is based on a massive trade-off designed to bridge the North-South gap, if the two sides only agree to take it into account. But the device also illustrates the problems with environmental trade-offs: compensation provides an immediate transfer of resources but has an air of bribery; in fact, the term *compensation* itself is frequently avoided in favor of "financial inducements" (a seemingly more loaded expression) or "safeguards and assistance." On the other hand, compensation for an action (conversion to nonpolluting materials, for example) is essentially no different than compensation for a good (purchase of a plot of land, for example) in that both cover current value as well as current and future use. Indeed, the compensation question has become "the focal point of the ozone-layer negotiations," according to Patrick Széll in Chapter 3. Properly constructed, compensation can be an answer to a major problem particularly prevalent in North-South environmental discussions—the problem of the free rider. No matter the device, the solution must be structured so that individual parties are not able to enjoy its benefits as a public good while opting out of its obligations. The misuse of environmental consensus to turn others' obligations into free riders' advantage is sadly well shown in the abuse of exceptions under the International Whaling Convention.

Incremental formulations find specific illustration in all of the cases studied. Indeed, in most of the examples, the initial or salient negotiation laid out the basic formula and the subsequent negotiations filled in and revised the details. Negotiations moved from the question of *whether* in the main round to questions of *when, how,* and *what* in later meetings. The formulating negotiations are termed the main round, or salient, negotiations because they are not usually the first meeting on the subject; instead they are preceded by preparatory and partial negotiations of their own, as well as other events, as might be expected. Often the incremental process begins bilaterally and even nongovernmentally, and the main round serves to collect and coordinate these diverse efforts around a coherent formula; the conventions on marine pollution and hazardous wastes are examples.

Each issue's process of incremental construction follows its own path. The 1972 United Nations Conference on Human Environment (UNCHE) in Stockholm that created the United Nations Environment Program (UNEP) was the starting point for many incremental processes, notably the Mediterranean Action Plan of 1975 and then the more binding Barcelona Convention the following year. But on the issue of marine pollution itself, UNCHE was preceded by GESAMP in 1967 and the Intergovernmental Working Group on Marine Pollution (IWGMP) in 1971. On the ozone layer, the Vienna Convention negotiations of 1982-1985 with subsequent workshops led to the Montreal Protocol negotiations of 1986-1987, followed by the Helsinki Statement of Intent of 1989 and the London Amendments signed in 1990. This incremental process also led to the establishment of the Intergovernmental Panel on Climate Change (IPCC) in 1988, with the framework convention of global warming expected at the UNCED meeting in Brazil in 1992. In a further twist, incremental formulation often leads to bilateral implementation in detail, as the International Atomic Energy Agency (IAEA) negotiations after 1986 laid the ground for the Swedish agreement on nuclear accidents with Denmark and Norway in 1986, Finland in 1987, the former Soviet Union in 1988, and the German Democratic Republic in 1989.

Other cases of incrementalism have been less straightforward. On the Sahel (Chapter 9), the United Nations Conference on Desertification of 1977 produced action recommendations and attempts to bring political will, resources, and programs to bear on the problem; yet there is still no regime for the problem. Despite the Ségou Declaration of 1989, efforts remain essentially hortatory. In a contradictory set of experiences, the Ramsar Convention on Wetlands of International Importance Especially as Waterfowl Habitat, through its lack of binding obligations, encouraged states to join the convention and then to become morally entrapped in their commitments; yet the Bonn Convention on Conservation of Migratory Species remained limited in its impact by its signatories' commitment only to "endeavor" to improve conditions. On the other hand, another interesting example of the process of formulation found in both the ozone and the nuclear-accident conventions shows the use of trade-offs in obligations to build a formula incrementally: parties exchanged their signature for an exception, or agreed to a stringent obligation in exchange for a derogation, leaving in place a nonbinding guideline to which they then found themselves committed without exception in the next round. Even in the unfortunate case of the International Convention for the Regulation of Whaling, where exceptions threatened to destroy the regime, member states undertook to enforce bilaterally what the multilateral treaty was unable to make binding. Not all regimes become more and more binding nor do formulas become incrementally more coherent, but the general trend is present nonetheless.

Strategy

The same process of agglomerating issues, interests, and payoffs is characteristic of the strategies used by negotiating parties. Experience, as opposed to distant observation, shows that the much-vaunted epistemic community is a result, rather than a motor, of environmental negotiations.[1] It may come into being as the issues arise and are brought into focus, but the point of strategy is to bring about its creation rather than to rely on its prior existence. The transnational cooperation of science, technology, and business is one type of coalition that can be built as a basis for an environmental bargain, but it is generally not enough. It is merely the grouping that constitutes one side of the negotiations, and it then must use its pluralistic resources—knowledge, skill, and money—to raise the consciousness of alert political leaders. By its description, the strategy clearly appears to be the equivalent of the incrementally aggregating process already noted on the issue side.

The other type of coalition-building is international—among, rather than across, states. In this the political leaders are the motor, with science, technology, and business in their advisory groups. The building blocks of such coalitions are frequently regional identity groups, but may also be caucusing groups based on issue-related common interests. Strategies are drawn from the three classic baskets labeled coalesce, cut up, and confront. Groups seek to aggregate other groups and parties into a growing winning coalition, or to divide opposing groups into smaller parts so as to absorb or weaken them or to work out a deal with them. The Mediterranean Action Plan appears to have resulted from an expanding coalescing strategy; the OECD group divided up its opposition to produce an agreement on hazardous wastes, and the ozone conventions and protocols resulted from a dialectical confrontation in which the Toronto Group faced the European Community to strike a deal, and then the newly developed states' consensus faced the less developed countries. Since regional groups frequently contain very diverse interests in regard to the environmental issue involved, the international coalition-building strategy involves a clash between solidarity-making (regional) and problem-solving (technical) groups and a development of issue awareness that is helpful in making global bargains.

One strategy can be considered that of leadership or orchestration versus coalition. As opposed to the acephalic conglomerating strategies of coalition, orchestration strategies depend on a designated conductor or leader who agglomerates parties into a consensual process. Each party pursues its own interests and is brought in to play its own score in order to produce a harmonious result. The interstate nature of environmental negotiations means that the conductor cannot be sovereign and cannot have an agenda related to personal interests. But the multilateral conference nature of the negotiations means that procedural requirements call for a disinterested leader to provide some order to the proceedings. Thus many environmental conferences give a prominent role to the secretary general, conference chair, secretariat, or other organizing agency. States rarely aspire to this role, for many reasons: no state is powerful enough to be hegemonic, interests are usually defensive and partial rather than global, and every potential leader is, above all, a regional and interest group player and so is tainted. In this situation, the procedural conductor is actually welcome, since he or she allows the state parties to pursue their own interests more effectively and facilitate agreement.

Whether through strategies of coalition or of orchestration, states usually enter environmental negotiations with the purpose of furthering or defending their own corner of interests, rather than exercising global leadership. Their substantive strategies can take one of the three forms outlined by Sjöstedt (Chapter 5): driving, braking, or modifying behavior, all of which are oriented to the pursuit of specific interests. A driving strategy seeks to have a particular measure or position incorporated in the final agreement. A braking policy tries to oppose such a policy, but, in the absence of a successful brake, a modifying strategy attempts to limit or slow down the effect of a drive. To these three strategies, two others must be added. One is an exit strategy, implemented through the use of exceptions and derogations. The other is compensation, which trades acceptance for inducements and side payments. Participants may be more or less open to the legitimacy of other parties' interests on other subjects than their own, and therefore more or less willing to engage in trade-offs to achieve their own offensive or defensive purposes. It is this strategic picture of "each defending a corner" that makes for the ad hoc and incremental nature of the environmental negotiating process.

Each strategy—transnational or international coalition, orchestration, driving, braking, modifying, exit, and compensation—has been used in environmental negotiations. In most cases, there has been a motor group using coalition tactics to build support for its desired agreement, essentially following a driving strategy. In opposition they met a braking or modifying strategy or, when these failed, an exit strategy through exceptions.

Conclusions

In the mid-1980s, as the Third World New International Economic Order (NIEO) campaign drew to a close, a study identified 10 ways in which North-South confrontations could be rendered more productive (Zartman, 1985, 1987). They included a timely shift away from confrontation to a joint attack on the problem, joint diagnosis, encompassing formulas, trade-offs, realistic deadlines, incremental and flexible agreements, partial participation, international organizations as mediators and orchestrators, and alertness to ripe moments to galvanize action. It is striking not only that all of these are employed in environmental negotiations but that they are its main characteristics, producing a process so different from the confrontations of the 1970s that practitioners asked whether it was negotiation at all. And still problems remain. It is probably fair to recall that the environmental process, in general, has been remarkably smooth and productive compared with the New International Economic Order standoff, largely because the current process has been loose, flexible, incremental, inchoate, and aggregative.

Analysis and practice then are faced with two opposing questions. On one hand, is it possible to tighten up the process to make it more efficient or, in other words, can formulation be something other than an ad hoc process? On the other hand, can environmental negotiations in the future continue to rely on momentum, hoping that, as in the past, loose and unstable agreements will fall forward and turn into tighter, self-enforcing systems of obligations? The first is unlikely, since formulation is necessarily an inventive process; the best that can be achieved is a greater awareness of more innovative ways of cobbling together mutually satisfying agreements (Raiffa, 1982; Sebenius, 1991b). The second is more threatening. This loose process is bound to tighten as time goes on. The unfolding nature of scientific questions relating to the environment will become more clear; "Arrangements devised in one multilateral environmental treaty have a tendency to become irresistible precedents," as Széll notes. And obligations become firmer; formulas and definitions crystallize; and trade-offs become urgent and expected. The result is less of a scientific conference and more of an adversarial bargaining among clear—if shifting—sides made up of political units. Plenty of examples of growing consensual bargaining on environmental and other topics have fallen apart under such conditions, from the International Convention for the Regulation of Whaling to the Law of the Sea. In this perspective, it is crucial to devise clear trade-offs so that parties are locked into agreement by a balance of obligations and rewards rather than simply by a consciousness-raising process. Not only *may* environmental negotiations of the 1990s come to resemble the NIEO confrontations of the 1970s but they *will* do so, in part because they take on a North-South character. The lesson that screams for attention is the need for both sides to become aware of the potentialities for trade-offs between environment and development, so that the failure and bitterness of NIEO can be avoided for the future.

It may well be that the argument of last resort concerning this problem is the need for political education. It is striking that many accounts of environmental negotiations carry the message of an agreement that is possible among technicians but is made more difficult by the need to deal with governments. In Chapter 1 the authors speak of the need to draft a treaty "in such a way that it is strict enough to be useful but not so strict as to make the state in question unwilling to ratify it." Thacher notes, in Chapter 7, "Soft law works so long as governments don't think they're being pushed around too much, or that a 'super government' is under construction." Governments are necessary to engage and enforce compliance on environmental matters, yet they balk at the constraints environmental agreements impose on them as governments. Short of conversion as the result of consciousness-raising, governments act out of interest from constituency pressure. The bridge between state and science is business, a link that is more effective in developed than in developing countries. The challenge of international negotiations on the environment, as is often the case, is to develop domestic coalitions that support international trade-offs.

Note

1. An epistemic community includes individuals who share cognitive understanding of the environmental issue concerned.

15

Third-Party Roles:
Mediation in International Environmental Disputes

JEFFREY Z. RUBIN

Whenever conflict exists between two or more parties, it can be settled in several ways. This volume addresses one of the most important and ubiquitous of these approaches, namely, negotiation. A close cousin of negotiation and the subject of this chapter is third-party intervention.[1] The term *third party* is used to denote an individual, group, or organization that in some way stands apart from, or external to, the primary conflict between the first and second parties, and intervenes in this conflict to help bring about settlement.[2] This chapter examines the possible roles and functions of third parties in the settlement of a conflict, particularly environmental conflict. While there are many possible third-party roles (including those of mediator, arbitrator, fact-finder, go-between, ombudsman, and conciliator), this chapter primarily focuses on perhaps the most common of these roles, that of mediator.

While mediation typically occurs when the parties to a dispute seek out the services of an external individual, group, or organization, third-party intervention can occur just as readily as a result of the *internal* dynamics of a negotiation. Thus, while complex international environmental negotiations may be helped as a result of the intervention of some international organization, or through the intervention of a mediator who deliberately has been invited to offer analysis and recommendations for settlement, mediators also can emerge from within the ranks of the negotiators themselves. Over time, the work of multiple parties addressing multiple issues can be expected (frequently) to spur the emergence of leadership among the parties to the dispute. Such leadership, when designed to bring about negotiated agreement, can be seen as another form of mediation.

As the case analyses in this book have made clear, third-party intervention in environmental disputes is as likely to be the result of internal dynamics and emergent leadership as it is to be the outcome of a call for external expertise. Environmental negotiations may require the formation of work or task groups, charged with the analysis of a particular subset of issues. Whoever assumes leadership of such subgroups eventually may be required to use "good offices" to mediate disputes. The reader therefore is encouraged to consider in a broad context the possible contributing roles and functions of a mediator.

Before proceeding further, two implicit assumptions warrant explicit statement. First, while Guy-Olivier Faure and Jeffrey Z. Rubin (Chapter 2) have pointed out that international environmental conflicts have certain distinctive attributes, which also apply to third-party intervention, it is assumed that effective intervention has similar properties—regardless of the particular context in which it occurs. That is, the principles of effective third-party intervention apply in a broad range of conflicts, whether these are interpersonal, intergroup, interorganizational, or international in scope. Second, while third parties often can help move disputants toward a settlement of their conflict, there is nothing certain about such benefits. Indeed, third parties are just as capable of making an already bad conflict even worse as they are of helping to produce agreement.

Functions of a Third Party

Mediators perform two fundamental functions: helping the parties *diagnose* their problem(s), and then offering *solutions* in the form of suggestions that bear on settlement of the conflict. Most of the research on the work of mediators has focused on the latter topic, examining the kinds of things that mediators say and do to move disputants out of an impasse and toward settlement. With respect to the matter of diagnosis, it typically is assumed that the disputants recognize that they have a problem, and approach the third party with some awareness of its nature and importance.

Thus the area of mediator diagnosis largely has been taken for granted or neglected. Yet, in the arena of international environmental disputes, such diagnosis may be of paramount importance.

Third-Party Roles

While it may be reasonable to assume the existence of conflict in many situations—for example, a labor dispute, a marital squabble, an international border dispute—in environmental disputes, one cannot automatically make this assumption. Thus one of the mediator's primary tasks is to ascertain whether or not there *is* a problem. The industrialized nations of the North may consider global warming, and the environmental factors contributing to this trend, as a problem worthy of immediate global attention; the less affluent nations of the developing South, on the other hand, may consider their own development to be the most pressing problem(s) at hand, and may regard global warming as an issue that is largely irrelevant, or at least secondary, to a host of more pressing concerns. If some parties believe there is a problem in need of a negotiated solution, while others do not see it that way, then one of the first steps a third party must take is to clarify perceptions and assumptions, then help forge some provisional agreement about whether or not there *is* a problem.

In Chapter 7, Peter S. Thacher describes the unusual (and helpful) role played by scientists in marine-pollution negotiations. In September 1974, the United Nations Environment Program (UNEP) sponsored a workshop in Monaco that was attended by 40 scientists. Based on their assessment of the facts, these scientists were asked to present their opinions on research priorities, and these priorities then were taken into account to ascertain the extent of a problem.[3] Far more troubling is Michael Mortimore's account of the Sahel conflict (Chapter 9), in which the parties could not even agree on an acceptable definition of *the Sahel,* let alone whether there was a problem.

Even if all sides agree that an environmental problem exists, there may be disagreement about the likely short-term and long-term implications of this problem. Some disputants may acknowledge a short-term problem, while denying the existence of any evidence supporting long-range concern. Others may consider an environmental issue to pose no problem in the short term, while believing that the long-range consequences will be severe for all. A good illustration of such disagreement can be seen in Chapter 6, which deals with acid-rain negotiations in North America and in Europe. As Roderick W. Shaw points out, scientific uncertainty has been treated very differently in these parallel acid-rain negotiations. The

United States, in particular, has used the (almost inevitable) uncertainty in establishing cause-effect relationships regarding the impact of acid rain to justify delaying the introduction of an emission-reduction strategy. While the United States apparently would prefer delaying action at the risk of possibly irreversible and costly damage, Canadian negotiators would prefer the risk of acting unnecessarily, at great expense. Meanwhile, much of the same scientific uncertainty (as least as played over the long run) among Europeans has led to the use of available knowledge, regardless of how imperfect, in the establishment of strict environmental protection provisions.

In summary, a first step that a mediator is likely to be asked to take in an international environmental dispute is to help the parties diagnose their problem. Is there a problem? Does it have consequences in the short term? In the long run? In helping the disputants to answer such questions, the mediator, in effect, is called upon to help ascertain the facts. This is a departure from intervention in many other kinds of conflict, where the facts are indisputable (for example, either wages and fringe benefits are of a certain magnitude, projected to increase at a certain rate, or they are not). In evaluating the facts in an international environmental dispute, the mediator may have to decide (or advise the disputants about how to decide) among various sources of expertise. *Whose* knowledge to rely upon thus becomes a second-order question that the mediator may have to help answer; the expertise one chooses may incline the parties toward differing views of the facts.

Once diagnosis has taken place—and it has been ascertained that there is a conflict, with all sides in acknowledgment—the mediator can review possible suggestions for moving forward. Naturally, much of the mediator's work focuses on *substantive* suggestions, as when the third party helps the disputants to identify the issues, and then proposes possible settlement packages. In addition, and often neglected in analysis of third-party effectiveness, are the various *process* suggestions and interventions that mediators use to help motivate disputants to take their conflict seriously, to view the conflict as soluble, and to help create an environment in which a productive exchange of ideas can take place.

Given the importance of process considerations in the settlement of international environmental disputes, and given the limited attention that such considerations generally have received, much of the remainder of this chapter addresses the matter of third-party process. Before examining this topic, however, a few additional observations are in order regarding the substantive work of third-party intervenors in international environmental conflict.

First, mediators help disputants substantively by focusing on the available options for settling their conflict. In environmental disputes, the identification of options becomes a particularly important and occasionally problematic task. Thus, if the disputants are inclined to disagree about whether a conflict even exists to begin with, they are even more apt to disagree about the legitimacy of various options for its settlement.

Second, environmental disputes, more than many other kinds of disputes, contain an extraordinary variety of costs and benefits. Often the mediator helps to identify these costs and benefits. Options for dispute settlement typically have many strings attached. We know, for example, that many pollutants have a harmful effect on the global ecosystem. The elimination of these pollutants, perhaps by imposing strict restraints on industrial manufacturers, involves significant costs. These costs are not only economic but political in nature, and a skillful mediator may be required to help reinforce the idea that long-term benefits could follow from the willing acceptance of short-term costs. Thus the identification of options for conflict settlement is inextricably related to some assessment of the costs and benefits associated with these options, a task in which third-party assistance can prove invaluable.

Let us now turn to the role of third parties in the development of process suggestions that bear on settlement. As the case analyses in this volume illustrate, most instances of international environmental negotiation involve multiple parties and multiple issues. Successful negotiations thus require the management of enormous informational and organizational complexity. Under these multilateral negotiating circumstances, mediator assistance can prove invaluable. The third party, functioning as an individual or as an international organization, can help the disputants develop a list of topics to be discussed and eventually negotiated, identify the order in which these topics should be addressed in the upcoming agenda, and determine which parties should be invited to attend a multilateral negotiation—including the order in which such invitations should be extended.

Multilateral negotiations, including the sort that typify international environmental disputes, usually either require or endorse the value of *consensus.* That is, it is assumed that a comprehensive negotiated settlement can be said to have been reached only or especially when every participant in the negotiations accepts the proposal(s) on the table. Such a decision-making rule, or emphasis, places extraordinary power in the hands of each negotiator—since each is capable of blocking agreement. In turn, it places enormous responsibility and pressure on the would-be third party charged with finding some way of creating a process that encourages consensual decision making.

The time to begin working toward consensus is not at the negotiating table itself, but before the disputants ever arrive. It is during the *pre-negotiation* phase of the process that mediators perform some of their most important work: helping to identify possible coalitions that may cut across lines of ideological division; helping to identify individuals who may emerge in leadership positions, and may be able or willing to use this position to guide the group toward consensus; helping to identify possible deviates, disputants who may hold out and block an emerging consensus. This is work best done informally, often behind the scenes and before parties ever sit down at the negotiating table.

Third-Party Approaches

In addition to recommending particular solutions to the conflict, an effective third party often focuses on various process considerations that, in turn, make dispute settlement more likely. Mediators do this in three related ways: first, by attempting to increase the disputants' motivation to reach agreement; second, by modifying, or making suggestions about the modification of, the physical and social structure in which negotiations will be conducted; and third, by making suggestions about the way in which the parties structure the issues under discussion.

Increasing the motivation to reach agreement. In order for disputants to be motivated to work toward negotiated settlement, it may be necessary that they first understand the benefits associated with agreement and/or the costs associated with the failure to reach one. While there are a number of steps a mediator can take in this regard, several are of particular importance.

First, the mediator needs to search for the ripe moment. This is the point (or series of points) when disputants are ready to get to work. To push the disputants before the moment is ripe is to run the risk of them not taking the conflict seriously, and dismissing various ideas for moving forward. To intervene too late (once the moment of ripeness has passed) is to risk entering at a point when the disputants already have locked themselves into intransigent positions and refuse to budge—no matter how creative or helpful an intervention idea may be. The third party's challenge, in environmental and other disputes, is to find the right moment to intervene.[4] A mediator in the acid-rain disputes between Canada and the United States in 1978 would have had precisely such an opportunity to seize the ripe moment. As Shaw describes in Chapter 6, a series of articles appeared in Canadian newspapers in 1978 on the harmful effects of sulfur dioxide emissions. These articles, Shaw points out, appeared just at the moment when the public was becoming sufficiently sensitive to the problem of acid rain. No such stirring of public opinion occurred in Canada's neighbor to the south, which may help to explain why the Canadians have been far more willing than the Americans to move ahead with negotiated solutions to the problem of acid rain.

The mere passage of time also can have an impact on creating a ripe moment for international environmental negotiations. This can be seen in the negotiations on ozone-layer depletion, as described by Patrick Széll in Chapter 3. Széll explains the contrast between the 38 months required to negotiate the Vienna Convention for the Protection of the Ozone Layer and the far shorter nine months required to complete the Montreal Protocol on Substances that Deplete the Ozone Layer partly in terms of the fact that as time passed, the scientific evidence about ozone depletion and its effects became clearer and more compelling. Similarly, Gunnar Sjöstedt (Chapter 5) points out how the mere passage of time (during which the Chernobyl disaster occurred in the former Soviet Union) may help to explain why there were no serious negotiations on nuclear security in 1983, whereas the same issues could be handled so smoothly during the 1986 Vienna Conventions.

A ripe moment, of course, can be *created* by an effective mediator—rather than merely being sought out or awaited. Secretary General Maurice Strong appears to have created a ripe moment (Chapter 7) when he opened meetings by presenting a list of marine pollutants ranked by the severity of their impact. What he achieved, in effect, was to remind the parties to these negotiations about the severity of the threat posed by marine pollution to the world. In so doing, he succeeded in engendering some sense of the ripe moment, rather than merely waiting for it to occur on its own.

Second, an effective mediator should be able to evaluate the state of the disputants' emotions, and act accordingly. When such emotions—particularly negative emotions—run high, it may be time to introduce a cooling-off period, thereby preventing the sort of direct confrontation that could make a bad situation even worse. If such a cooling-off period is not practical, perhaps because of severe time constraints, the third party also can help alleviate angry emotions by serving as the willing target of the disputants' displays of anger. Much as a psychotherapist can personally absorb some of the angry discharge when helping a couple deal with their anger, so too can a mediator deflect negative emotion. If, as a result, the parties in conflict can better sort out the substantive problems from the so-called people problem, then they are more likely to reach agreement. Finally, mediators can use humor to mitigate angry exchanges, turning a potentially bitter moment into an occasion for laughter; witness, in this regard, Henry Kissinger's use of humor during his 1973-1975 shuttle diplomacy mediation in the Middle East (Kissinger, 1975).

A third way of motivating disputants to take the conflict seriously, and to work toward settlement, requires the third parties to capitalize on their reputation. The mediator who is seen as trustworthy, whose ideas are credible, and who has a reputation for honesty, fairness, and effectiveness, is also a mediator whose proposals are likely to gain acceptance. In international environmental negotiations, it thus may make sense to attempt to enlist the services of third parties who can seize the moment through their well-established reputation. Whether it is an individual (see, for example, James Sebenius's description in Chapter 11 of Ambassador Tommy Koh's personality and persuasive appeal during the Law of the Sea Conference) or a respected international organization, a well-respected third party often can make a great difference.[5]

This, then, is a partial list of the moves and maneuvers that may be at the disposal of the mediator who wishes to increase motivation. As stated at the outset, the available techniques consist of an amalgam of anticipated benefits and foreseeable costs associated with reaching agreement—or failing to do so.

Modifying the physical and social structure. Almost any aspect of the negotiating environment can be varied or manipulated by a skillful third party. Negotiations take place within a physical context (time limits, access to communication, etc.) and a social context (the number of parties to the exchange, the formation of subgroups, etc.). By judiciously suggesting ways of modifying these structural elements, the mediator can encourage a process that facilitates dispute settlement.

First, the mediator may wish to create a climate of motivation to reach agreement through the judicious formation of subcommittees and other task groups. In most international environmental negotiations, multiple parties and multiple issues are involved. Instead of trying to work with the group as a whole, it often makes sense to organize a subgroup, consisting of members who share the mediator's concern about working toward agreement. This subgroup, in turn, can proliferate into other subgroups, and in this way a critical mass can develop that is of sufficient magnitude to generate the momentum necessary for reaching agreement.

Second, the mediator may wish to stimulate the formation of certain coalitions. Perhaps by using the formation of working groups as an acceptable rationale, the mediator can cross over existing lines of division and conflict, and create smaller groupings consisting of individuals acceptable to the parties in conflict: as a case in point, witness Tommy Koh's efforts during the Law of the Sea Conference (Chapter 11). The result may be the emergence of cross-cutting ties that bridge opposing views in new and creative ways. In even the most strongly divisive conflicts, there usually are individuals who can play this bridging role. By identifying such people, then bringing them together in a forum that allows new ideas to be put forth, the mediator can give the negotiations strong encouragement and support.

Third, the mediator may wish to make use of opportunities for informal exchange as a way of getting things unstuck. If the formal process of offer and counteroffer, as it takes place at the negotiating table, is being used to state extreme positions in public, and the disputants have reached an impasse, it may be wise to create opportunities for more informal arrangements. UNEP Executive Director Mostafa K. Tolba appears to have done just this during the Montreal Protocol negotiations on the depletion of the ozone layer. As Széll points out (Chapter 3), Tolba made extensive use of "informal consultations" designed to help narrow the gap between the divergent views of negotiators on central issues, and accomplished this away from the plenary session.

This informal approach is what U.S. diplomat Joseph Montville has referred to as "track two diplomacy"; if formal exchange is the single track that most diplomats typically pursue, then a second track may be necessary to support the movement toward agreement. Others have referred to this as "supplemental diplomacy," denoting the work that supplements (and thereby advances) the work in primary channels. Whatever the label, the point is this: multiple links between and among disputants can facilitate the process of moving toward agreement. Such links cannot reasonably be reserved for the formal and public exchanges, but must be created in other, often more appropriate, settings. It is the informality of such settings (a conference retreat, a meeting over dinner, a casual drink before retiring), coupled with the knowledge that no binding decisions will be made, that encourages the invention of creative options that may satisfy the interests and concerns of all sides.

Fourth, an effective third party can use opportunities for prenegotiation to create the proper climate and setting for the upcoming exchange. *Prenegotiation* means almost everything that comes before the negotiations proper, and that helps make these negotiations more likely to take place and succeed. International environmental disputes are laden with examples of prenegotiation. It is during this time that the mediator helps to identify the parties to the negotiations, to devise the best order in which to extend invitations to participate, to identify the issues to be discussed, and to set priorities in terms of the order in which these issues will be taken up.

As an example of the place of prenegotiation in international environmental negotiations, consider the work of Strong prior to the 1972 Stockholm Conference on marine pollution. As described in Chapter 7 by Thacher, Strong began meeting informally with delegations two full months before assuming responsibility for the Stockholm Conference. Beginning in November of 1970, Strong developed a preparatory action plan designed to improve the intellectual level of the discussion by identifying areas of consensus and major gaps in present knowledge.

The aforementioned possibilities bear primarily on the modification of social structure. But various physical adjustments also can have an impact. Hence, a fifth way of modifying structure entails the possible imposition of time limits. The mediator, sensing that the disputants are not sufficiently motivated, may choose to impose a time limit on the negotiations. Time limits increase the pressure on disputants to make the necessary concessions for settlement.[6]

Sixth, a mediator can make suggestions about site location that may have an impact on the ensuing negotiations. Locating the negotiations on one party's home turf may shore up the legitimacy of that side; it also may increase the pressures on this party to play the role of the proper host, and to act more conciliatory than might be expected of the guests. The guests, in turn, are deprived of the technical, physical, and social support of their home environment; in exchange, they have an opportunity to leave the negotiations, perhaps on the grounds of having to check with their constituency before accepting some proposal. In complex international environmental negotiations, site location often assumes enormous symbolic meaning in relation to such considerations. The choice of Rio de Janeiro, Nairobi, or Geneva for a conference conveys a powerful message about the legitimacy, value, and importance of the host country. The choice of some clearly neutral site, so often possible in other kinds of negotiations, may be difficult or impractical to imagine in an environmental context; so many of the environmental problems confronting the world are so truly global in scope that there really is no neutral corner into which the negotiations can retreat.

Seventh, and related to the matter of site location, is the mediator's judgment about site openness. Open-site negotiations that allow various observers to witness the exchange confirm for all that no secret handshakes are taking place and that no side deals risk compromising the various interested parties. On the other hand, open-site negotiations also encourage grandstanding, adopting extreme positions (for political or personal reasons) that become very hard to escape; public posturing (witness Saddam Hussein's saber rattling in the fall of 1990) cannot easily be disregarded, or explained away, without risking loss of face. Given these potentially costly consequences, it often is wise for mediators to recommend closed-site negotiations, at least at the outset. Once agreements have been reached, at least tentatively, it may make sense to open the negotiating site to various observers, including the media; indeed, such openness at this point even may help to solidify the commitment to agreement reached in the negotiations.

Another possible form of modification entails the introduction by the mediator of additional resources. If disputants regard a conflict as zero-sum, such that one side can only do well at the other's expense, then suggestions that expand or enlarge the conflictual pie may open the way to possible agreement. Clearly, not all third parties are in a position to increase the pie through the introduction of additional resources. Some, however, can help in this way, as when they represent relatively affluent nations interested in a particular agreement. Moreover, even if third parties cannot offer resources, they can pave the way for other parties to help in this regard.

Modification of issue structure. When all is said and done, the issues themselves—and the way in which they are arranged or presented—determine whether negotiations succeed or fail. Expressed in another way, the management of physical and social structural arrangements—even the management of motivation—is the preliminary step before working on the issues themselves. In this regard, a mediator can do many things.

First, the mediator can help advance the negotiations by encouraging the disputants to move from unilateral assertions of position to analysis of underlying interests. Whereas positions (for example, "I'll have to have that" or "You can have this") may lead to a model of concession-making in pursuit of some point of convergence, analysis of underlying interests opens the way to a more creative exploration of opportunities for mutually acceptable (so-called win-win) solutions. Thus, independent of the particular issues on the table, a third party can help by encouraging analysis of interests in the taking of positions.

Second, a mediator can help by making recommendations about the sequencing of issues. There may be occasions where it makes sense to start negotiations with small, relatively easy issues; then, after successfully addressing these, the disputants may be poised to move on to tougher problems. This approach makes it more likely that momentum can be generated by succeeding with easy issues, then transferring that success to the more intractable ones. The salami tactic (or "fractionation") approach to conflict settlement often works very well.[7] In Chapter 5, which examines negotiations on nuclear pollution, Sjöstedt points out the political importance of the executive secretariat of the International Atomic Energy Agency (IAEA) in developing a draft agenda that could be accepted and approved before the beginning of a 1986 conference of government experts began.

On the other hand, it also may occasionally make sense for a mediator to encourage work in the reverse sequence. If the tough issues are so pressing that they simply must be addressed directly and without delay (perhaps because they could become even tougher with the passage of time), then it may be necessary to encourage work on the tougher issues before moving on to allegedly easier problems.

Third, a mediator may believe that progress is most likely to occur only or especially if the disputants refrain from addressing issues one at a time, and instead generate possible agreement packages. Instead of encouraging stepwise movement among a set of issues, the mediator thus may wish to support efforts to make a series of preliminary proposals on all the issues under discussion, without commitment to agreement on one single issue. After passing packages back and forth, the mediator can then advise the negotiators about which package, if any, seems most plausible and most likely to prove acceptable to all sides.[8] In a variation on the same idea, the mediator may prefer to suggest another overarching framework; UNEP accomplished this in helping to develop the 1974 Mediterranean Action Plan. As described by Thacher in Chapter 7, Strong explained UNEP's capacity to mobilize and coordinate various mechanisms in the management of the ocean as an ecological whole.

There are many occasions where the kind of overarching framework introduced by a mediator is of a special form. Indeed, this form—relying for its effectiveness on the so-called method of constructive ambiguity—is so important that it warrants mention its own right. In Chapter 10, which addresses the topics of biological conservation and biological diversity, John Temple Lang argues for the importance of writing an initial treaty so that it is strict enough to be useful but not so strict as to make the state in question unwilling to ratify it. In this fourth approach to the modification of issue structure, then, the intervening individual or organization tries to invent a framework that is sufficiently ambiguous in its construction that virtually all of the parties to the exchange can find something in the framework that appeals to their interests and concerns. United Nations Resolution 242 has produced this effect in the ongoing conflict between Israel and its Arab neighbors. There are also numerous examples in the international environmental realm. To cite one illustration, recall Széll's description (Chapter 3) of the importance of a "framework instrument" in obtaining early commitment to protection of the ozone layer. The key, as he observes, was the development of a framework containing deliberately "nonspecific obligations," "nebulous entitlement," as well as "general requirements for further research." It was precisely the generality of this instrument that made it possible for the signatories to begin to work toward a broader, long-term agreement.

Fifth, a mediator can suggest new issues, previously overlooked by the disputants, whose inclusion may increase opportunities for agreement. In addition, the third party can help the disputants see the issues in conflict in new ways that could facilitate agreement. One version of this occurs when a third party introduces a "decommitting formula," allowing the disputants to evaluate the conflict in some way that promotes settlement. In the case of the Persian Gulf crisis, which marked the beginning of the 1990s, one wonders what sort of formula could have been introduced to allow Hussein to declare his actions as a "complete and total victory," then withdraw from occupied Kuwait without going to war.

Conclusions

International environmental disputes contain an extraordinary number of opportunities for third-party intervention. These opportunities, in turn, are the result of the equally extraordinary complexity of environmental disputes. In closing, it may be fruitful to return to the framework chapter of Faure and Rubin (Chapter 2) to recall the special circumstances of international environmental disputes and the implications for outside intervention.

First, the presence of multiple parties and multiple roles means that it certainly will be difficult for the antagonists themselves to gather sufficient perspective on their exchange to invent ideas for settlement. When you are in the lion's den, with threats (ferocious lions) coming at you from every possible angle, it is impossible to observe events with dispassionate objectivity. A third party can help.

Second, the presence of multiple issues in international environmental disputes makes it extremely difficult to weave one's way through the morass of possible trades and points of linkage to find a solution that all disputants can accept. As discussed in this chapter, there are many steps a resourceful mediator can take to frame or sequence these multiple issues to increase the chances of settlement.

Third, the fact that so many environmental disputes cross national boundaries means that third parties can help identify the transcendent quality of these disputes. Thus, a mediator may be better positioned than the disputants themselves to help the parties understand the non-zero-sum nature of the conflict—the fact that if solutions are not found, *both* sides stand to lose.

Fourth, international environmental conflicts are characterized by considerable scientific or technical uncertainty. As the chapters in this book have pointed out, one of the most difficult stumbling blocks in these conflicts comes at the very beginning, when the parties concerned are trying to agree on the extent to which a problem exists, its likely time frame, and the urgency of developing some sort of jointly negotiated response. Clearly, mediators can be enormously helpful in this regard.

Fifth, many environmental problems are characterized by power asymmetry. Witness, in this regard, Christophe Dupont's analysis of the Rhine River pollution problem (Chapter 8); he points out that downstream nations are more vulnerable (less powerful) than their upstream counterparts—who are far less motivated to acknowledge the existence of a problem, let alone to negotiate a settlement. Under such power asymmetry, mediators can try several interventions, including moving the disputants out of a potential logjam by carefully choosing the site for negotiations, the openness of this site to various observers, the use of time limits, and so on. These considerations, and many others, are typically under the control of the mediator, and can be used to help create more of the equal power footing that may be necessary if negotiators are to come to the table.

Sixth, Faure and Rubin observe that environmental disputes typically contain elements of joint interest. Each nation, in isolation of its neighbors, may foster the illusion that it can have a free ride, that it is not accountable for its actions. In the presence of a mediator, this illusion of a free ride is quickly shattered. One way in which a mediator can enhance this awareness of joint interest, while pointing to the illusory nature of the so-called free ride, is by addressing the need for an inconvenience distribution. Faure and Rubin point out that as long as the painfulness of the situation does not justify immediate action, environmental disputes are evaluated prospectively—which is not the most powerful leverage to get negotiations started or progressing efficiently. Mediators can help the disputants to focus on future costs, costs that disputants may try to overlook.

Seventh, international environmental negotiations, because they so often extend over long periods of time and require so many different kinds of expertise, often contain changing actors. Under these circumstances, it becomes especially important to monitor who knows what, who has spoken with (or should speak with) whom, and so on. A mediator can help by providing the overarching perspective on the proceedings that offers some modicum of stability and oversight in what might otherwise be a chaotic arena.

Eighth, Faure and Rubin observe that international environmental disputes are often played out on the pages of the world press, and before the eyes of countless television cameras. Research has demonstrated the tendency of antagonists, under these circumstances, to take extreme positions from which they are reluctant to budge—lest they risk the loss of face. By interposing themselves between the disputants and the domain of public opinion—that is, by serving as gatekeepers who manage the disclosure of information between negotiators and the world—mediators may be able to shield the disputants from the pressure of public opinion.

Ninth, Faure and Rubin point out that it simply is not enough to reach a negotiated agreement in an environmental dispute. Ways must be found to ensure the successful implementation of such an agreement. While this problem exists in any negotiation, it is particularly difficult in environmental disputes where—because of the number of actors involved and the extended temporal landscape—implementation requires the institutionalization of solutions. Here, too, an effective individual or organizational third party can help, using its resources to intercede with governmental and nongovernmental agencies to ensure the implementation of negotiated accords.

In conclusion, *any* dispute offers many opportunities for effective third-party intervention. Because of their distinguishing attributes, international environmental disputes, in particular, are extraordinarily complex. And this very complexity makes the kinds of helpful services that an effective mediator can provide all the more important.

Notes

1. Perhaps a clearer way of understanding the relationship between negotiation and third-party intervention (particularly mediation) is to view the two processes as residing along a single continuum of conflict settlement techniques. Effective negotiation requires some minimal understanding of the rules of third-party intervention, since most negotiators have found themselves caught in the middle, between the demands of an adversary and the pressures of their constituency. Similarly, effective third-party intervention requires some understanding of the elements of negotiation—since negotiators and negotiation typically invoke the services that a third party has to offer. Given this comment, it should be clear that the observations on negotiation processes by I. William Zartman, in Chapter 14, will bear close relation to the observations presented here.

2. The fact that the third party stands apart in no way implies that this outsider is necessarily impartial or disinterested. Third parties often *are* impartial or disinterested, but the presence of such an attribute is in no way a necessary condition for effective third-party intervention.

3. In this sense, scientists themselves can be regarded as third parties, interposed between nature and its possible abuse or exploitation by humanity.

4. Some view this hypothetical ripe moment as coming only once, a window of opportunity that, if not utilized to the best advantage, will shut; such an approach invites the use of threat and extortion, in the service of seizing this once-in-a-lifetime opportunity. My own guess is that it is wiser to proceed from the assumption that there are many such ripe moments; nevertheless, while there may be other opportunities to move forward, it makes sense to seize the present moment and take advantage of the available opportunities.

5. The argument here actually is twofold. First, the third party's reputation can help create the motivation necessary to move out of impasse toward settlement. Second, the best time for a well-regarded, highly reputable mediator to intervene is at the moment of ripeness; in particular, there may be some danger that if the third party intervenes prematurely, his or her input may be discounted, and it may be difficult (if not impossible) for further work by this

individual to take place. Is this what happened when Secretary General Javier Perez de Cuellar attempted to mediate the 1990 Persian Gulf crisis perhaps a bit prematurely?

6. Unfortunately, the imposition of time limits may also (unwittingly) encourage a game of chicken, in which each side resists making a concession on the grounds (and in the hope) that the other will give in first. If both sides reason the same way, then neither will concede, and an impasse will result.

7. There is an inherent danger in this approach: Should one fail to reach agreement on the relatively easy issues under discussion, there is virtually no hope of succeeding with the tougher problems.

8. The reader may wonder when it makes sense for a mediator to encourage stepwise negotiation among a series of issues, and when it instead makes sense to encourage negotiation on a single, all-encompassing package. When negotiations are stuck at a point of impasse, some sort of momentum-generating approach is likely to prove most helpful, and this probably can be accomplished best through a piecemeal approach. On the other hand, if the negotiators already appear motivated to reach agreement, then work on packages may prove most productive, and indeed is likely to produce agreements that are most Pareto-optimal.

16

Conclusion

GUNNAR SJÖSTEDT
BERTRAM I. SPECTOR

Environmental issues are beginning to receive the attention they deserve from a global audience that, for the most part, is now willing to confront these problems directly and act. It is certainly high time, since in many cases resolution of these issues is acknowledged to be a matter of global survival.

International negotiation processes have become the principal approach in dealing with global and transboundary environmental disputes and problems. To date, most environmental issues have been addressed to some extent through negotiation processes, though with varying success, as indicated by the case studies in this volume.

One of the major goals of this book is to have an impact on policy. Thus, in the first part of this chapter, lessons learned from past experience for decision making are examined and presented as recommendations for the practitioner. These proposals are intended to enhance policy-making and support greater effectiveness in future environmental negotiations.

The preceding analytical chapters present several insightful conclusions about this increasingly prevalent subject of negotiation. They address the propositions posed in the opening sections of this book and confirm the distinctiveness of the international environmental negotiation process. Still, much remains to be understood and explained about environmental negotiations. As a result, an additional set of issues and problem areas ripe for further research are presented in the second section of this chapter in the form of a *problematique*. A formal research agenda is needed to examine these issues. This list of prioritized research topics was derived on the basis of salient policy needs.

Policy Recommendations

External advisers are often commissioned by decision makers to provide policy recommendations and support decision making in specific choice situations. Typically, these advisers suggest strategy alternatives to decision makers that are most likely to achieve desired objectives, as well as tactics that are most likely to be effective given certain situations. Advisers may also give counsel on realistic aspiration levels with respect to specific goals.

These types of policy recommendations can also be helpful for national decision makers participating in international negotiations on environmental issues. A government may want, for instance, to become better informed about what it could obtain from another country in exchange for a concession, such as a domestic regulation or requirements for industry to invest in new technologies. A government may want assessments from external advisers on how best to influence public opinion in a desired direction with respect to a certain environment problem, for example, nuclear waste.

In this chapter, we approach the work of such external advisers from a somewhat different perspective. We observe the need for policy recommendations that support collective action on international environmental issues, not decision making in just one country. The external advisers' clients, therefore, are more difficult to define precisely. They include those who want to accelerate international problem solving on environmental issues. The normative basis for their policy recommendations is different as well. Rather than supporting a single nation's objectives, the adviser seeks to accelerate global and collective problem solving to avoid mutual catastrophes, some of which are quite imminent. Support that, in principle, is given to the overall process does not exclude advice given to particular actors such as individual governments.

Certainly, some actors may be willing but not technically competent to support or participate in a project aimed at increasing regional or global environmental security. Such nations may be activated by the technical support, analysis, and information provided by an impartial external adviser. What kind of support can such external advisers provide that indeed would be meaningful to a multinational set of actors, each with different interests and objectives in environmental negotiations? The case studies in Part II contain direct as well as indirect evidence of how the processes of international negotiations on environmental problems could become more effective. It is our belief that this knowledge can be truly supportive to negotiators and decision makers concerned with resolving future international environmental issues. Making the lessons learned from past negotiations practical and operational for other practitioners is the purpose of this chapter. Chapter 11 by James K. Sebenius is an instructive case study demonstrating how policy-relevant lessons may be learned from a process of negotiation, which is useful for the analysis of other negotiations.

Policy recommendations may be linked to all of the aspects of the negotiation process that were defined by Guy-Olivier Faure and Jeffrey Z. Rubin in Chapter 2: actors, structure, strategies, process, and outcomes.

Actors. The case studies and analyses in this volume suggest that environmental negotiations are often characterized by problems related to the mobilization of actors into the negotiation process. These problems can be partly remedied by external support activities. (How actors perform and conduct themselves in the negotiation will be dealt with as a strategy issue.)

Actor mobilization is a problem of great significance. In several environmental cases in this book, effective negotiations were started too late in relation to the seriousness of the problem. The actors who should have been mobilized were not. It would have made a great difference, for example, if the negotiations on the ozone layer discussed by Patrick Széll in Chapter 3 had been started and had achieved their initial results 10 or 15 years earlier.

Michael Mortimore's Sahel case (Chapter 9) gives some critical insight into the problem of actor engagement and mobilization in a Third-World context and the manifold difficulties of introducing external adviser support. Two contradictory facts serve to describe this case. First, swift international negotiations are vital to cope with the environmental problems of this region. Second, the prospects for such constructive conflict resolution and international cooperation are very slim at this time. One of the major obstacles seems to be that in the Sahel region, there are practically no actors willing to enter into such critical problem solving. Hence, without actors there are no negotiations.

External adviser support activities that could contribute to actor mobilization in this case would be highly desirable. A simplified diagnosis of the Sahel case suggests that the situation may not be sufficiently mature for comprehensive international action, be it in the form of imminent crisis management dealing with water supplies or longer term problem solving related to desertification, for instance. As Mortimore points out, the overall social and political structure of the peoples and nations in the Sahel region are such that the small political elite are neither moved nor constrained by political demands coming from below.

The logical policy recommendation resulting from this diagnosis is to urge the respective governments to establish comprehensive communications concerning these environmental problems with their affected populations. The populations suffering directly from these problems should be:

- Properly informed about the damaging effects of environmental destruction.
- Enlightened as to viable and realistic solutions, including costs.
- Advised on ways to organize to gain access to decision makers in their governments.

Such policy recommendations may be considered illegitimate interference and unacceptable by government policymakers. However, one important mission that public or official international organizations might accept would be to develop strategies to disseminate information about the environmental problems and the possibilities for remedial action to selected target groups in the affected countries. Much of the prenegotiation activities that have taken place in the Sahel case were clearly due to the intervention of international organizations, although at the national level. According to Mortimore, educational programs are required, organized by international organizations and targeted at societal organizations in the various Sahel countries or perhaps at the masses. Their objective should be to increase the general awareness of the existing threats and opportunities. With such information in hand, citizens may force national actors to mobilize for negotiations. Similar efforts should be made in other geographical areas—notably in the developing world—where from an objective point of view, international environmental negotiations should already be under way. One example would be negotiations on water rights, resources, and environmental degradation in rivers and other waterways throughout the Third World.

In the Sahel case, the mobilization of actors implies the activation of relevant interests. In the end, the negotiated outcome should represent an accommodation of these interests in a collective decision. Such interests are correlated with power. Nations lean on their respective power bases to promote their interests. When an aggregate of interests are introduced into the negotiation late in process, the process will become disturbed. For instance, if external actors, and notably international organizations, try to mobilize support for international negotiations on the Sahel problems without taking existing power relationships into consideration, the effort may backfire. One lesson for advisers is that all support attempts should be preceded by careful assessment of the situation. Another lesson is that levels of ambition should be set relatively conservatively.

It should be noted that important interests and strong power bases do not always go hand in hand. John Temple Lang refers to the extreme case in his case study of biological diversity negotiations (Chapter 10). He indicates that threatened species of plants or animals cannot defend their own interests in international negotiations however important they are in a future-oriented ecological perspective. These and other common interests of a similar kind need representatives. To a large extent, that role has been performed until now by national representatives speaking from an idealistic platform. Dependence on uncertain idealism is very shaky ground on which to base future global problem solving on biological diversity or any other environmental issue. Yet the studies show that consciousness raising is an important and necessary aspect of mobilizing actors.

Thus it is important to search for better methods of bringing undefended collective environmental interests into the multilateral negotiation process. Several approaches could be explored.

- Establish rosters of independent and highly qualified experts by means of international agreement in some appropriate international organization. From this roster, one expert or a team of experts could be selected to serve as representatives for undefended or weakly defended environmental interests. These representatives should not play the role of a mediator or that of a secretariat servicing a particular negotiation round. Neither should they have responsibilities to national delegations. Such representatives would constitute a new kind of actor in environmental negotiations truly representing collective global interests.

- Develop institutional structure and administrative support to epistemic communities. Such transnational groups have emerged to function as driving forces in several negotiation processes discussed in this book, notably the negotiations on pollution in the Mediterranean and the ozone problem.

- Enhance the access of nongovernmental organizations and selected international interest groups into the negotiation process. In many past negotiations, national governments as well as the leadership of international organizations have been reluctant to permit such representation at the negotiation table. One reason is that some nongovernmental organizations (NGOs), such as Greenpeace, have been skillful in mobilizing national and international opinion in the area of environmental problems. Therefore, the participation of such NGOs in international environmental negotiations has added an element of uncertainty. Notably, NGOs have been capable of upsetting tentative agreements by revealing the real trade-offs of governments or by punishing a government or policymaker for taking the wrong position in a negotiation.

The rate of participation of NGOs in environmental negotiations has increased in recent years. This development is particularly evident in the prenegotiation process leading up to the United Nations Conference on Environment and Development (UNCED) in Brazil in 1992. At the meeting of the preparatory committee in Nairobi in August 1991, one of the most contentious issues causing highly intensive discussions was the role of NGOs in the UNCED process. Influential NGOs demanded increased access to, and participation in, the negotiations; these requests were largely obliged. It is interesting to note, however, that the NGOs becoming involved in the UNCED process, for the most part, represent interests of the developed countries. Actually, a strong constellation of developing countries resisted the increased presence of NGOs, as such organizations in the Third World in the 1990s generally favor environmental concerns before the needs of development.

It seems clear that NGOs can make important contributions to environmental negotiations in the future. They may not only mobilize support for the negotiations generally, but also contribute to the structuring of the agenda by helping authorities set priorities. A new task for NGOs, which will probably increase in importance in the future, is to assist in the implementation of agreements in the area of environmental problems. One way that this may be accomplished is by actual supervision of governmental activities. The root cause of many environmental problems can be traced to the social behavior of individuals or to their common life-styles. Therefore, educational programs can be expected to play an important role in the implementation process by recommending modified behavior and life-styles. NGOs may become important channels for such crucial educational programs.

Another way that external advisers situated in international organizations can help mobilize actors is to create a negotiation setting that will effectively engage affected parties. Their mission would consist of defining the environmental problem in terms that make them amenable to negotiated outcomes. This requires that:

- All interested parties are in fact involved and have identified positive interests to defend in the negotiation.
- The definition of the problem situation clearly points to solutions that are economically feasible and realistic.

• Cost compensation schemes are offered from the very beginning to ensure active participation of all relevant actors.

Structure. The case studies demonstrate the major role played by international organizations in influencing the negotiation process through its principal function of structuring the process. These organizations have often been the primary channels for supplying decision support to negotiators and policymakers as well.

In Chapter 13, Oran R. Young argued that international organizations (IOs) are often engaged in particular environmental negotiations for reasons that are less than altruistic. Their engagement may result from power plays between IOs to gain control over certain issue areas, for example. Once linked to a particular negotiation process, an organization can have a great impact on it. The competence and organizational culture of the IO may considerably condition how issues are defined, what negotiation solutions are deemed feasible, and which national agencies send experts to the negotiation sessions.

In many cases, it is logical to expect several IOs to be interested and involved in environmental talks. Young suggests that, in such cases, the work should be distributed among them. Accordingly, research studies should analyze the appropriate distribution of work. Such analysis should ideally be related to the UNCED process before, as well as after, the final conference in 1992. One of the main tasks of the UNCED process is to coordinate the work on the environment in different negotiation forums and organizations. Another set of studies should be undertaken on how to formulate effective expert task forces from several organizations. Yet another set of research studies can examine if and how environmental issues can be considered within the context of ongoing nonenvironmental negotiations. One illustration is how environmental consequences of international trade should be handled within the GATT talks.

Strategies. Nations do not naturally possess appropriate and adequate capabilities and resources to exercise their political will and pursue their interests in international negotiation. They are not always able to carry out planned strategies intended to achieve their objectives.

An observer of large multilateral negotiations on the environment would quickly note that many developing countries are passive or perhaps not even present at sessions. There are various explanations for such inaction. Passive countries may feel they have political or moral obligations to take part in negotiations, but wish to keep a low profile. Alternatively, passive countries may be active free riders, allowing other nations to negotiate, and benefiting from the results, while not sharing any of the costs. A still more probable explanation for passivity in the negotiation process is that such nations lack sufficient actor capability. Even if they wanted to, they may not possess the requisite resources to contribute appropriately.

One obstacle to active participation in negotiations may be the lack of statistical and other systematically collected data that policymakers require to develop a most preferred position with respect to the issues under negotiation. Another obstacle may be the lack of analytical resources to evaluate correctly the implications of assessments and propositions made by other parties to the negotiation. Yet another impediment to participation may be the lack of technically competent and experienced negotiators.

Accordingly, external advisers and international organizations can provide decision support services to countries with such deficient informational resources. Obviously this type of support would have to be carefully designed to fit the special needs of the host country. It could focus on enlightening government policymakers so that they can actively defend their interests in negotiations. The support would include information and policy analysis of particular negotiation issues, as well the general negotiation context. It would also include educational activities—seminars and workshops by technical experts on the negotiation process as well as on the substantive issues to be negotiated.

Finding the most effective way of enhancing actor capability in environmental negotiations is so important that it should be the focus of further research. For example, the relative value of the following methods of decision support could be evaluated:

- Producing or reformulating relevant statistics.
- Developing independent and unbiased policy analyses that examine all possible negotiation options and outcomes.
- Stationing of technical experts from international organizations in a country's ministries or national agencies.
- Training negotiators in the process and substance of upcoming talks.
- Acting as an external adviser during the negotiations.

Process. In Chapter 14, I. William Zartman concludes that intensified systematic research on the process and dynamics of multilateral negotiation may help practitioners anticipate and avert unnecessary pitfalls in future international talks on environmental problems. Sebenius in Chapter 11 describes how such process analysis can be used to draw lessons from one negotiation process for another. He also highlights the considerable opportunity costs involved in not profiting from the systematic elucidation of the process properties of complex negotiations.

In Chapter 15, Jeffrey Z. Rubin discusses ways in which third-party intervention could help move negotiations forward and bypass potential stalemates and other pitfalls tied to process properties. In particular, Rubin emphasizes the opportunities for effective third-party mediators in the prenegotiation period, but does not elaborate on how they should be selected. One answer can be found in Chapter 13 by Young dealing with the role of international institutions in environmental negotiations. International organizations and their secretariats perform functions in multilateral negotiations that are similar to those of the third-party mediator described by Rubin. For instance, the secretariat may supply objective information needed to clarify issues, summarize proceedings, and undertake systematic comparison of key elements in national position papers. Such activities may help find common ground among negotiating parties.

Still, the role of secretariats is fundamentally different from that of a true mediator. One reason is that the secretariat often does not retain the necessary freedom of action (one exception is the Commission of the European Community). Normally, the secretariat functions as a mediator at the request of nations who belong to the secretariat's mother organization. Under such circumstances, the secretariat often has difficulties intervening at will when it considers the time to be right. This is a serious handicap given Rubin's assessment that timing is crucial for successful mediation intervention. Moreover, when the secretariat becomes an active and integral part of the negotiation, it may lose its status as an impartial mediator in the eyes of the national actors.

To the extent that the secretariat manages to influence the negotiation by means of its own initiatives, its character can be viewed in more of a leadership role than as a mediator. This leadership role was clearly illustrated in Gunnar Sjöstedt's case study of the nuclear-security negotiations (Chapter 5), in which the secretariat was extremely active during the early stages of the prenegotiation. Also recall the active and leading role performed by the UNEP Secretariat in several of the cases investigated in this book, notably in the negotiations on the Mediterranean (Chapter 7) and hazardous waste (Chapter 4).

To serve effectively as an independent mediator, an international organization could arrange for a special mediation team drawn from the organization. Alternatively, these mediators could be drawn from an independent roster of experts. The team could consist of a group of specialists who would be accepted as independent, honest brokers by all negotiating parties and would be integrated into the organizational infrastructure of the negotiations from the start. It would have to be given a mandate to intervene any time it judges that such action would be constructive. If the team loses the confidence of the parties during the negotiations, a new preselected team should be installed.

Research is called for to study how such mediation teams should be organized to perform effectively and under what circumstances they are likely to be viable. Experiences may be drawn from the functioning of some international organizations. One such example is the panel system in the General Agreement on Tariffs and Trade (GATT). Panels consist of a few independent experts who decide whether the country being scrutinized has performed in line with GATT rules. It should be possible to use this GATT panel system as an example for mediation concerning environmental problems. Another kind of mechanism for mediation that has been used in the Organization for Economic Cooperation and Development (OECD) and in other organizations is the consultation of a group of "wise men." These acknowledged experts are typically used to clarify the agenda for international consultations or negotiations. This approach is particularly useful for mediation in the prenegotiation stage. Research should be undertaken to investigate in more detail how such mechanisms might be transferred effectively to facilitate the resolution of environmental conflict. A hypothesis to be tested is that prearranged mediation would be particularly useful when the power distribution is relatively symmetrical. In such situations, the probability of stalemates is comparatively high and active mediation may help avoid such impasses. The contrary hypothesis to be tested is that mediation is effective when the power distribution is relatively asymmetrical. In these situations, the weaker party may be unable to get their interests considered in early stages of the negotiation. Another possibility is that weak actors, with little chance of influencing the prenegotiations, will choose to exit at the end of the negotiations and refuse to sign the final agreement. This can lead to coalitions being formed by weaker actors that can block the road to consensus. Active mediation can help the weaker parties have a stronger voice in prenegotiations. Thereby, they may become more committed to the negotiation process and its outcome.

Policy advice pertaining to process may also focus on the communication between different categories of actors actively engaged in international environmental negotiations, for instance, professional diplomats, international lawyers, and technical experts. Several case studies indicate that communication difficulties between these and other types of actors can be particularly pronounced in environmental negotiations.

One reason is simply the complexity of issues from a purely technical point of view. This complexity is further enhanced due to the relative lack of knowledge that has been a common feature of many negotiations on the environment. It has often been necessary to build up knowledge during the ongoing process of negotiation. As a consequence, scientists have been given a key role in negotiations, such as those concerning the Mediterranean, ozone depletion, and climate change. The contribution of scientists has often become a sine qua non for the attainment of a feasible outcome of the negotiations. Furthermore, transnational cooperation between scientists in different countries has sometimes functioned as one of the most important driving forces in the negotiations. Thus the relatively high active involvement of scientists is in many ways a positive phenomenon: a factor that may help improve the quality of the outcome, as well as the speed with which such agreements are attained. There is also another side to the coin. Other participants may experience difficulties in understanding the assessments made by scientists, particularly their probabilistic evaluations of future developments or the expected consequences of ongoing processes.

These circumstances suggest that one important contribution of an external policy adviser may be to find ways to facilitate communication between scientists and other categories of actors in the negotiation process. Measures to attain this sort of facilitation of communication may be of at least two different kinds: educational and organizational.

Educational measures should aim at giving diplomats and international lawyers hard facts about the environmental problem under negotiation. It is equally important to sensitize all actor categories to the professional subculture attitudes of the other groups as well as to commonly held knowledge. If due consideration is not taken of these factors there is a risk that the negotiation process may become unnecessarily protracted due to misunderstandings.

Organizational measures largely concern the coordination of work and the procedures for communication within national delegations or between the ministries and agencies that direct or support them. There are numerous factors to consider, such as the question of who leads the delegation. Under some circumstances, it may be preferable that the foreign ministry exercises strong leadership and control over the delegation, notably when negotiations concern the formal codification of informal agreements that have been reached in earlier rounds. In other instances, it may be better if negotiation work is coordinated by the ministry of environment. One illustration is the case where the aim of the negotiations is to reach an agreement quickly that does not need to become clothed in a formal convention. In such a case, it may be preferable to rely on the ministry that retains the most effective lines of communication to the scientific experts who represent indispensable sources of knowledge and information.

Most of the case studies in this volume demonstrate the high degree of complexity inherent in international environmental negotiation processes.

An important objective of external decision support, therefore, should be to assist parties in coping with complexity that hinders or delays progress in the negotiation. Three approaches to decision support can be considered:

(1) Computer models can be used to calculate the consequences for individual nations if given proposals are implemented. Sebenius in Chapter 11 describes such a model used in the Law of the Sea Conference. The importance of that model was that it enabled negotiating parties to anticipate possible gains from concessions made and compare alternative concessions. Another example is the RAINS model developed at IIASA, which has been successfully used for approximately the same purposes in the negotiations on acid rain in Europe.

In complex multilateral negotiations, much work is undertaken by the negotiation teams themselves to develop formulas which pave the way for bargaining over details—the actual exchange of concessions that is the ultimate basis for agreement. Model building seeks to reduce the complexity of this negotiation process.

There are difficulties attached to building and using such computer models in the context of negotiations. First, participants in the negotiation are not likely to have the competence to build such models themselves; they are dependent upon researchers who, in turn, may not have the requisite practical experience in negotiations to add a necessary dimension of realism to the models. Second, the computer models may become so constrained by political considerations and compromises that they may become technically deficient. Therefore, it should be explored how independent competent national or international organizations (such as IIASA) can be commissioned to develop models that would compare gains with concessions in complex negotiations over environmental issues.

(2) Decision support to help negotiators deal with process properties that hinder negotiations need not be as elaborate or sophisticated as computer modeling. Systematic policy analyses by external advisers might also be useful. For instance, lessons learned from successes in similar earlier negotiations can be supportive, as well as illustrate the conditions for such successful outcomes.

(3) Role-playing exercises and games are another useful form of decision support for negotiators and policymakers. For example, the negotiations situation described by Christophe Dupont that dealt with pollution in the Rhine (Chapter 8) has been used by the same author in training simulations. The Rhine exercise, in turn, would be a meaningful case for policymakers concerned with water rights and pollution in other rivers.

Outcomes. The negotiation outcome is the result of the interplay of all the other aspects of a negotiation: actors, strategies, process, and structure. Thus all policy recommendations pertaining to these dimensions also indirectly relate to the outcome.

It may be argued that policy recommendations concerning the outcome are unrealistic or normative. However, the case studies in this volume suggest at least one dimension of the outcome that could benefit from external advice. In his study of the biological diversity negotiations, Temple Lang points out that the professional background of negotiators, which tend to be similar across all nations, has a tendency to influence irrationally the type of negotiation outcome that is ultimately sought. He indicated that legal drafters of a convention often give priority to legal exactitudes over practical usability, although a text with vague formulations may sometimes lead to swifter policy changes than a more satisfactory convention text.

This observation suggests the need for external assessments of the true objectives of specific negotiations, what purposes the outcome will serve, and how the outcome can be designed to achieve those purposes. For example, negotiated outcomes can serve the following purposes:

- To establish rules of the game that hold for formal dispute settlement.
- To create a general framework for coordination of national policies.
- To sustain a platform for future negotiation.
- To develop a regime of confidence building that helps nations avoid open conflict.

Different purposes require, or permit, different forms of agreement. Determinants of such agreements are factors like precision in language, hard or soft law requirements, and the exclusion or inclusion of mechanisms for the implementation and supervision of the agreement.

An Agenda for Further Research

Faure and Rubin in Chapter 2 outline an analytical framework for the case studies in Part II. Their purpose is to present a picture of what is special or typical of international negotiations on environmental problems. These properties of negotiations may be summarized as follows: (1) Multiple parties and multiple roles represented in delegations; (2) multiple issues; (3) meaningless boundaries; (4) scientific and technical uncertainty; (5) power asymmetry derived from the way nations are affected by the environmental problem under negotiation; (6) joint interest of actors to deal with the environmental problem concerned regardless of their special interests; (7) negative perceptions of immediate outcomes; (8) long time frame; (9) changing actors during the negotiation process; (10) public opinion; (11) institutionalization of solutions; (12) new regimes and rules.

The propositions concerning these properties of environmental negotiations were formulated primarily on theoretical grounds. The case studies in this book can be viewed in terms of the extent to which they give support to these properties.

While some significant insights can be drawn from the case studies in this respect, the lessons learned are not conclusive. Many historical cases are not represented in the study; for example, the current negotiations on climate change. Other missing examples are environmental negotiations on waterways other than the Rhine and seas other than the Mediterranean. A third set of missing cases is concerned with preserving particular species of animals threatened with extinction, such as polar bears or whales. It is important to keep these omissions in mind when assessing the general properties of environmental negotiations.

The authors of the case studies largely support Faure and Rubin's propositions. No case study author explicitly objects to the propositions made in Chapter 2 about the particular character of international environmental negotiations. However, some distinctions or differences in emphasis can be made between the 12 propositions brought forward by Faure and Rubin.

The characteristic of changing actors is one of Faure and Rubin's assertions that has gained only modest support from the evidence of the case studies, although Széll emphasizes this factor in his analysis of the negotiations on ozone-layer depletion. In the very short negotiations over nuclear security following the Chernobyl accident in spring 1986, the problem of changing actors was clearly not relevant at all. In his description of the negotiations over hazardous waste (Chapter 4), Willy Kempel explicitly notes that the practice of changing actors was not a problem. Dupont witnesses the fact that in the case of the Rhine, new actors (agencies, expert groups, etc.) emerged within the government structure as a result of the gradual widening of the agenda for the negotiations. This is not considered to be much of a problem, however, and Dupont does not mention that it resulted in a substitution of actors.

Meaningless boundaries are typical for most of the cases studies in this book. The perception of this particular kind of interdependence no doubt influenced developments in most of the negotiations. An exception should be mentioned: the negotiations over acid rain in North America. In Europe, meaningless boundaries were evidently highly significant and influenced negotiations in many different ways, for instance, by requiring the development of a trade model for the measurement of transboundary flows of air pollution. Once established, this model considerably facilitated the search for feasible negotiation solutions. However, in North America the concept of meaningless boundaries was only perceived by one of the two parties involved, namely, Canada. For the United States, borders were seemingly quite meaningful. U.S. decision makers clearly thought that they could ignore environmental degradation north of the border regardless of the source of pollution. In this case, perhaps the asymmetrical power relationship between the parties neutralized the significance of other often salient factors such as meaningless borders and joint interest.

The characteristic of scientific and technical uncertainty also warrants a few comments. In most of the cases, this factor was typical for the negotiations concerned and, furthermore, had a strong impact on how they evolved and produced outcomes. In at least one case, the elimination of scientific and technical uncertainty seems to have been decisive not only for the outcome of the negotiation process but also for its initiation in the first place. This is the case of atomic security. Chernobyl effectively eliminated the uncertainty with respect to the key factor in the prenegotiations on atomic security, the actual risk of a nuclear accident. Three Mile Island strongly indicated that nuclear catastrophes were real possibilities. Chernobyl transformed this possibility into reality; it demonstrated that the notion of a serious nuclear catastrophe was not merely a theoretical scenario but an actual fact. No doubt, this change of risk perceptions was a decisive force behind the exceptionally rapid negotiations on atomic security in the summer and autumn of 1986. With this caveat taken into consideration it should be noted that the factor Faure and Rubin call scientific and technical uncertainty was critical in most cases of environmental negotiations discussed in this book. Uncertainty influenced not only *if* an actor was to participate in the negotiations but also *how* this should be done.

Other properties of environmental negotiations that are particularly emphasized in the case studies are the complexity caused by multiple issues and actors, power asymmetry, negative perceptions of immediate outcomes, and institutionalization of solutions. Several cases (atomic security, ozone depletion, acid rain, hazardous waste, and the Mediterranean) also demonstrate that public opinion plays a particularly important role in connection with environmental negotiations. Several cases also indicate that the role of public opinion and the performance of NGOs may be different in environmental negotiations as compared with other negotiations. This is an area in which existing research is particularly wanting.

The typical properties of environmental negotiations suggested by Faure and Rubin represent a significant area of research in their own right. A comparative examination of the cases also highlights a further set of issues worthy of closer analysis. These issues represent problematic relationships, inconsistencies, ambiguities, and possible disconnects in the behavioral process of negotiation. Many of these issues are unique to international environmental negotiation, although some share features with other types of negotiations. These issues demand examination and testing against additional case studies, in a similar way as the attributes in Chapter 2 were examined against the cases in this volume.

Scientific and technical logic versus policy formulation. International environmental negotiations rely heavily on complex scientific and technical information. This is one of the major characteristics that distinguishes these types of negotiations from many other types of international negotiations. Scientists, engineers, technologists, and futurists must sit side by side with professional diplomats for the problems to be understood, solutions to be devised, and progress to be made.

The bridge between these two domains has yet to mature fully, leading to some potential problems and ambiguities. The first issue that arises is one of negotiating about uncertain parameters. In very few of the cases described in this book can it be said that all of the scientific issues being negotiated were completely understood and their future implications projected reliably. Certainly, scientific measurements often result in the very identification of the problem that is being negotiated. But, there are so many scientific parameters of environmental problems that are uncertain and so many correlations that reasonably cannot be stated as causal relationships, that the substance of what is being negotiated, what are appropriate trade-offs, what are reasonable fallback positions, and what are effective outcomes can become rather nebulous.

At the same time, since the potential environmental consequences are often catastrophic, professional negotiators are left in the unenviable position of having to negotiate issues that are ill defined. The dilemma they face is negotiating in this state of uncertainty only to find later that the problem was not as significant as once thought versus delaying negotiation until substantial scientific results are available only to find out then that irreparable damage has been done.

Széll points out that despite wide initial scientific uncertainty about the problem and its causes, the negotiations on the depletion of the ozone layer did proceed in a forthright way in the late 1970s and early 1980s. This is a case of preemptive risk aversion. In the acid-rain negotiations between the United States and Canada, on the other hand, Shaw explains that the perception of scientific uncertainty was so high on the part of the United States that it resulted in a veritable impasse in the negotiations. Too, major negotiations on desertification in the Sahel according to Mortimore have essentially been deferred until recently because the problem remains too ill defined and scientific controversy shrouds the causes of the problem. In these two cases, the actors are apparently willing to suspend judgment and negotiations until the problem and its possible solutions are more fully elucidated by the scientific community. Whether these approaches are rightfully cautious or foolhardy should be studied further to see if early indications can be identified for use in other cases.

A related question was asked by Zartman in Chapter 14: Are environmental negotiations exercises in problem solving or true negotiation? The situation is viewed differently from the unique perspectives of the scientific expert and the diplomat. The position of the expert is that the environmental problem is just that, a problem that one seeks to resolve logically in the most effective and efficient way possible. Interest conflicts between different national actors are extraneous and inconsequential; environmental problems are scientific-technical issues that demand systematic research and analysis to uncover valid solutions. Once the optimal solution is identified, the rational thing to do is to implement it. To them, systematic problem-solving approaches are the common medium for communication.

Diplomats, on the other hand, view environmental talks as situations in which conflicting interests must be satisfied through compromise. From their perspective, optimal technical solutions are only as good as the feasibility of concluding multilateral agreements that apply them. Conflicting objectives among interested parties must be resolved somehow in the formulation of negotiated outcomes for them to be widely acceptable. Thus the optimal scientific solution to an environmental problem may not correlate strongly with the suboptimal negotiated outcome.

Certainly, these two perspectives of the negotiation process can be accommodated. The role of the expert is to identify each scientific solution and how effective each is likely to be in resolving the environmental problem. The role of the negotiator is to cobble together an agreement, hopefully that utilizes the solution sets at the most effective end of the continuum to maximize parochial interests, while offering positive pay-offs to all other parties.

These are not inconsistent roles if the roles and the negotiation process are adequately defined. The experts should not run the show, but the professional negotiators must pay heed to the scientific implications of the alternative solutions. Negotiation outcomes that fall short of solving the true environmental problems or delay the process, though they are politically expedient, can be more damaging than no outcome at all. The structuring of their roles and perceptions of the problem demand additional study.

The third related issue deals with the translation of technological solutions into policy options. A common language to discuss the problem is essential, both within and among negotiating teams. The expert needs to understand the requirements of the negotiator and vice versa so that they can collaborate closely in defining meaningful solutions.

The process by which this translation occurs is most interesting to understand. Are the negotiators dependent on the experts or do they have a sufficient background themselves in the scientific field? Have they developed a good working relationship? If they have not, they may be at a disadvantage in developing a full range of viable policy options.

Preemption versus crisis management. There is a tendency to treat international environmental problems in a crisis posture. Unfortunately, a real or imminent catastrophe is most often the event that precipitates the need for negotiation. An obvious instance in this volume is Sjöstedt's case of the Vienna Conventions dealing with nuclear accidents. After the Chernobyl incident, these negotiations were summoned and concluded rapidly—a prime example of the catalytic impact of crises—which is in sharp contrast to earlier, slow-moving attempts by the IAEA to motivate multilateral interest and action on the very same issues. The negotiation outcome provided a crisis management mechanism for use in future incidents.

Rarely do actors deal formally with incipient problems based upon some early warning of its future emergence. It is not often that one observes the development of a multilateral negotiation regime to deal with a dispute in the making, though such noncrisis joint problem solving might be the most rational approach. An exception, not discussed in this volume, is the successful negotiation in 1987 of a regime to deal with the environmental management of the common Zambezi River system (United Nations, 1987). Given the foresight of the five riparian states, an approach and action plan were adopted prior to the outbreak of any dispute or environmental damage.

Both the ozone-depletion and Mediterranean Sea pollution negotiations in this volume, while conducted in reaction to various levels of environmental damage, are viewed by the authors as largely preemptive negotiations, keeping the problem from reaching catastrophic proportions. The analysis of preconditions that facilitated these processes should be extended to other incipient environmental problems to see how such noncrisis regimes can be replicated.

Ambiguity of national objectives and interests. National objectives related to environmental negotiations are often schizophrenic. They reflect a push-pull phenomenon. On the one hand, national actors emphasize the costs of regulation and the significant constraints that regulation will place on the domestic labor force and the economy in general. As a result, they tend to act cautiously so as not to upset these interest groups. Temple Lang points this out in the case of biological conservation treaties in particular. On the other hand, negotiated agreements that constrain emissions, for example, can be a boon to industry that now can reap the benefits of newly created markets for control and substitute technologies. These opportunities attract national actors to negotiated agreements that might stimulate such technological development.

Many actors, with the exception perhaps of Japan, have not resolved this push-pull conflict in their national interests and objectives. This results in an ambiguous approach to international environmental talks that yields indecision and delay. In large part, this ambiguity can be traced to pluralism within national actors. As environmental issues are often emotional, domestic interest groups on all sides of the issue are stimulated and mobilized, complicating attempts to devise coherent national negotiating objectives. In the case of environmental degradation in the Sahel, Mortimore suggests that for many of the nations involved, negotiation objectives are not ambiguous, but entirely unformulated. Little consensus can be found among government interests on environmental problems because of political volatility and competing objectives focused on economic development. Moreover, educated public opinion and differentiated interest groups on these issues simply have not matured in these societies. The internal bargaining process among governmental and nongovernmental interests directed at formulation of a set of national negotiation objectives is an interesting subject for future research.

Coordination. International environmental negotiations proceed at many different levels, which can result in what appears to be ostensibly uncoordinated activity. The stimulation of interest group activity on environmental issues in pluralistic nations leads to extensive intranation negotiations during and prior to internation negotiations. As indicated above, this tends to complicate the development of a coherent set of interests and objectives. In the case of the pollution negotiations on the Mediterranean, Thacher explains that for each national actor, the number and diversity of interest groups and government ministries involved in the domestic debate on national policy formulation was a function of the multiple dimensions from which the negotiations were viewed—maritime commerce, fisheries, health, environment, and tourism, to name a few. Skillful internal negotiations were required to achieve a sense of positive-sum outcome among these varied domestic groups.

When dealing with coalition behavior, as with the European Community (EC) in the ozone-depletion negotiations, another level of coordination is required. Széll indicates that the strains and divergence of interests within the EC coalition prior to the Vienna Convention were many and required extensive intracoalition bargaining before an integrated single approach could be generated.

On a different dimension, a complex interaction has been described in the cases in this volume between the scientific and technical track and the diplomatic track as negotiations progress over time. These interchanges often occur over such long periods of time, with significant changes of personalities and misperceptions in communication and nuance between the two communities, that it is surprising that binding agreements can be developed at all. The interaction across stages and communities leaves wide open the possibilities for disconnected and inefficient communication.

In the Mediterranean pollution negotiations, for example, Thacher points out that the 1972 Stockholm Conference Secretariat recognized a difference in the nature of the interchange between experts and diplomats and, as a result, encouraged the use of soft-law techniques to benefit from these differences. More frequent informal exchanges among technical experts were promoted to build the technical norms, standards, and agreements that the negotiators could then use to resolve disputes at the policy level. Thus the mode of communication and the roles played by these two groups of actors was structured to ensure that they were complementary.

In a similar vein, Temple Lang asserts strongly in the case of biological conservation negotiations that the design of treaty implementation structures must take into account the difficulties in communication that sometimes plague scientific and diplomatic players in negotiation. He suggests that implementation is best left to independent scientists, rather than diplomats or administrators, who can regularly assess needed improvements in the operation of a regime based on the evolution of scientific and technical knowledge in the field.

At the same time, some negotiation cases have exhibited effective coordination between the technical experts and diplomats. Again in the Mediterranean pollution case, a multidisciplinary group of experts assembled from various interested UN organizations established a common definition of the problem and a common language that facilitated discussions at the policy level. The IAEA draft conventions on nuclear safety developed by technical experts served a similar purpose of enhancing communication among the policymakers once the negotiation got under way.

A third potential source of uncoordinated activity stems from the fact that while environmental issues, by their very nature, may have to be negotiated at the international level, they are implemented and regulated at much lower levels. For implementation to be a faithful representation of the intent of negotiated agreements, existing local regulations must be adaptable and local authorities induced to be compliant. Again, to cause these local actors to behave as intended may require extensive domestic negotiations. For example, in the case of acid-rain regulations in the United States and Canada, the standards imposed by Clean Air Acts or any future negotiated agreement must be implemented by the states and provinces, respectively, who will not be direct participants in the negotiations themselves. In biological conservation negotiations, local and regional authorities, of necessity, play a significant role in the implementation of land-use and natural reserve plans that are agreed to in negotiation.

Coordination problems can often be solved through restructuring the formal institutions or informal processes of negotiation. Further study into reorganization and reformulation approaches is warranted.

Asymmetry in negotiation. More so than in many other types of negotiation, environmental talks exhibit asymmetrical qualities. Wide differentials can and do exist in accessibility to scientific and technological information, for example. The countries of the North usually have the resources at their disposal to gather and analyze data, thus giving them a definite advantage in terms of examining possible solutions and trading off benefits against likely impacts on domestic interests. In an age when information is power, this differential gives the North a definite advantage over the South. Sjöstedt demonstrates that asymmetry in information resources was a contributing factor to the more passive participation of Southern countries at the Vienna talks on nuclear accidents.

Moreover, such asymmetry in information yields dependencies for information that can easily foster suspicion. This point was pertinent especially in the case of the negotiations concerning the transboundary movement of hazardous waste, which pitted the North against the South in sharp relief. As victim, the developing countries were highly dependent on the industrialized nations for information during the negotiations and were concerned that the final resolution of the Basel Convention would not go far enough in banning transboundary movement. The resulting actions of the African countries are particularly telling. As a bloc, the African states adopted a joint declaration highlighting issues of critical interest to them that they were fearful would not receive appropriate treatment at Basel. In addition, none of the African countries signed the Final Act of the Basel Convention on the spot.

Another dimension of asymmetry between actors in environmental negotiations deals with the use of strategy and power. The limited resources and assets of the South can easily lead to a prevalence of blocking strategies on their part. Sometimes, the only card held by the weaker party is to deprive the stronger actor of what it desires. While the South might not get what it wants out of the negotiation, it can see to it that the North will not get what it wants either. Although not an enlightened or progressive strategy, it may be the only way the weak can project its objectives to the strong. An example of this strategy was vividly portrayed by several large developing countries at the London meetings on ozone depletion who explicitly threatened to withhold their support for further restrictions on emissions if significant financial incentives were not forthcoming.

How can the negative effects of asymmetry be averted? Research strategies that focus on the creative distribution of information—common decision support systems, for example—or restructuring possible trade-offs might facilitate the process.

Freshness and creativity. The case studies in this book suggest that increasingly fresh approaches and proposals are required to deal with future environmental disputes. This is due to the pervasive complexity and uncertainty in the science of environmental issues and the global nature of these problems. Reliance on precedent established by previous environmental negotiations may not be sufficient to resolve tomorrow's problems. Creative ideas that somehow refocus the problem and modify the current reality of objectives are needed to identify solutions that yield positive sums covering all sides (Spector, 1991). As Pruitt (1987) has written, this may be accomplished by broadening the size of the pie, offering side payments, trading off low priority issues that are viewed as high priority by the other side, minimizing the costs incurred by accepting the other side's interests, or satisfying the true interests of both sides.

In the preparations leading to the Mediterranean pollution talks, the Stockholm Conference Secretariat found it useful to make analogies to earlier expert analyses concerning the health effects of atomic radiation. Referring to analogies is a common approach to stimulate creative results. Too, in the ozone-depletion negotiations, the secretariat found it effective to institute an independent legal drafting group during the London meetings to act as a nonevaluative brainstorming group, outside the more formal meeting structures. Again, a creativity technique was used to push the negotiations beyond particular stumbling blocks or potential impasses.

What additional creativity techniques can be institutionalized to avoid deadlocks and yield a step-level change in the joint image of successful negotiated outcomes? The research field is ripe with creative approaches that can be tested.

Linkages to sustainable development. Several negotiations discussed in this volume, while convened ostensibly to handle environmental disputes or problems, have been linked inextricably with economic development issues brought forward by the developing countries. To these countries, the linkage is a matter of equity. They believe that their societies should not be deprived of the benefits of certain critical, though polluting, technologies merely because they have arrived at this stage of development later than the industrialized countries.

The argument of tying environmental issues to development is a legitimate linkage. The imposition of environmental controls and regulations often does inhibit opportunities for economic growth in developing nations unless alternative or substitute technology is employed. But these technologies are usually more expensive and less available than the existing polluting options.

Several negotiation cases in this volume have addressed this linkage— the ozone-depletion, the Sahel, the hazardous-waste, and the biological diversity cases, in particular. But none has focused specifically or analytically on the linkage issue. This is what requires further research, particularly in the light of the 1992 UNCED trade-offs.

How does the linkage between environment and development change the calculus in international environmental negotiations? For one thing, it makes already complex issues more complex. Cost-benefit trade-offs must be extended to deal not only with the differentials between increased regulation constraint and improved environment, but with balancing this regulation constraint and the demands of sustainable development as well. The design of a formula that encompasses these divergent interests into a positive-sum solution is indeed difficult to generate. Thus the linkage between environment and development demands creative approaches; drawing upon precedent will not do.

The linkage of these two often emotional and conflicting objectives suggests a negotiation situation in which strategies and the use of power are more likely to be used in a negative fashion. Blocking strategies by developing countries that threaten noncompliance with new environmental controls are natural reactions to fears that their demands will not be satisfied.

The restructuring of the process of environmental diplomacy, as described in the Salzburg Initiative (Salzburg Seminar, 1990), addresses many of the linkage problems in negotiation. It establishes an agenda for research and practice that would reform current practice and make the negotiation process dealing with environmental and development linkages more manageable.

A new system of negotiation? Faure and Rubin in Chapter 2 suggest a conceptual model of the negotiation process that is claimed to be applicable to all types of negotiation. If their model is valid, the apparent differences noted in international environmental negotiations are truly variations on a common theme. These differences can be explained through our understanding of the model.

However, Victor A. Kremenyuk and Winfried Lang, in Chapter 1, suggest that a new system of international negotiation, based upon principles of interdependence and global security, is emerging. Are the differences noted in environmental negotiations in this book just the tip of an iceberg that represents this new system? If so, these differences may denote not a variation on a common theme, but an entirely new formulation of the negotiation process, with new types of structures, strategies, and outcomes—perhaps a new negotiation model. Additional research and a continual monitoring of the changing nature of international negotiation are required to make this assessment of possible transition to a new global negotiation system.

References

Abbots, A. (1980). Nuclear power after Three Mile Island. *Business and Society Review, 18.*

Abbots, A. (1981). Nuclear power after Three Mile Island. *Business and Society Review, 19.*

Adede, A. O. (1987). *The IAEA Notification and Assistance Conventions in Case of a Nuclear Accident: Landmarks in the multilateral treaty-making process.* London: Graham & Trotman/Martinus Nijhoff.

AMCEN. (n.d.). *The Cairo Programme for African Cooperation.* Nairobi: AMCEN.

AMCEN. (1989). *Reassessment of AMCEN's operational and organizational structures.* AMCEN Task Force Meeting, 28-30 November, AMCEN, Nairobi, Kenya.

Arbatov, G. A. (1988, October 17). *Glasnost, Peregovory, Razoruzhenie* [Openness, negotiations, disarmament]. *Pravda.*

Archer, C. (1983). *International organizations.* London: George Allen & Unwin.

Avtal. (1987a). *Sveriges överenskommelser med främmande makt* (SÖ 12).

Avtal. (1987b). *Sveriges överenskommelser med främmande makt* (SÖ 16).

Avtal. (1987c). *Sveriges överenskommelser med främmande makt* (SÖ 26).

Avtal. (1988). *Sveriges överenskommelser med främmande makt* (SÖ 5).

Barbour, K. M., Faniran, A., & Oguntoyinbo, J. S. (Eds.). (1974). *River basin development in Nigeria.* Ibadan, Nigeria: Ibadan University Press.

Batisse, M. (1990, June). Probing the future of the Mediterranean basin. *Environment, 32,* p. 5.

Benedick, R. E. (1989). U.S. environmental policy: Relevance to Europe. *International Environmental Affairs,* Spring.

Benedick, R. E. (1990a). Lessons from the ozone hole. *EPA Journal, 16*(2), 41-43.

Benedick, R. E. (1990b). *Ozone diplomacy.* Washington, DC: World Wildlife Fund, Conservation Foundation, and Georgetown University Institute for the Study of Diplomacy.

Benedick, R. E. (1991). *Ozone diplomacy: New directions in safeguarding the planet.* Cambridge, MA: Harvard University Press.

Bergman, L., Cesar, H., & Klaassen, G. (1990). *A scheme for sharing the costs of reducing sulfur emissions in Europe* (Report No. WP-90-5). Laxenburg, Austria: IIASA.

Birnie, P. (1988). The role of international law in solving certain environmental conflicts. In J. Carrol (Ed.), *International environmental diplomacy.* Cambridge: Cambridge University Press.

315

Boulier, F., & Jouve, Ph. (1988). *Etude comparée de l'évolution des systèmes de production Saheliens et de leur adaptation à la sècheresse* (No. R3S-SP). Montpellier, France: Département Systèmes Agraires.

Browne, M. W. (1990, June 30). 93 nations agree to ban chemicals that harm ozone. *The New York Times*, p. A1.

Brydges, T. (1987). *Some observations on the public response to acid rain in Canada*. Paper presented at the Svante Odén Commemorative Symposium, Skokloster, Sweden.

Buchanan, J. (1975). *The limits of liberty: Between anarchy and leviathan*. Chicago: University of Chicago Press.

Bunge, T. (1989). *International agreements in responsibility means doing without—How to rescue the ozone layer*. Berlin: Umweltbundesamt.

Buxton, V. (1988). The Montreal protocol. *European Environment Review, 2/2*(July), 46-48.

Carroll, J. E. (Ed.). (1984). Pollution across borders: Acid rain—Acid diplomacy. *Proceedings of the Conference Pollution Across Borders*. Durham: University of New Hampshire, Department of Forest Resources, Program in Environmental Conservation.

CEC. (1983). *Public opinion in the European Community: Energy*. Brussels, Belgium: CEC.

CESI. (1971). NOTE/29, 8 February.

Chayes, A. (1990). *Managing the transition to a global warming regime or what to do until the treaty comes*. Unpublished manuscript, Harvard Law School, Cambridge, MA.

Chen Lung-chu. (1989). *An introduction to contemporary international law*. New Haven, CT: Yale University Press.

Chossudovsky, E. (1989). *East-west diplomacy for environment in the United Nations*. New York: UNITAR Publication.

Clean Air Act. (1977). 42 *U.S.C.*, 7457 (b), Washington, DC.

Cline-Cole, R. A., Falola, J. A., Main, H. A. C., Mortimore, M. J., Nichol, J. E., & O'Reilly, F. D. (1990). *Wood fuel in Kano* (Final Report of the Kano Rural Energy Research Project). Tokyo: United Nations University.

Contini, P., & Sand, P. (1972). Methods to expedite environmental protection. *American Journal of International Law*, January.

Deutscher Bundestag. (1988). *Schutz der Erdatmosphäre: Eine internationale Herausforderung* (Zwischenbericht der Enquete-Kommission des 11. Deutschen Bundestages). Bonn, Germany.

ECE. (1990). *The state of transboundary air pollution: 1989 update* (Report ECE/EB.AIR/25). New York: United Nations.

Eckholm, E., & Brown, L. (1977). *Spreading deserts: The hand of man* (Paper No. 13). New York: Worldwatch.

ECOSOC. (1971). *The sea: Prevention and control of marine pollution* (Report of the Secretary General, E/5003, 7 May, Economic and Social Council). New York: United Nations.

Ehrlich, P. R., & Ehrlich, A. H. (1990). *The population explosion*. New York: Simon & Schuster.

Environment Canada. (1988). *Canadian achievements in controlling acidic emissions* (Information sheet). Ottawa: Environment Canada.

Evensen, J. (1986). *Working methods and procedures in the Third United Nations Conference on the Law of the Sea*. The Hague, the Netherlands: Hague Academy of International Law.

Ezenwe, U. (1984). *ECOWAS and the economic integration of West Africa*. Ibadan, Nigeria: West Books Publisher Ltd.

FAO. (1971). *Report of the FAO Technical Conference on marine pollution and its effects on living resources and fishing* (FIRM/R99). Rome: FAO.

Farmer, G., & Wigley, T. M. (1985). *Climatic trends for tropical Africa: A research report for the Overseas Development Administration.* University of East Anglia, UK, Climatic Research Unit.

Favre, D. S. (1989). *The international trade in endangered species: A guide to CITES.* Amsterdam: Kluwer.

Fouéré, E. (1988). Emerging trends in international environment agreements. In J. E. Carroll (Ed.), *International environmental diplomacy: The management and resolution of transfrontier environmental problems.* Cambridge: Cambridge University Press.

Frankel, G. (1990, June 30). Governments agree on ozone fund. *Washington Post.*

"The global fallout." (1986, September 8). *U.S. News and World Report.*

Gorse, J. E., & Steeds, D. R. (1985). *Desertification in the Sahelian and Sudanian zones of West Africa* (Technical Paper No. 61). Washington, DC: World Bank.

Grainger, A. (1982). *Desertification: How people make deserts, how people can stop and why they don't.* London: Earthscan.

Gregoire, E. (1980). *Etude Socio-Economique du Village de Gourjai* (Département de Maradi, Niger). Paris: Université de Bordeaux II.

Grenon, M., & Batisse, M. (Eds.). (1989). *Futures for the Mediterranean basin.* New York: Oxford University Press.

Grubb, M. (1989). *The greenhouse effect: Negotiating targets.* London: Royal Institute of International Affairs.

Grubb, M. (1990). The greenhouse effect: Negotiating targets. *International Affairs, 66*(1), 67-89.

Haas, P. (1989). Do regimes matter? Epistemic communities and Mediterranean pollution control. *International Organization, 43*(3).

Haas, P. (1990). *Saving the Mediterranean: The politics of international environmental cooperation.* New York: Columbia University Press.

Haass, R. (1990). *Unending conflicts.* New Haven, CT: Yale University Press.

Hamson, F., & Mandell, B. (Eds.). (1990). *Managing regional conflict.* Baltimore, MD: Johns Hopkins University Press.

Hardin, G. (1968). The tragedy of the commons. *Science, 162,* 1243-1248.

Homans, G. (1961). *Social behavior.* San Diego, CA: Harcourt Brace Jovanovich.

Hordijk, L., Shaw, R., & Alcamo, J. (1990). Background to acidification in Europe. In J. Alcamo, R. Shaw, & L. Hordijk (Eds.), *The RAINS model of acidification: Science and strategies in Europe.* Dordrecht, the Netherlands: Kluwer.

IAEA. (1982). Report, July, Vienna, Austria.

IAEA. (1984). INFIRC/321, Vienna, Austria.

IAEA. (1985). INFIRC/310, Vienna, Austria.

IAEA. (1986a). GOV/INF 497, Vienna, Austria.

IAEA. (1986b). GOV/OR. 649, Vienna, Austria.

IAEA. (1986c). *Summary record of the Final Plenary Meeting of Governmental Experts to Draft Agreements on Early Notification and Mutual Assistance.* 15 August. Vienna: IAEA.

IAEA. (1987). Legal Series No. 14, Vienna, Austria.

IAEA. (1990). *Regional and multilateral agreements relating to cooperation in the field of nuclear safety.* Vienna: IAEA.

International Bank for Reconstruction and Development. (1990). *Conserving the World's Biological Diversity,* World Resources Institute, World Conservation Union, Conservation International and World Wildlife Fund, Washington, DC.

IUCN. (1988). *The IUCN Sahel studies, 1989.* Nairobi, Kenya: International Union for the Conservation of Nature, Regional Office for Eastern Africa.

IWGMP. (1972). UN Document A/CONF.48/IWGMP.1/5.

IWRB. (1972). *Proceedings: International Conference on Conservation of Wetlands and Waterfowl,* Waterfowl Research Bureau, Slimbridge International, Goucestershire, United Kingdom.

Jackson, C. I. (1990). A tenth anniversary review of the ECE Convention on Long-Range Transboundary Air Pollution. *International Environmental Affairs, 2*(Summer), 217-226.

Josserand, H., & LeClerq, V. (1990). A world premiere: Food aid charter for the Sahel. *Club du Sahel Newsletter, 7,* 57.

Kaufmann, J. (1988). *Conference diplomacy* (Vol. 1). Dordrecht, the Netherlands: Martinus Nijhoff.

Kaufmann, J. (1989). *Conference diplomacy* (Vol. 2). Dordrecht, the Netherlands: Martinus Nijhoff.

Keohane, R. (1989). *International institutions and state power: Essays in international relations theory.* Boulder, CO: Westview.

Keohane, R., Nye J. (1989). *Power and interdependence* (2nd ed.). Glenview, IL: Scott, Foresman.

Kindler, J., Warshall, P., Arnould, E., Hutchinson, D. F., & Varady, R. (1989). *The Lake Chad conventional basin: A diagnostic study of environmental degradation.* Nairobi, Kenya: UNEP/UNSO/UNDP/LCBC.

Kiss, A. (1989). *Droit International de l'Environment.* Paris: Pedone.

Kissinger, H. A. (1975, August 11). *International law, world order, and human progress.* Speech presented to the American Bar Association Annual Convention, Montreal, 11 August 1975 (U.S. Department of State Press Release). Washington, DC: U.S. Department of State.

Knowles, G. H., & Pratt, D. J. (1990). *Sustainable drylands development strategy.* Rome: FAO.

Koh, T. T. B., & Jayakumar, S. (1985). The negotiating process of the Third United Nations Conference on the Law of the Sea. In M. H. Nordquist (Ed.), *United Nations Convention on the Law of the Sea 1982: A commentary.* Boston: Martinus Nijhoff.

Kokoshin, A., Kremenyuk, V., & Sergeev, V. (1989). Voprosy issledovaniya mezhdunarodnykh peregovorov [Problems of research of international negotiations]. In *Mirovaya ekonomika i mezhdunarodnye otnosheniya,* November.

Kolawole, A. (1987). Environmental change and the South Chad Irrigation Project. *Journal of Arid Environments, 12*(13), 169-176.

Krasner, S. (Ed.). (1983). *International regimes.* Ithaca, NY: Cornell University Press.

Kremenyuk, V. (1989, July 17). Serious challenges. *Moscow News.*

Kremenyuk, V. (1991). *International negotiation: Analysis, approaches, issues.* San Francisco: Jossey-Bass.

Kuwabara, S. (1984). *The legal regime of the Protection of the Mediterranean Against Pollution From Land-Based Sources.* Dublin, Ireland: Tycooly International Publishing.

Lang, W. (1986). Luft und Ozon Schutzobjekte des Volkerrechts. *Zeitschrift für Ausländisches Öffentliches Recht und Völkerrecht, 46*(2), 261-285.

Lang, W. (1988, Diplomatie zwischen ökonomic und ökologie, das Beispiel des Ozonvertrages von Montreal. *Europa-Archiv, 43*(4), 105-110.

Lang, W. (1989). *Internationaler Umweltschutz.* Vienna: Orac.

Lang, W. (1991a). Is the ozone depletion regime a model for an emerging regime on global warming?. *UCLA Journal of Environmental Law and Policy, 9*(2), 161-174.

Lang, W. (1991b). Negotiations on the environment. In V. Kremenyuk (Ed.), *International negotiation.* San Francisco: Jossey-Bass.

Lashof, D., & Tirpak, D. (1989). *Policy options for stabilizing global climate.* Washington, DC: U.S. Environmental Protection Agency, Office of Policy, Planning, and Evaluation.

Luce, R., & Raiffa, H. (1957). *Games and decisions.* New York: John Wiley.

Lyster, S. (1985). *International wildlife law.* Cambridge: Grotius Publications.

Mabbutt, J. A. (1987). A review of progress since the UN Conference on Desertification. *Desertification Control Bulletin (UNEP),* No. 15, pp. 12-23.

MacNiell, J., et al. (1991). *Beyond interdependence.* New York: Oxford University Press.

Manne, A. S., & Richels, R. G. (1990). *Global CO2 emission reductions: The impacts of rising energy costs.* Menlo Park, CA: Electric Power Research Institute.

Mathews, J. T. (1989). Redefining security. *Foreign Affairs, 68,* 162-177.

Milburn-Hopwood, S. (1989). *The role of science in environmental policy-making: A case study of the Canadian acid rain policy.* Unpublished master's thesis, Environmental Studies, University of Toronto, Toronto, Ontario.

Ministerial Conference on Atmospheric Pollution and Climate Change. (1989, November 7). *Noordwijk Declaration for the Ministerial Conference on Atmospheric Pollution and Climate Change.* Noordwijk, the Netherlands: Author.

MOI. (1983). *Report of Work Group 1 on impact assessment, United States-Canada Memorandum of Intent on Transboundary Air Pollution.* Downsview, Ontario: Atmospheric Environment Service.

Moomaw, W. R. (1990). *A modest proposal to encourage unilateral reductions in greenhouse gases.* Unpublished manuscript, Tufts University, Medford, MA.

Mortimore, M. (1989a). *Adapting to drought: Farmers, famines and desertification in West Africa.* Cambridge: Cambridge University Press.

Mortimore, M. (1989b). *The causes, nature and rate of soil degradation in the northernmost states of Nigeria* (Working Paper No. 17). Washington, DC: World Bank.

NAPAP. (1990). *Integrated assessment of the National Acid Precipitation Assessment Program: Questions 1 and 2.* Washington, DC: National Acid Precipitation Assessment Program.

NAS. (1983). *Acid deposition: Atmospheric processes in eastern North America.* Washington, DC: National Academy Press.

NAS. (1986). *Acid deposition: Long-term trends.* Washington, DC: National Academy Press.

Nash, J. F. (1950). The bargaining problem. *Econometrica, 18,* 155-162.

Nelson, R. (1988). *Dryland management: The desertification problem* (Working Paper No. 8). Washington, DC: World Bank.

Nilsson, S., & Duinker, P. (1987). The extent of forest decline in Europe: A synthesis of survey results. *Environment, 29*(4), 4.

Nuclear News Magazine. (1984, August).

Odingo, S. (1990). *The definition of desertification and its programmatic consequences for UNEP and the international community.* Paper prepared for the *Desertification Control Bulletin,* UNEP, Nairobi, Kenya.

OECD. (1983-1986). [Various documents]. Paris: Nuclear Energy Agency.

OECD. (1988). *The Sahel facing the future: Increasing dependence or structural transformation.* Paris: OECD.

OECD/CILSS. (1989). *Final report of the Ségou Regional Encounter on Local Level Natural Resource Management.* Paris: OECD.

Plantey, A. (1980). *La négociation internationale. Principes et méthodes.* Paris: Editions du CNRS.

Pruitt, D. (1987). Creative approaches to negotiation. In D. Sandole & I. Sandole-Staroste (Eds.), *Conflict management and problem-solving: Interpersonal to international applications.* London: Frances Pinter.

Raiffa, H. (1982). *The art and science of negotiation.* Cambridge, MA: Harvard University Press.

Repetto, R. (1989). Balance-sheet erosion—How to account for the loss on natural resources. *International Environmental Affairs, 1*(Spring), 103-137.

Richardson, E. L. (1980). Power, mobility and the law of the sea. *Foreign Affairs, 58,* 902-919.

Riker, W. (1962). *The theory of political coalitions.* New Haven, CT: Yale University Press.

Riktlinjer. (1989). Riktlinjer för tillämpning av avtalet mellan Konungariket Sveriges regering och Socialistiska rådsrepublikernas unions regering angående tidigt varsel rörande en kärnenergiolycka och rörande utbyte av information angående kärntekniska anläggningar, 1989.

Riordan, C. (1990). Acid deposition: A case study of scientific uncertainty and international decision making. In *Environmental Management Case Studies.* Washington, DC: National Academy Press.

RMCC. (1988). *Assessment of the state of knowledge on the long range transport of air pollutants and acid deposition* (Report of the Federal/Provincial Research and Monitoring Coordinating Committee [RMCC]). Downsview, Ontario: Atmospheric Environment Service.

Robson, P. (1985). Regional integration and the crisis in sub-Saharan Africa. *Journal of Modern African Studies, 23*(4), 603-622.

Rönnow, H.-H. (1988). Blå ögon i rymden. *Internationella Studier, 18.*

Rosenau, J. (Ed.). (1991). *Governance without government: Change and order in world politics.* New York: Cambridge University Press.

Rosseland, B., Skogheim, O., & Sevaldrud, I. (1986). Acid deposition and effects in nordic Europe: Damage to fish populations in Scandinavia continue to apace. *Water, Air and Soil Pollution, 30,* 65.

Ruchay, D. (1990). *Inland water case study: Negotiation of the Rhine.* Notes from a meeting at IIASA, July, Laxenburg, Austria.

Rummel-Bulska, I. (1986). Recent developments relating to the Vienna Convention for the Protection of the Ozone Layer. In *Yearbook of the Association of Attenders and Alumni of the Hague Academy of International Law* (Vol. 54-56). The Hague, the Netherlands: Hague Academy of International Law.

Salzburg Seminar. (1990). *The Salzburg initiative: Improving the process of environmental diplomacy. Salzburg, Austria: Salzburg Seminar.*

Sand, P. (1985). Protecting the ozone layer—The Vienna Convention is adopted. *Environment, 27*(5), 18-43.

Sand, P. (1987). Air pollution in Europe: International policy measures. *Environment, 29*(10), 16-29.

Sand, P. (1990). *Lessons learned in global environmental governance.* Washington, DC: World Resources Institute.

Sandford, S. (1984). *The management of pastoral development.* Chichester, UK: John Wiley.

Sands, P. J. (1989). The environment, community, and international law. *Harvard Law Journal,* Spring.

SAS. (1990). *Surveillance des Acridiens au Sahel: Lettre d'information.* Montpellier, France: CIRAD/PRIFAS.

Schelling, T. (1960). *The strategy of conflict.* Cambridge, MA: Harvard University Press.

Schmandt, J., & Roderick, H. (Eds.). (1985). *Acid rain and friendly neighbors: The policy dispute between Canada and the United States.* Durham, NC: Duke University Press.

Sebenius, J. K. (1981). The computer as mediator: Law of the sea and beyond. *Journal of Policy Analysis and Management, 1,* 77-95.

Sebenius, J. K. (1984). *Negotiating the law of the sea.* Cambridge, MA: Harvard University Press.

Sebenius, J. K. (1990). *Negotiating a regime to control global warming.* Unpublished manuscript. (September).

Sebenius, J. K. (1991a). Designing Negotiations Toward a New Regime: The Case of Global Warming. *International Security, 15*(4), pp. 110-148.

Sebenius, J. K. (1991b). Negotiation analysis. In V. A. Kremenyuk (Ed.). *International Negotiation: Analysis, Approaches, Issues.* San Francisco: Jossey-Bass.

Shaikh, A. (1990). After Ségou: A coordinated donor approach. *Club du Sahel Newsletter, 7,* 12-13.

Sinclair, I. (1984). *The Vienna Convention on the Law of Treaties* (2nd ed.). Manchester, UK: Manchester University Press.

Skolnikoff, E. (1990). The policy gridlock on global warming. *Foreign Policy, 79,* (Summer).

Snrech, S. (1990). Regional cereals markets: The results of the Lomé Seminar. *Club du Sahel Newsletter, 7,* 8-10.

Somerville, C. M. (1986). *Drought and aid in the Sahel: A decade of development cooperation.* Boulder, CO: Westview.

Spector, B. I. (1991). *Freshness in negotiation: Creativity techniques that can break impasses* (Technical Report). Laxenburg, Austria: IIASA.

Stein, J. (Ed.). (1989). *Getting to the table.* Baltimore, MD: Johns Hopkins University Press.

Stone, C. (1990). The global warming crisis, if there is one, and the law. *American University Journal of International Law and Policy, 5*(2), 497-511.

Strong, M. (1974, April 1). *The scramble for the oceans: Towards anarchy or order.* Presented at the Gabriel Silver Memorial Lecture, Columbia University, New York.

Széll, P. J. (1985). The Vienna Convention for the Protection of the Ozone Layer. *International Digest of Health Legislation, 36*(3), 839-842.

Széll, P. J. (1988). The Montreal Protocol on Substances That Deplete the Ozone Layer. *International Digest of Health Legislation, 39*(1), 278-282.

Temple Lang, J. (1982). The European Community directive on bird conservation. *Biological Conservation, 22,* 11-25.

Temple Lang, J. (1986). The ozone layer convention: A new solution to the question of community participation in "mixed" international agreements. *Common Market Law Review, 23,* 157-176.

Temple Lang, J. (1987). The ERTA judgment and the court's case law on competence and conflict. *Yearbook of European Law 1986,* 183-218.

Temple Lang, J. (1990). International and legal aspects of conservation of Irish bogs. In Schouten & Nooren (Eds.), *Peatlands, economy and conservation.* The Hague, the Netherlands: SPB Academic Publishing.

Thacher, P. (1973, Spring). Assessment and control of marine pollution: The Stockholm recommendations and their efficacy. *Stanford Journal of International Studies.*

Thacher, P. (1977). The Mediterranean action plan. *Ambio, 6*(6).

Thacher, P. (1990a). Alternative legal and institutional approaches to global change. *Colorado Journal of International Environmental Law and Policy, 1*(1), 101-126.

Thacher, P. (1990b). *Global security and risk management: Background to institutional options for management of the global environment and commons.* Geneva: WFUNA.

Timberlake, L. C. (1985). *Africa in crisis: The causes, the cures of environmental bankruptcy.* London: Earthscan.

Tolba, M. (1989). A step-by-step approach to protection of the atmosphere. *International Environmental Affairs, 1*(4), 307.

UNITAR. (1971). *Wider acceptance of multilateral treaties.* New York: UNITAR.

United Nations. (1971). General Assembly Resolution 2861 (XXVI), 20 December, New York.

United Nations. (1972). Document A/CONF.48/8, 7 January, General Assembly, New York.

United Nations. (1973). Report of the Conference, A/CONF.48/14/Rev.1, General Assembly, New York.

United Nations. (1974). *UNEP approach to Mediterranean* (Internal paper, 25 October). Nairobi, Kenya: UNEP.

United Nations, 26-28 May 1987, *Final Act,* Conference of Plenipotentiaries on the Environmental Management of the Common Zambezi River System, Harare.

UNEP. (1975). *Report of the Intergovernmental Meeting on the Protection of the Mediterranean, Barcelona, 28 January-4 February 1975* (UNEP/WG.2/5 [11 February]). Nairobi, Kenya: UNEP.

UNEP. (1985). *First African Ministerial Conference on the Environment, Cairo,* 16-18 December. Nairobi, Kenya: UNEP.

UNEP. (1989a). *Register of international treaties and other agreements in the field of environment* (UNEP/GC. 15/Inf.). Nairobi, Kenya: UNEP.

UNEP. (1989b). *Synthesis report* (UNEP/OzL.Pro. WG.II(1)4, 13 November). Nairobi, Kenya: UNEP.

UNEP. (1990a). *Report of the Ad Hoc Working Group of the work of its second session in preparation for a legal instrument on biological diversity of the planet.* Nairobi, Kenya: UNEP.

UNEP. (1990b). *Report of the Second Meeting of the Parties to the Montreal Protocol on Substances That Deplete the Ozone Layer* (UNEP/OzL.Pro.2/3, 29 June). London: UNEP.

UNESCO. (1974). *Report of the IOC/GFCM/ICSEM International Workshop on Marine Pollution in the Mediterranean* (Workshop Report No. 3). Paris: UNESCO.

U.S. Accounting Office. (1985). *International nuclear safety* (GAC, NSIAD-85-128). Washington, DC: Government Printing Office.

USAID. (1989a). *Sahel Development Programme 1986-1988.* Report to Congress, Washington, DC.

USAID. (1989b). *The Ségou Roundtable on Local Level Natural Resource Management in the Sahel.* Ségou, Mali, May 22-27, 1989: Report to USAID, Washington, DC.

USAID. (1989c). *The Ségou Roundtable.* Washington, DC: USAID.

U.S. Congressional Record. (1986). AQ ch. 5]

U.S. Council of Economic Advisers. (1990). *Economic report of the president.* Washington, DC: Government Printing Office.

U.S. Office of Technological Assessment. (1984). *Nuclear power in the age of uncertainty.* Washington, DC: Government Printing Office.

Walton, R., & McKersie, R. (1965). *A behavioral theory of negotiations: An analysis of a social interaction system.* New York: McGraw-Hill.

Warren, A., & Agnew, C. (1988). *An assessment of desertification and land degradation in arid and semi-arid areas* (IIED Issue Paper No. 2). London: International Institute for Environment and Development.

Williams, R. H. (1989). *Low cost strategies for coping with carbon dioxide emission limits.* Princeton, NJ: Princeton University, Center for Energy and Environmental Studies.

Winsemius, P. (1990). *Guests in our own home.* Amsterdam: McKensie & Company.

WMO. (1990). *Intergovernmental panel on climate change: First assessment report overview.* Geneva: WMO and UNEP.

World Bank. (1988). *Annual report.* Washington, DC: World Bank.

World Bank. (1990). *Annual report.* Washington, DC: World Bank.

World Commission on Environment and Development. (1987). *Our common future.* Oxford: Oxford University Press.

Young, O. (Ed.). (1975). *Bargaining: Formal models of negotiation.* Urbana: University of Illinois Press.

Young, O. (1989a). *International cooperation: Building regimes for natural resources and the environment.* Ithaca, NY: Cornell University Press.

Young, O. (1989b). The politics of international regime formation: Managing natural resources and the environment. *International Organization, 43*(Summer).

Young, O. (1991). Political leadership and regime formation: On the development of institutions in international society. *International Organization, 45*(Summer), 281-308.

Zaelke, D., & Cameron, J. (1990). Global warming and climate change: An overview of the international legal process. *American University Journal of International Law and Policy, 5*(2), 249-290.

Zartman, I. W. (1985). Negotiating with asymmetry. *Negotiation Journal, 2,* 121-138.

Zartman, I. W. (Ed.). (1987). *Positive sum: Improving north-south negotiations.* New Brunswick, NJ: Transaction Books.

Zartman, I. W. (1989). *Ripe for resolution.* New York: Oxford University Press.

Zartman, I. W. (1991). The structure of negotiation. In V. Kremenyuk (Ed.), *International negotiation.* San Francisco: Jossey-Bass.

Zartman, I. W., & Berman, M. (1982). *The practical negotiator.* New Haven, CT: Yale University Press.

Zhurkin, V., Karagnov, S., & Kortunov, A., (1987). New challenges to the national security. *The Kommunist,* April.

Index

About the Contributors

Richard Elliot Benedick is a U.S. career diplomat with extensive negotiating experience. As Deputy Assistant Secretary of State, he was responsible for international environmental policy and was chief U.S. negotiator for both the Vienna Convention and the Montreal Protocol on protecting the ozone layer. He is currently Senior Fellow at World Wildlife Fund and recently wrote *Ozone Diplomacy: New Directions in Safeguarding the Planet.*

Christophe Dupont is professor of negotiation at the Faculty of Business Administration, Lille University, France, and an adviser to the *Centre de Recherches et d'Etudes des Chefs d'Entreprises* (CRC), Jouy-en-Josas. He is the author of *La Negociation: Conduite, Theorie, Applications.*

Guy-Olivier Faure is associate professor of sociology at the Sorbonne University, Paris, where he teaches international negotiation. His major research interests are in business negotiations, especially with China and Asian countries, focusing on strategies and cultural issues. He is concerned particularly with developing interdisciplinary approaches. Among his latest publications are the following coauthored books: *International Negotiation: Analysis, Approaches, Issues* (V. Kremenyuk, Ed.), *Processes of International Negotiations* (F. Mautner-Markhof, Ed.), *Evolutionary Systems Design: Policy-Making Under Complexity* (M. Shakun, Ed.), and *Conflits et Negociations dans le Commerce International: L'Uruguay Round* (Messerlin and Vellas, Eds.).

Willy Kempel is a member of the Austrian Foreign Ministry currently posted in Tel Aviv. He represented Austria at the negotiations for the Basel

Convention on the Control of Transboundary Movements of Hazardous Wastes and Their Disposal.

Victor A. Kremenyuk is deputy director at the Institute for USA and Canada Studies, Russian Academy of Sciences. His areas of interest are international conflict resolution, crisis management, foreign policy, and the negotiation process. He has published more than 100 hundred works in Russian and other languages and, most recently, edited a state-of-the-art compendium sponsored by IIASA entitled *International Negotiation: Analysis, Approaches, Issues* published by Jossey-Bass (1991). Some of his contributions include: "Processes of International Negotiation" (F. Mautner-Markhof, Ed.), "Windows of Opportunity" (G. Allison, W. Ury, and B. Allyn, Eds.), and "Cold War as Cooperation" (R. Kanet and E. Kolodziej, Eds.). He is an IIASA research associate in the Processes of International Negotiation Project.

Winfried Lang is an Austrian career diplomat and professor of international law and international relations at the University of Vienna and Austria's Ambassador to International Organizations in Geneva. He chaired the OECD Transfrontier Pollution Group (1977 to 1982) and presided over UN conferences on the protection of the ozone layer (1985), on biological and bacteriological weapons (1986), and on substances that deplete the ozone layer (1987). He has published several books and articles on integration policy, protection of the environment, international negotiations, neutrality, and the law of treaties.

Michael Mortimore taught in Nigerian universities for most of his career before becoming an independent researcher on environmental and developmental issues in African drylands, including the West African Sahel. He has authored several books, articles, and reports sponsored by the World Bank and other organizations on problems relating to dryland management, including *Adapting to Drought: Farmers, Famines and Desertification in West Africa* (1989).

Robert H. Pry is the former director of IIASA. He was founding president of the Center for Innovative Technology, adjunct professor at the Massachusetts Institute of Technology, vice-chairman (technology) and executive vice-president (research and development) at Gould, Inc., and vice-president (research and development) at Combustion Engineering, Inc. A fellow of the American Association for the Advancement of Science, he has authored many publications in the fields of management, technology assessment, and material science.

Jeffrey Z. Rubin is professor of psychology at Tufts University, Associate Director of the Program on Negotiation at Harvard Law School, and Adjunct Professor of Diplomacy, Fletcher School of Law and Diplomacy, Tufts University. He is the author, coauthor, or editor of more than a dozen books and numerous articles on interpersonal and international conflict and negotiation, as well as on the role of third-party intervention in the dispute settlement process. His recent books include *Social Conflict: Escalation, Stalemate, and Settlement* (with D. Pruitt), *Leadership and Negotiation in the Middle East* (with B. Kellerman), *When Families Fight* (with C. Rubin), and *Negotiation Theory and Practice* (with J. W. Breslin).

James K. Sebenius, professor at the Harvard Business School and formerly on the faculty at Harvard's Kennedy School of Government, specializes in analyzing and advising on complex negotiations. He coauthored (with D. Lax) *The Manager as Negotiator.* With Howard Raiffa, he now co-chairs the Negotiation Roundtable, which has focused on global-warming negotiations. He served as an adviser to Ambassador Elliot L. Richardson with the State Department's Delegation to the Law of the Sea negotiations from 1977 to 1980. Author of *Negotiating the Law of the Sea,* he was elected a term member of the Council on Foreign Relations in 1984.

Roderick W. Shaw is leader of the Environment and Development and Climate Change Projects at IIASA. For several years, he was a research scientist in air-pollution meteorology for the Atmosphere Environment Service in Toronto. From 1975 to 1980, he was chief of the Air Pollution Control Division, Environmental Protection Service in Halifax, Nova Scotia, carrying out monitoring and control work in both local air pollution and acidic precipitation. He also participated in the activities under the U.S.-Canada Memorandum of Intent on Transboundary Air Pollution.

Gunnar Sjöstedt is a senior research fellow at the Swedish Institute of International Affairs and also associate professor of political science at the University of Stockholm. His research work is concerned with processes of international cooperation and consultations in which negotiations represent an important element. He has studied the OECD as a communication system and the external role of the European Community, and is currently working on a project dealing with the transformation of the international trade regime incorporated in GATT and its external relations.

Bertram I. Spector is leader of the Processes of International Negotiation Project at IIASA. He has directed research in the field of international negotiation and decision support techniques for foreign policy analysts and policymakers at two research organizations in Washington, D.C. In particular, he has conducted research and published papers on the impacts of perceptual and personality factors on negotiation processes and developed econometric models in support of the Camp David negotiations on the Middle East in 1978. He is currently studying the prenegotiation processes of the UN Conference on Environment and Development and is investigating the use of creativity heuristics as mechanisms to resolve negotiation impasses.

Patrick Széll is head of the International Environmental Law Division at the Department of the Environment in London. He has worked extensively on the environment aspects of international and European Community law. Among the treaties with which he has been closely associated as Legal Adviser to the United Kingdom delegation have been the Vienna Convention, Montreal Protocol, Basel Convention on the Control of Transboundary Movements of Hazardous Wastes and Their Disposal, and Cartagena Convention for the Protection and Development of the Marine Environment of the Wider Caribbean Region.

John Temple Lang is now a director, Directorate General for Competition, Commission of the European Communities and from 1974 to 1988 was one of its legal advisers. He has lectured on various areas of law at Trinity College, Dublin, intermittently from 1959 to 1990. He is the former chairman, European Section, International Council for Bird Preservation and author of *The Common Market and Common Law* (1966) and more than 120 articles on legal and nature conservation issues.

Peter S. Thacher is senior counselor at the World Resources Institute, a nonprofit, policy-research organization in Washington, DC. He is also senior adviser to Maurice F. Strong, the secretary general of the UN Conference on Environment and Development (UNCED). He is the former deputy executive director of the UN Environment Program (UNEP) in Nairobi, and played a major role in creating the Mediterranean Action Plan in the mid-1970s. He was a program director for the UN Conference on the Human Environment (1972) with responsibility for pollution and institutional aspects. Recently, he has worked with NASA and UNEP in the establishment of GRID—the Global Resources Information Database—a part of UNEP's Global Environmental Monitoring System (GEMS), operating in Geneva, Nairobi, and Bangkok.

Oran R. Young is director of the Institute on Arctic Studies at Dartmouth College. He has authored many books in the field of international negotiation, including *The Intermediaries: Third Parties in International Crises* (1967) and *Bargaining: Formal Theories of Negotiation* (1975). His current areas of research include negotiation regimes, international organizations, and natural resource management. He is a member of the editorial board of *International Organization.*

I. William Zartman is Jacob Blaustein Professor of Conflict Resolution and International Organization at the Nitze School of Advanced International Studies (SAIS) of The Johns Hopkins University. He is author of *The Practical Negotiator* (with M. Berman) and *Ripe for Resolution,* and editor and coauthor of *The 50% Solution, The Negotiation Process,* and *Positive Sum,* among other books. He is organizer of the Washington Interest in Negotiations (WIN) Group and director of the Conflict Reduction in Regional Conflicts (CRIRC) Project conducted by SAIS and the Institute for USA and Canada Studies of the Academy of Sciences of the USSR.